Hidden Hillsborough

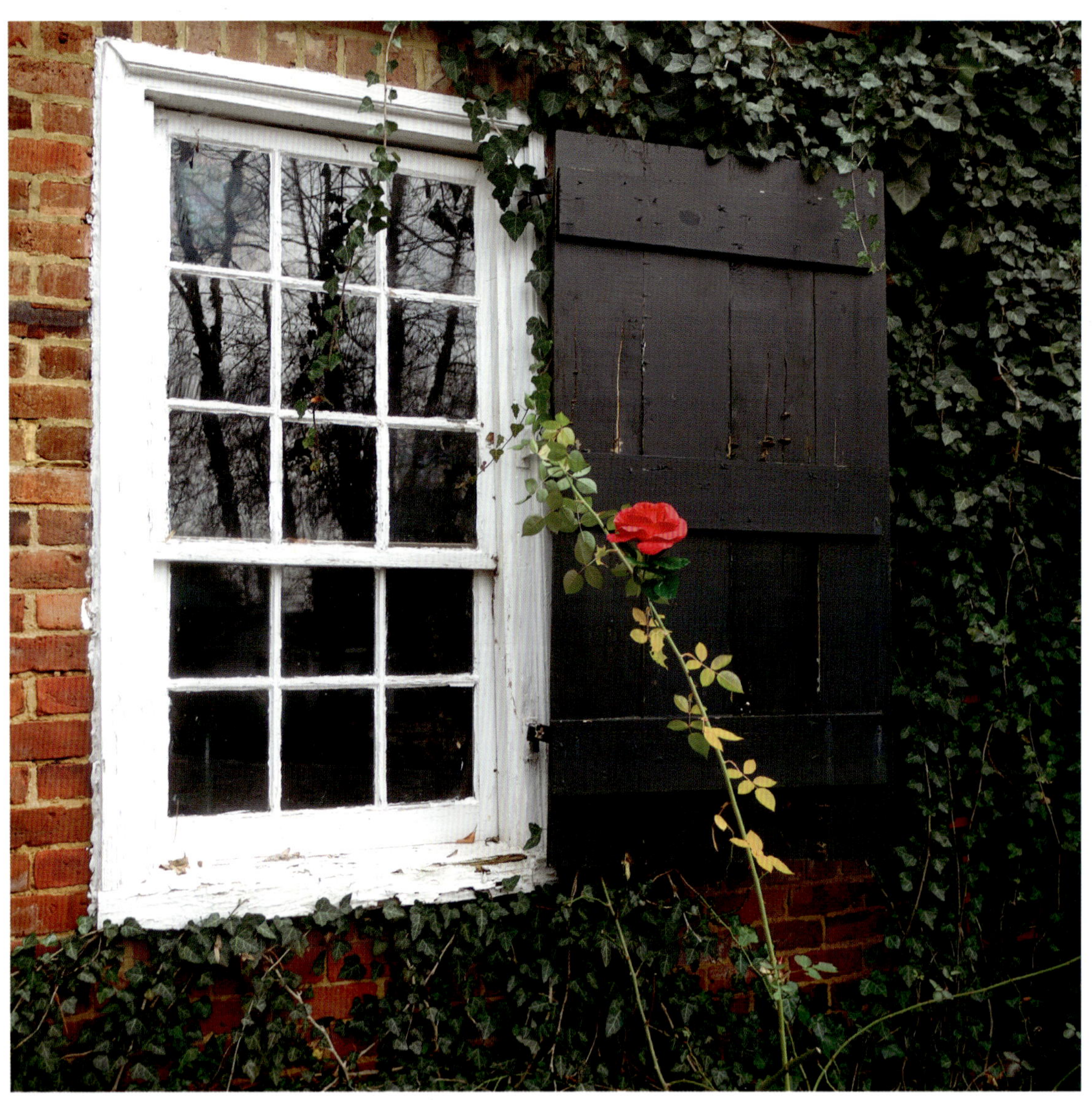

Hidden Hillsborough

Historic Dependencies and Landscapes in a Small Southern Town

Photographs by Elizabeth Matheson

Maps by Stewart E. Dunaway

A PROJECT OF THE PRESERVATION FUND OF HILLSBOROUGH, NORTH CAROLINA

Hidden Hillsborough: Historic Dependencies and Landscapes in a Small Southern Town

Eno Publishers
P.O. Box 158
Hillsborough, NC 27278
www.enopublishers.org

Paperback edition: ISBN: 978-0-9973144-3-4
Library of Congress Control Number: 2017906085

Hardcover edition: ISBN: 978-0-9973144-2-7
Library of Congress Control Number: 2017933521

Book jacket photographs by Elizabeth Matheson
Design & production by BW&A Books, Inc., Oxford, NC
All photographs are by Elizabeth Matheson, unless otherwise noted
Frontispiece caption: Burnside kitchen, west window.

Printed in China.

Dedicated to the Founding Board Members
of the Preservation Fund of Hillsborough

Acknowledgments

This book owes a debt of gratitude to the help and enthusiasm of friends, neighbors, and local residents of the Hillsborough community, as well as those working more broadly for the State of North Carolina and its educational and other institutions.

First, to those who opened their doors and back gates to members of this committee, or contributed information about or any other help with the subjects of our research, we owe you most cordial thanks for your spirit of collaboration and discovery: Nancy and Steven Demorest, Dinah and Larry Dozier, Susan Frankenburg, Nancy and Craufurd Goodwin, Mary Banks and Stuart Knechtle, Fran and David McCullough, Lauri and Kirk Michel, Mary Ann Plambeck, Maureen Quilligan and Michael Malone, Gwenyth and William Reid, Tom Roberts, Lee Smith and Hal Crowther, Virginia Smith and Mark Bell, Bobbie Strickland, Bryan Stuart, Linda Swain, David Terry, Elizabeth Woodman and Eric Hallman, Janie Trumbull, Barbara and Clifford Younger.

We also wish to thank the librarians, consultants, technical experts, preservationists, town officials, and organizations, and local historians who generously offered their time, knowledge and skills in aid of our project: Steven B. Burke and Randy Campbell, Bill and Schatzie Crowther, Betty Eidenier, Kathleen Faherty, Jeanne L. Frederick, the Rev. N. Brooks Graebner, Margaret Hauth, Nancy Kaiser, Rosetta Moore, Tom Magnuson, Steve Peck, Evelyn Poole-Kober, Holly Reid, Amy F. Roach, Mary Rocap, Dean Ruedrich, Rebecca Ryan, Peter Sandbeck, Cynthia Satterfield, Richard Shaw, Stephanie Trueblood, Bob Ward, the Alliance for Historic Hillsborough, the Burwell School, the Hillsborough Historic District Commission, the Orange County Historical Museum, Preservation North Carolina, St. Matthew's Episcopal Church, and the Southern Historical Collection at the University of North Carolina at Chapel Hill. A special note of thanks to Holden Richards for his help with the photographs.

Elizabeth Woodman of Eno Publishers volunteered her editing skills for this book, for which we owe her our most profound and sincere thanks. Thanks are also due to BW&A Books and in particular to Chris Crochetière and Julie Allred, for their helpful guidance and thoughtful visualization of this book.

Finally, the Hidden Hillsborough Committee wishes to thank the Preservation Fund of Hillsborough (PFH) for sponsoring the production of this book. PFH was established in 1980 as a revolving fund with support from the Z. Smith Reynolds Foundation, the Mary Duke Biddle Foundation, and other donors. Its stated mission is "to direct attention to sites, buildings, residences, and gardens, and other places of historical or architectural interest . . . and to increase and diffuse knowledge about and appreciation of such places." Since that time it has sponsored a number of local preservation projects, among other initiatives: the moving and renovation of the Alexander Dickson House and Office (Visitors Center for Hillsborough and Orange County, 1982–84); the moving and renovation of the Hughes Academy, the last remaining one-room schoolhouse in Orange County, to Cameron Park in Hillsborough (1997); the restoration of the Cadwallader Jones (Norwood) Law Office on the courthouse square (1997–2001); and the restoration and reconstruction of the Great Burnside Icehouse, whose foundations were restored and consolidated below ground, and missing portions of its superstructure were entirely reconstructed (2007).

We wish to honor the members of the founding board of the Preservation Fund of Hillsborough by dedicating this book to them: Leigh Cameron, Stephen A. Dennis, Craufurd Goodwin, Giles Gunn, Helen Hill, J. Myrick Howard, John P. Kennedy Jr., Margaret Moore, Dr. H.W. Moore, Dr. Robert J. Murphy, Cecil Sanford, John Seelye, Lucy Strickland, Roscoe L. Strickland Jr., Larry Tise, and Evan Turner. A special tribute is due to Craufurd Goodwin, for both his dedication to this project and to historic preservation in Hillsborough over the past forty years. It has been an inspiration to work alongside him.

—*The Hidden Hillsborough Committee of the Preservation Fund of Hillsborough*:
Barbara Hume and Callie Connor, co-chairs, Jean Anderson, Bill Crowther,
Stewart E. Dunaway, Craufurd Goodwin, the Rev. N. Brooks Graebner,
Elizabeth Matheson, Pip Merrick, Jim Parsley, Mary Ann Peter, Ellen C. Weig

Contents

List of Maps / xi
Maps, *Stewart E. Dunaway* / xii
Preface, *Callie Connor* / xxiii
Introduction, *Barbara Hume* / 1

1 An Evolving Townscape: The Location and Early Importance of Hillsborough
Barbara Hume and Stewart E. Dunaway / 5

2 Historic Kitchens
Callie Connor / 19

3 Slave Houses
Jean B. Anderson / 33

4 Smokehouses
Jim Parsley / 43

5 Springs and Spring Houses, Wells and Well Houses
Mary Ann Peter / 48

6 Barns
Jean B. Anderson / 59

7 Other Dependencies
Icehouses: *Stewart E. Dunaway*
Dining Rooms: *Barbara Hume*
Laundries: *Barbara Hume*
Necessary Houses: *Jim Parsley* / 76

8 Trees and Gardens
Callie Connor / 92

9 On the Streets
Stewart E. Dunaway / 104

10 Offices and Law Offices
Craufurd D. Goodwin / 123

11 Schools and School-Related Buildings
Callie Connor / 133

12 Cemeteries
Ellen C. Weig and Pip Merrick / 143

Conclusion
Callie Connor / 170

Notes / 175
Selected Bibliography / 185
List of Contributors / 187
Index / 189

List of Maps

Note: All maps were designed and produced by Stewart E. Dunaway, unless otherwise attributed.

Map 1
Sauthier Map of Hillsborough, 1768. Earliest record of town layout, including buildings and landscape features (© British Library Board, K.TOP.122.59) / xii

Map 2
Detail, Sauthier Map of Hillsborough (© British Library Board, K.TOP.122.59) / xiii

Map 2B
Detail, Sauthier Map, with superimposed plan of original Town Lots / xiv

Map 3
Map of Hillsborough, 1892, showing Town Lots and stages of expansion of the town / xv

Map 4
Major Buildings and Properties, with map key on facing page / xvi–xvii

Map 5
National Register Historic District (1973) and Adjacent National Register Plantations / xviii

Map 6
Mansion House Complexes / xix

Map 7
Dependencies by Category / xx

Map 8
Landscape Features by Category, showing approximate locations of surviving traces / xxii

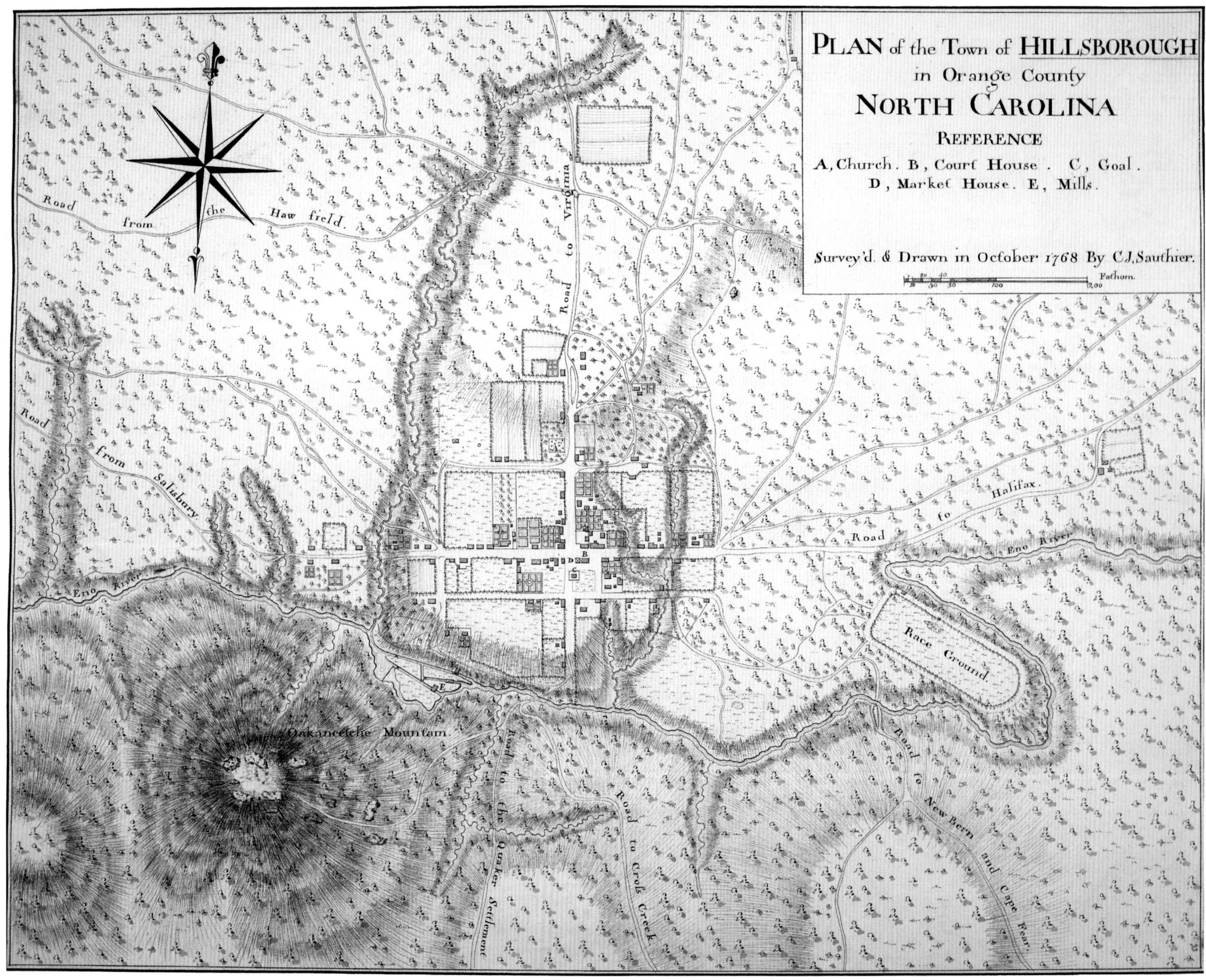

Map 1 / Sauthier Map of Hillsborough, 1768. Earliest record of town layout, including buildings and landscape features (© British Library Board, K.TOP.122.59*).*

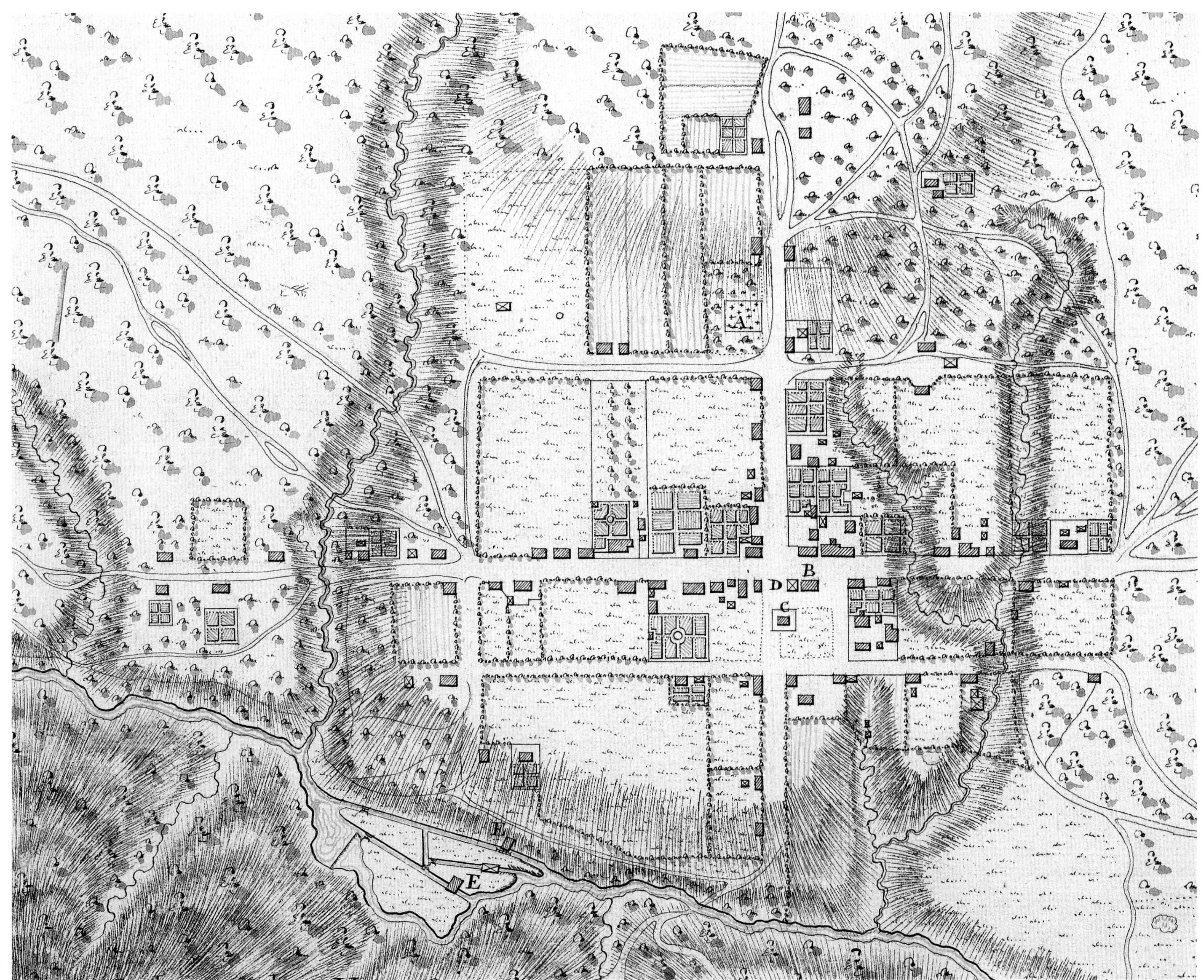

Map 2 / Detail, Sauthier Map of Hillsborough (© *British Library Board,* K.TOP.122.59).

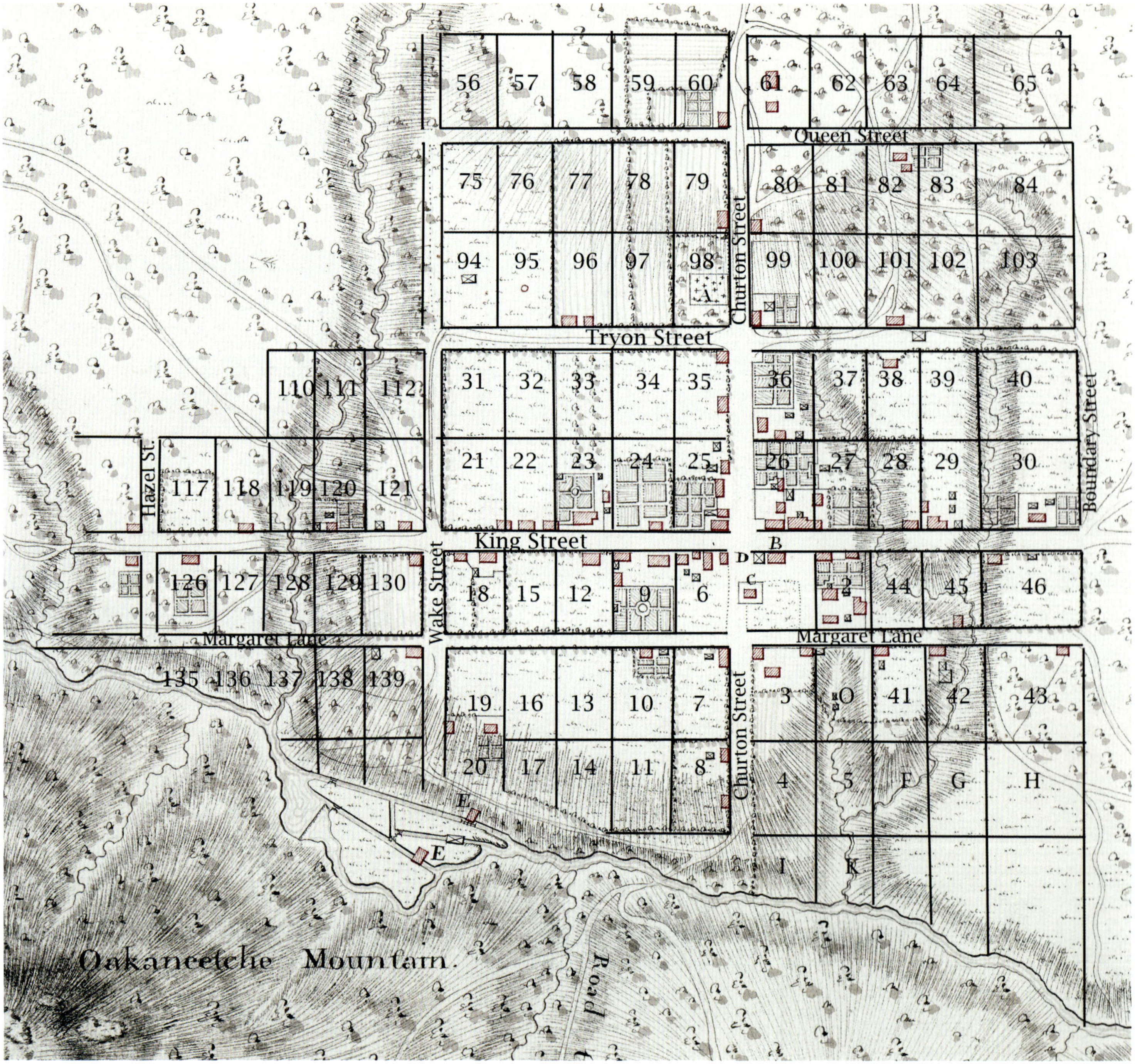

Map 2B / Detail, Sauthier Map, with superimposed plan of original Town Lots.

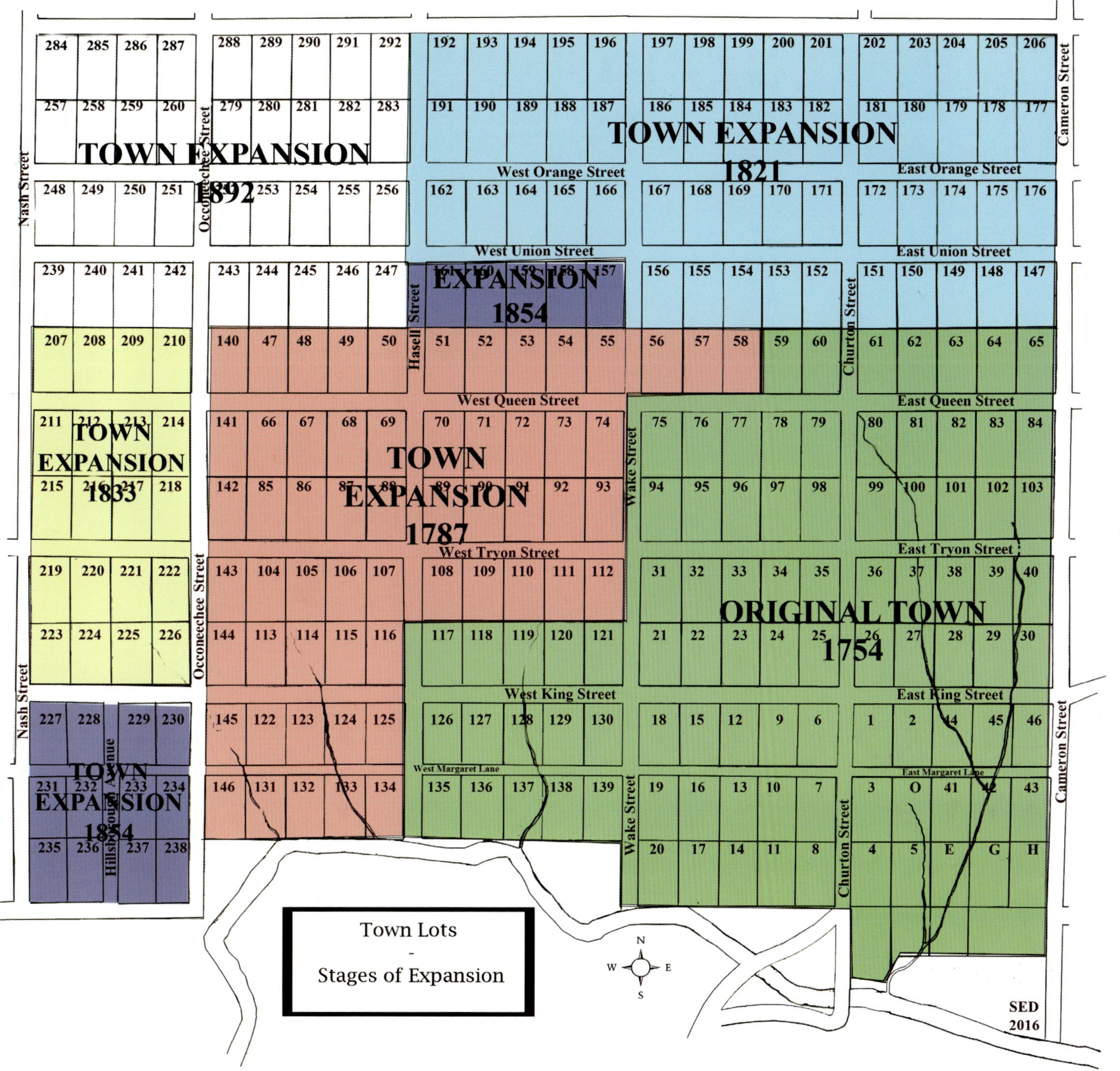

Map 3 / Map of Hillsborough, 1892, showing Town Lots and stages of expansion of the town.

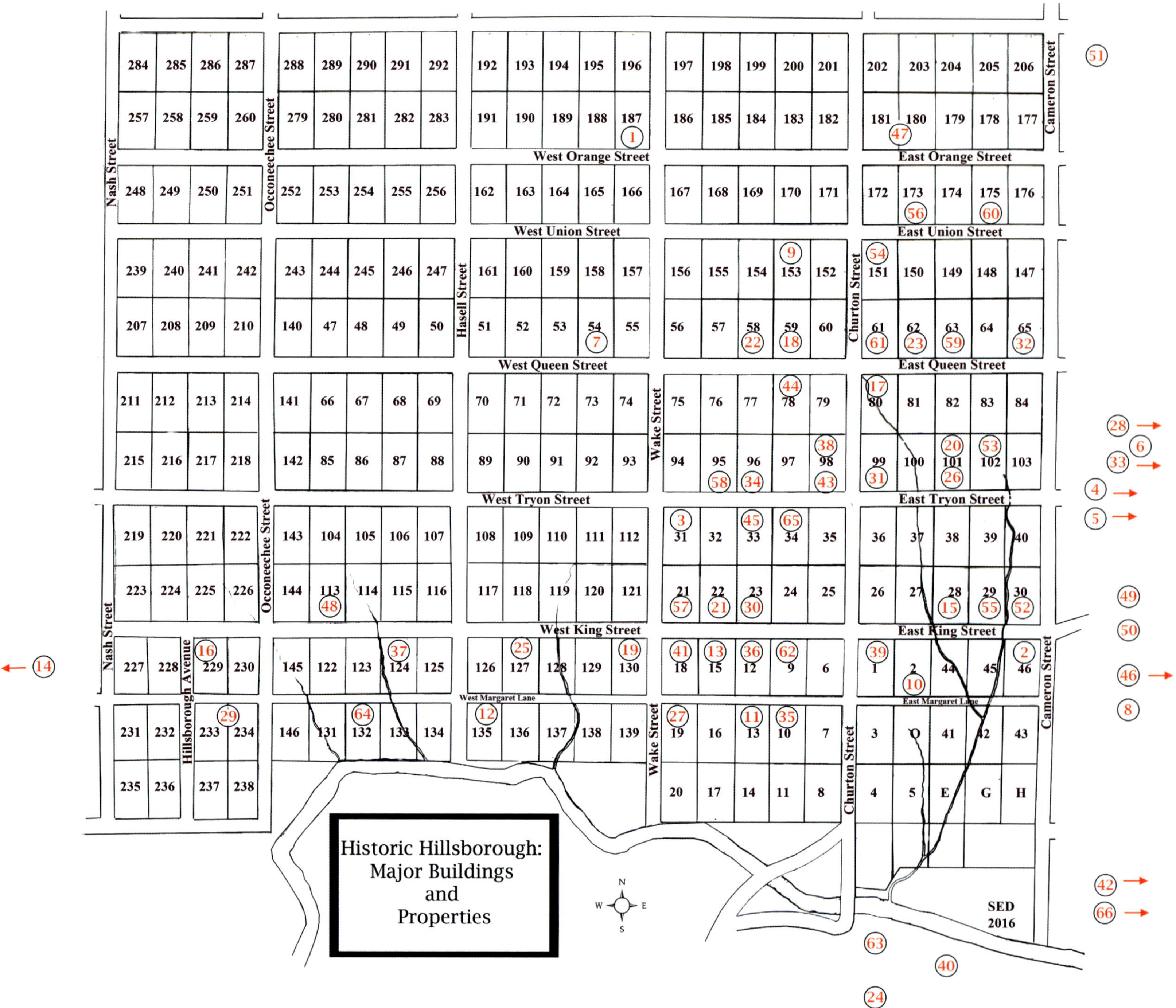

Map 4 / Major Buildings and Properties, with map key on facing page.

1. Academy, site (ca. 1821–44)
2. Alexander Dickson House and Office (ca. 1780)
3. Ashe House (ca. 1840)
4. Ayr Mount (ca. 1815)
5. Ayr Mount Cemetery
6. Bellevue (ca. 1790; 1853)
7. Berry Brick House (1805)
8. Burnside (1834; 1858)
9. Burwell School (1821; 1837–57)
10. Cadwallader Jones, (Norwood) Law Office (mid-19th century)
11. Cameron-Nash Law Office (1801; ca. 1839)
12. Carpenter's House (1820)
13. Colonial Inn (1838)
14. Commandant's House (1859)
15. Courtney's Yellow House (ca. 1768)
16. David Anderson House (1840s)
17. Dickerson Chapel (1790 courthouse)
18. Dr. Edmund Strudwick's Kitchen (1819)
19. First Baptist Church (1860–70)
20. Gattis House (East Tryon St.)
21. Gattis Well House (West King St.)
22. Hasell-Nash House (Pilgrim's Rest, 1819)
23. Heartsease (ca. 1786)
24. Highlands (ca. 1844)
25. House, Lot 127 (19th century)
26. Lockhart-Phillips Cemetery
27. Mallett Mill House (ca. 1820)
28. Mangum-Ruffin House (ca. 1840; ca. 1875)
29. Margaret Lane Cemetery
30. Masonic Hall (1823)
31. Mason's Ordinary (before 1790)
32. Midlawn (ca. 1881)
33. Montrose (ca. 1820; 1890; 1898)
34. Nash-Hooper House (1772; 1820)
35. Nash-Kollock School, site (1801; 1859–90)
36. Nash Law Office (1818; 1839)
37. Old King Street Tavern (ca. 1800; ca. 1840)
38. Old Town Cemetery (1757)
39. Orange County Courthouse (1845)
40. Over-the-River (1820)
41. Parks-Richmond House (Inn at Teardrops) (late 18th century; 19th century)
42. Poplar Hill (ca. 1794; mid-19th century)
43. Presbyterian Church (1816; 1892)
44. Robertson-Cheek House (mid-19th century)
45. Roulhac-Hamilton House (ca. 1840)
46. Ruffin Law Office (1818)
47. Ruffin-Roulhac House (Town Hall) (1823; 1830)
48. Ruffin-Snipes House (ca. 1820; ca. 1840)
49. Saint Matthew's Cemetery
50. Saint Matthew's Episcopal Church (1824–26)
51. Sans Souci (ca. 1812)
52. Seven Hearths (ca. 1800)
53. Spring Lot (Town Lot 102)
54. Tamarind (1903)
55. Teer House (1870)
56. Turner-Strudwick House (1833; 1889)
57. Twin Chimneys (ca. 1768; ca. 1817)
58. United Methodist Church (ca. 1859)
59. Webb House (ca. 1817)
60. William J. Bingham House (ca. 1833; 1903)
61. William Whitted House (late 18th century; mid-19th century)
62. Whitted-Johnston House (ca. 1800)
63. Eno Lodge (ca. 1825)
64. Thomas Faucett House (ca. 1840)
65. Scott House (ca. 1840)
66. Holeman-Gates House (ca. 1800; 1981)

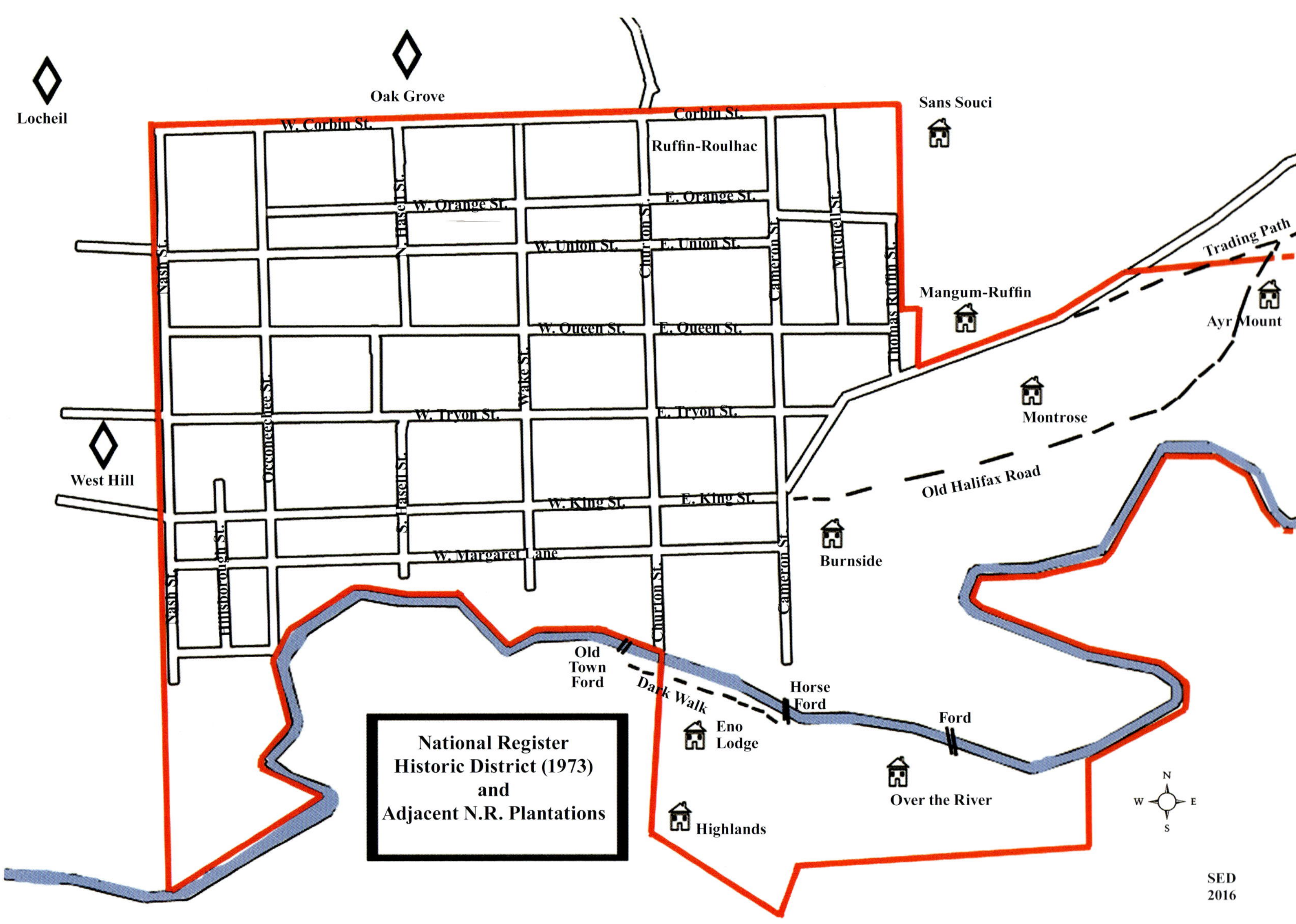

Map 5 / National Register Historic District (1973) and Adjacent National Register Plantations.

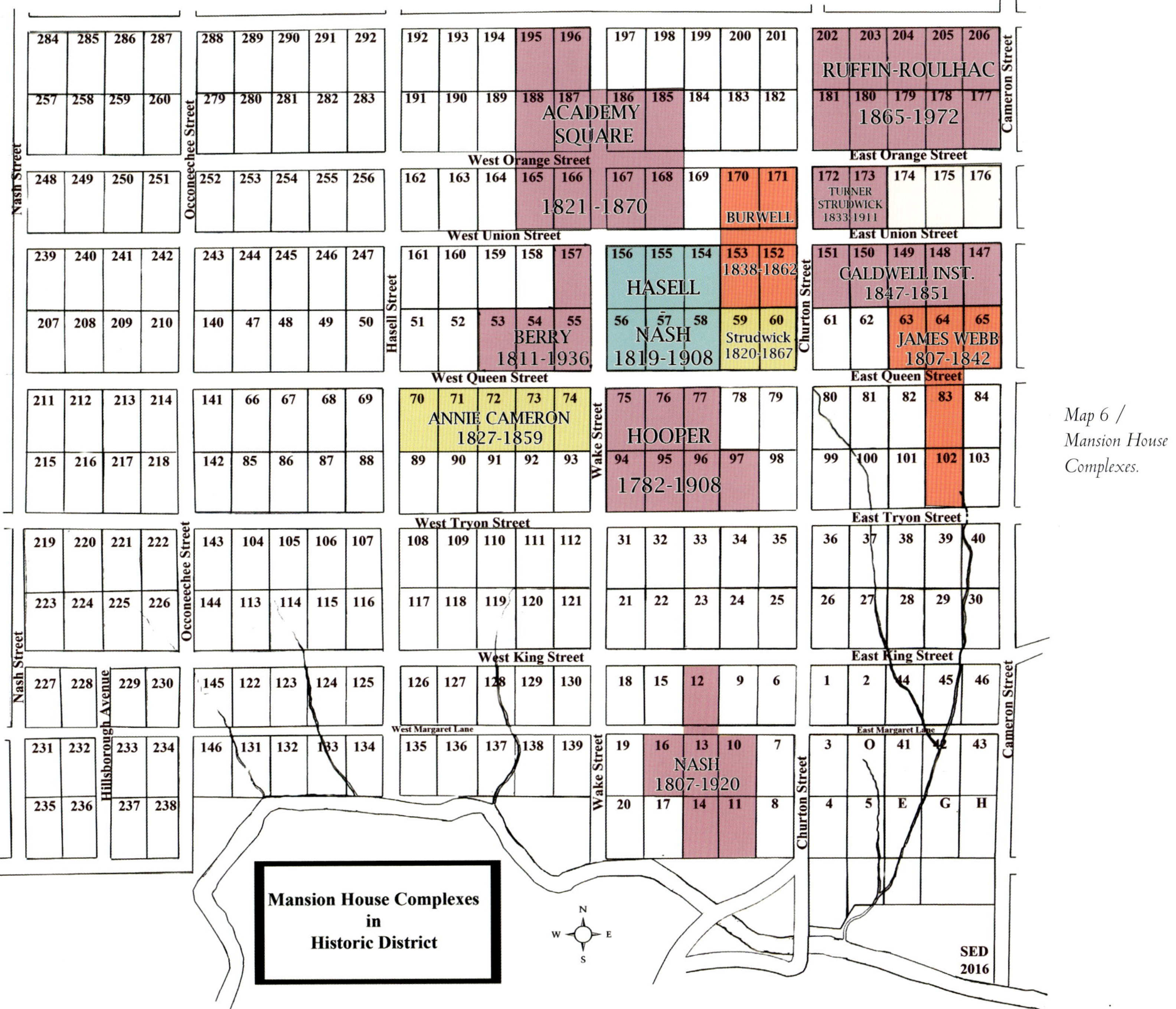

Map 6 / Mansion House Complexes.

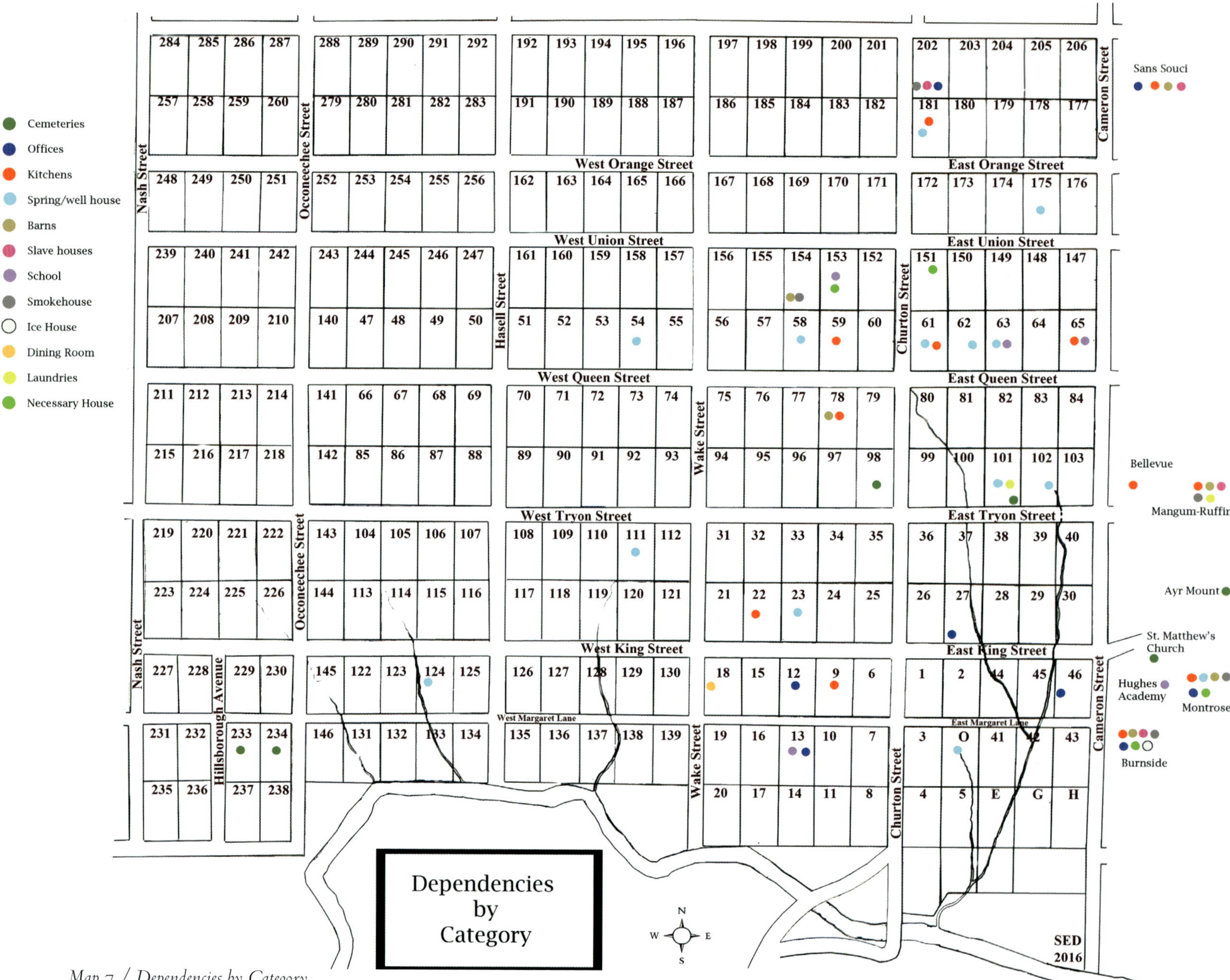

Map 7 / Dependencies by Category.

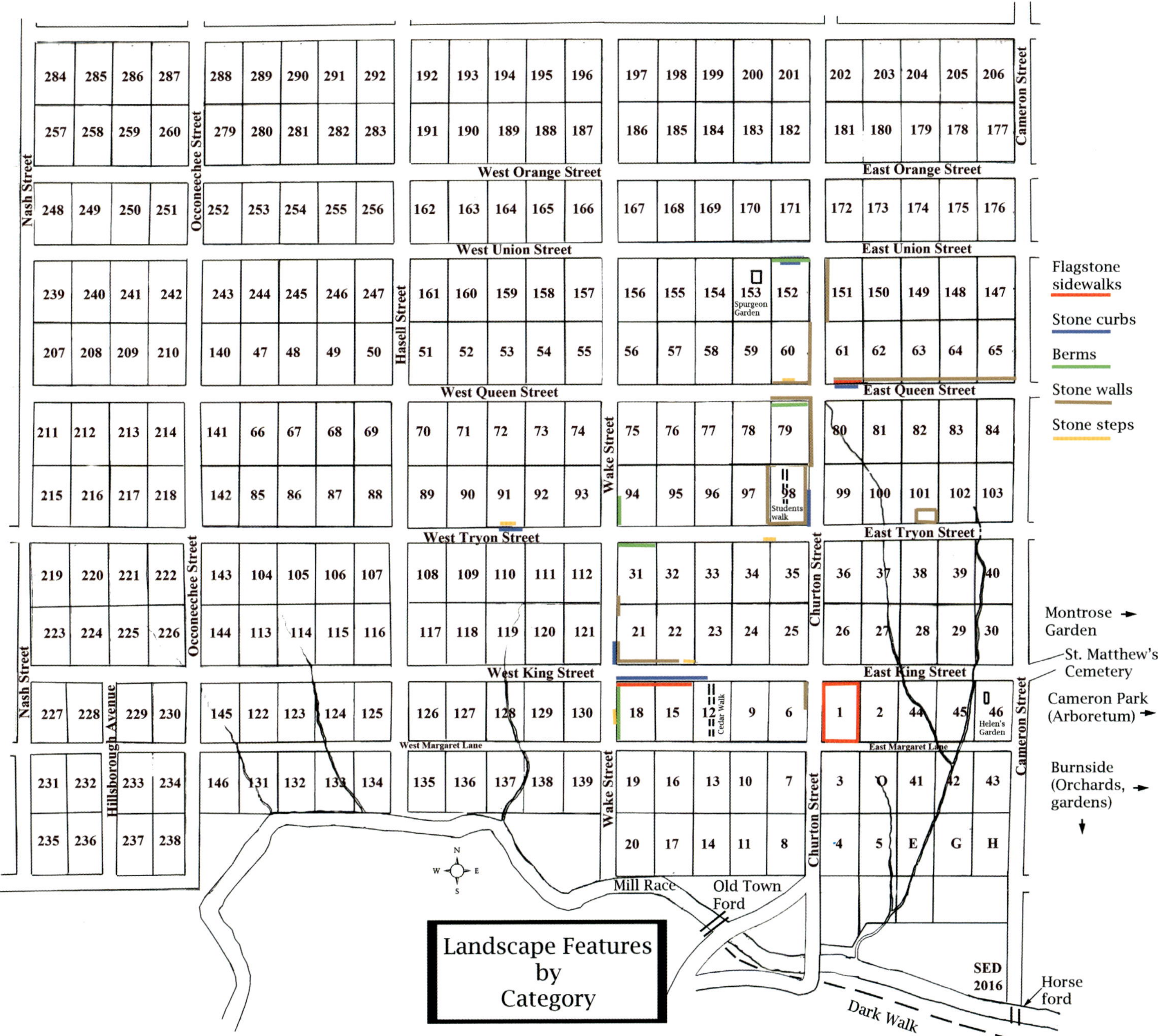

Map 8 / Landscape Features by Category, showing approximate locations of surviving traces.

Preface

The term *hidden* in the title of this book is to be understood both literally and figuratively, for seeing Hillsborough today implies a task for both the eyes and the imagination. Behind the gracious houses and their thick hedges, sometimes partially obscured by trees—often altogether invisible and inaccessible to a visitor or, in some cases, right in plain sight—are signs of a past that evoke the intimate story of a small Southern town and its life and people a century and a half, or two, or three, ago.

In *Hidden Hillsborough* we seek to understand and interpret the secondary buildings, or dependencies, that dot the townscape seemingly randomly, preserved here and there along the streets or in backyards. The book also calls attention to various types of landscape features that appear in our peripheral vision, but are difficult to explain or are taken for granted, and therefore usually ignored. *Hidden Hillsborough* hopes to guide the reader to a way of seeing these traces of the historic town in a fuller sense, including and beyond the visual, in a perception of what is present today, but whose implications are not immediately apparent—things barely observed and easily overlooked.

THE GENESIS OF *Hidden Hillsborough* dates to a 2011 board meeting of the Preservation Fund of Hillsborough at which a committee was formed of some of its members and volunteers to research and catalog the dependencies and landscape elements of the town environment that we live with daily. Among these are the historic kitchens, offices, school-related buildings, well houses and spring houses, smokehouses, barns, and slave houses, and, yes, necessary houses (or privies). Alongside them, scattered along the quiet streets, are aspects of the terrain whose origin and function have been somewhat of a mystery: stone walls that start and stop abruptly, stone steps and curbs in strange places, rolling berms, receding paths, whispers of past gardens, silent gravestones, and ancient, sidewalk-heaving shade trees. These do not immediately carry meaning for most of us. How could they? For how could the passerby possibly sense that those carefully formed berms once supported flagstone sidewalks that kept the long, rustling skirts worn by nineteenth-century ladies away from the muddy, unpaved streets? Sidewalks were just one of the features that rendered this an exceptionally sophisticated and well-appointed town.

The mission of the Hidden Hillsborough Committee was to record the persistent presence of these easily overlooked buildings and features, along with their historic resonance and rationale. This book is our modest attempt to give them a voice as to the kind of life they witnessed and the very different rhythm and pace of the times for which they were created. Our wish to let the past speak for itself was, in part, to encourage the preservation of these precious testimonials, as so many were in danger of slipping into decay or being cast aside for new, more modern materials or tastes or simple necessities such as concrete sidewalks or sewer lines. The rest was sheer curiosity: We wanted to know more about our historic town.

Four years later, the committee had photographed, researched, and mapped as many of these town features as possible. We confined our inquiry to the National Register Historic District along with the adjacent National Register properties on the immediate outskirts of town. Our timeframe was set generally from between 1754, when the town was founded, and World War I. As it happens with some happy collaborative endeavors, the committee realized that it was now looking at a story whose richness and historic value added up to more than the sum of its parts, and that the results of the project had indeed developed into a coherent record.

IF THE TRUTH be told, this study could not have happened without the responses of property owners—thereby avoiding embarrassing confessions and apologies, remorseful admissions that zealous committee members had been peeping in the windows of their neighbors' outbuildings and over their back fences in search of data. How shocking! This could never happen in Hillsborough! But in fact, homeowners warmly complied with our requests for access, in order to study, measure, or photograph features of their properties. They unlocked their gates and opened the creaking doors on their little buildings—and their barns, too—to the researchers, and even produced deeds and other records to substantiate dating and agency. This outpouring of goodwill was galvanizing and inspiring to the committee, effectively turning the project into a joint venture, a palpable form of active engagement with the community.

Other felicitous forms of collaboration developed among the twelve Hidden Hillsborough Committee members themselves, who naturally came from diverse backgrounds and training. The immense talents of two in particular must be mentioned here. Elizabeth Matheson, a widely published and admired photographer, volunteered on the first day to do the photography for the project. Just like that! Soon after, Stewart Dunaway, who had recently completed the first of his books, *Hillsborough, NC: History of the Town Lots,* came on board as our historian-mapmaker. Working as a team, committee members thus correlated their individual essay subjects with the needed documentation in the form of maps and photographs of the town.

The committee met monthly around the conference table in the Cooke-Lawrence Room at St. Matthew's Episcopal Church, a peaceful and serious setting, with afternoon light streaming across the table through the ancient trees in the adjoining cemetery. The meetings generated their own energy as the volunteers brainstormed and problem-solved while individually pursuing their own chosen essay topics. Categories were shuffled and redefined as the project clarified in its scope, structure, and purpose, and gradually took shape as a publication that might serve the community in a number of ways. The distinct voices and interests of individual authors are evident within the collaborative process.

SEVERAL OTHER BOOKS with similar goals served as models along the way: John Allen's *Uncommon Vernacular: The Early Houses of Jefferson County, West Virginia* was a lofty example of expert photo-documentation of an historic landscape. John Michael Vlach's *Back of the Big House: The Architecture of Plantation Slavery* was of particular value for its treatment of dependencies as separate categories of buildings worthy of interpretation.

Eno Publishers' *27 Views of Hillsborough,* with its forays into the exceptional literary resources of the town, offers a complimentary perspective to this book in its evocative stories and fascinating rambles penned by local authors. *Hidden Hillsborough,* however, offers glimpses and insights into the quirky physical makeup of the town with its disproportionately large number of secondary buildings, seemingly untouched by time, views captured in literary sources of the banal and everyday aspects and rhythms of daily life in the past—combined with the presence of some extraordinary figures in the state's history—while simultaneously demonstrating the startling fact of the preservation of so much tangible evidence. Such features as this book explores were already cited years ago by the historian Mary Claire Engstrom as fodder for research, and so we in a sense picked up where she left off.

Finally, *Hidden Hillsborough* echoes a small book by Elizabeth Matheson and Elon Eidenier entitled *Sense of Place: a Hillsborough Memoir* (1991), with its timeless images and lyrical voices from the past. Alongside these, we hope our work will prove an informative, beautiful, and lasting companion as well as a gentle incentive to preserve our history.

—*Callie Connor* for the Hidden Hillsborough Committee
of the Preservation Fund of Hillsborough
January 2016
Hillsborough, North Carolina

Introduction

BY BARBARA HUME

"Hillsborough rather exceeded my expectations; it is far from being a disagreeable town, as to appearance, and there is a remarkable handsome church in it." Thus wrote James Iredell, future justice of the United States Supreme Court, in 1778, after having dined "with great satisfaction" in a "most elegant tavern."[1] The town was described in 1786 as containing "forty dwelling-houses, a church, court-house, and academy" and embracing "a very genteel society."[2]

Unlike most other county seats in the Piedmont of North Carolina (e.g., Raleigh, Durham, and Greensboro), Hillsborough has experienced slower population growth in the last century and a half. Beginning about 1830, population expansion in Orange County shifted to Chapel Hill and the vicinity of the University of North Carolina campus. Changing fortunes in the Piedmont's furniture and textile industries in the last half of the twentieth century resulted in the closing of factories. Hillsborough became a sleepy courthouse town. Then, toward the end of the twentieth century, its appeal as a peaceful, walkable community with no parking meters, beautiful old houses, and a commitment to historic preservation attracted newcomers who joined the descendants of the early inhabitants. Today, the town is known for its writers, its historic buildings, its thriving shops and eateries, and its charm.

Today, Hillsborough remains a small, quiet town noted for its surviving collection of historic buildings, which are still being lived in, still being used for business and for government, still functioning as churches. Its historic architecture, located mostly in the central section of the town, draws visitors who stroll about the streets admiring the old houses.

But hidden between and behind these larger and more dominant houses are other significant, but smaller eighteenth- and nineteenth-century buildings, known as dependencies, that served a number of different types of functions useful to the landowner or community, considering that this was before the introduction of electricity and a municipal water system in the early 1900s. These dependencies include, for example, well houses, kitchens, offices, and smokehouses. Landscape features range from stone curbs to steps and walks that now lead nowhere. Many of these escape the notice of the casual observer, but are important in understanding the evolution of the townscape. The town's somewhat mysterious small buildings and landscape features merit consideration in the context of a bygone era and are the subject of *Hidden Hillsborough*.

The timeframe of the book spans the period of the town's history from its beginnings in 1754 to about 1915. The geographic area included in this study has been defined by the boundaries established in the original nomination of Hillsborough to the National Register of Historic Places in 1973, and by the National Register properties located just east and south of those boundaries (Map 5).

In Chapter One, following an overview of factors in the history of the town's development, we address the question of the circumstances that dictated Hillsborough's need for its particular collection of dependencies. A juxtaposition of in-town "mansion house complexes" with the outlying plantations to the east of the town center reveals common needs that were met in both cases by the construction of dependencies serving the principal house on a property, regardless of the scale.

In Chapters Two to Seven, we explore the individual categories of dependencies, one after the other. The aim is to define not only the types of structures but also the way in which they evoke aspects of private life and social contexts of the home. Chapters Eight to Eleven concern the dependencies or features that relate more to public life as it was experienced within the community. Finally, Chapter Twelve, "Cemeteries," focuses on the end of life. It examines physical features and changing customs of burials, including symbols of death and the afterlife.

In this book, the historic designs on the land are placed in the context of modern-day Hillsborough. Elizabeth Matheson's illuminating photographs and Stewart Dunaway's original maps, referenced throughout the text, allow us to envision the bustling pattern of life in the past, as our seemingly random little outbuildings and abandoned hedges assume the role of guides. Combined with the essays of committee members, the photographs and maps together evoke the story of life in a small Southern town.

Over the years the original need for most of the dependencies, hidden or not, has disappeared. The spaces that were once occupied by the large gardens and lots for horses have been sold and filled by modern, and usually smaller, houses. Laundries and kitchens have been moved inside the houses. Modern offices, which demand more space than a single room, are now located in office buildings, often outside the town center. The surviving dependencies have frequently been adapted to other uses, but some have been allowed to remain as architectural ornaments in the landscape, reminding us of our not-too-distant past. Their seemingly haphazard placement in the town must perplex newcomers, but when viewed in the context of the historic town they contribute a meaningful and intriguing dimension to the experience of seeing Hillsborough today.

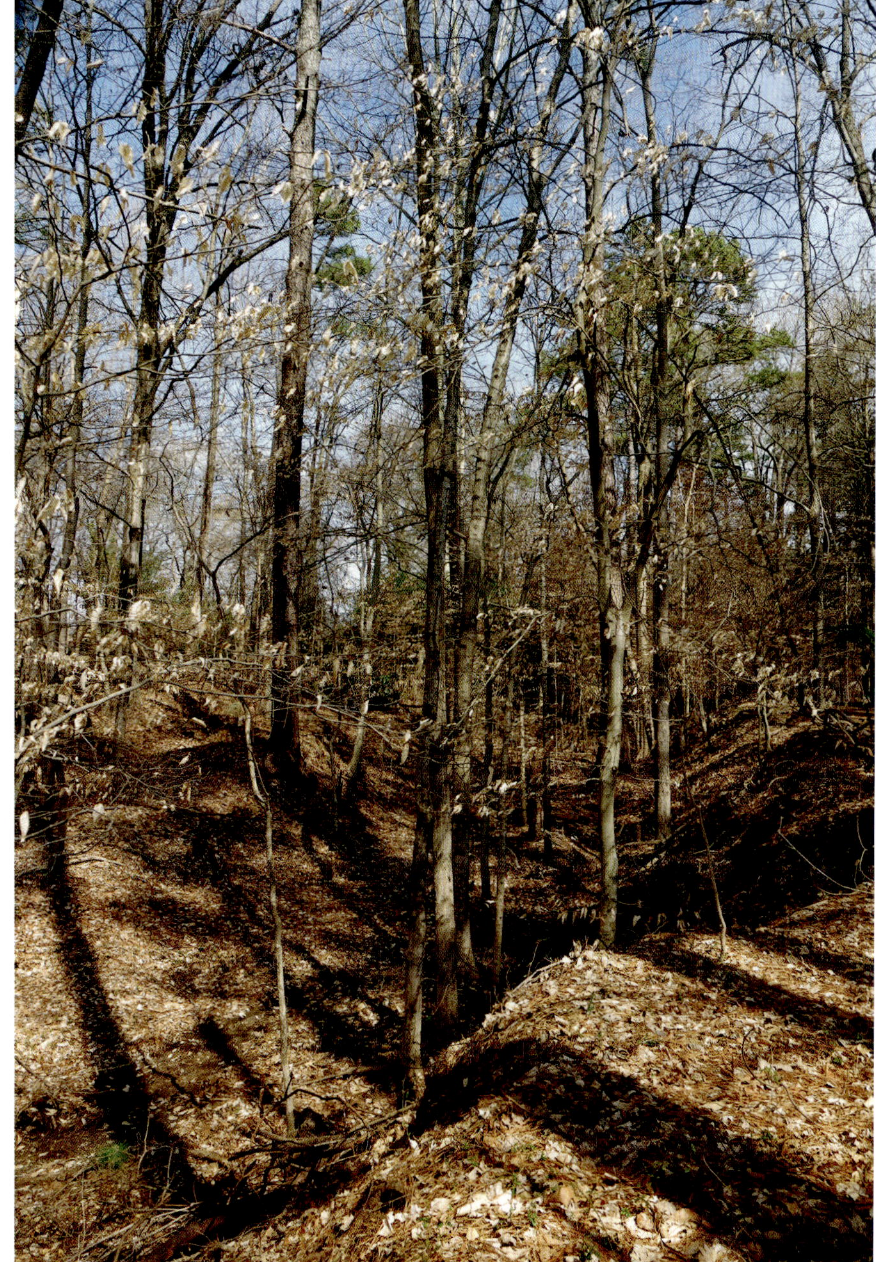

Figure 1.1 / View of the Old Indian Trading Path from a vantage point at Ayr Mount, where it appears as a deep, wide trough, dense with undergrowth and trees.

One

An Evolving Townscape

The Location and Early Importance of Hillsborough

BY BARBARA HUME AND STEWART E. DUNAWAY

From the time the first Native Americans inhabited this area, paths traversed the landscape that would one day become Hillsborough. When European explorers and trappers began to arrive in the early eighteenth century, they documented these paths, the most famous of which is known today as the Old Indian Trading Path.

The Old Indian Trading Path and Early Hillsborough

By Stewart E. Dunaway

The Old Indian Trading Path ran diagonally across North Carolina for centuries. Substantial traces of this ancient road can be seen in several spots around Hillsborough today. The road now consists of a twelve-foot-wide trough, and although cluttered with grown trees and brush, the evidence of its long use as a path, and then a coach and wagon road, is apparent. *Trading Path View,* at a bench located at the northern end of Poet's Walk on the Ayr Mount property, offers a clear view of a section of the Old Indian Trading Path (Figure 1.1).

Another stretch of the Trading Path runs into the woods near the southeast side of the intersection of St. Mary's Road and Highway 70 Bypass. Much of St. Mary's Road as it continues to the northeast is built directly on the Trading Path, but occasionally one can see it running parallel to the modern paved road. Another section, known as the Halifax Road, was one of many branches of the trading path. It continued east from the eastern end of King

Street, across the present-day Board of Education property, and rejoined the main route of the Trading Path at the Few farm on what is today Ayr Mount. Perhaps an alternate branch of the Old Indian Trading Path ran north of town and crosses the Eno at the ford below Faucette Mill northwest of Hillsborough (see Maps 1 and 5 for these detectable sections of the ancient Trading Path). Early explorers also found that the area's streams and creeks could be forded at unique geological locations, called low-stream embankments, where broad, shallow streams made it possible to cross these watersheds at times of low water.

When the colonial government was established in the eighteenth century, the evolution from trail to roadway began. Laws were enacted in 1715 that established roadways, including bridges and ferries, and delegated their approval and maintenance to individual counties.[1] Roads and wooden bridges began as simple one-lane thoroughfares with a mandated ten-foot width.

As migration increased and commerce demanded larger wagons, transportation routes continued to increase in size (width) and scope (distance). Ford locations at larger rivers were upgraded with wooden bridges, allowing for uninterrupted travel, especially improving "time-to-market" for produce or mail. Hillsborough's town ford, situated just west of where Churton Street crosses the Eno, near the present-day Exchange Park concrete bridge, was equipped with a twelve-foot-wide wooden bridge in 1788 at a cost of £123.10.0 (approximately $23,034).[2]

Because landscapes change over the years, most of these ancient roadways are no longer extant or have left few traces. Some are actually underneath current highways; others can be detected in the woods, sometimes appearing as ditches. A number of the early-eighteenth-century roadbeds still exist in the general area of Hillsborough.

The earliest map of the area, drawn by Edward Moseley in 1735,[3] shows roads in the province of North Carolina and documents the Old Indian Trading Path as a single roadway entering North Carolina from Virginia and running southwest. It crossed the area called Occoneechee (the name of the Native American village)—that is, the present town of Hillsborough—by fording the Eno River once. A survey by the province's surveyor, Matthew Rowan, in 1738 shows the Old Indian Trading Path meandering in a more east-west direction, crossing the Eno River three times before heading to the Haw River.[4] The Fry-Jefferson map of 1751 shows a single route similar to that shown on the Moseley map.[5]

The earliest detailed map of Hillsborough showing not paths but roads—both town streets and long-distance trade routes—dates to the October 1768 map (see Maps 1 and 2) by famed French cartographer Claude J. Sauthier.[6] Of the ten towns Royal Gov. William Tryon commissioned Sauthier to survey and map,[7] Hillsborough had more named roads than any other location, although several of the towns were in the coastal region and had been established decades earlier. This highlights the importance of the county seat and its role as a central hub for travel via roadways. Sauthier's map with its alternate routes for roads illustrates the continual proliferation of and changes to roads referenced in earlier maps. More than three decades after Moseley had drawn his map of the area, Sauthier included in his map a new road to Halifax and another leading toward New Bern; the latter was better known in the mid-nineteenth century as Fish Dam Road.

As it matured, Hillsborough, like other villages, experienced an evolutionary change in transportation routes within its town limits, as well as those interconnecting to other towns. Within Hillsborough, numerous roadways were consolidated and other, older roadways discontinued as the town expanded and new town lots were sold.[8] Hillsborough established and maintained a grid-like street system, running north and south, as well as east and west (see Maps 2B and 3). As travel increased between the central part of the state and Virginia, the major road-traffic patterns changed from an east-west main thoroughfare, with patterns of movement being predominantly via King Street, to a north-south one via Churton Street. In addition, town streets were widened and sidewalks added in accordance with local needs and village life, requiring a shift in land ownership and dimensions: The size of town lots decreased from an acre to seven-eighths of an acre.

Shaping the Colonial Town

By Barbara Hume

Having considered the patterns of the earliest roadways and the evidence of early maps, we move to features of colonial settlement.

There were five major factors that determined the location and early importance of Hillsborough, among which transportation was perhaps the most crucial, as explained above. Hillsborough was platted where there was an established ford in the Eno River on the Old Indian Trading Path, which ultimately connected the port in Petersburg, Virginia, with the southwestern part of North Carolina (via Salisbury), and even beyond.[9] This transportation factor resulted immediately in the second factor, the commercial one. Stores were established in Hillsborough with wholesale connections to Petersburg and beyond that to the mercantile companies in such cities as Glasgow and Dumfries in Scotland. Several stores in Hillsborough were part of an archipelago of branch stores that were managed by young Scottish merchants, such as William Kirkland, sent to the town for that entrepreneurial purpose. Thus, Hillsborough, with its important early market house, located at the intersection of Churton and King streets in the center of town (see Maps 1 and 2), quickly became a market town for the surrounding area.

The third factor giving Hillsborough its early prominence was its designation as the county seat of Orange County. The town was the site of the courthouse serving a large area that would gradually be divided into a number of counties as population increased.[10] The courthouse drew lawyers, aspiring lawyers, and judges to the town, as well as people requiring legal services. The influx of travelers and salesmen for even a short period required the presence of taverns and ordinaries, such as Mason's Ordinary and the Old King Street Tavern, to accommodate them.[11] The presence of educated members of the legal profession encouraged the fourth factor, the establishment of educational facilities in Hillsborough. Lawyers took young men into their offices to read law. An academy, noted in the Introduction as already existing in the town in 1787, was followed by numerous day and boarding schools for girls and for boys, and, eventually, even a military school. These educational institutions became known all over the region and the country for their excellence.

The fifth factor that attracted people to Hillsborough was its climate. Located in the small range of the Occoneechee Mountains, it was considered to be a healthy place for year-round residence and a desirable location for summer homes, or even for an extended summer visit at a local tavern or hotel. The summer heat at the coast and the threat of associated sickness drove those who could afford it to retreat to the safer, more salutary mountains of the Piedmont plateau around Hillsborough.

These factors brought together teachers, merchants, ministers, and lawyers in the eighteenth-century town. The construction of the buildings brought carpenters and joiners (most notably Martin Palmer), brick masons and bricklayers (such as Samuel Hancock), stonemasons, turners, painters, and other craftsmen to the growing town. Just before 1800, lawyer Duncan Cameron[12] and physician James Webb[13] moved to Hillsborough. They were among the first arrivals of a series of professional men whose family origins and education led them to expect a more enhanced quality of life, and in the case of Dr. Webb, a determination to promote it.

The Architectural and Landscape Development of Hillsborough from 1754 until 1800

The Sauthier map of 1768 documents the appearance of the town only fourteen years after it was founded. Hillsborough had been laid out about 1754 by the surveyor William Churton. His original plan divided a portion of its four hundred acres into one-acre lots, according to a grid plan, with a large commons, in the northwest quadrant of town. In later years additional blocks of town lots were formed (Map 3, "Town Expansion 1892"). Settlers bought anywhere from one to many lots, depending on their wealth and needs. Speculation motivated some; others required space. Because the town was designed as the county seat, the courthouse and jail at its center became the hub of activity, and around them clustered merchants, tavern-keepers, artisans, and lawyers on lots divided and subdivided again and again as the value of the lots increased. In direct contrast, ringing the town just outside its periphery were estates and small plantations of those with ample means, perhaps involved in commercial investment or modest agricultural activities (see Map 5).

Churton used a Gunter's (or surveyor's) chain, which is sixty-six feet long. The terrain was divided into town lots, each approximately one acre, or two and a half chains by four chains. All of the major streets were one chain wide, and narrow Margaret Lane was a half chain (thirty-three feet) wide. The roadways and sidewalks of these major streets have been located within those sixty-six feet ever since. During the nineteenth century the sidewalks were paved with large, flat stones from a nearby quarry. Although a few of these sidewalks were on approximately the same level as the adjoining roadway, most were elevated on a berm somewhat above street level (see Chapter 9 for more about berms and sidewalks). Almost all of these old, flagstone-paved sidewalks have now been replaced with concrete sidewalks, but in some instances the stones have simply been set in concrete in order to maintain a more regular and level surface. In others they have been obscured by grass or been taken up and transferred to walks and gardens on nearby properties. Today, the foremost example of a flagstone sidewalk can be seen in front of the Inn at Teardrops on King Street near the intersection of Wake Street (see Figures 9.4 and 9.6).

The stone curbs and flagstone-paved sidewalks were not intended to define the widths of the streets; instead, stone walls erected during the early history of the town delineate the property boundaries.[14] In the first block of West Queen Street where the dry-stack stone walls (those constructed without mortar) survive on both sides of the street, the walls are exactly sixty-six feet, or one chain, apart.

Perhaps the most overlooked stones in Hillsborough today are the old mounting blocks that were used when mounting a horse or climbing into a carriage. These stones were positioned in front of most if not all houses standing before about 1910. Today, they can be found hidden away in a corner of a yard, sometimes being used as a step into a house, as at the David Anderson House on West King Street.[15]

Although many early stone landscape features survive today, other designs on the land have mostly disappeared. A noteworthy landscape feature in the Sauthier map is the allée, or tree-lined avenue, that had been planted on or before 1768, running from Tryon Street to Edmund Fanning's house (Lot 33 and the northern part of Lot 23 [see Map 2B]).[16] No trace of this allée remains. Another prominent feature of Hillsborough's garden design illustrated in Sauthier's plan, but missing today, was the division of gardens into parterres, or small ornamental planting plots. Drawings of the Nash-Kollock School gardens on Margaret Lane from the late nineteenth century indicate both flower and vegetable gardens, arranged in squares and rectangles, and separated by walks.[17]

The Mansion House and its Dependencies: The "Mansion House Complex"

The Sauthier map of 1768 documents the appearance of the town only a short time after it was founded. Even at that early date, Hillsborough contained many houses with supporting dependencies and gardens. Although these original houses were probably mostly one-story or one-and-a-half story frame buildings, many would have been known as *mansion houses.*

During the early history of the town, a mansion house was "a dwelling house; the primary residence of a landowner," according to the Acts of the North Carolina General Assembly of 1766. It specified that the purchaser of a town lot or lots "shall, within two years . . . erect, build, and finish on each lot, one brick, stone, or frame house, at least twenty feet long, sixteen feet wide, and nine feet pitch in the clear, with brick or stone chimney."[18] Thus, in that period and up to the Civil War, the term *mansion house* was not used exclusively to describe large or pretentious houses; it could also designate a small house. The point was that they were to be substantial houses, built to last, and for residents who aimed to remain in place.

These mansion houses were not usually isolated dwellings standing alone. In Hillsborough, most of them were situated on a tract that included several adjoining town lots and encompassed from two to six or more acres. A mansion house, itself, and its supporting dependencies, taken together, comprised a *mansion house complex,* or small town estate (see Map 6 for locations of the mansion house complexes). These clusters of lots were anchored by the mansion house, but also included many of the dependencies of a plantation, albeit on a smaller scale. Absent from these town complexes were the vast acres reserved for croplands and woodlands seen on large agricultural plantations. Present in both the rural plantation and the typical town mansion house complex were the main house, a lot[19] and stable for horses, a small pasture and shed for cows, a large vegetable garden, and access to a well or spring. In addition, both would have included other dependencies such as a kitchen, laundry, office, smokehouse, woodshed, slave house, icehouse, dairy, carriage house, barn, etc., of various dimensions and sizes.

The best preserved and most complete example of a mansion house complex within the historic town limits of Hillsborough is the Ruffin-Roulhac House, now owned by the Town of Hillsborough and operated as the Town Hall. With its ten town lots (Lots 177–81 and 202–6), it was the largest in-town complex, and was bounded by Churton, East Corbin, Cameron, and East Orange streets; today it retains four of its original lots, 180–81, 202–3 (see Figure 1.2 for a site plan and view of the house and dependencies; see Maps 4 and 6 for location of the complex).

The handsomely restored main house faces East Orange Street, and behind and beside it can be seen its dependencies, in clockwise order: the well house with its well shelter, smokehouse, slave house, office, carriage house, barn, water tower foundation, kitchen, and adjoining pantry (see photos on the jacket on the front and back covers). Some of the dependencies have been restored or moved from their original positions on the property. At different

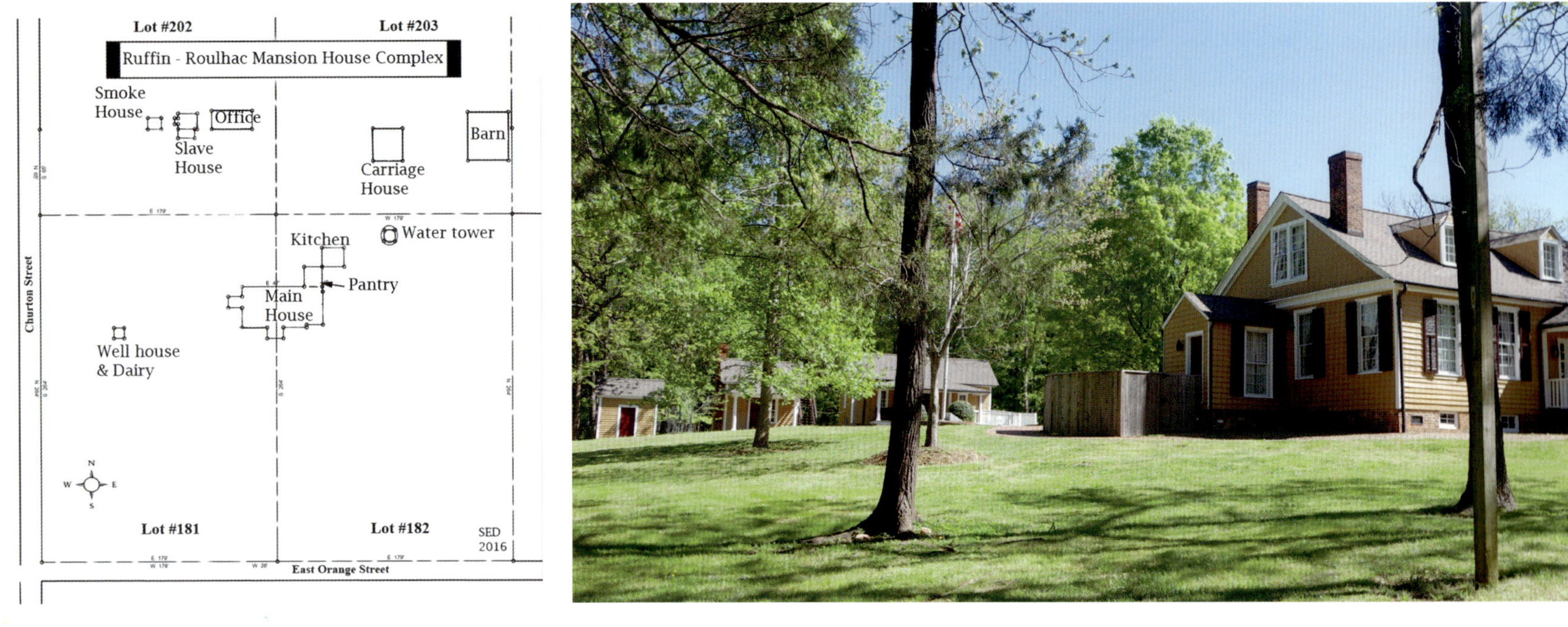

Figure 1.2 / Site plan of Ruffin-Roulhac House complex showing house and surrounding dependencies; on the right is a view of the house and dependencies from the southwest.

times, this property was owned by the Rev. Francis Lister Hawks[20] and by Thomas Ruffin, chief justice of the North Carolina Supreme Court.

The Architecture and Landscape of Historic Properties Adjoining the Town

Immediately to the east of Hillsborough and its town lots are five country estates, all of which were once small plantations with a main house and dependencies, farm outbuildings, and agricultural land. These are Sans Souci, the Mangum-Ruffin House, Montrose, Ayr Mount, and Burnside (see Map 5 for their locations).

The historic house Sans Souci, along with its associated dependencies, illustrates the makeup of the country plantation, as compared with the in-town mansion house complex

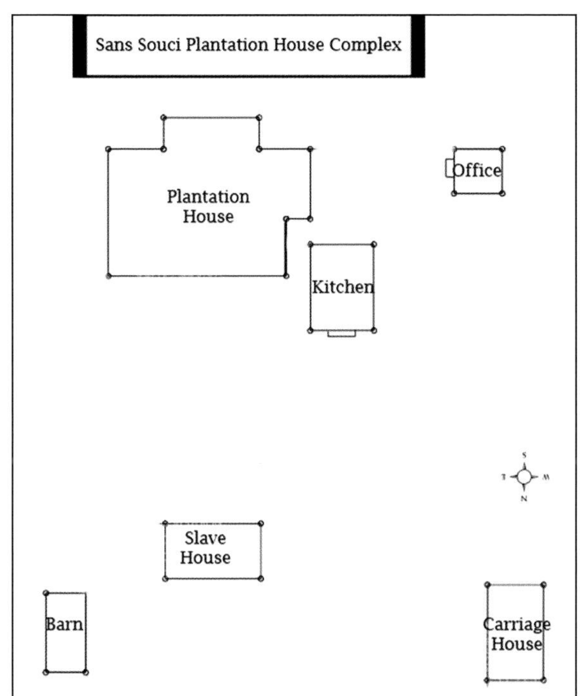

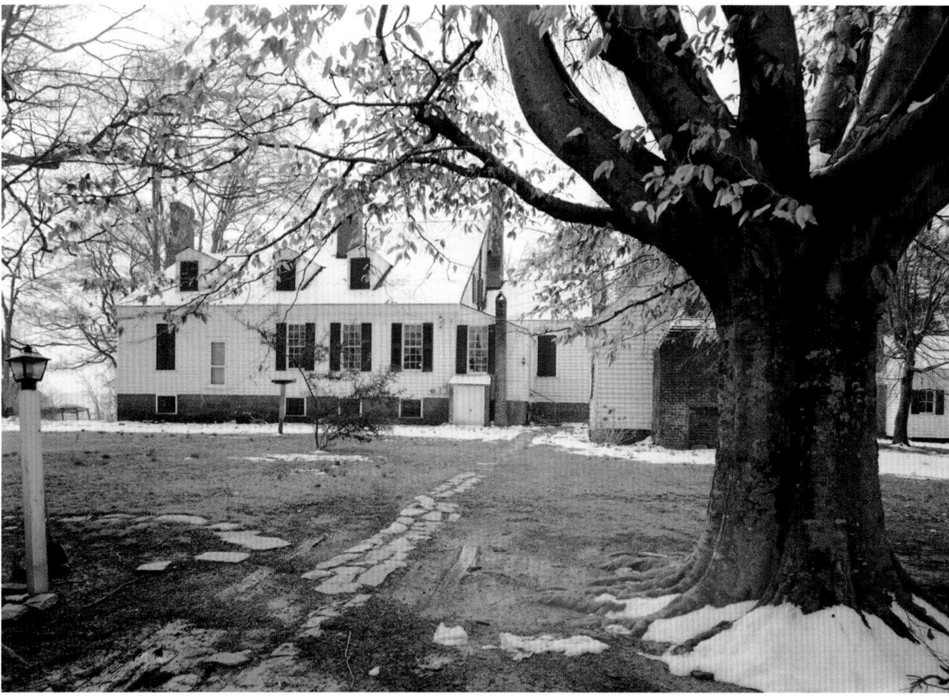

Figure 1.3 / Site plan of Sans Souci, showing plantation house and surviving dependencies. On the right is a view from the north, showing the rear of the house, the separate kitchen, and the office. (Photograph, circa 1938; Historic American Buildings Survey. Courtesy, Library of Congress, No. NC*-221-1.)*

just discussed. Sans Souci began as a plantation, but in recent years its agricultural lands have been subdivided and sold for modern houses; however, it still retains its historic kitchen, office, carriage house, slave house, and barn, clustered around the main house (see Figure 1.3, site plan of Sans Souci).

Two other examples of plantation complexes that were also formerly associated with traditional farming activities are the Mangum-Ruffin House and Montrose. Although they have each lost at least one main house to fire, they both retain a collection of supporting dependencies, mostly on their original sites. Montrose is also distinguished by the retention of about sixty-two acres.[21]

The historic plantation house, Ayr Mount, built around 1815, retains significant acreage, but it has lost all of its supporting dependencies, with its only remaining historic landscape features being a picturesque family cemetery and a section of the Old Indian Trading Path. Burnside, another historic plantation once consisting of some seventy acres (a portion of the earlier 263-acre grant to Francis Corbin), retains its mid-nineteenth-century house and a large number of dependencies, including an office, kitchen, smokehouse, necessary house, dairy, corn crib, icehouse, barn, and even vestiges of the design of its agricultural landscape.

Early Public and Religious Buildings and Cemeteries

Two lots in the original town plan were reserved for important buildings: the church, on Lot 98; and the courthouse, jail, and market house, all on Lot 1 (also known as the courthouse square). The church was allocated its own separate town lot, probably because an adjoining cemetery had already been established there or at least was anticipated. The government buildings were clustered together in or near the courthouse square.

The church, constructed about 1770–71, was St. Matthew's Church, the "remarkable handsome church," noted by James Iredell in 1778 (see Introduction). Since Hillsborough was a county seat, the Church of England, the established church before the Revolution, located St. Matthew's on the lot reserved for it in the town plan; the adjoining cemetery is known as the Old Town Cemetery. The church served as the site of the North Carolina Constitutional Convention of 1788. Although the building has disappeared, a plan and an elevation of the church survive. Both of these drawings have been attributed to the architect, John Hawks, and date circa 1769.[22] After the Revolution, St. Matthew's Church was remodeled by carpenter/joiner Martin Palmer to be an academy. Later, after the building had deteriorated, it was ordered to be sold and the lot cleared. The Presbyterian church was built on the church lot in 1816. About 1824–26, a replacement for the first St. Matthew's was constructed just east of town with a cemetery adjoining it on land donated by State Supreme Court Chief Justice Thomas Ruffin (1787–1870) (see Map 4 for the locations of these buildings and cemeteries).

In addition to the two cemeteries associated with an adjoining church, there are three other cemeteries in the study area. One, of unknown date, is located on a hill in the western part of town and is known as the Margaret Lane Cemetery (Lots 233 and 234). It has traditionally been associated with the African American community in Hillsborough. Abandoned about 1931, it suffered from want of care until its restoration by the town in 1987. Another in-town cemetery is known as the Lockhart-Phillips Cemetery, located on Lot 101. It is enclosed by a stone wall. The fifth cemetery, also a family cemetery, is on the grounds of Ayr Mount, William Kirkland's plantation mentioned above.[23]

An important colonial artifact that has been associated with several of the public buildings in Hillsborough is the Old Town Clock.[24] An undated elevation of the colonial St. Matthew's Church shows a circular space about the size of the clock face reserved in the church's tower. Although the exact date the clock was installed in the tower is unknown, it was certainly there by 21 August 1787, when the clockmaker in Guilford County, who had recently inspected the clock, described it as being "on the church in Hillsborough."[25] After the church building was confiscated and converted into an academy, the clock was moved to the market house.[26] Later, after the market house was razed, it was stored for a time and then moved to the cupola of the new courthouse in 1846,[27] where it still marks the time today. Its original two faces were supplemented with two additional ones, all four of which are visible today in the cupola soaring above the town. To see the clock itself one must climb the steps inside the cupola.

Evolving Expectations and Expanding Influences on the Architecture of Hillsborough, 1800–61

Around 1800, the architectural landscape of Hillsborough was not as promising as it had been at the time of the Revolution, in spite of some growth that occurred in that period. The houses were still small, usually only one story or one-and-a-half stories in height and one room in depth, and constructed using wood framing.[28] Its two most ambitious buildings, the original St. Matthew's church (circa 1768–70) and the brick courthouse (1778), were gone, replaced by a vacant church lot and a modest frame courthouse. (See Maps 4 and 5 for building and site locations.)

Gone also were the energetic, ambitious, but mostly transient men, such as Nathaniel Rochester, who had settled in Hillsborough in the early years to take advantage of its position as the courthouse town of a county covering a great expanse of land to make a quick financial profit.[29] By about 1800 these men had moved on to western North Carolina, Tennessee, Kentucky, or other places with fresh possibilities to make money, or they had relocated to the country and become planters. They were replaced by distinguished men, including doctors, lawyers, and teachers, who came to establish homes, practice their professions, raise families, and stay the remainder of their lives. Among those men were Frederick Nash,[30] Dr. Edmund Strudwick,[31] William A. Graham,[32] and the aforementioned Dr. James Webb.

The transformation of the architecture of the town in the early 1800s reflected this change in the goals and objectives of its inhabitants. Beginning in the early part of the nineteenth century, the prominent citizens in town began to enlarge these houses (e.g., Twin Chimneys, the Whitted-Johnston House, Courtney's Yellow House) or to construct more substantial and imposing houses (e.g., Hasell-Nash House, Mallett Mill House).

Two buildings stand out as important examples (circa 1815) of this movement: the large, impressive brick plantation house, Ayr Mount, in the final phase of construction, and the brick church that replaced St. Matthew's on the church lot. That church, which immediately became the Presbyterian church, helped attract to Hillsborough its first resident minister, the Rev. John Knox Witherspoon, a grandson of a Signer of the Declaration of Independence. That church is today the oldest church building in town that was built to be a church. About 1824–26, a replacement for St. Matthew's, designed by the noted architect, William Nichols, and also constructed in brick, was erected on a bluff overlooking the town. Today, there are three other antebellum churches scattered throughout the historic district.[33]

In 1845 the town finally replaced its frame courthouse, constructed in 1790, with a brick courthouse designed by John Berry. Today, the courthouse square (Lot 1) is still the site of that courthouse and still serves some needs of the county government, although a newer courthouse, completed in 1954, is now the primary location of the judicial functions of the county. Another building originally on the courthouse square in the Sauthier plan of Hillsborough was the jail; although it is long gone, a modern jail still adjoins the courthouse square on the east.

When a new brick courthouse was constructed in 1845, the 1790 frame courthouse was moved two blocks north on Churton Street and converted into a church, now Dickerson Chapel. Today, three courthouses, or former courthouses, line Churton Street in the four blocks north of the Eno River, and the cupolas or towers of all three can be seen above the tree line when crossing the river and entering the town from the south.[34]

About 1818, English-born architect William Nichols appeared in Hillsborough, and his buildings had a profound effect on local architecture for the next couple of decades.[35] His influence was due not only to his design ability and knowledge of current movements in architecture, but also to the advanced training he gave to a couple of local craftsmen: John Faucett, a carpenter, and John Berry, a brick mason, who worked on the construction of the Masonic Lodge.[36] Nichols was responsible for both the design of the Masonic Lodge and, as previously mentioned, the new St. Matthew's Episcopal Church. He was also almost certainly the designer of Lochiel, a grand plantation northwest of town (see Map 5), and the important villa constructed for Eliza Hasell, which she named Pilgrim's Rest.[37] Both of those elegant houses were distinguished by interior chimneys flanked by lighted alcoves entered through arched openings, an appealing design feature immediately replicated by other owners and future builders of houses in Hillsborough.[38] When Nichols's design and construction abilities were united with the desire of the professional class for improved housing, the result was the collection of historic houses that are the pride of Hillsborough today.

Hidden Treasures: The Legacy of Hillsborough's Historic Architecture and Landscape

The dependencies that were built in association with both mansion houses and plantations were so essential to the operation of a household that their presence was invariably mentioned in advertisements for the sale of a house. For example, when advertising his house for sale, John Witherspoon described his outbuildings associated with it:

> Adjoining the house is a dining room, 30 by 16, well finished. The other improvements on the lot are a kitchen, smoke house, barn, stable, carriage house, &c. and a well of excellent water within a few feet of the kitchen door.[39]

However, dependencies were so ubiquitous that they were frequently lumped together in a collective abbreviated phrase such as "There is a good Office on the lot, with two rooms, a Well, Barn, and Stables, and every necessary Out House."[40] Dependencies and their locations need to be understood in relation to their original association with mansion or dwelling houses; then their presence in the townscape has meaning.

Hillsborough still retains historic buildings and landscape features within a block or two of the center of town in all directions. And scattered about, hidden among and behind these buildings, are the small surviving dependencies that were so essential to life in the eighteenth and nineteenth centuries, but today have outlived their original, important purposes. These buildings, together with the stone walks, walls, and curbs that still delineate the original spatial divisions of Hillsborough, are preserved today as important contributing features of our historic town. This preserved townscape defines Hillsborough and gives it its unique character, so cherished by its present-day inhabitants.

Two

Historic Kitchens

BY CALLIE CONNOR

The kitchen has always been the most critical space for a household's smooth operation. In eighteenth- and nineteenth-century Hillsborough, the cooking was done either in cellar kitchens or in freestanding kitchens. There are at least twelve preserved historic kitchens in Hillsborough—that is, self-contained buildings used for cooking, sometimes referred to as summer kitchens. They are among the most richly evocative reminders of a past way of life (see Map 7).

These kitchens were usually located a short distance from the main house for several reasons: to protect the occupants of the main house from the noise, odors, and heat involved in the preparation of food; and to lessen the danger of a cooking fire spreading to the main house. In social and symbolic terms, regardless of where the kitchen was found, its location accentuated the divide between those who were served and those who did the serving (Figure 2.1).[1]

It may seem surprising that such a large number of exterior kitchens survives; however, they were usually sturdily built structures, small and charming in external appearance, and so could easily be put to a number of other purposes when kitchens became integral to the interiors of houses in the South after the Civil War. With the abolition of slavery, exterior kitchens were no longer manageable without the slaves who had once carried food the distance from the kitchen to the dining room. In the later decades of the nineteenth century, kitchens were moved to be adjacent to the main house and integrated into its fabric, for

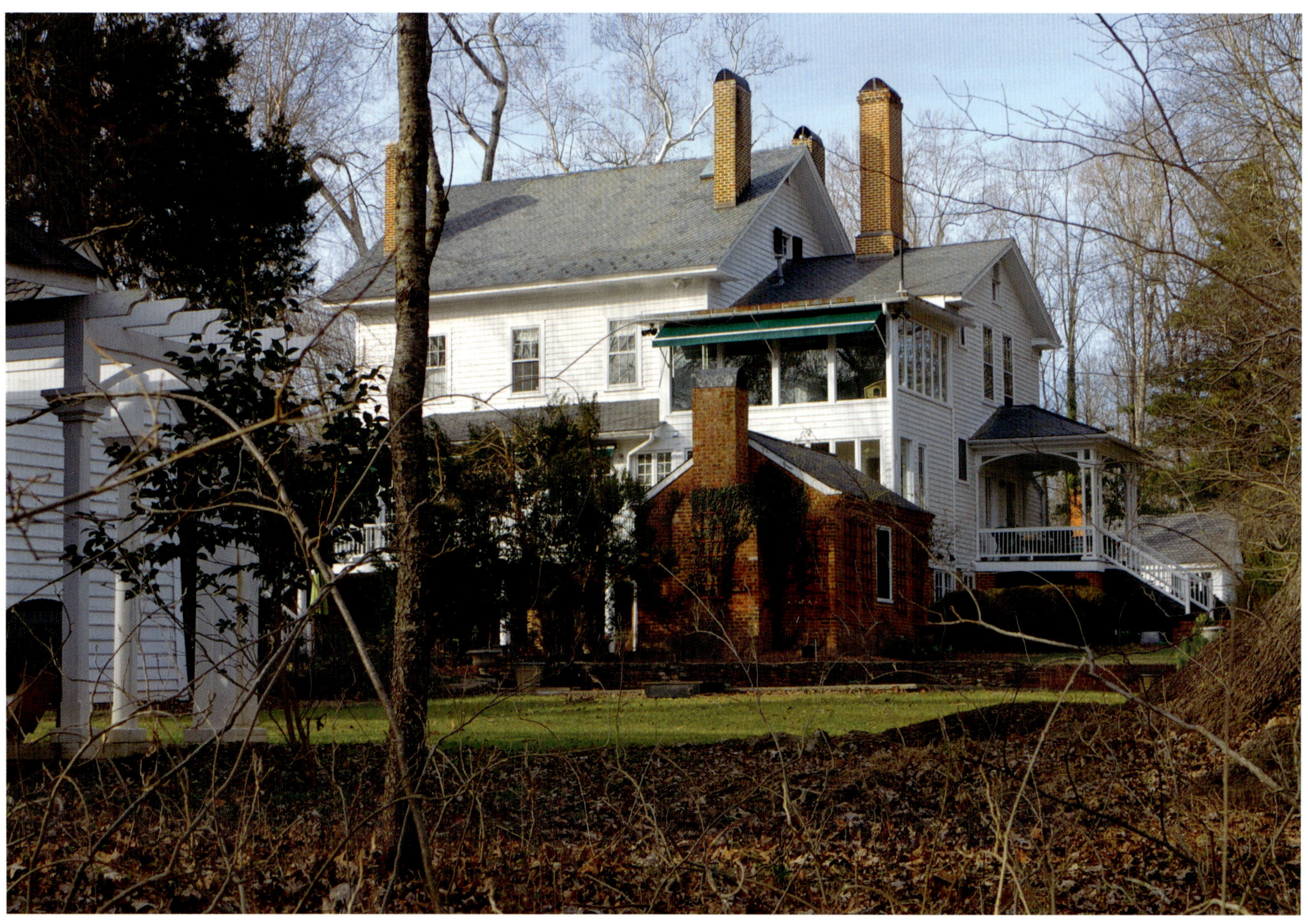

Figure 2.1 / Kitchen at Burnside, showing location behind the main house.

convenience; others were simply joined to the house by a dogtrot or other connector, to consolidate everyday routines into a less labor-intensive lifestyle.

Those freestanding kitchens that remain are located behind or beside the main house, and are much easier to identify than those that have been incorporated or joined to an ell at the rear of a house. Those that were moved were usually of wood frame construction as opposed to brick, which would have been much more difficult to move.

The exterior kitchen could be one of a number of small dependencies arranged in a row or clustered behind or beside a main house. Dependencies typically included slave quarters, a smokehouse, dairy, office, or self-contained pantry. Kitchens are distinguishable as one- or two-room, square or rectangular, single-story buildings with small attics and prominent chimneys large enough to accommodate a cooking fireplace; many had a central chimney serving the two rooms; others had chimneys at both ends of the building. Some kitchen fireplaces were large enough to step into, and could be eight to ten feet in length, but most were sized in more familiar terms, with an opening closer to three to four feet high, and between three and four feet wide, and up to two feet deep. Examples of kitchens that were incorporated into the main house are found at the Whitted House, Whitted-Johnston House, and Twin Chimneys, where they form ells extending toward the rear of the house. In the case of the Twin Chimneys kitchen, which measures fourteen by eighteen feet, the very large original fireplace with brick bake-oven was downsized and rebuilt as a smaller fireplace when the frame building was moved adjacent to the house in the 1870s (Figure 2.2); according to the owners, ghostmarks of the dimensions of the old fireplace are easily detectable on the former chimney wall.[2]

In some cases kitchens are two-room buildings with two entrances; larger than one-room kitchens, they measure around fifteen by thirty feet, with a center chimney opening into both rooms and allowing for supporting functions in the second room, such as a servant's room, a laundry, or sometimes a family dining room, as in the Mangum-Ruffin House kitchen (Figure 2.3).

In yet another design possibility, the rooms are combined in a duplex arrangement with two entrance doors, and chimneys on both gable ends. At Bellevue, with its end chimneys, the kitchen appears to have served two functions, such as cooking in the room at the south end, and slave quarters in the other, for there are two doors side by side on the long side of the building (Figures 2.4 and 2.5).

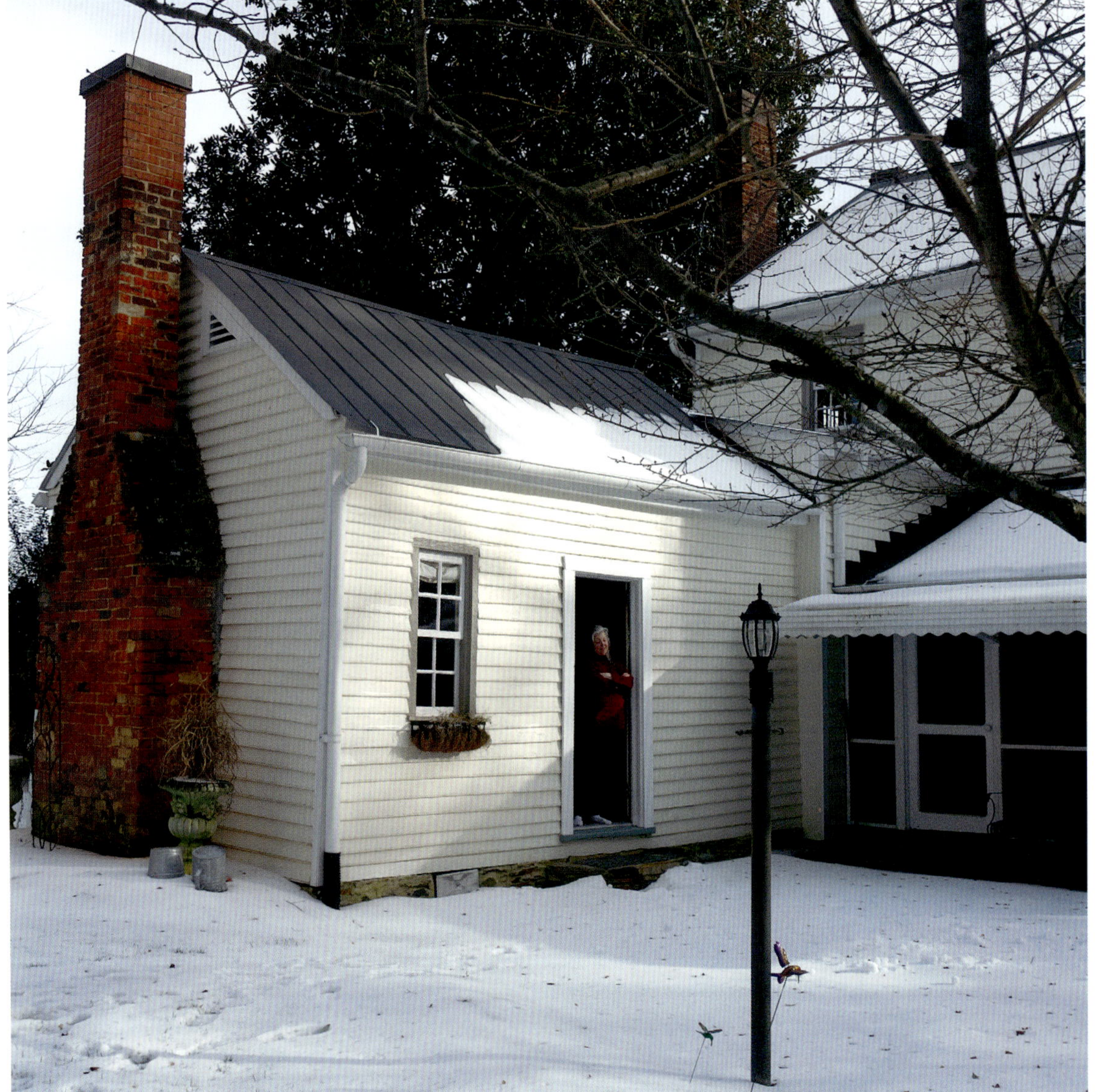

Figure 2.2 / The Twin Chimneys kitchen was moved and joined to the back of the main house.

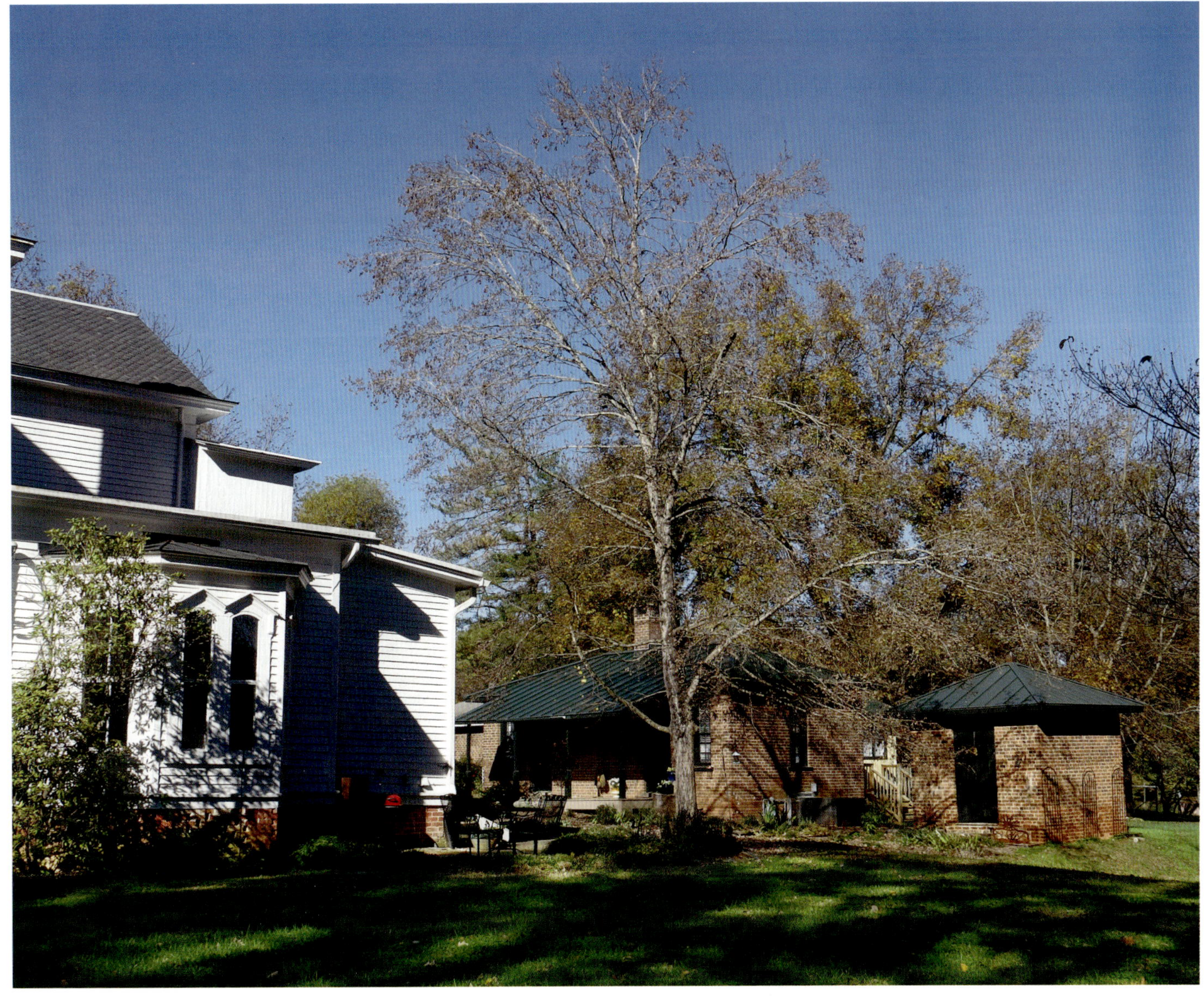

Figure 2.3 / Mangum-Ruffin House, two-room kitchen building.

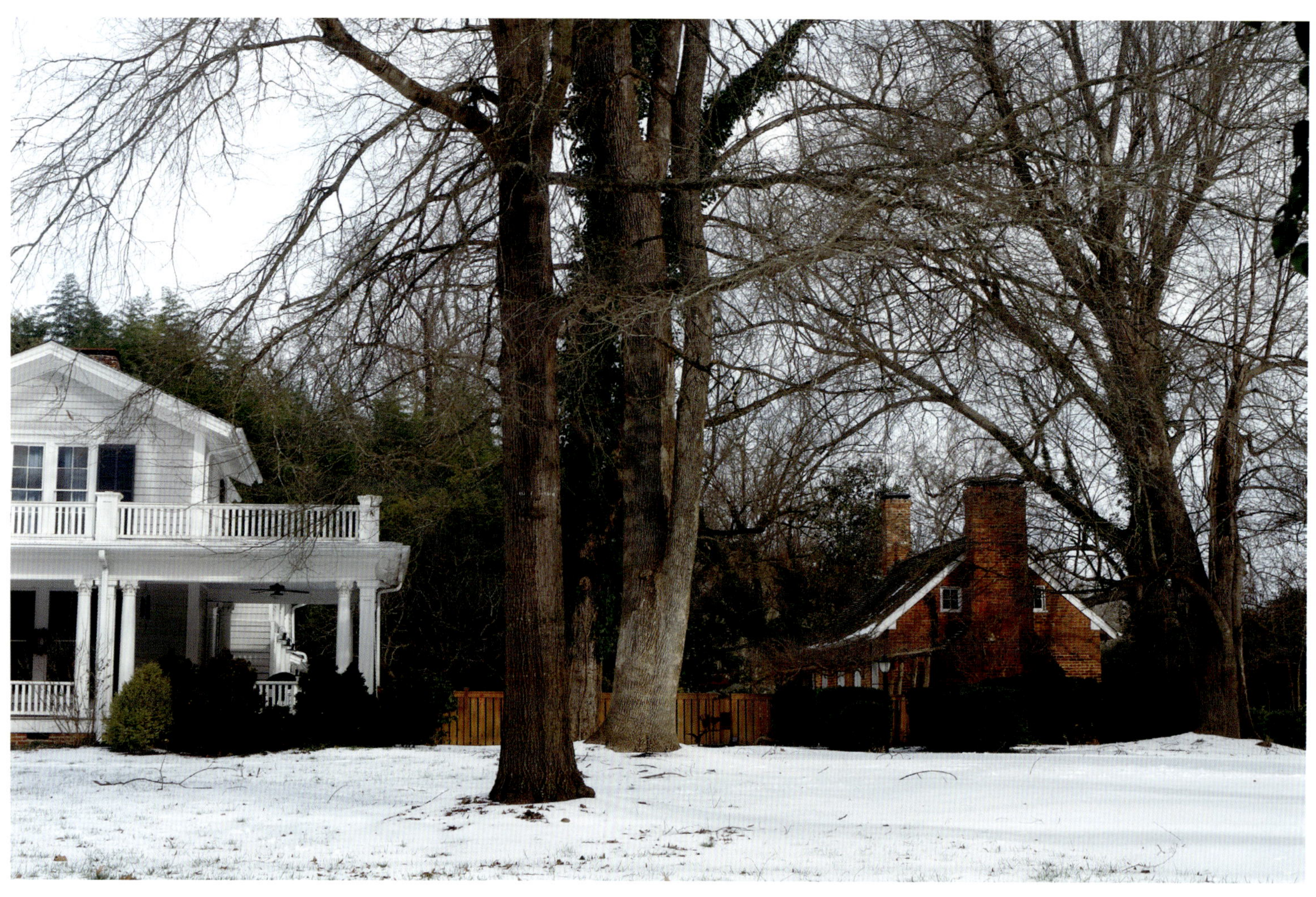

Figure 2.4 / Bellevue, showing brick kitchen positioned to the east of the main house.

In addition, there is a loft room, which likely served as living space for the cook, accessible by a steep, winding stairway (Figures 2.6 and 2.7). The Bellevue kitchen also preserves the firebox with a crane for suspending heavy pots over the fire; there is also a bake-oven built into the side of the fireplace.

Freestanding, one-room kitchens built of brick survive at the Robertson-Cheek House, Burnside, and at the site of the home of Dr. Edmund Strudwick, although that main house was demolished and recently replaced. The Strudwick kitchen is well preserved, with its arched firebox equipped with a crane for hanging heavy pots over the fire (Figures 2.8 and 2.9).

One-room kitchens have floor plans that are simple rectangles, with a hip or gable roof and several side windows. The proportions of the little Robertson-Cheek House kitchen with its diminutive hip roof are particularly pleasing; it has been adapted as a guest cottage (Figure 2.10). At Burnside the summer kitchen is a small brick building with a tiny loft above, probably for the cook (Figure 2.11); it now serves as a potting shed.

Former cellar kitchens can be detected in a few instances. The Robertson-Cheek House is a particularly interesting case, for it has two adjacent cellar rooms with fireplaces, one perhaps used for cooking and the other to heat a room used for dining or another purpose. Both are accessed from the south side of the house near the freestanding brick kitchen. The Mallett Mill and Hasell-Nash houses also show signs that basement rooms served as kitchens.

Many features and design possibilities are represented in the kitchens of Hillsborough. They encourage one to imagine the constant traffic in the vicinity of such buildings, with slaves constantly traversing the route to the main house where the food would be consumed. In an account of the Nash-Kollock School by a former student, the kitchen is described as being located behind the main building, near the slave quarters, while the dining room for the students was in the basement of the main house.

> The kitchen was a long distance from the back porch, and even when the slaves had reached this shelter without mishap, the bearers of the heavy serving trays still had the steps, the butler's pantry, and the hall to negotiate before they reached the dining room. In spite of the unavoidable delay, the food under its heavy covers almost always arrived hot and steaming.[3]

In terms of its extended functions, the kitchen was the hub of a great deal of activity; not only was the cooking and baking done around the fireplace, but all food had to be prepared in or near the kitchen; storage and preserving, or "putting up," of food was orchestrated

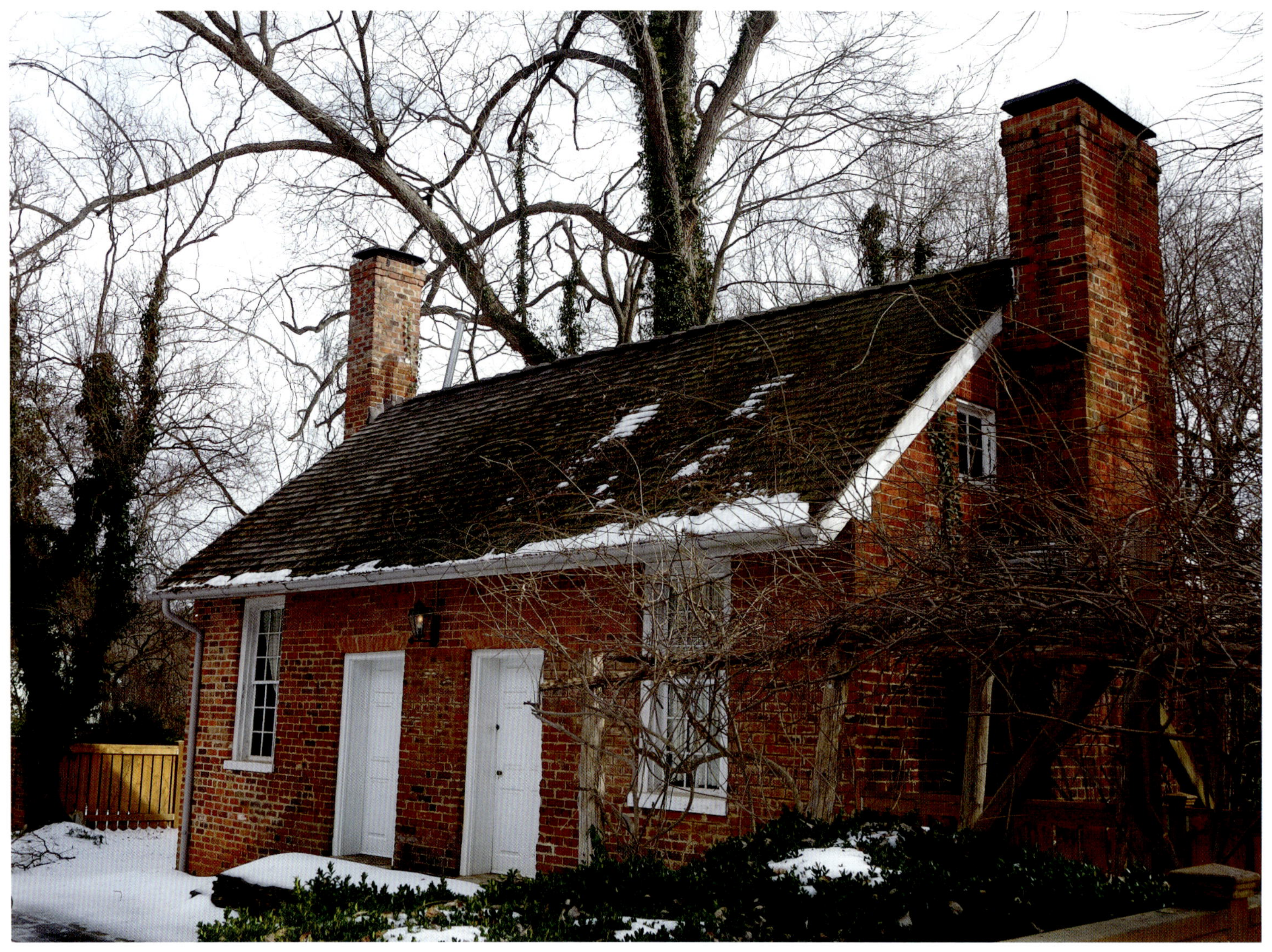

Figure 2.5 / Bellevue, brick kitchen with end chimneys and two entrance doors.

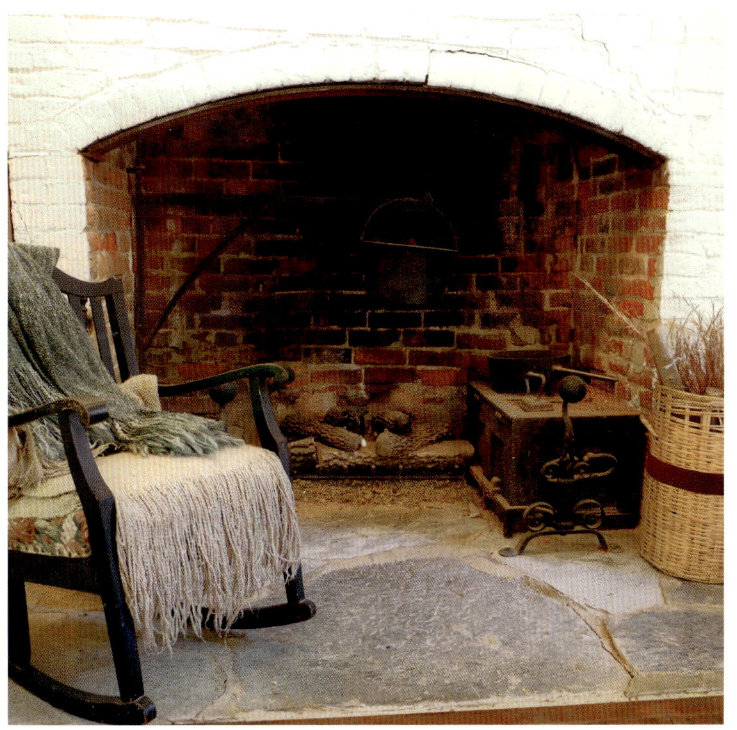

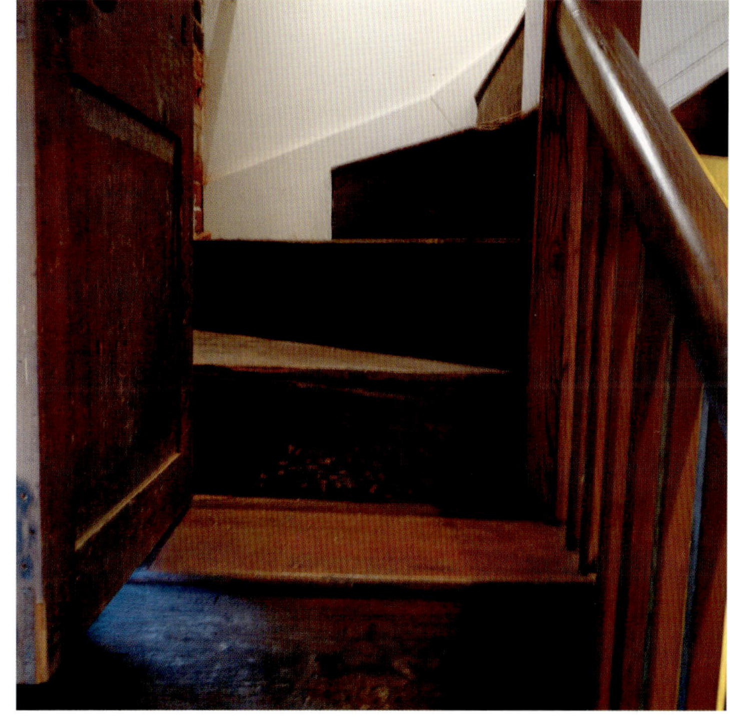

there, as well as the storage of cooking vessels and utensils, perhaps in conjunction with the loft above the kitchen or with a part of the building that contained cupboards or shelves and served as a pantry. At Sans Souci, such a pantry forms a separate room with its own entrance on one end of the kitchen, for there is a table along one side, probably used for putting up and preparing food, and storage shelves on the other (Figure 2.17). Such a pantry would have been accessed constantly during the preparation of a meal. A ready supply of fresh water carried in buckets from the well was necessary for kitchen operations; vegetables or other crops from the gardens had to be brought into the kitchen for washing and preparation, just as did flour from the mill, milk from the milk house or dairy where it was stored, eggs from the hen house. The frame kitchen at Montrose, for example, which stands thirty yards from

(above, left)
Figure 2.6 / Bellevue brick kitchen, showing firebox with crane for hanging heavy pots.

(above, right)
Figure 2.7 / Bellevue kitchen, showing winding stairs leading to the loft.

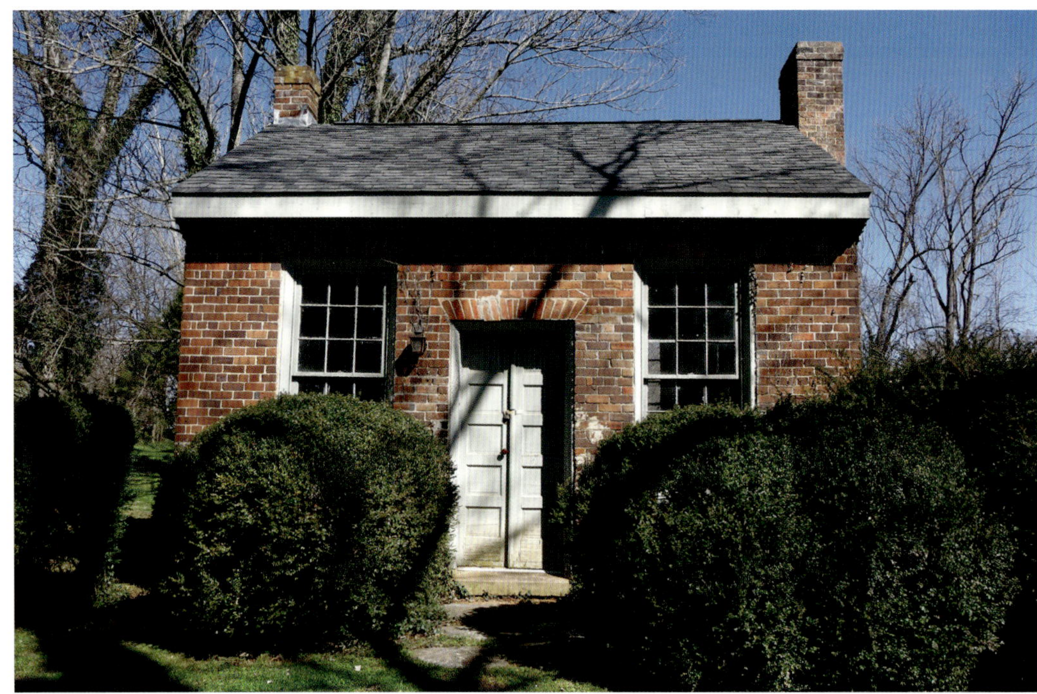

Figure 2.8 / Dr. Edmund Strudwick's brick kitchen.

the back of the main house, is joined by a dogtrot to a complex of outbuildings that includes the well shelter and a dairy. The butchering and processing of animals for food had to be accommodated in an outside area before cooking could take place, perhaps explaining the outside hearth at the north end of the Sans Souci kitchen (see Figures 1.3, right, and 2.17). Still other commodities used in meal preparation had to be purchased and carried from the market house, which stood at the intersection of King and Churton streets in Hillsborough until the mid-nineteenth century.

Baking involved a scenario all its own, as recaptured in a description of the kitchen of the Nash-Kollock School:

> In the center of the kitchen there was a large stump, its top worn to the smoothness of satin by years of friction. Here the biscuit dough was mixed and beaten, and the

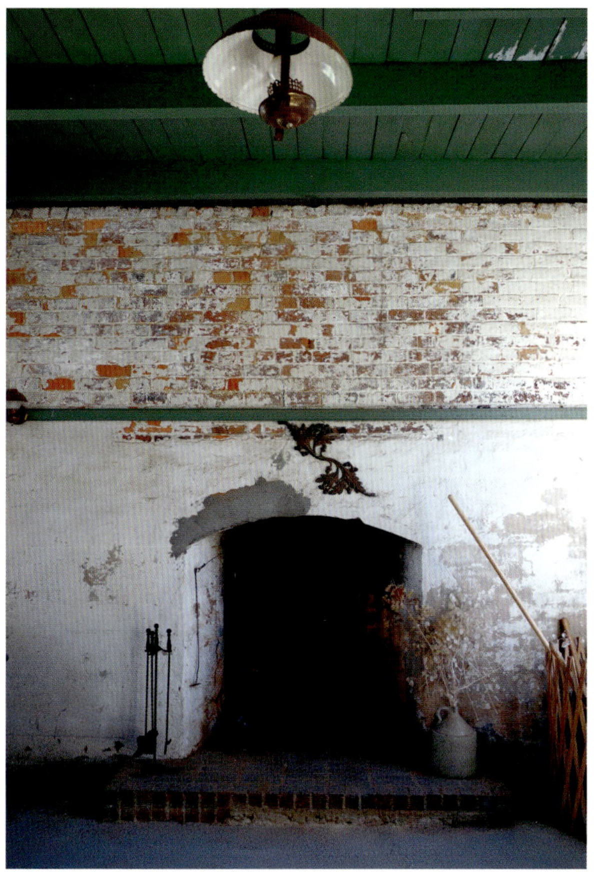

Figure 2.9 / Dr. Edmund Strudwick's brick kitchen showing firebox with crane.

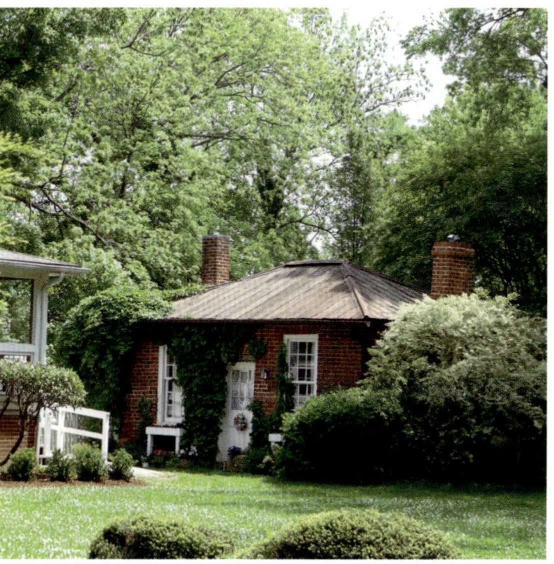

Figure 2.10 / Robertson-Cheek House kitchen.

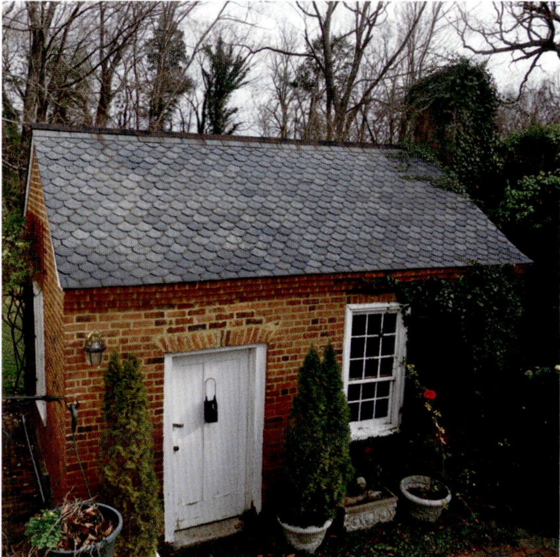

Figure 2.11 / Burnside kitchen.

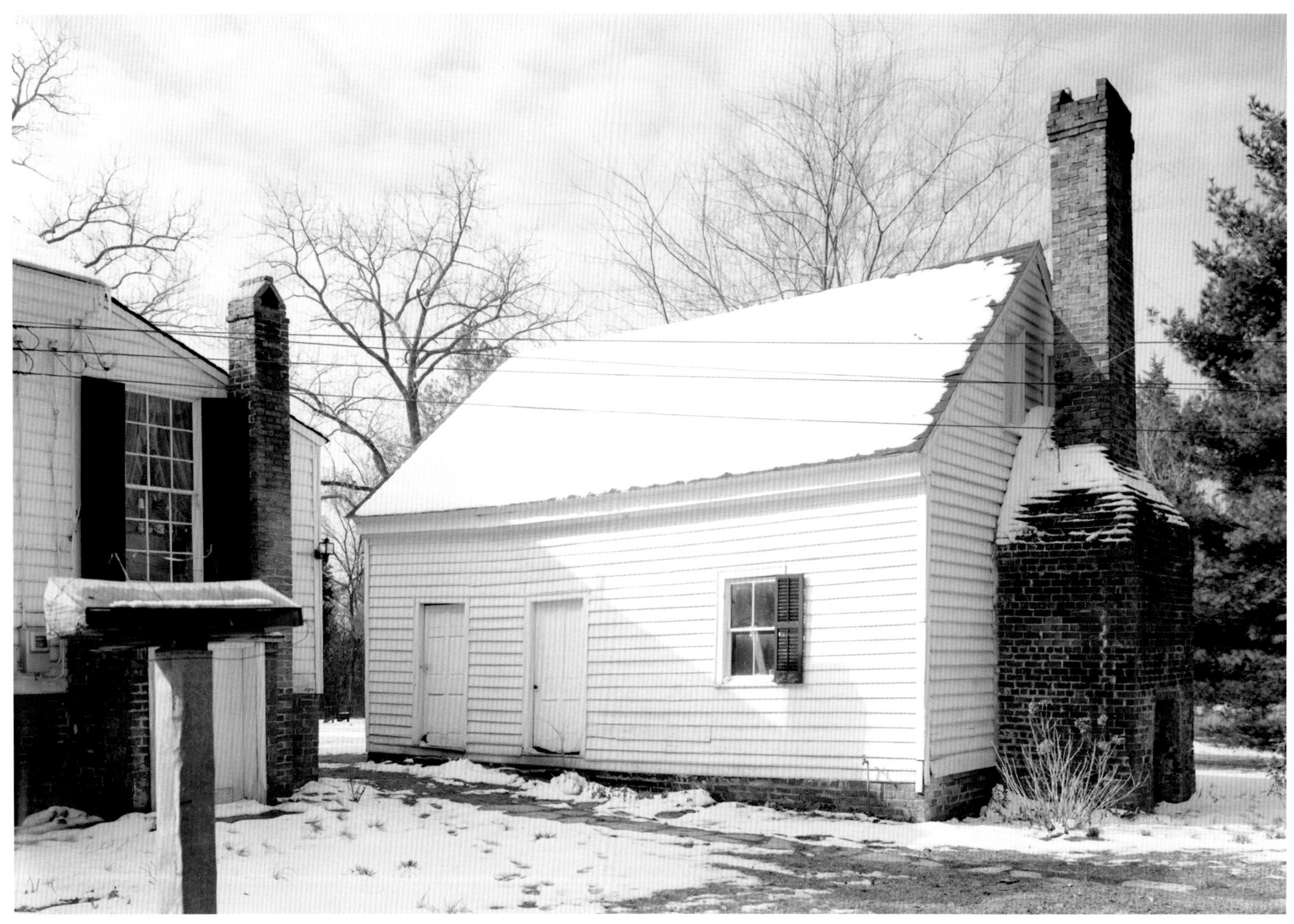

Figure 2.17 / Kitchen at Sans Souci. (Photograph from the 1930s; Historic American Buildings Survey. Courtesy, Library of Congress, No. NC-221-A-1.*)*

> first sound you would hear in the morning would be the blows of the rolling pin in perfect time to whatever hymn the presiding genius had chosen for her early devotions. Some of the cooks had lovely voices, and this morning concert furnished a pleasant introduction to the new day, especially if you were still in bed, drowsily waiting for Becky to open the shutters and make the fire.[4]

A bake-oven was sometimes built into the chimney, as at the Bellevue kitchen, and would require its own utensils and constant surveillance. An account of such an oven in Hillsborough survives in a short memoir by Mary Elizabeth Strayhorn Berry, who lived at Twin Chimneys during the Civil War:

> The kitchen was 100 or more feet from the dwelling house, with a nice walk made of flagstones, extending from the house to the kitchen. The fireplace accommodated 8 foot logs, an iron rod or crane extended from jamb to jamb from which hung pots, kettles, etc., the baking was done on the hearth, in ovens and skillets, the finest fruit cakes, loaf bread, and light corn bread was cooked in these ovens. On the side of the chimney was a Dutch oven also for baking or roasting.[5]

The wood supply to keep the fire going in the firebox or coals ready for the bake-oven would require constant vigilance; the proximity of a woodshed or, at the very least, a woodpile had to be accommodated. Those who tended to these roles—the cook, slaves, or servants, in the case of a large or well-off household—would have negotiated the space in and around the kitchen constantly throughout the day. This role would otherwise be required of the housewife, with or without help from a servant or hired helper, children, or extended family members. In this case, the kitchen would also have been a natural gathering place for parents and children seeking a warm atmosphere for a number of homely activities or chores.

The following are the thirteen houses or sites in Hillsborough with surviving kitchens: Bellevue, Burnside, Dr. Edmund Strudwick's house, Mangum-Ruffin House, Midlawn (Figure 2.12), Montrose (Figure 2.13), Robertson-Cheek House, Ruffin-Roulhac House (Figure 2.14), Twin Chimneys, Whitted House, Whitted-Johnston House (Figure 2.15), Henderson Jones House kitchen moved to Montrose (Figure 2.16), and Sans Souci.

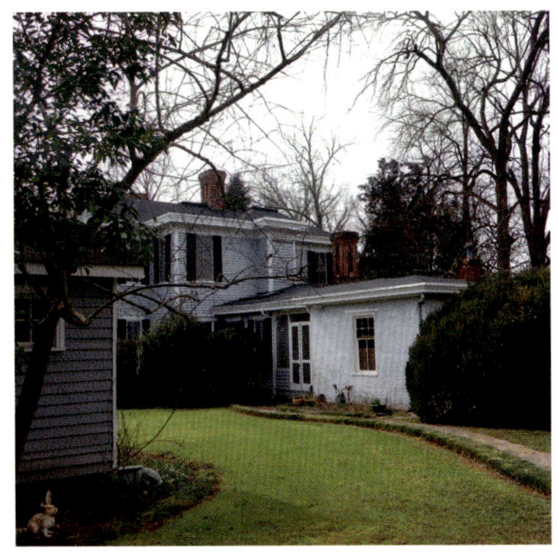

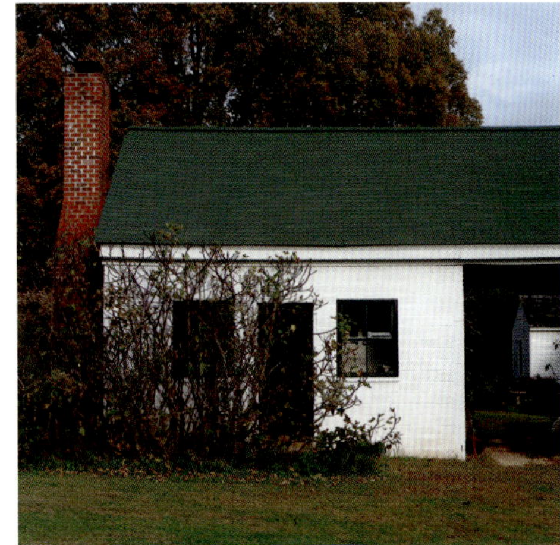

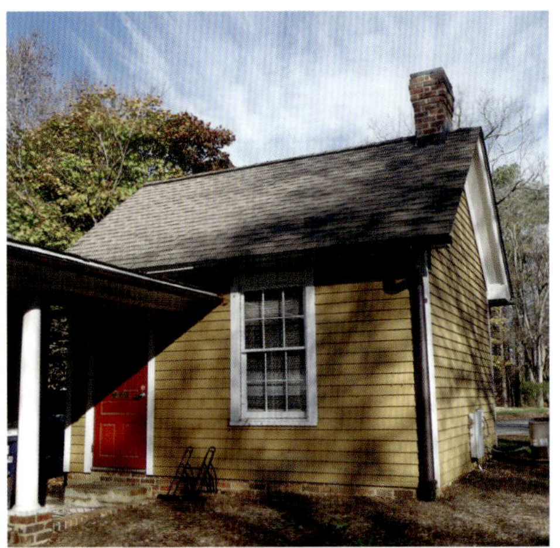

(left to right)
Top row: Figure 2.12 / Kitchen at Midlawn.
Figure 2.13 / Kitchen at Montrose.
Figure 2.14 / Kitchen at Ruffin-Roulhac House.

Bottom row:
Figure 2.15 / Kitchen at Whitted-Johnston House, incorporated in ell.
Figure 2.16 / Henderson Jones House kitchen, moved to Montrose.

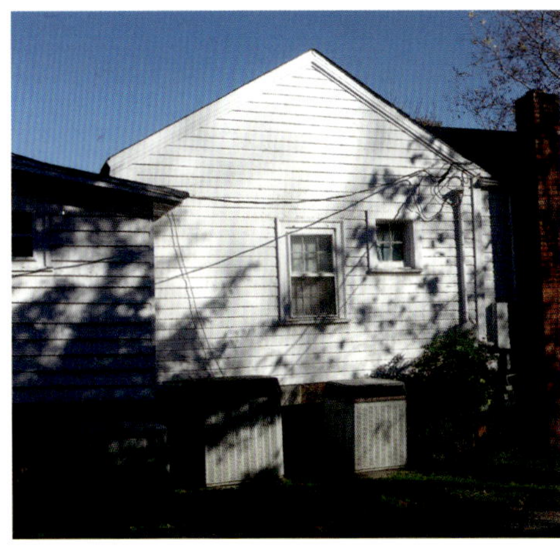

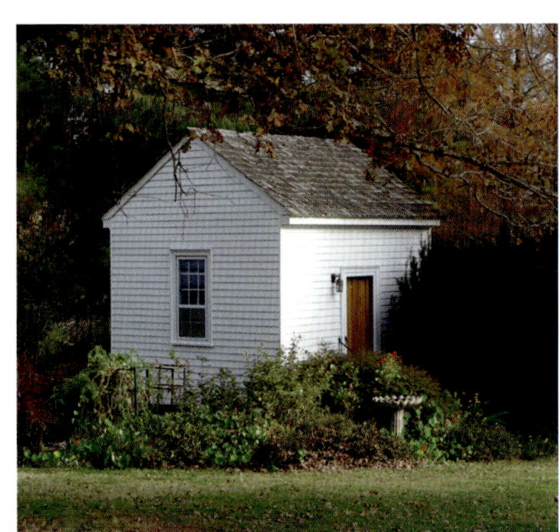

Three

Slave Houses

BY JEAN B. ANDERSON

Slave houses make up a small minority of the historic structures still surviving in Hillsborough, but they fill a very important role in American history (see Map 7). They give voice to those who had no voice, enslaved African Americans. The houses relate to the traditions, music, food, language, and arts that have only recently been incorporated into our written histories, our museums, and our national heritage. These houses can evoke a variety of reactions: regret, perhaps shame, for the system of slavery that is mirrored in their existence; empathy with the people who lived in them; curiosity about the homes of ancestors and of the past generally.

Because North Carolina was primarily settled by yeomen farmers, only a third of families in our state owned slaves; thus fewer slave houses were built than other outbuildings—and fewer remain. In Hillsborough and vicinity, four have been identified, but others are possibly encased within other houses, unrecognized, and their origins lost. It is not surprising that Hillsborough's remaining slave houses are found mostly on the outskirts of town. Those that were once in town probably stood on lots separated from the main houses they served. After the Civil War, when the structures were no longer occupied, the lots they sat on, which had become too valuable to hold, were sold off; the old buildings were then either destroyed or repurposed and new houses constructed on them. Consequently it is on the estates and small plantations outside the town limits, on land less valuable, that the remaining examples are more likely to be found.

At Burnside, the once-seventy-acre homestead of Paul Carrington Cameron (1808–91),

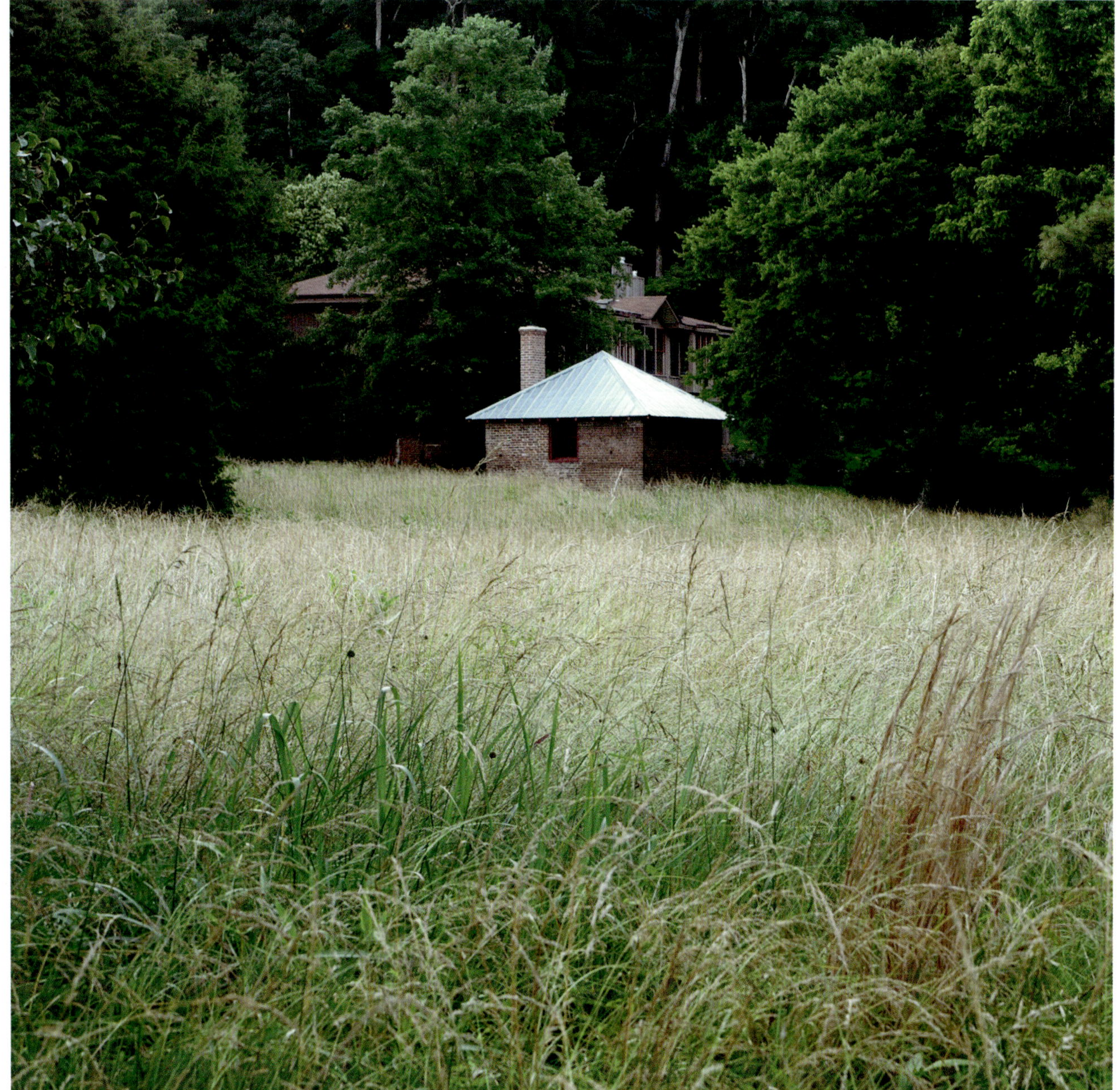

Figure 3.1 / Burnside, Coachman's House.

there is the Coachman's House, a house for the estate's groomsman. This dwelling apparently was built in conjunction with the nearby stable. Formerly a ruin, the Coachman's House, like the stable, has recently been restored by its owners (Figure 3.1).[1]

In the same style as the barn, the Coachman's House was built of brick laid in the American bond pattern of three stretcher rows to one header row. Experts who have examined it think it was built about the same time as the stable—in the late 1850s. It has a single room measuring approximately eighteen feet square on the exterior, with a rebuilt chimney and hearth. That size, incidentally, is close to that of the rooms in the slave cabins that Paul Cameron built at Stagville, the nucleus of his vast plantation complex, at about the same time.

The little building's roof was gone and the tops of the walls were missing when the current owners decided to restore it; therefore the walls' height and the shape of the roof had to be guessed at in the reconstruction. Today it has a pyramidal roof, a common shape of cap for antebellum small outbuildings, and is covered in tin.

The building's most notable feature are two bricks with markings obviously etched into them with difficulty and discernible as *5 Dec. [18]65*. It is thought that the occupant was recording a date very important to him. A shrewd guess has identified that date with the ratification of the Thirteenth Amendment to the United States Constitution by North Carolina on 4 December 1865. It was the amendment that abolished slavery.[2]

Another common style of slave house, a duplex, can be found on a tract of land on the north side of St. Mary's Road close to Cameron Park Elementary School. It stands somewhat at a distance and slightly to the west side of the Mangum-Ruffin House on the same tract (Figure 3.2). Each of the two rooms would have housed a slave family, but not many years ago the brick structure was rehabilitated, added onto, and converted to a single-family dwelling. Originally it was identical to the old kitchen that stands directly behind the Victorian dwelling. Both kitchen and slave house are built of the same kind of brick laid in an American bond pattern. The dimensions of both were originally the same, about sixteen by thirty-two feet, two rooms wide and one deep, with a chimney placed slightly off center between them.

Each room had its own door, opening to a small, covered porch, which extended across the fronts of both buildings. The former slave house now lacks its porch. Each room has a window of nine panes over nine flanking the doors. Although the slave house's low-pitched roof is now covered by modern shingles, originally it would have had either cedar shingles or a standing-seam tin roof like that on the old smokehouse standing beside the kitchen. As with the kitchen porch, the slave house porch would have had an engaged roof supported by four plain wooden square posts.

These two buildings and the smokehouse were clearly all built at the same time, probably in the 1840s during the tract's ownership by Priestly Mangum (ca. 1795–1850), a prominent lawyer, county solicitor, and younger brother of Sen. Willie P. Mangum. Priestly Mangum lived on this tract of land from 1824 until his death.[3] Thomas R. Cain (1831–82), who succeeded Mangum as owner and lived there even after the junior Thomas Ruffins moved in with him in 1870, could also have built the brick outbuildings. However, the earlier date is the more likely.

A third known slave house, also a duplex, still exists at Sans Souci, just outside town limits (Figure 3.3). Situated behind and to the north of the plantation house, this slave house unlike the other two is built of wood. Each of its two rooms has its own entrance with a window beside it, like the slave house on the Mangum-Ruffin property described above. It stands on a brick foundation with a central chimney. Lacking a porch, a stoop of three steps provides entry to each door. The roof while now of tin might once have been cedar shingles. Today the slave house has a shed room built across the back, divided into a very small bathroom, mudroom, and pullman kitchen to make the house habitable as a modern dwelling. It is now painted white like all the other outbuildings and the main house.

The Sans Souci slave house may date to the ownership of David Yarborough, who bought the property in 1812. It is very much of a piece in appearance and age with other outbuildings on the tract (except for a much later carriage house); but all of them likely date from the period when William Cain Jr. (1784–1857) owned Sans Souci (1830s–1856). The Cains acquired Sans Souci from Yarborough, according to Cain's will, but no deed or other document gives a date for the deal. Since the Cains sold their house at Burnside to Paul Cameron in 1834, the year William Cain Jr.'s father died, it seems possible that they moved about that time. It is almost certain that it was the Cains, wealthy landowners, who added a wing to the house and made other improvements from the 1840s on. Consequently, it seems probable that the outbuildings, including the slave house, were part of that improvement effort.[4]

The only slave/servant house remaining in the town historic district stands in a row of outbuildings behind the early nineteenth-century Ruffin-Roulhac House, now used as the

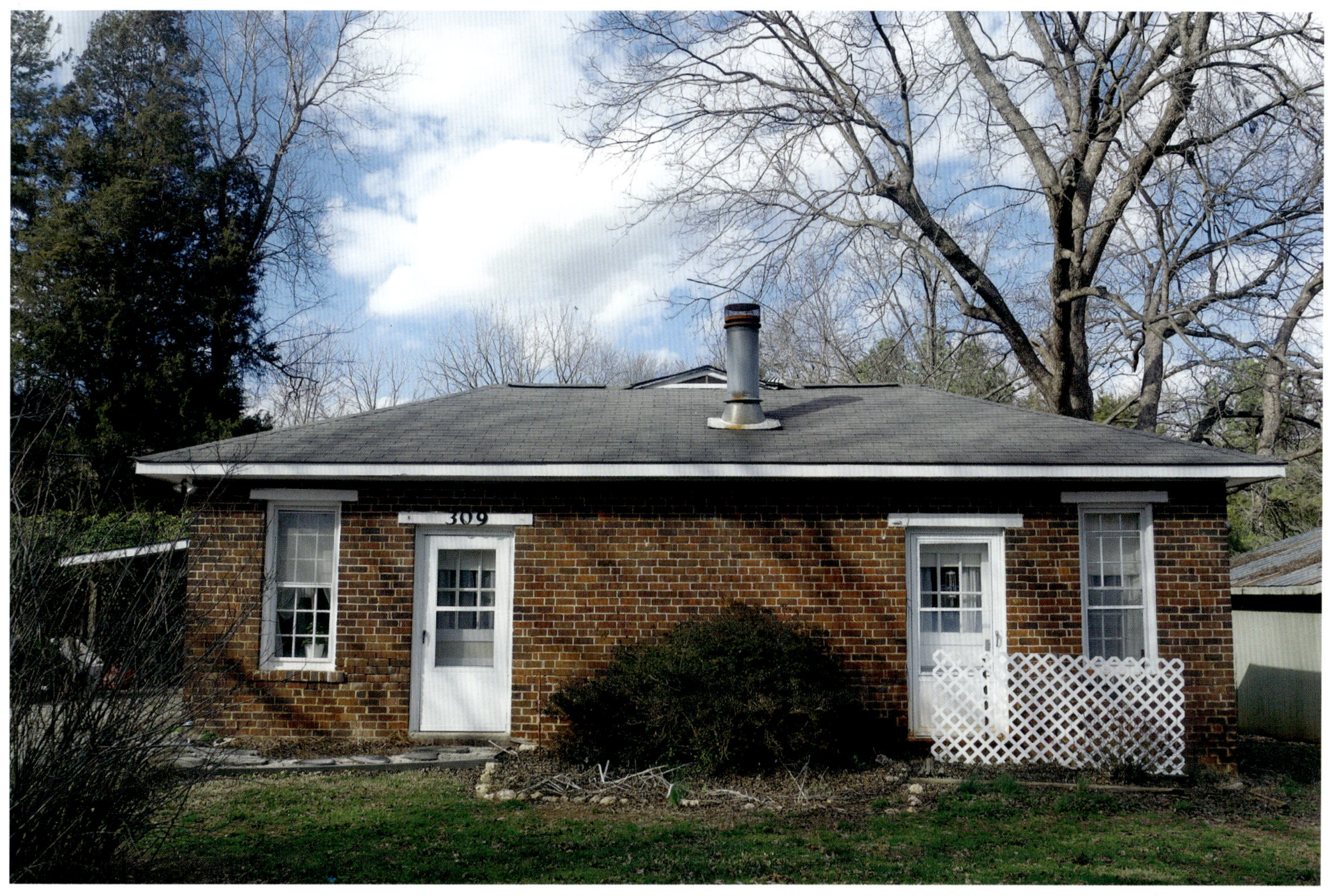

Figure 3.2 / Mangum-Ruffin slave house.

Hillsborough Town Hall. The tract of ten acres they stand on was bought by the town in 1972 and lies between East Corbin, Cameron, East Orange, and Churton streets. At the time of the purchase, all the buildings were in poor condition, and the carriage house unsalvageable, but old photographs enabled the town to restore or reconstruct them exactly as they had been.[5]

The former slave house (Figure 3.4) stands between the law office and the smokehouse. It is a one-room building, about fourteen by twelve feet, with a pitched roof and large exterior chimney on the west side. A miniature hip roof covers the front porch, identical to the neighboring law office (see back of book jacket). Beside the door is one small window with four panes over four. On the east side is an exterior, narrow staircase leading to a loft door, probably not an original feature. On either side of the chimney stack in the loft is a tiny four-paned window. The building appears to have been built at the same time as its neighboring buildings, the whole now forming a very neat and pleasing appearance.

One of the last inhabitants of the slave house was Price Boyd, who was born a slave. Boyd is well remembered by older Hillsboroughans as the coachman for the Roulhac family, descendants of Judge Thomas Ruffin (1787–1870). The Ruffins and Roulhacs successively owned the place from 1866 to 1972. "Uncle Price," as the neighbors called him, was a very old man when he told them he was twelve years old at the time he was freed.[6]

The first house on the site had been built by William H. Phillips in 1823. He sold it in 1825 to Francis L. Hawks, the grandson of the architect of Tryon Palace in New Bern, who probably made improvements; but it was Frances Clark Pollock Connor Blount (later Hill), owner of the house from 1830 to 1865, who expanded the main house and possibly built the many outbuildings there today. The problem with this theory is that she owned only two lots on Orange Street at the corner of Churton Street, and all the outbuildings are now in a row on adjacent lots to the north. One must conclude either that she built the original outbuildings, which were later moved to their present location, or that the Ruffins, who later owned all ten lots in the block, built them where they stand.[7] If the latter was true then the little house must be called a servant's house, as it postdates slavery.

Two pieces of evidence bear on the subject. An old photograph of Mrs. Hill's house with a string of outbuildings close beside it proves that there were a number of dependencies on her lots that could have been moved. In addition, the office in the present row next to the slave house is said to have been moved from beside her house; hence it is not unreasonable

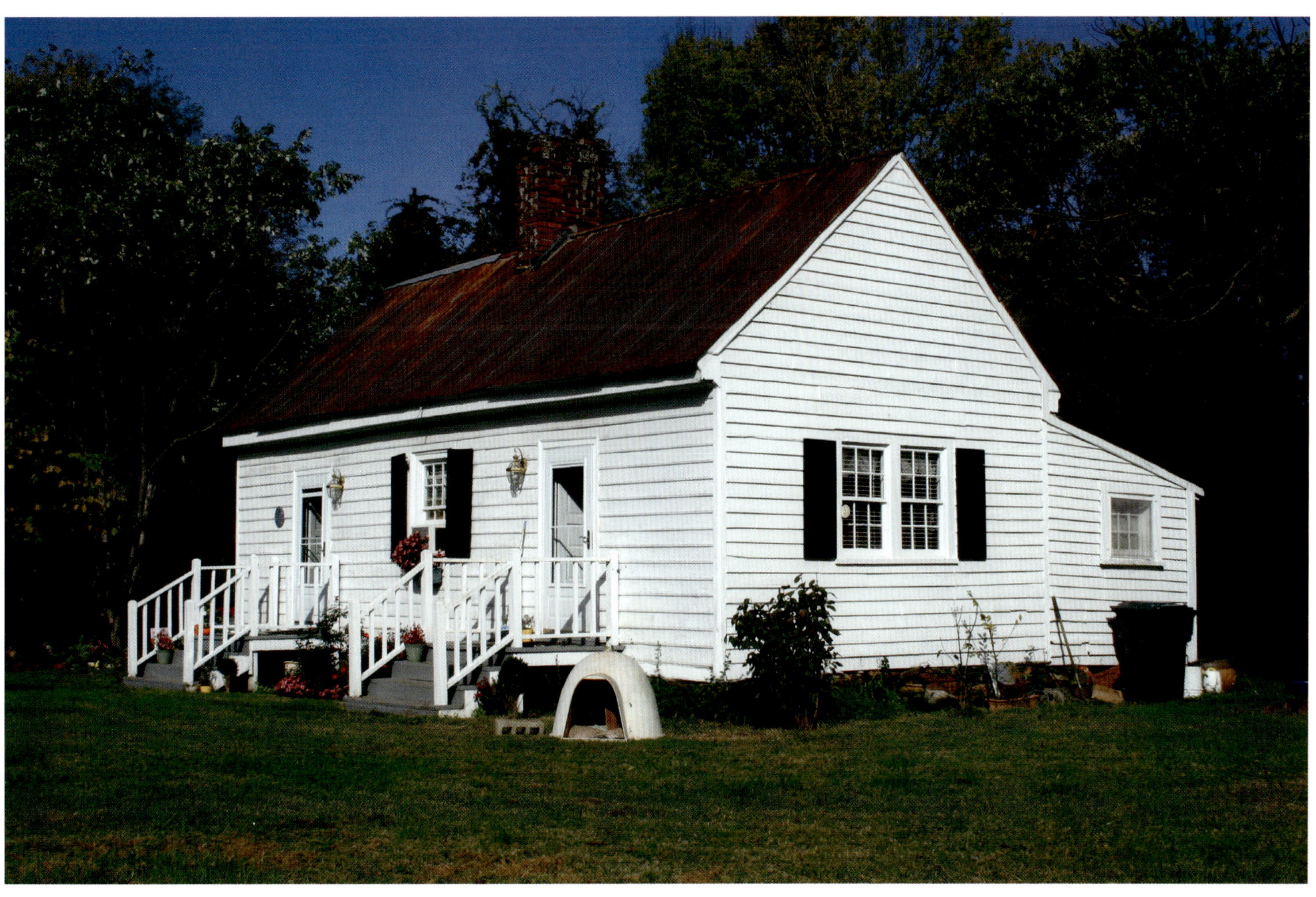

Figure 3.3 / Sans Souci slave house. (Photograph by Heather Wagner, 2012. Courtesy, N.C. Department of Cultural Resources, State Historic Preservation Office, Image 12.)

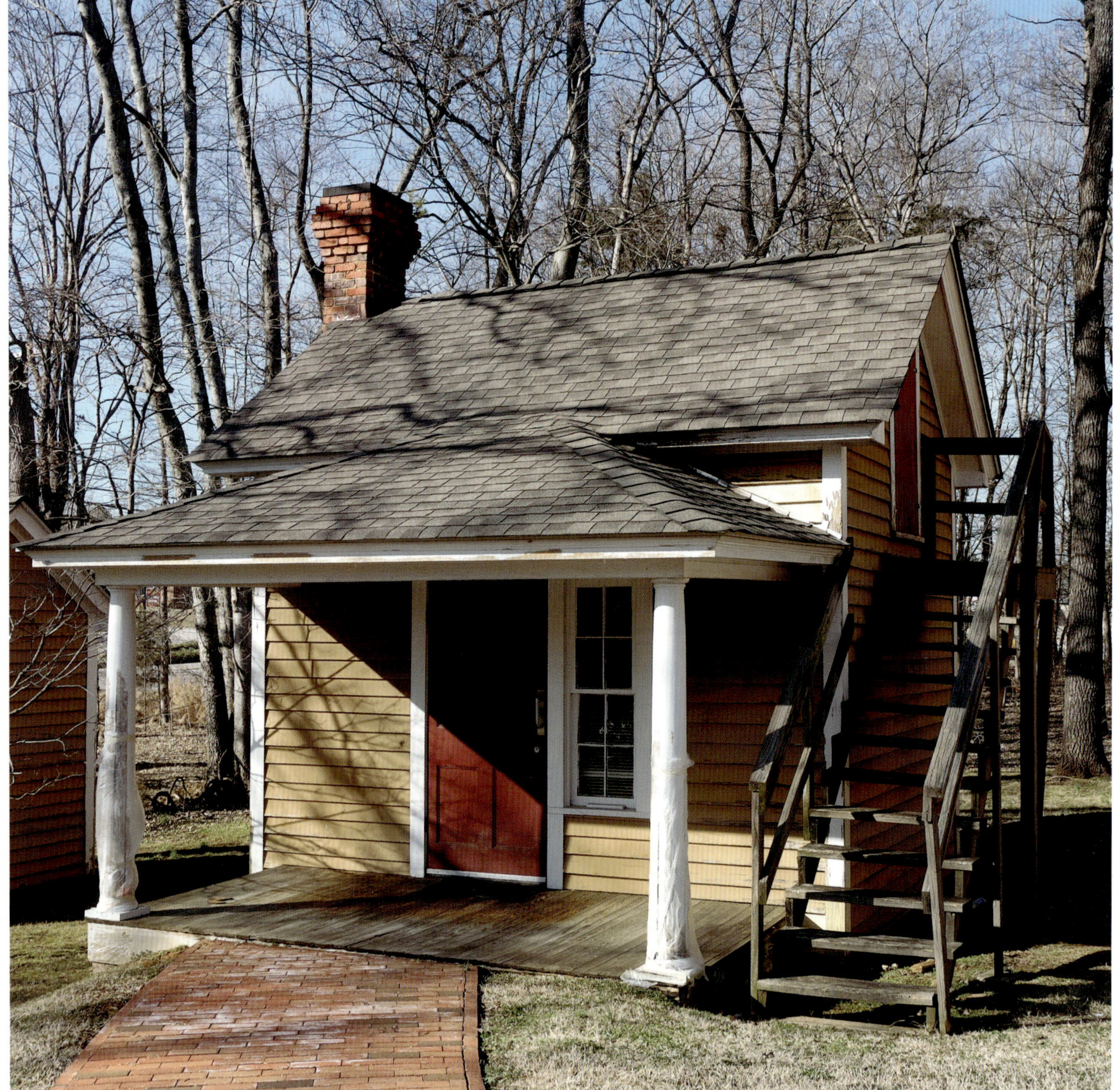

Figure 3.4 / Ruffin-Roulhac slave house.

to think the others were moved as well.[8] Besides the main dwelling with its handsome interior woodwork, there was at the time of the restoration a carriage house in ruins, barn, office, kitchen, slave/servant's house, smokehouse, well house, and kitchen. Little Hawfields, as Thomas Ruffin called the place, now exemplifies for visitors the complete, antebellum, in-town homestead.

As these examples show, slave houses varied in size, construction, and appearance. They most commonly were one- or two-room structures (usually without lofts) built of logs, wood, or brick, depending on the wealth and whim of the master. Chimneys of duplexes could be in the center of the two rooms, a variety now called saddlebag, or on the gable ends. If there were a breezeway between the two rooms with a common roof, that variety would be called a possum-trot or dog-run house. A planter with multiple slave houses was likely to group them or place them in rows. Such multiple arrangements were referred to as slave quarters. Some wooden houses were insulated with interior brick infill in the walls, like those remaining at Historic Stagville in Durham County. Some, however, did not even have foundations and stood on bare ground with or without flooring to cover the earth. Some had large square rooms as much as eighteen feet square, others as small as fourteen by twelve feet; the contrast is observed in the diversity of examples illustrated above.

Hillsborough is fortunate to have a variety represented: both brick and wood, single and duplex. As few as they are, they still fill a gap in the historical record. Now that slavery and African American culture in general have been incorporated into the national narrative, perhaps additional research will further humanize the slave houses, as it has the masters' homes, with the names and stories of those who lived in them.

Hillsborough's four slave houses are identified by the house or property names where they are located: Burnside Coachman's House, Mangum-Ruffin slave house, Ruffin-Roulhac slave or servant's house, Sans Souci slave house.

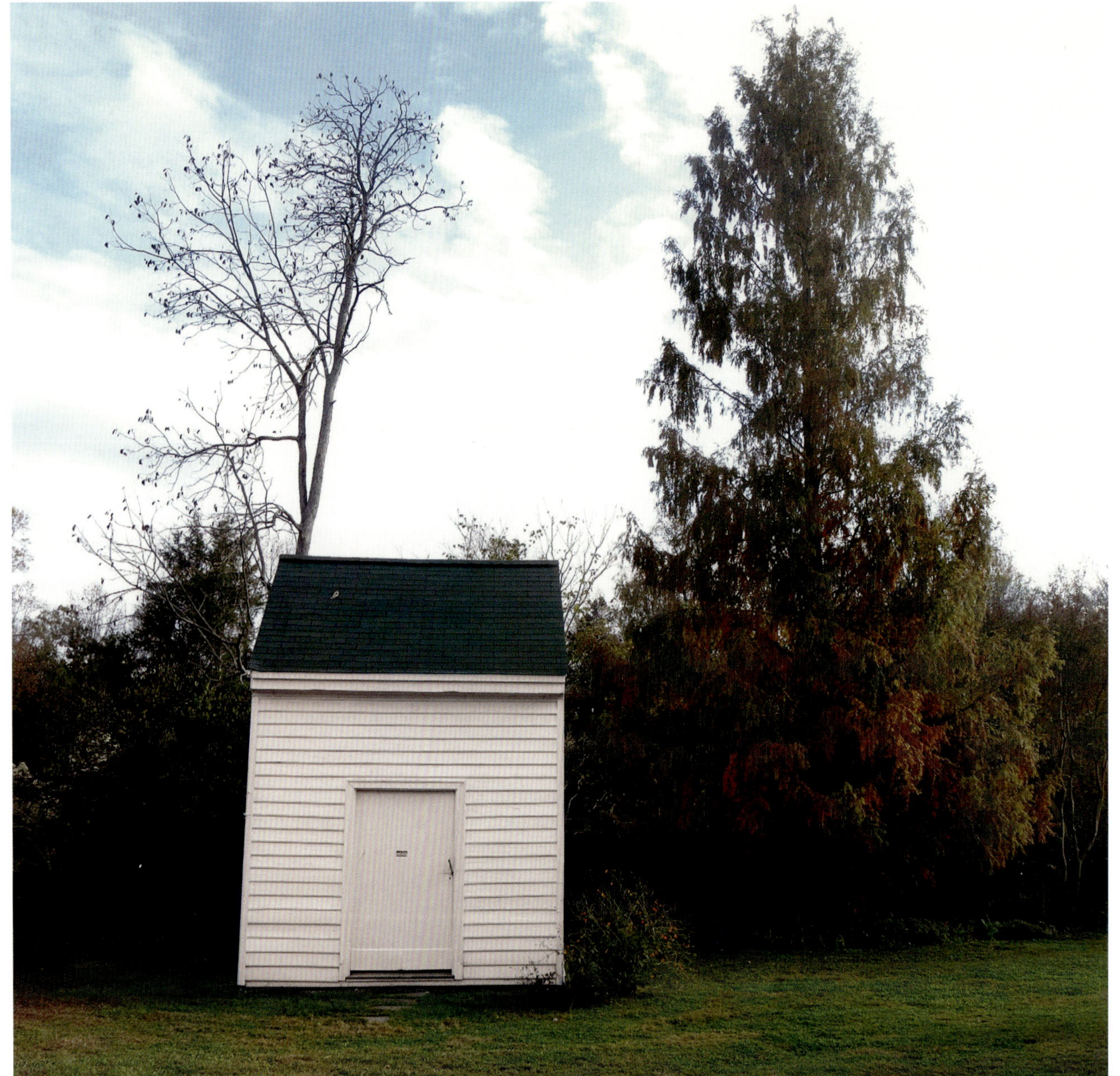

Figure 4.1 / Montrose smokehouse.

Four

Smokehouses

BY JIM PARSLEY

The Hillsborough family that was fortunate enough to frequently enjoy meat at its meals probably preserved and stored much of it in a smokehouse close to the main house. In the age before refrigerators, fresh meat could not be kept from spoiling for more than a few warm days unless it was cured. Curing a piece of fresh meat involved coating it with salt, sometimes other chemicals, and sugar, letting it age and dry out, often slow-cooking it in very warm, smoky air from a hardwood fire. By using a smokehouse, one could efficiently cure substantial quantities of meat and safely store them for months.[1]

Many Hillsborough residents kept smokehouses, otherwise known as *meat houses,* to preserve enough meat to keep their families and dependents well fed year-round. These were small freestanding buildings where the curing could be done, and where cured meat could be safely stored in cool, protected conditions and in a self-contained space where it would not add its odors to the main house. *Meat house* is perhaps a more general term for a building used to cure and store cured meat. If the building was also designed and built for smoking and curing a quantity of meat, then it might be called a *smokehouse.* Smoking enhanced the curing process by making it faster and contributing to the flavor of the cured meat.

The typical smokehouse was a small building with a single entrance that could be tightly closed. A good example is found at Montrose. There are no windows, and the ceiling is elevated (Figure 4.1).

The Montrose smokehouse, with its wood frame construction, is combined at the rear with a necessary house (see Figure 7.6). The building was tightly constructed to keep in the

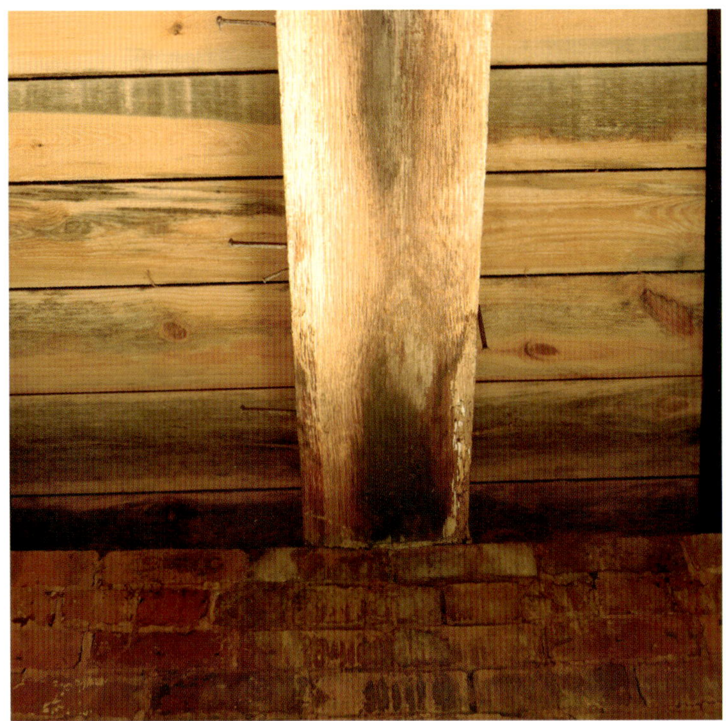

Figure 4.2 / Mangum-Ruffin smokehouse interior, showing soot on beams and roof from the smoky fire, and nails on which meat was hung.

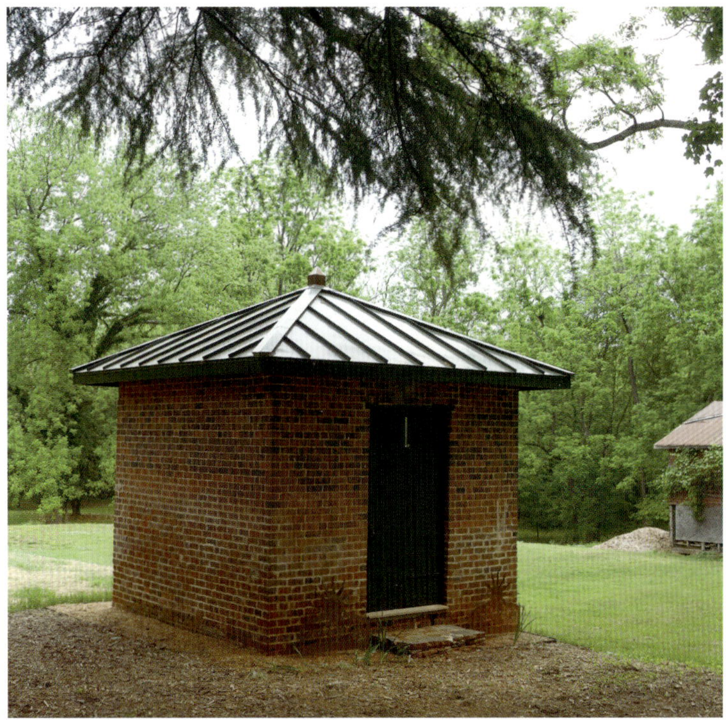

Figure 4.3 / Mangum-Ruffin smokehouse.

heat and smoke (though some smokehouses had a vent opening to discharge excess heat and smoke to the outside).

Smoke for the process was produced either by a small, wood fire burning on the floor or in a stove inside the building, or sometimes burning on a hearth or stove outside the building but ducted into it. All the upper interior surfaces would be black from the soot of the fire, as seen here at the Mangum-Ruffin smokehouse (Figures 4.2 and 4.3).

The smokehouse at the Mangum-Ruffin House is built of solid brick walls, with a standing-seam metal roof. The inside floor was dirt, which easily absorbed ashes and drippings.

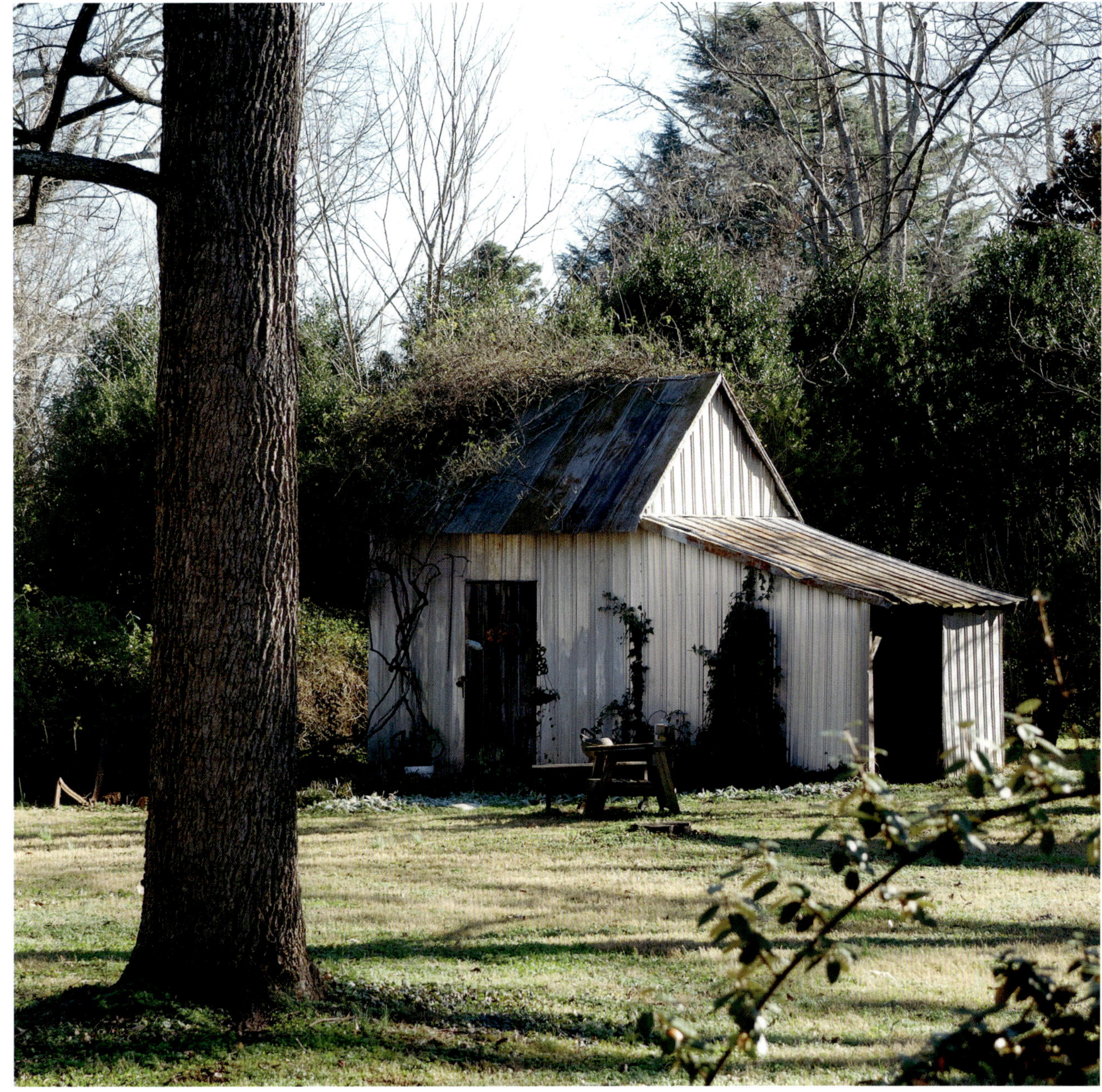

Figure 4.4 / Dozier smokehouse.

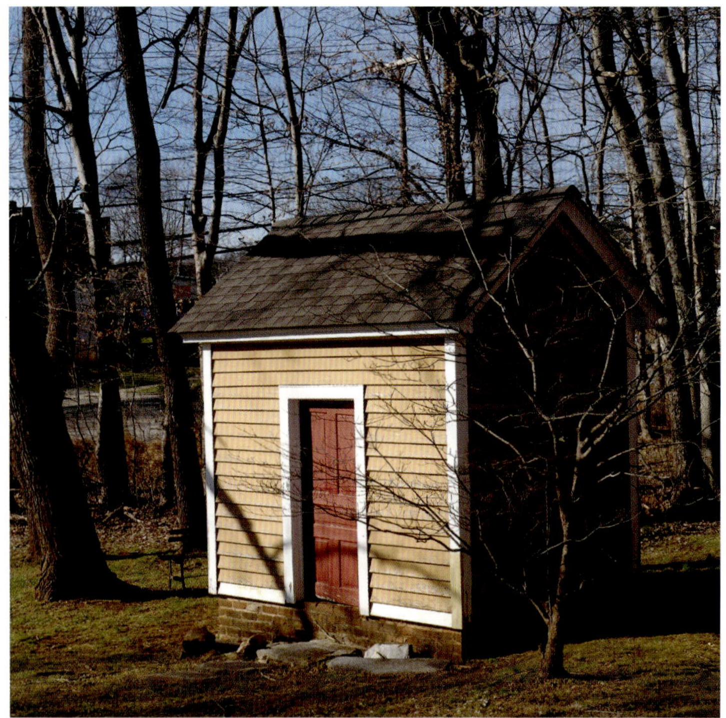

Figure 4.5 / Ruffin-Roulhac smokehouse.

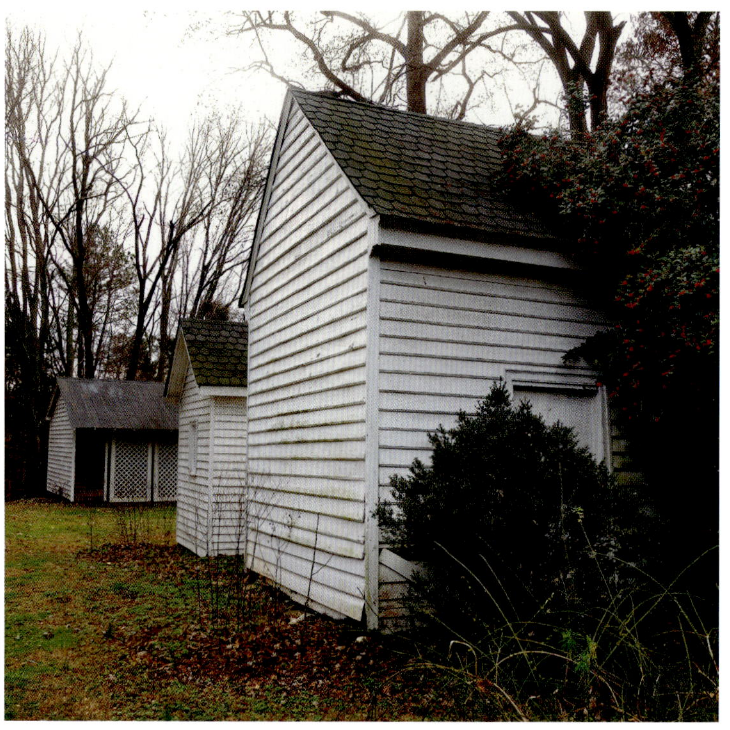

Figure 4.6 / Burnside smokehouse, in foreground, with the necessary house and a dairy behind it.

Smokehouses might be made of wood (logs or frame/siding) or masonry (brick), depending upon how much investment the owner wanted to make. They were usually built solidly, to securely protect the valuable meat from animals or thieves. Since they produced smoky odors and had some risk of fire, smokehouses were located away from inhabited buildings.

Hardwood, sometimes from fruit trees, was burned to produce the desired smoky flavor. The fire had to be carefully maintained to keep the smokehouse temperature hot enough to dry out the meat, but not so hot as to roast or bake it, nor cause it to dry excessively or become too tough or split. The meat was exposed to the hot, smoky air for several weeks or more, until the cook was satisfied. Cured meat was often left in the cold smokehouse, stored there until it was needed.

To preserve the fresh meat, a coating of salt was applied to pull moisture out of the meat and out of any microorganisms that may have collected on the meat surface. This also slowed the oxidation process. Sugar was often added to the coating to offset the salty flavor and to promote the growth of beneficial bacteria. All this extended the storage life of the meat so that it could be kept unrefrigerated for long periods.

Hillsborough has several examples of smokehouses or meat houses remaining from long ago, though none of them are being used for that purpose today. All are located on properties where their owners have respected and maintained structures that represent a link with the past. The Dozier smokehouse is of wood frame construction with functional sheet metal used for the roof and siding, whereas the Ruffin-Roulhac smokehouse appears more as a diminutive landscape ornament (Figures 4.4 and 4.5).

The Burnside smokehouse appears in a row of dependencies extending behind the main house, starting with the kitchen, then the smokehouse, necessary, and corn crib (Figure 4.6).

The pungent scent of cured meat is no longer present in these old buildings, which have evolved into storage outbuildings. Some now have floors, windows, even electricity.

Hillsborough's smokehouses are found on five properties: Burnside, the Dozier House, the Mangum-Ruffin House, Montrose, and the Ruffin-Roulhac House. (See Map 7.)

Five

Springs and Spring Houses, Wells and Well Houses

BY MARY ANN PETER

Hillsborough author Ann Strudwick Nash tells us that a mineral spring located at Poplar Hill, an estate on the south side of the Eno River,[1] was "generously placed at the disposal of the town"; here the "water bubbled up cold and clear and we drank deep drafts of it, regardless of possible impurities."[2] Another, more accessible spring was located on the Spring Lot in town where there was a public spring located between Lots 3 and 41 on East Margaret Lane. It is listed as alpha Lot O. The Sauthier map indicates the spring on Lot O as being at the head of a stream that flows south through Lots 5 and K down to the Eno (see Maps 2 and 2B). Two spring houses on Lot O are depicted as small rectangles. The Act of Assembly in 1766 states that spring lots are to be convenient, free, and reserved for supply water for the inhabitants of the town.[3]

Streams fed by springs also had another use. On the west side of Churton Street, Sauthier's map shows a broad stream that originates north of town and flows due south through town Lots 119, 128, and 137 to the Eno River. In 1768 there were no buildings indicated on these lots, likely because of the difficulty of crossing these streams. In 1778, ten years after the map was made, a deed documents that Lot 128 was sold, and in 1788, Josiah Lyons sold the same lot, which was then known as the Lyons' Stillhouse Lot. Likewise, on the east side of Churton, Lot 45 was called William Courtney's Stillhouse Lot.[4] Sauthier's map shows streams running through all three lots, providing essential water as well as the means to produce alcoholic spirits in colonial Hillsborough.

Spring houses were so common in the eighteenth century that little mention is made of them in colonial documents. Most of the preserved evidence concerning spring houses consists of reconstructions, plans, or photographs of exceptional buildings that survive intact.[5] The common colonial spring house was built into the slope of a bank to surround a spring. The slope was partially excavated and the foundation, or spring box, was built on the site. Then the spring house was built upon this foundation. Its walls were generally about one-and-a-half-feet thick and made of fieldstone. Colonial spring houses in the South were often made of logs or thick wood lumber, but were not long-lasting because of the constant dampness. The interior walls tended to be whitewashed to give the spring house a finished and clean appearance. It was typically located under trees to shade it from sunlight in the summer. The interior of a spring house contained a stone pallet for a floor, around which natural spring water flowed on three sides, usually about two feet deep. Here milk, cream, and butter could be stored in containers. Windows, if any, were small and recessed and used to ventilate the structure. Shelves were a universal feature; they were usually three or four feet above the water to keep items cool which could not be put into water, such as fruit and other perishables. Water would run through the pool in the spring house and out an opening where the outflow could be tapped to fill water troughs for animals and for fire protection readiness. The combination of the house being slightly underground, its constantly flowing water, thick walls, and ventilation helped keep the spring house's temperature around fifty-five degrees.[6]

The remnants of several of these structures exist in Hillsborough today, if we refer to Sauthier's map. What can be seen now? A stream begins at the base of a hill shared by Lots 83 and 84 on East Queen Street and flows south toward the Eno. Just to the south, we find the site of a spring box clearly visible on Lot 102 on East Tryon Street (see Map 2B). Passersby can still see the remains of the spring box's broad, stone foundation, approximately fifteen feet in diameter and three feet deep, which connects to a modern, stone-walled, cement-floored channel where the stream, known as Stillhouse Creek, flows south, under East Tryon Street; from there it flows toward the post office and into the Eno River beyond (Figures 5.1 and 5.2). No evidence of a spring house remains.

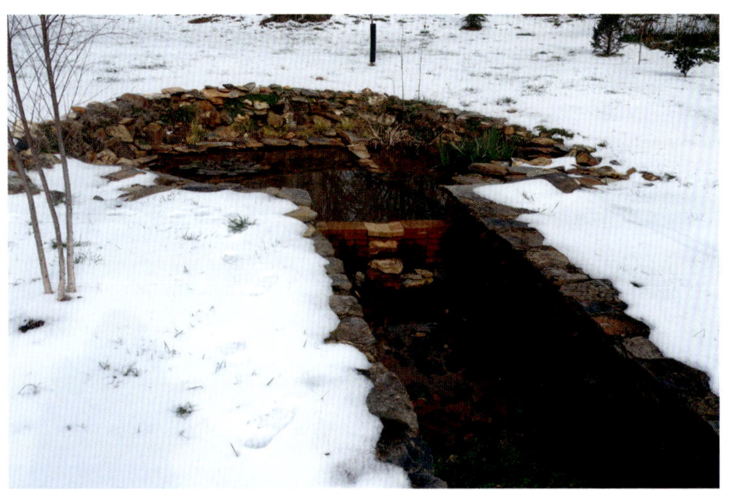

Figure 5.1 / Lot 102, spring box remains, showing pool and origin of runoff channel.

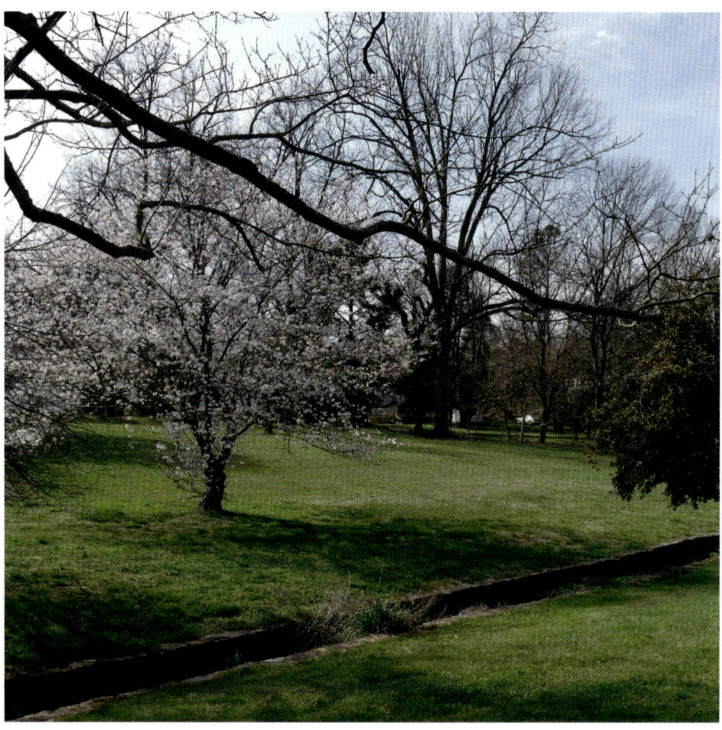

Figure 5.2 / Lot 102, springhouse runoff channel flowing away from the spring box.

Additional restoration by the historically sensitive owner is currently in progress in and around the spring box.

A second handsome spring box has been found hidden from passersby, nestled in a private garden on West Tryon Street, where several large trees, a boxwood, and a patch of white and pink Lenten roses stand sentry. This spring box is narrower and deeper than the one on East Tryon Street, measuring about eight feet long, five feet wide, and five feet deep. Its sides and floor are impeccably lined with flat, black fieldstones and its location is a stone's throw from a nearby stream that channels water toward the Eno (Figure 5.3).

Because of the impermanence of colonial wooden structures as well as the emergence of the well as a source of fresh water, no intact spring houses are known to exist today in Hillsborough. We are grateful to find a few enduring remains of spring boxes that give testimony to the significance of springs and spring houses to the early residents of Hillsborough.

In Hillsborough, as in other towns during the late eighteenth and nineteenth centuries, wells displaced the need for springs and their spring houses.[7] Because wells could be dug by hand and could be located near the houses they served, they offered greater protection from contamination than springs. Wells could be dug without the use of specialized equipment and demanded only the simplest water-raising equipment of rope and bucket. The well could hold a large volume of water in storage for times of high demand, as in the event of a fire.

The well was often sheltered by a small house, or by a roof supported on four corner posts. The well house not only helped prevent debris from tainting the water but also protected the ropes and pulleys used to draw the water buckets up from the depths. Some enclosed well houses offered shelves on which to store perishable foods.

Until the twentieth century, most wells were dug by hand, and therefore the diameter of a well needed to be large enough to accommodate one or more people using a pick and shovel. The excavation would stop when the diggers reached the water table, usually anywhere from about thirty to seventy feet below ground. The well was then lined with either stone or brick, and in many cases the lining extended above the opening to protect the water from contamination by people or animals (Figure 5.4).

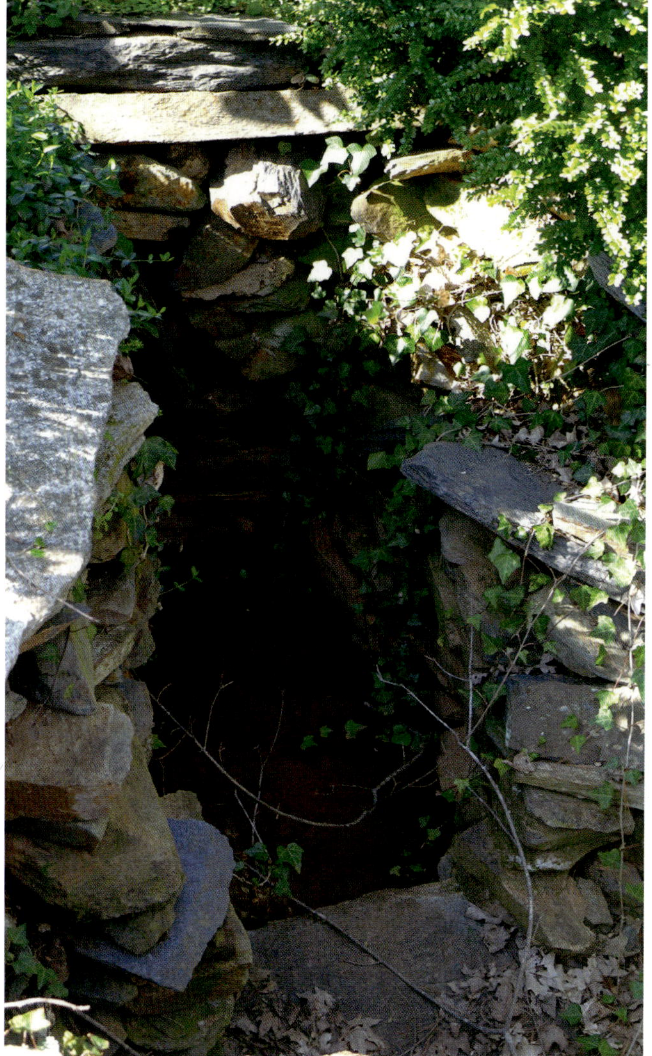

Figure 5.3 / Spring box on property on West Tryon Street.

Hillsborough, like most towns, depended on local sources for water, usually a mix of private and public wells. The Sauthier map of 1768 does not specifically locate wells, but a small circle thought to indicate a well is pictured on Lot 95 on West Tryon Street. The Sanborn map of 1888 shows a town well at the intersection of Churton Street and King Street, which was equipped with a wooden pump.[8] The date of the public well is not known, but there are indications that it was not adequately protected nor was the water quality monitored. The State Archives of 1825 reported that

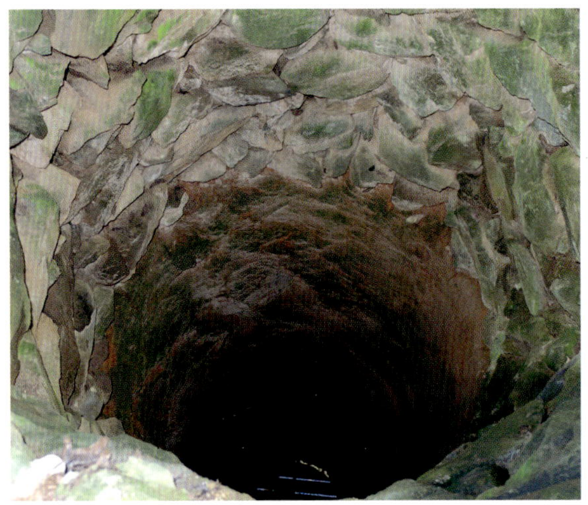

Figure 5.4 / Dug well shaft on West Queen Street property showing fieldstone lining.

Robert Jones was named by town commissioners to ensure that the pumps in the public well near the market house and on the public lot be kept in good repair, and allocated $300 for the year.[9] In 1852, a Hillsborough Pump and Spring Committee was formed and its members were named. And in 1881, the *Orange County Observer* scolded the public: "We would call the attention of the town authorities to the too frequent abuse of our town pump. Persons watering horses, cleaning out old buckets, washing hands, &c., don't seem to think the water is used by decent people for drinking purposes."[10] These were among a number of reasons homeowners began to dig more wells on private property, locating them where they were close to the house and access could be controlled.

Wells were particularly important assets on a property, and their well-house enclosures could vary greatly. When the Ruffin-Roulhac House, now the Hillsborough Town Hall on East Orange Street, was sold in 1865, a letter by the new owner declared it to "have one of the very best wells of water with a good pump."[11] Well houses survive as desirable yard structures because of their charm. Those walking in the historic district today may easily see the Ruffin-Roulhac well house from the street. It consists of an enclosed room, next to the wellhead with its crank and shaft protected under an open, shed-roofed covering (Figure 5.5).

The picturesque Berry Brick House, built circa 1805 on West Queen Street, has a simple, partially enclosed wooden well house in the front yard (Figure 5.6).

A fully enclosed and imposing well house stands a few blocks away beside the Judge Gattis House on West King Street; its hexagonal enclosure is capped by a hexagonal roof (Figure 5.7).

A well house behind the historic Turner-Strudwick House on North Churton Street is constructed of cedar corner posts that support a pyramidal roof with a distinctive decorative element at the apex. It is unusually large and its benches seem to invite a picnic party to gather in its shade (Figure 5.8).

The diversity of designs and sizes of well houses in Hillsborough might be a point of local pride, especially since most of them can be viewed from the street or sidewalk.

Ann Strudwick Nash's account of life at the Nash-Kollock School reminds us that the availability of fresh water was never taken for granted. Rain barrels stood all around

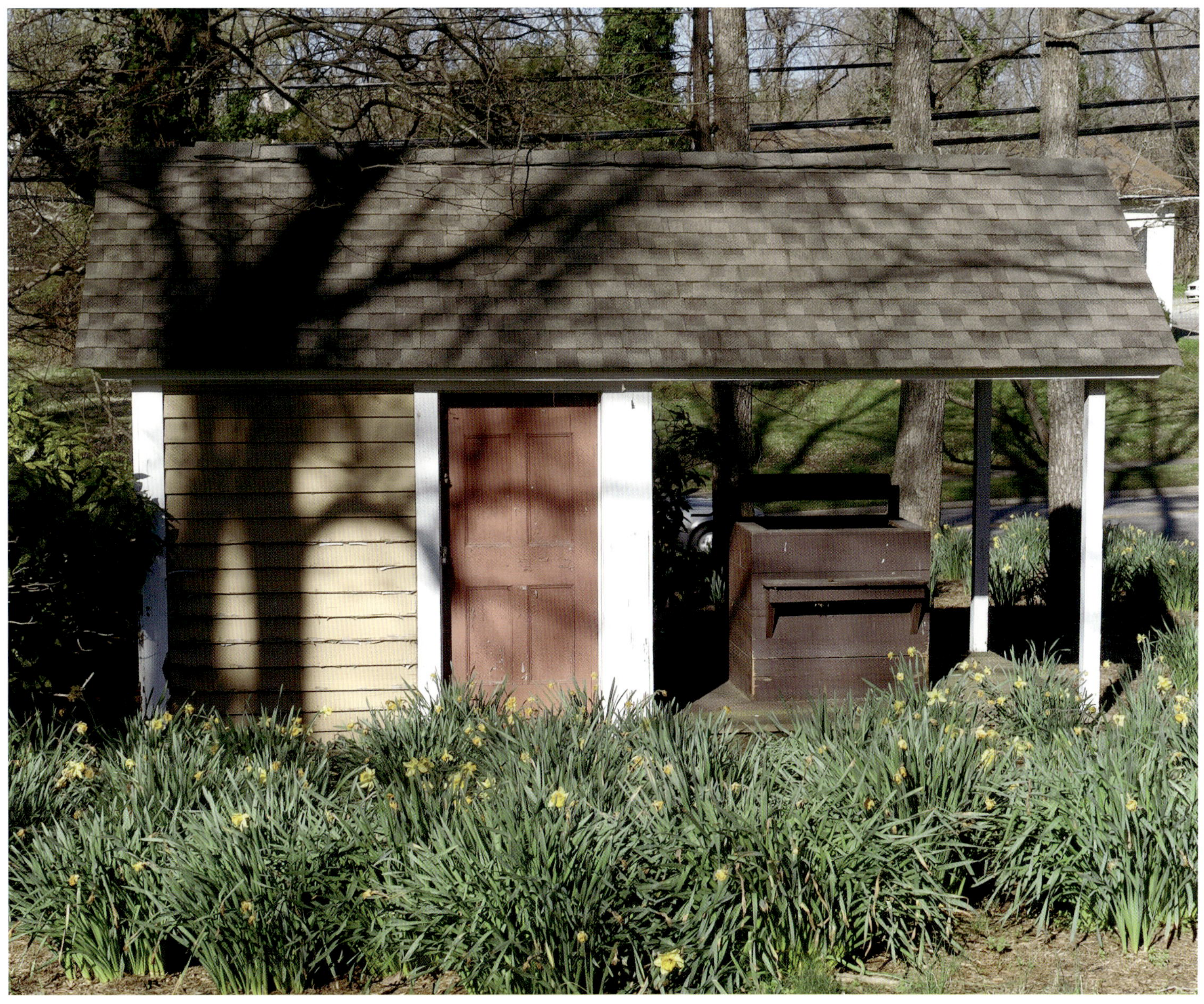

Figure 5.5 / Ruffin-Roulhac enclosed well house, showing wellhead shelter to one side and crank housing over the well.

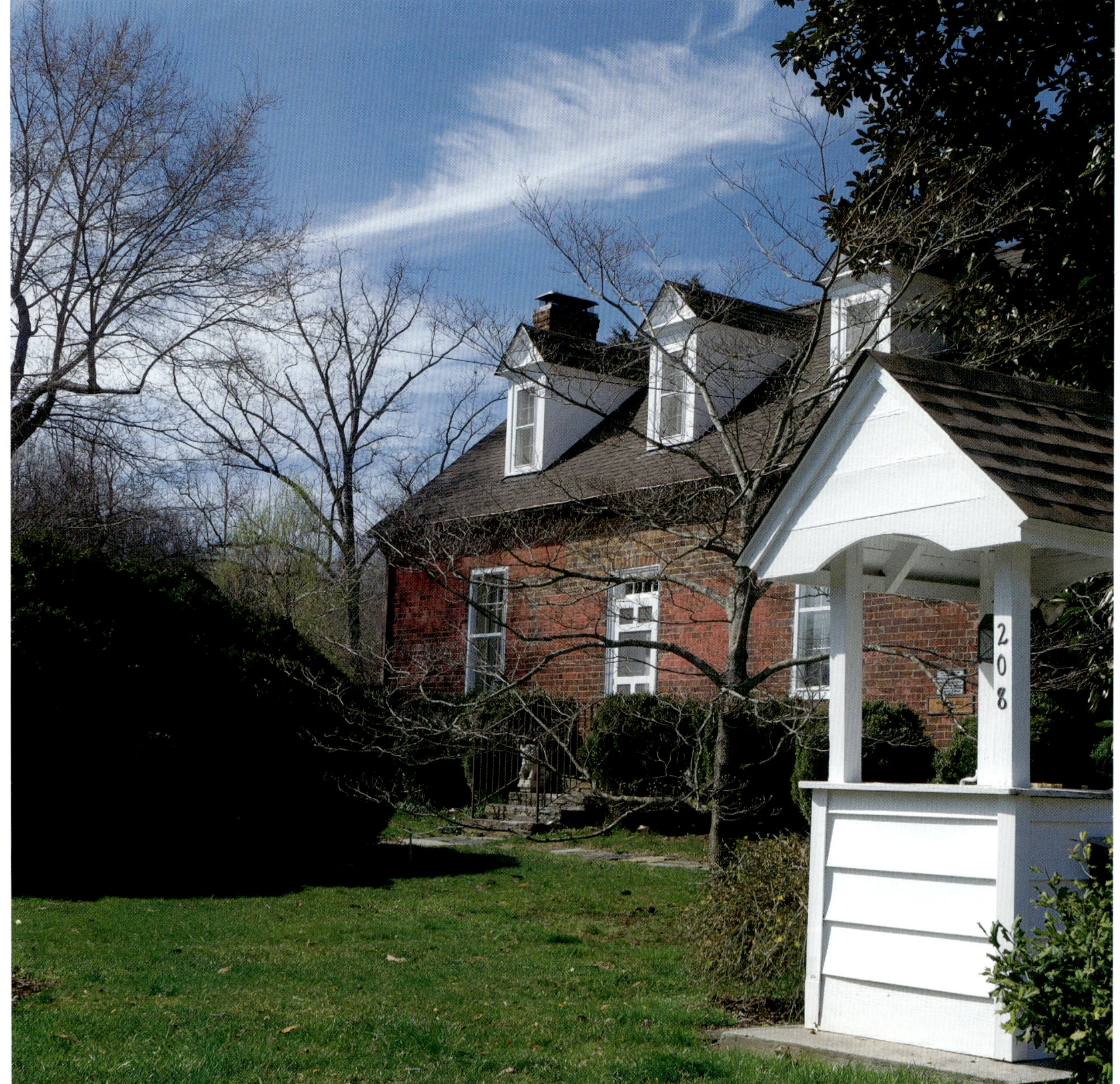

Figure 5.6 / Berry Brick House well house, with enclosed base.

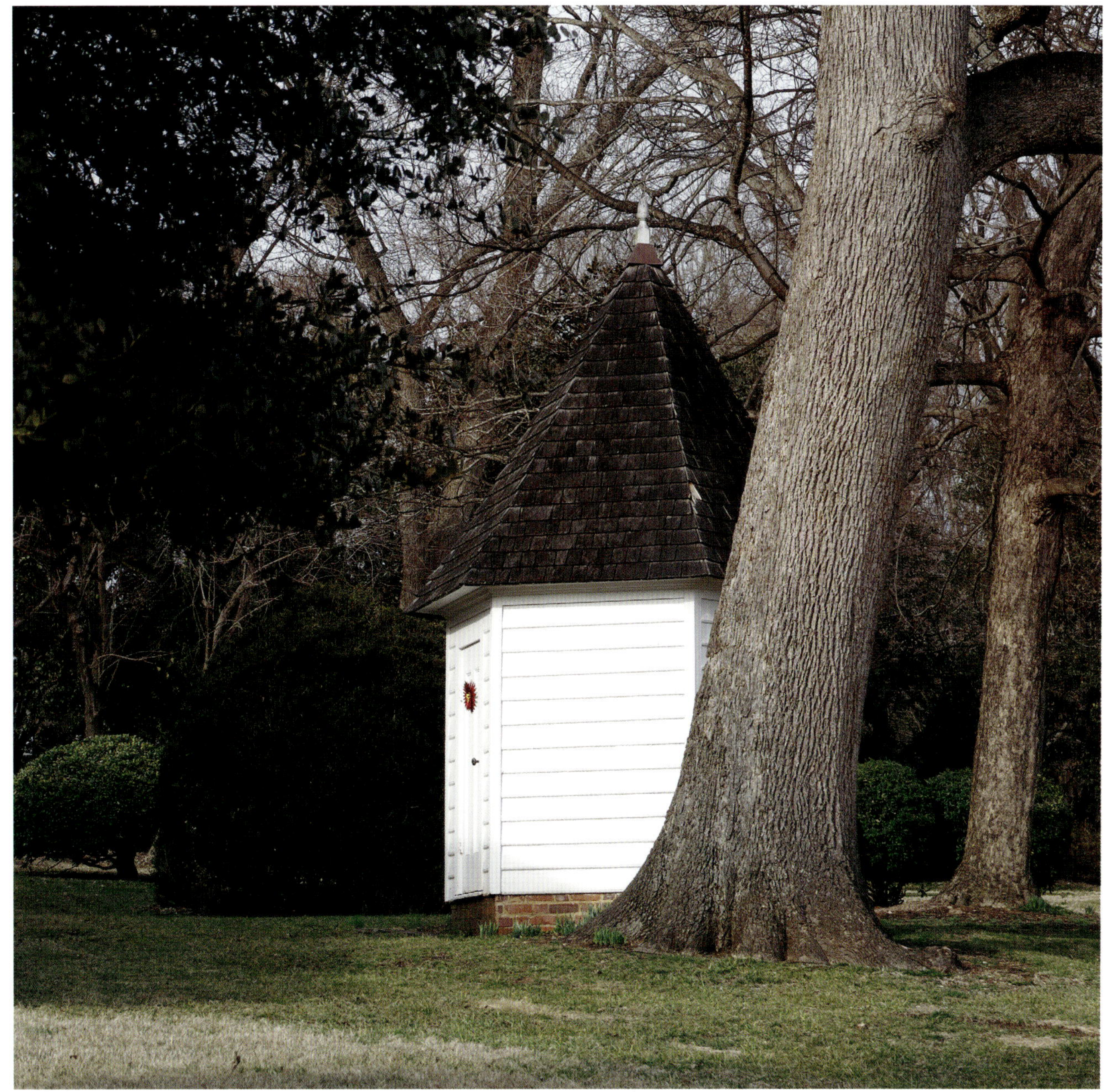

Figure 5.7 / Judge Gattis well house, a large hexagonal structure.

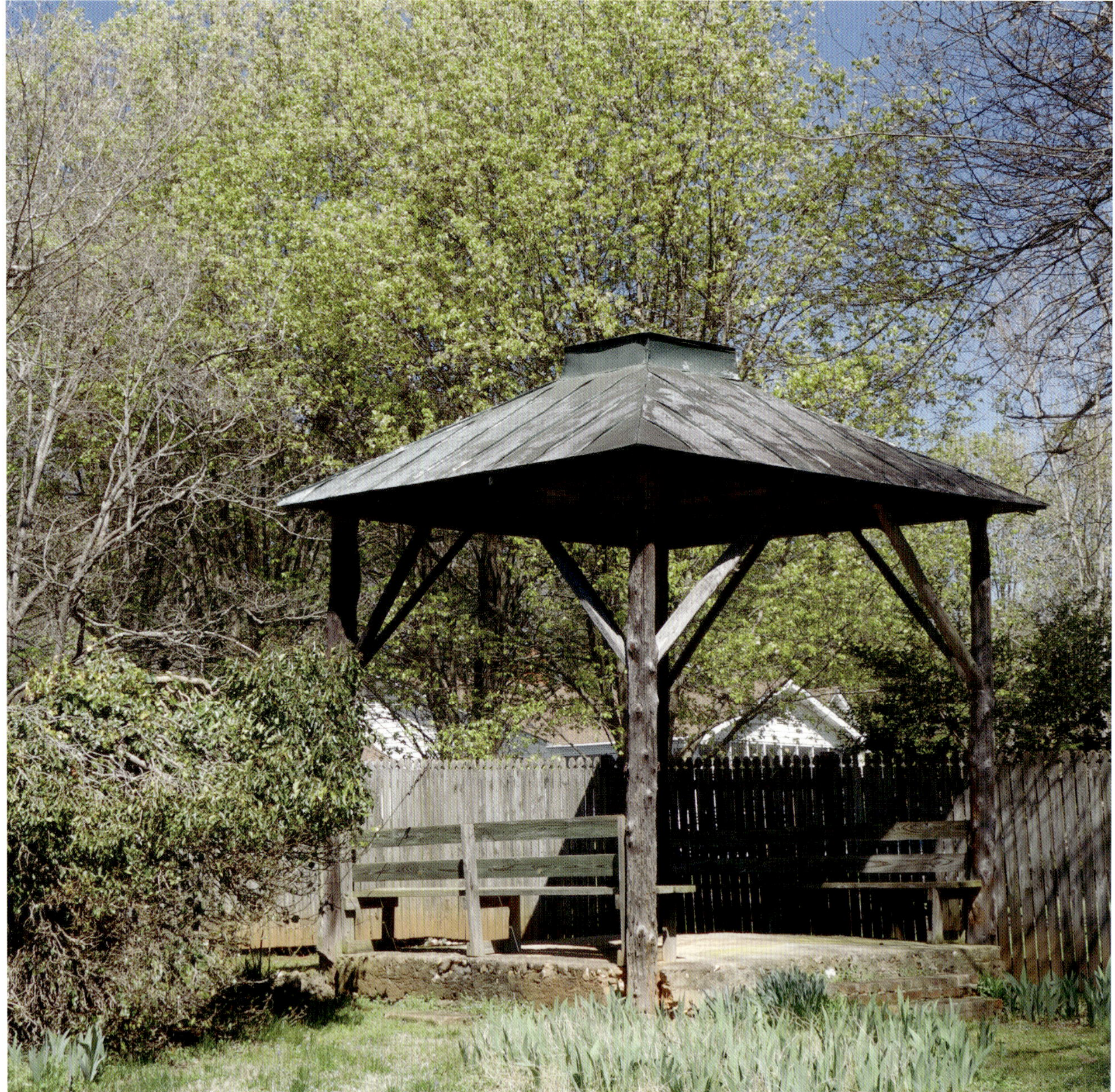

Figure 5.8 / Turner-Strudwick well house.

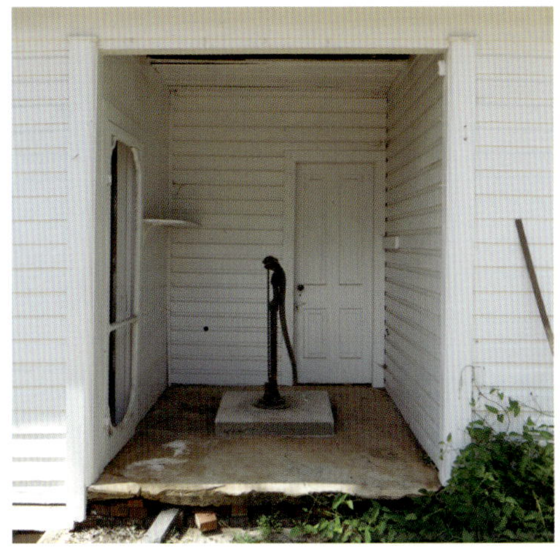

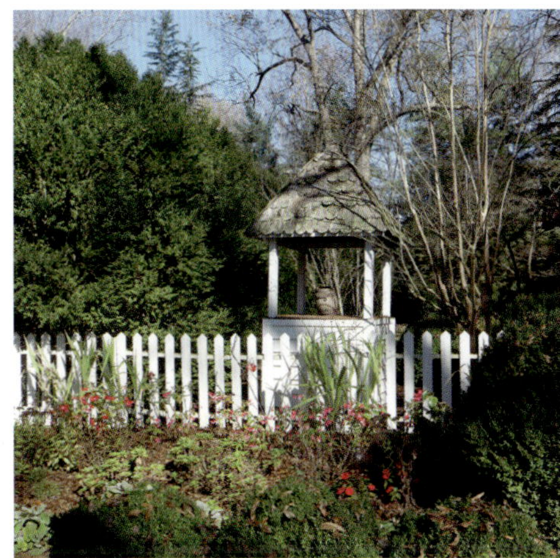

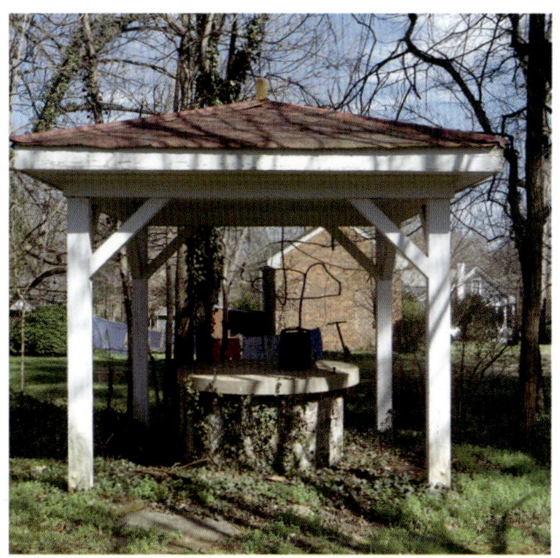

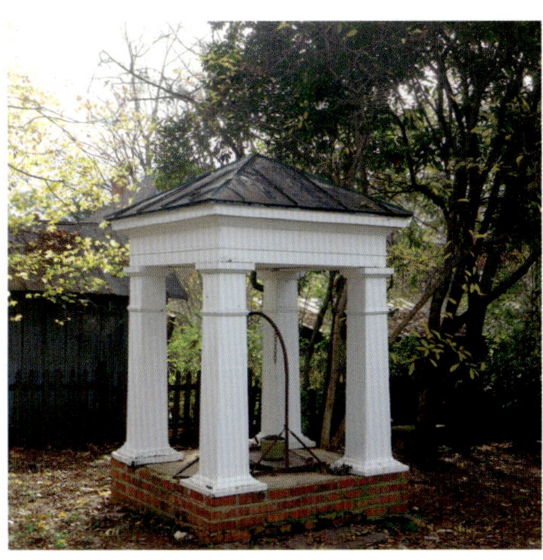

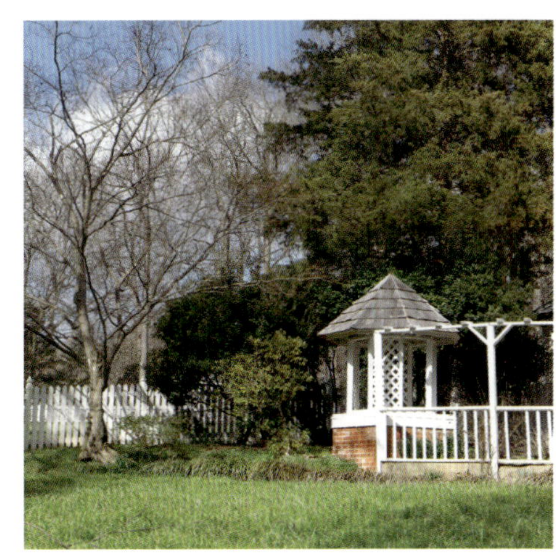

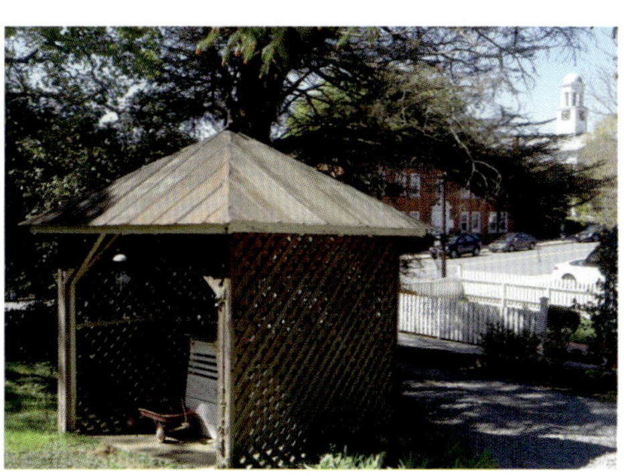

Top row (left to right)
Figure 5.9 / Well shelter with pump at Gattis House.
Figure 5.10 / Well house at Heartsease.
Figure 5.11 / Well house at Hasell-Nash House.

Bottom row (left to right)
Figure 5.12 / Well house at Tamarind.
Figure 5.13 / Well house at Whitted House.
Figure 5.14 / Well house at Courtney's Yellow House.

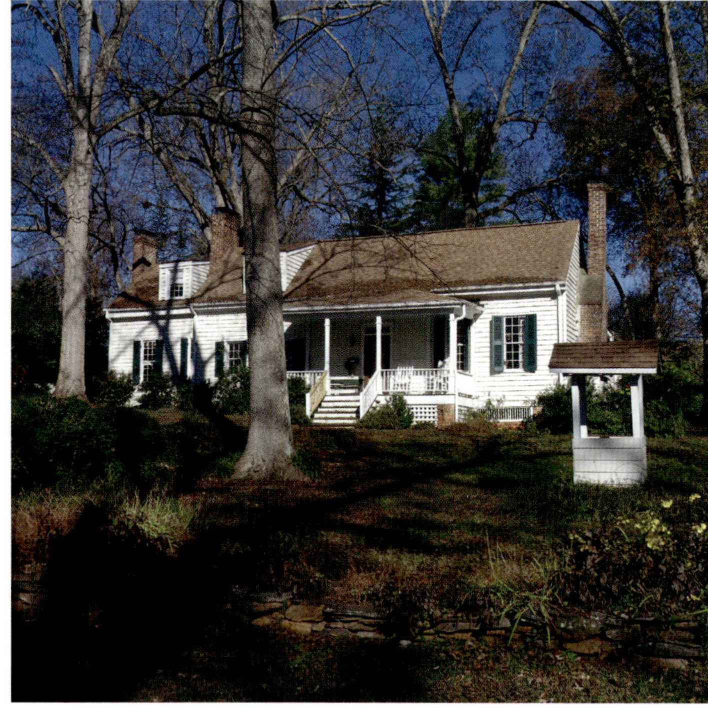

Figure 5.15 / Well house at Webb House.

the house to collect water for bathing and watering the gardens. One of her recollections is particularly vivid:

> The back porch, flooded with sunshine in winter and shaded by maple trees in summer, was a pleasant gathering place. . . . In one corner there was a shelf for the wooden bucket of drinking water brought fresh from the well several times a day. A shining tin dipper hung within reach and from it all who were thirsty drank. . . .[12]

The following twelve well houses are associated with historic houses: Berry Brick House, Gattis House (Figure 5.9), Heartsease (Figure 5.10), Hasell-Nash House (Figure 5.11), Judge Gattis House, Montrose, Ruffin-Roulhac House, Tamarind (Figure 5.12), Turner-Strudwick House, Whitted House (Figure 5.13), Courtney's Yellow House (Figure 5.14), Webb House (Figure 5.15). (See Map 7.)

Barns

Six

BY JEAN B. ANDERSON

In an agricultural county such as Orange, farm buildings once dotted the landscape, usually clustered around a dwelling. Most numerous among the outbuildings were barns. The word *barn* covers various structures: storage facilities for crops or food (animal and human); sheds for tools, farm machinery, wagons, or animals; buildings for carriages, and many other large pieces of equipment that needed cover outside the family dwelling. The uses and cost of the barns determined their size, shape, and quality of construction, and therefore, they came in many varieties. Some survive from the antebellum period, and many barns built after the Civil War and into the early twentieth century can still be found in both town and country.

When the town of Hillsborough was surveyed and planned by William Churton in 1754, a portion of its two hundred acres was divided into one-acre lots with a large commons,[1] from which in later years additional town lots were formed. Settlers bought anywhere from one to many lots, depending on their wealth and needs. Speculation motivated some; others required space. Because the town was designed as the county seat, the courthouse and jail at its center became the hub of activity, and around them clustered merchants, tavern-keepers, artisans, and lawyers on lots divided and subdivided again and again as the value of the lots increased. In direct contrast, ringing the town just outside its periphery were estates and small plantations of those with ample means, perhaps involved in commercial investment or modest agricultural activities.

Even in the town, small estates of up to five or ten acres could be found. The lawyer Duncan Cameron, for example, at the turn of the nineteenth century bought two lots on

Margaret Lane, and a year or two later added three more adjacent lots. When he had finished building on his five-lot property he had a story-and-a-half dwelling, office, kitchen (in addition to an old kitchen already on the site, probably used as a slave house), corn crib, well house, wagon shed, barn, dairy, smokehouse, carriage house, and stable.[2] This extensive establishment was not common in town; many inhabitants made do with only one or two lots and fewer outbuildings.

Because the only transportation available depended on horses or mules, however, not a few urban dwellers needed a barn, stable, or shed, if only for an old gray mare. Moreover, chickens, cows, and pigs were common contributors to the family diet and required food and shelter as well. Remember Mrs. O'Leary's cow in densely built Chicago, where animals were crowded in on the lots with the people. The same was true in Hillsborough on a smaller scale, even into the twentieth century, and barns, stables, and carriage houses can still be found, often repurposed for current uses, hidden behind the houses, and some slowly deteriorating in picturesque desuetude (see Map 7).

The most ambitious of the remaining barns in Hillsborough may be found just to the east of the town limits, off Cameron Street. It was built at Burnside, an estate of some seventy acres at the time the barn was constructed that had once been part of the original 263-acre grant to Francis Corbin. Over time the acreage dwindled under subsequent owners such as Thomas Pollock, James Hogg, and Thomas Ruffin. There, in 1857, Paul Carrington Cameron, Duncan Cameron's son, moved from his vast complex of plantations at Stagville in Durham County and bought back the house he had built in 1834 along with much of the land around it. He proceeded to add elaborate gardens, an arboretum, and ancillary buildings for agricultural and household needs. But Cameron had other plans for some of his land by the Eno River, which had been utilized first by the Occoneechee Indians and later during colonial days for a racetrack. He established oat- and cornfields and kitchen gardens so that he might "take my horses and cows out of my pocket."[3] Farther up the hill, he put orchards and formal gardens as well as a new stable, coach house, icehouse, servants' quarters, along with roads to access them.[4]

From Cameron's large construction effort, a few structures have survived. Now disguised as a beautiful dwelling is the stable or horse barn he built in the late 1850s (Figure 6.1). What remains of the barn are its original brick walls, built from bricks made on the site,

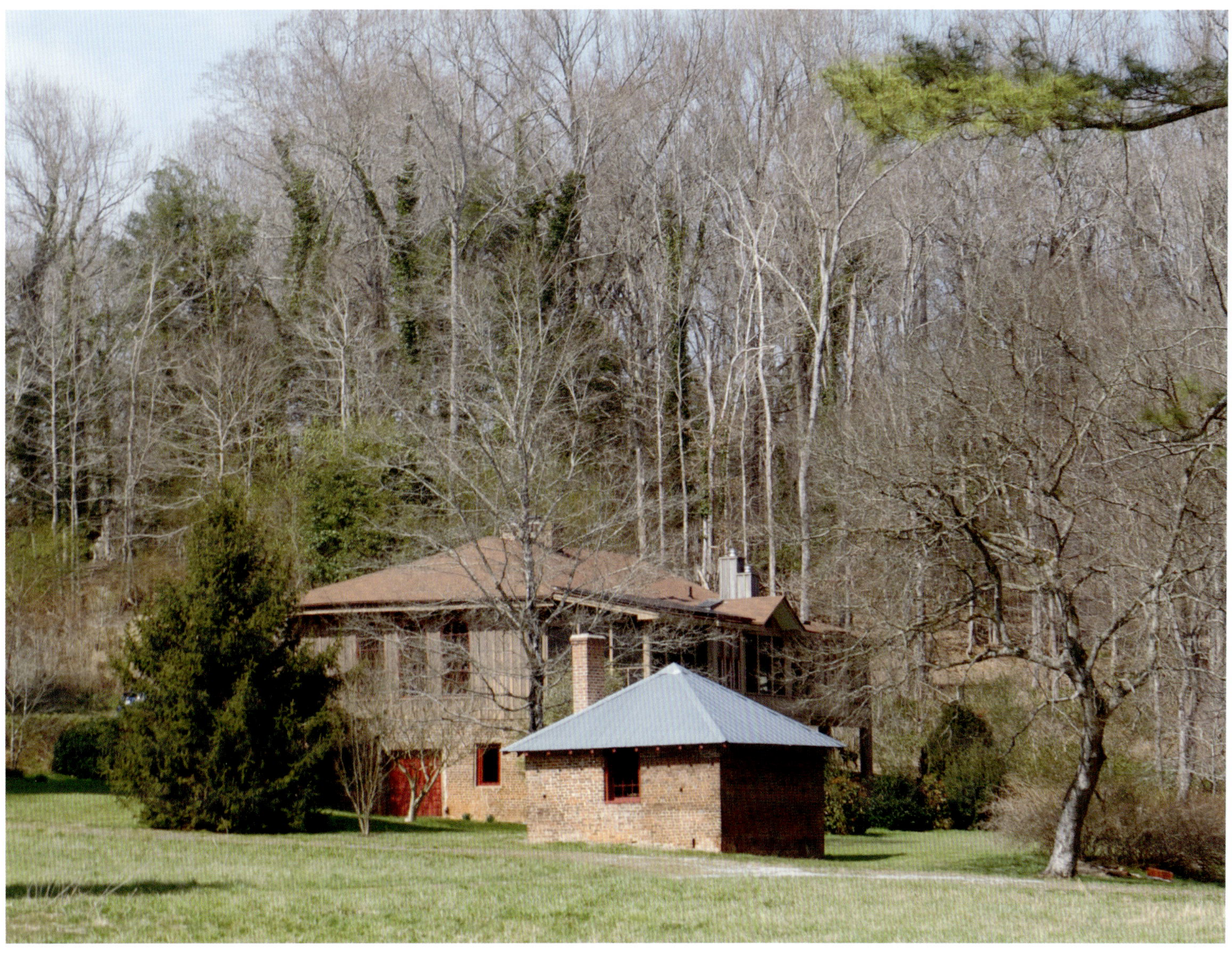

Figure 6.1 / Barn at Burnside, from the southeast, with Coachman's House in the foreground.

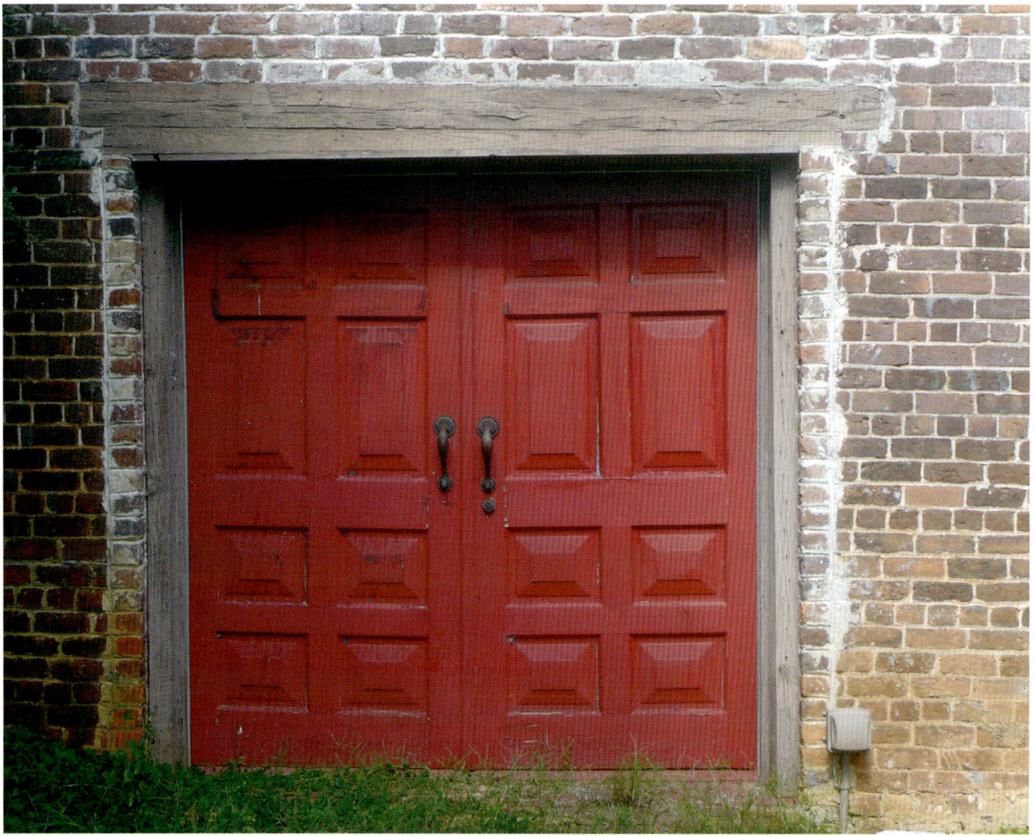

Figure 6.2 / Barn at Burnside, detail of main door (double door) of the barn (door leaves are modern replacements).

and huge frame and rafters, probably cut from trees on the grounds. Originally, the stable was a rectangular structure, two stories high, about sixty by thirty feet. Built on a slope, the modified bank-barn's northwest corner fit snugly into the rising ground, and its three-brick-thick foundation walls rose fourteen feet to the second story on the south and east sides. The bricks were laid in American bond, three stretcher rows to one header row. The stable's long sides faced east and west. On the ground floor in the south end nearest the river, a large double door, now outfitted with modern leaves, gave access to an aisle running north and south between two rows of stalls, ten to a side (Figure 6.2). The rows were interrupted in the middle by a cross aisle ending at an exterior door on the east side. On the ground level a room at the northwest corner held harnesses. No flooring covered the bare earth except the straw in which the horses and mules bedded down.[5]

The second story was of board and batten construction, in which the present house renovation follows suit. Centered over the stable door on the south end, another large opening gave access to the hayloft, but because of the slope, the north end of the loft was entered at ground level. Very large louvered openings in the lower brick walls and smaller scattered windows in the loft gave ventilation to animals and hay and prevented spontaneous combustion. The louvers have been retained over new glass windows. Huge hand-hewn beams running the length of the barn still support an original complex system of posts and rafters, rough oak floorboards on hand-hewn joists, and a hip roof. Because of the barn's great length, beams are joined lengthwise with beautiful scarf joints. The barn was covered with a standing-seam tin roof. The intricate system of rafters supporting the roof very much resembles that of the great barn that Cameron built at his Stagville plantation in 1860. (That barn along with slave houses and big house are now open to the public as a North Carolina Historic Site.)

The huge collection of Cameron Family Papers in the Southern Historical Collection in Wilson Library at the University of North Carolina at Chapel Hill contains several hand-drawn plans of the grounds at Burnside. In one of them the stable is shown in some detail exactly as found on the site with one exception: In the drawing an open shed is attached to the east side of the stable and designated for cows and pigs (see Figure 8.2).[6] What was actually built was a two-story enclosed structure that ran the length of the stable's east side with a shed roof, brick foundation, and board and batten second story slightly less tall than the stable itself and with five symmetrically placed windows in the east wall of the loft. This shed, too, stored hay. At the time of the barn's reconstruction in 1979, the shed had pulled away from the stable and lay in ruins. Pictures taken in 1938 from a distance, however, show the barn and shed still standing with their brick first levels painted white (Figure 6.3).[7]

During the reconstruction of the barn, the east wall was pulled back into plumb with cables and crank, and the sagging ceiling joists were tightened and reinforced, and the rough-cut floorboards for the second floor were re-planed and re-laid.[8] The beautifully reconstructed stable, now a dwelling, as previously mentioned, pays homage to the quality of the structure's materials and the expertise of the carpenters who originally built it.

Figure 6.3 / Barn at Burnside, 1938 photograph, from the east, showing first-level shed addition along the east wall (courtesy of Holly Reid).

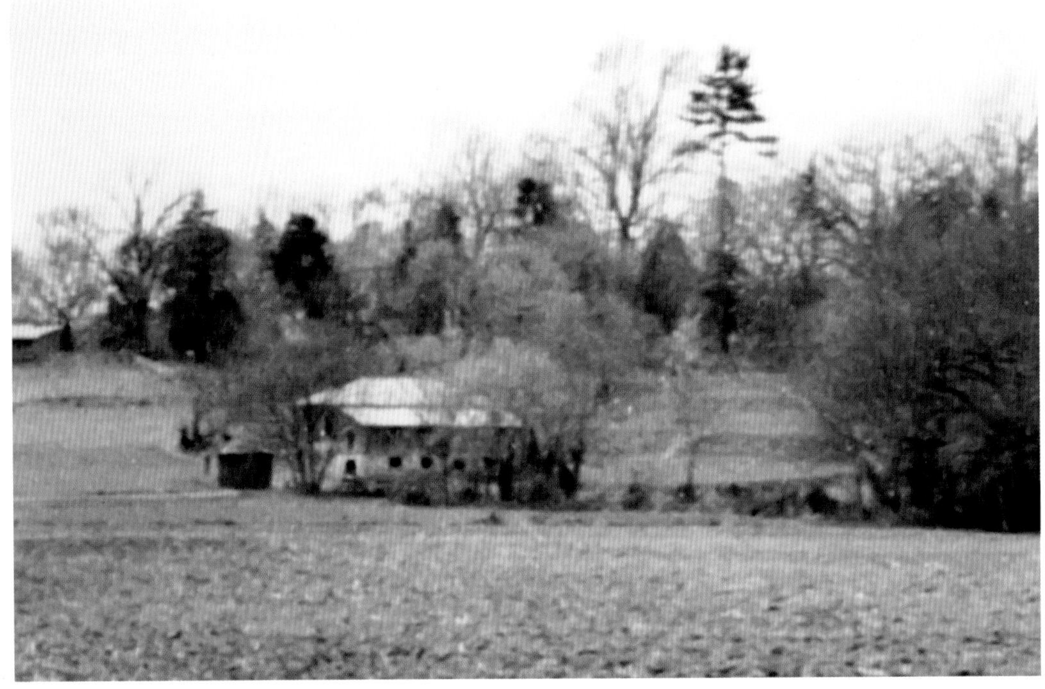

A very different multipurpose barn has survived in almost original condition at Montrose, the estate to the east of Burnside on St. Mary's Road (Figures 6.4 and 6.5). The barn is some forty to fifty feet square and two stories high, with a pitched, standing-seam tin roof. The frame of huge hand-hewn timbers, joined with pegs, is covered with horizontal board siding painted white. The doors are made of vertical boards, two with large, iron strap hinges (Figure 6.5). The loft has openings on all sides for ventilation. A one-story shed along one side is a much later addition, possibly for a tractor. The barn's lower floor was once partitioned into four rooms for different uses, but the space now is essentially two rooms. One area obviously used for stalls could have accommodated three horses or mules ("a pair and a spare"). Another sectioned-off space may have been reserved for farm machinery, since a corn-picking machine was found in that area.[9]

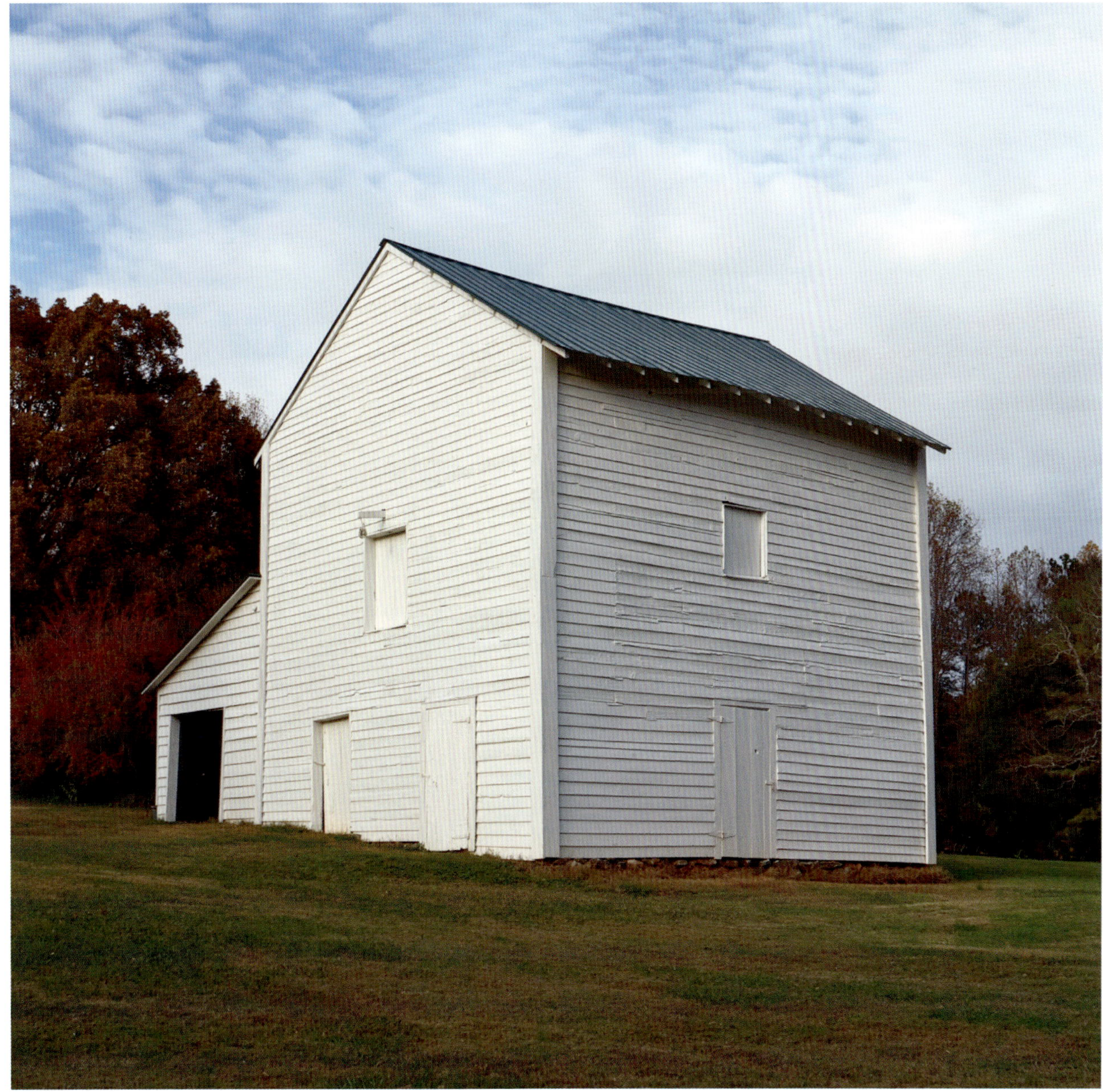

Figure 6.4 / Montrose barn.

Figure 6.5 / Montrose barn, detail of strap hinge.

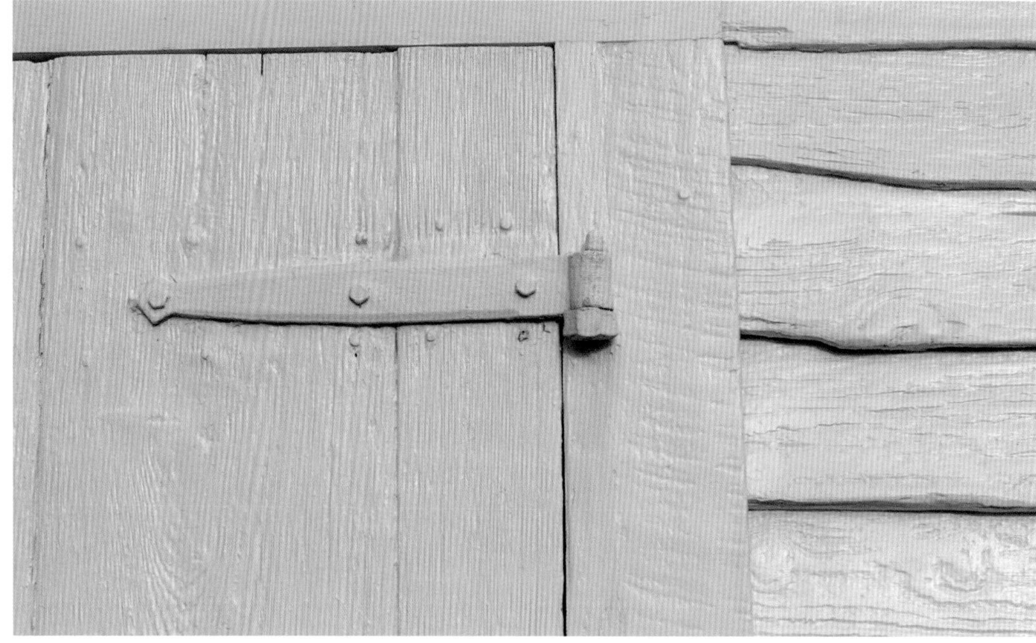

The barn's exact age is hard to determine. The Montrose tract was first developed as a home site when William Kirkland sold fifty-six acres to the Rev. William Mercer Green in 1825. After Green moved away in the late 1830s, the land reverted to Kirkland ownership, until Gov. William A. Graham bought it in 1842.[10] It remained in the Graham family until the 1970s. A fire destroyed the governor's house in 1869, after which he moved to the Nash-Hooper House on Tryon Street.[11] It may not have damaged any farm buildings, since Graham's law office was spared, and still stands much closer to the main house site than the other outbuildings. If Gov. Graham didn't build the barn, it is possible his son, John W. Graham, could have built it, after moving into a new house on the site in 1875 with his wife, Rebecca Cameron Graham, the daughter of Paul C. Cameron.[12] However, the barn's handmade construction suggests an antebellum building date. Therefore it was probably built during the governor's occupancy, in the 1840s. Whatever the barn's age it has had good care throughout its existence, and like a trim and well-preserved veteran, it is probably older than it looks.

Opposite Montrose on St. Mary's Road another barn, the Mangum-Ruffin barn, contrasts starkly with that at Montrose. A newer structure, its formerly red-painted surface weathered to a dusty pink, it resembles a child's drawing of a barn—a little wobbly and listing (Figure 6.6).

The barn has been repaired many times, and there is no evidence pointing to a clear construction date; historic restoration experts suggest a range anywhere from late nineteenth to the early decades of the twentieth century. The rectangular barn is about twenty by thirty feet, divided in half on the ground level by a passage for a wagon. On each side of the passage are two stalls, each with a small, almost square window in the outside walls. In the northeast corner is an enclosed room for harnesses with a door in the east wall. The exterior walls are a mishmash of plain, beaded-board, plank, and German siding indicating the many different times and periods in which the barn has been repaired. A second-story hayloft covers both lower sections of the barn and is topped by a low-pitched tin roof. The loft is ventilated by a window in each gable end. The barn is slated for demolition.[13]

Who built the barn is an open question. At the time Thomas Ruffin Jr. bought the land in the 1870s until well into the twentieth century, the tract consisted of forty-seven acres, with St. Mary's Road (then called the Oxford Road) as its southern boundary.[14] In 1928 the tract passed into the Mitchell family, one member of which wrote his name in black paint on a stall in the barn. During successive generations the land was subdivided until now the handsome Victorian house with its antebellum, brick outbuildings and the more recent barn stands on just under eight acres.

At the northeast corner of town, outside the old town limits, stands another, once-extensive estate known as Sans Souci. It contains examples of a variety of outbuildings along with its intact antebellum house. While the original house on the site was built by David Yarborough around 1812, it was later added onto and probably embellished by the next owner, William Cain Jr., who also owned a country plantation, Hardscrabble, on St. Mary's Road, inherited from his father. It was Cain who probably gave the humorously contrasting names to his two houses. He may also have been responsible for many of the outbuildings that remain.[15] A letter by young Joseph Norwood to his sister written in 1830 describes what

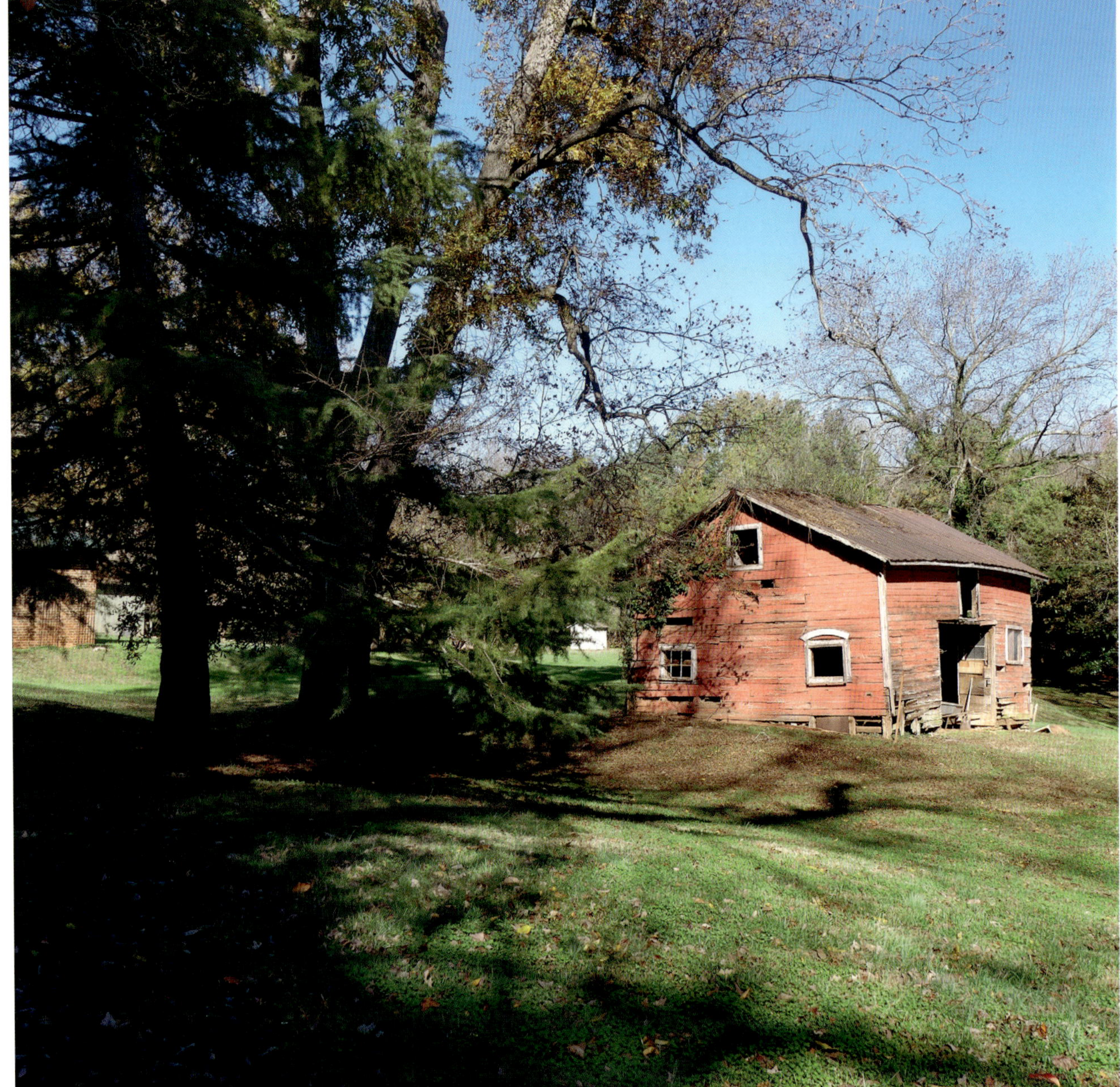

Figure 6.6 / Mangum-Ruffin barn.

he saw on a winter's stroll at sunset as he looked toward the town from the ridge across the river where the Norwoods lived. The Cains had not yet bought the place from Yarborough:[16]

> Mr. Yarborough's old place at once arrested my attention, whose wheat fields fretted by the long shadows and enlivened by the last beams of departing day, graced by the beautiful undulations of the ground, adorned by his beautiful house and all set off in a stronger light by the bleakness of the surrounding woods, presented quite a handsome landscape.

Sans Souci's many outbuildings differ from one other in style. Among them is a carriage house, now altered, enlarged, and refitted for housing. Its original function is now obliterated inside and out by a chimney and hearth, repartitioning of the interior space, and a brick addition. The original section stands on a low brick foundation and is covered by horizontal siding up to the second floor, which is shingled (Figure 6.7).

The current front door has been made smaller and replaces an original, wide carriage door, but upper windows on each side of it have kept their original rounded tops. The hip roof is unchanged except for dormers, which were added to give light to the second floor, and a chimney stack has changed the roof's silhouette.

The builder of the carriage house is almost certainly known. Bishop Theodore B. Lyman of the Episcopal Church bought Sans Souci at auction from William Cain Jr.'s son-in-law Pride Jones Jr., when Jones was financially forced to sell. Because of its appearance and construction, the carriage house can be safely dated to Bishop Lyman's occupation of Sans Souci from 1889 to 1893.[17]

Even within the town's historic district, barns can still be found. An excellent example stands on the Robertson-Cheek House property on the southwest corner of Queen and Churton streets (Figure 6.8).

It is a plain rectangular structure, around twenty-two by thirty feet, now so weathered that a faded red-brown wash is perceptible only here and there. It has not been altered or added to externally. On the longer north side a row of two doors and a window disclose the original interior's two-section arrangement. A large double door indicates where a carriage or wagon would enter the barn. Next to it a smaller but still large door leads to the section for the horses. Louvered windows on the west end ventilated the stalls and hayloft. Internally all divisions have been removed, but remaining joists suggest what was once there. The

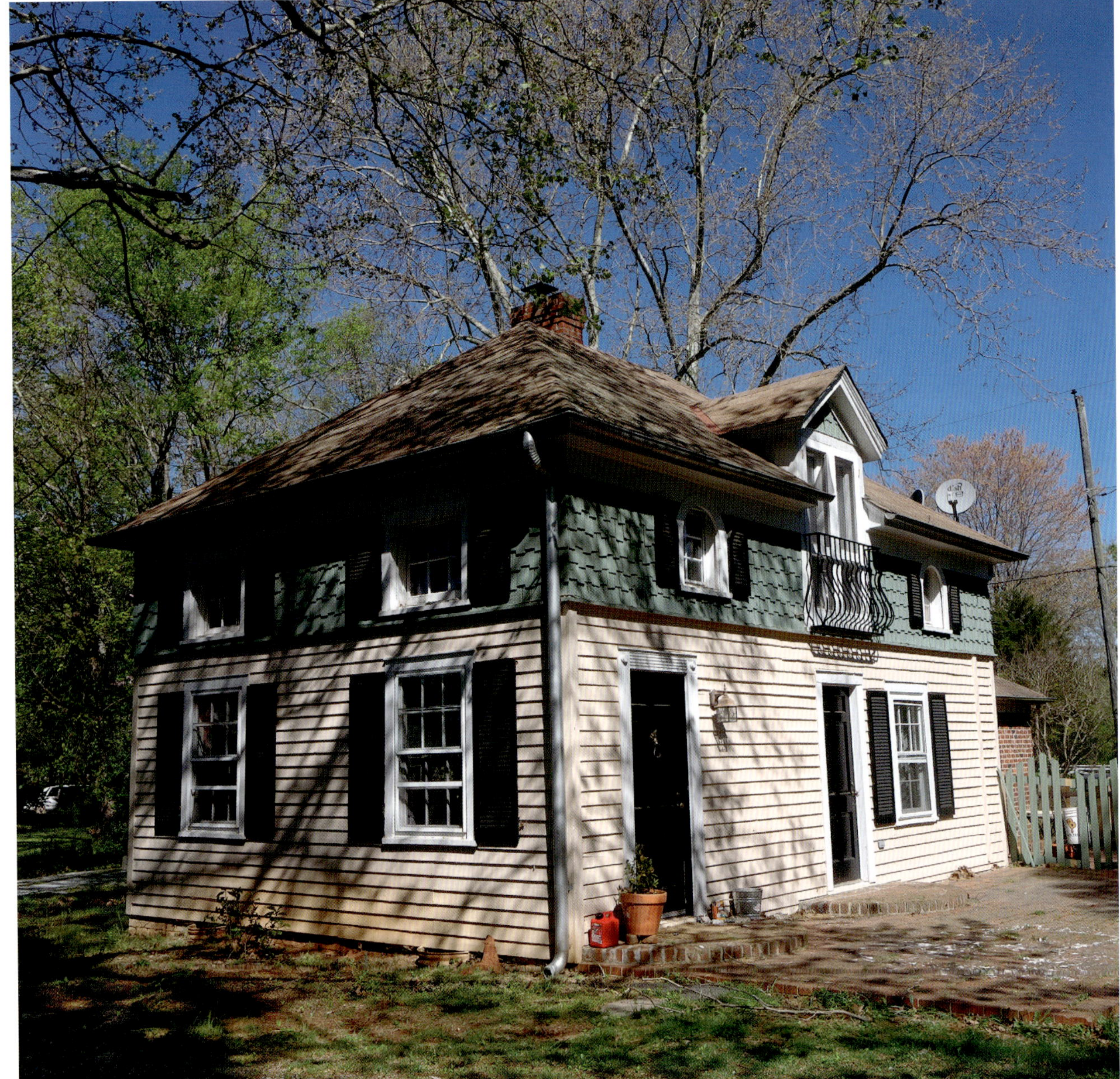

Figure 6.7 / Sans Souci carriage house, much altered and adapted as a residence.

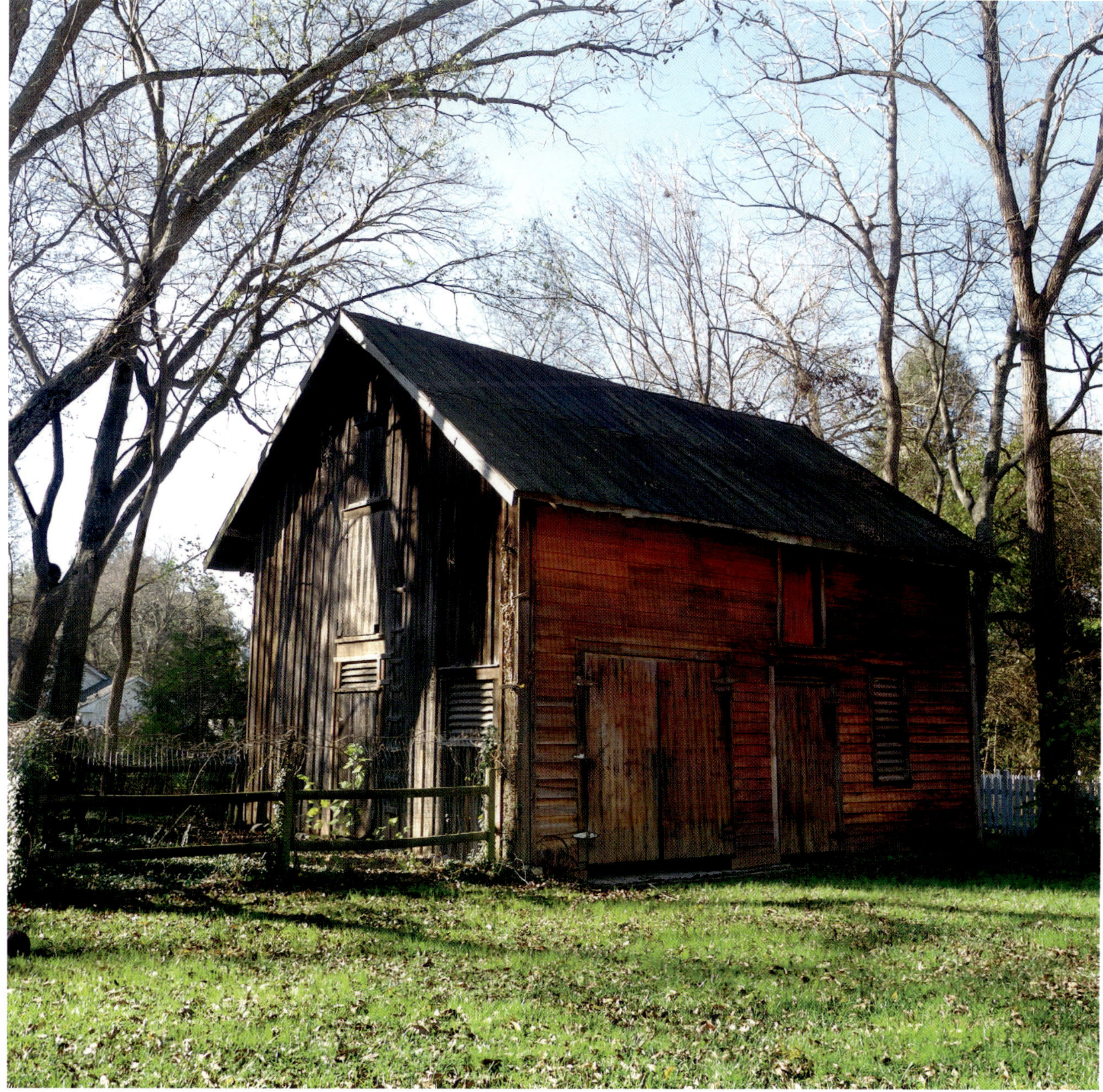

Figure 6.8 / Robertson-Cheek barn, from the northeast.

west end has a projecting shed roof over a loft door where a pulley lifted the hay into the loft. The pitched roof is high, accommodating three levels of windows or openings in the gable ends. The end sheathing is vertical board and batten while the sides have horizontal board siding.

Many clues to the barn's age can be found both inside and out: wrought iron nails, square iron locks on the doors, and oak ceiling joists. Rows of pegs on the wall were for harnesses and other tack. The barn has a low stone foundation. Although replaced elements can be identified on the exterior walls, the building as a whole suggests a date in the first half of the nineteenth century.[18] Unfortunately, the absence of a clear chain of title of the lot or other public records prevents even speculation about the barn's builder. An old building's survival often depends on the owners with whom it is associated; it is to be hoped that one of Hillsborough's many surviving manuscript collections may still reveal the builder.

A block away on the south side of West Union Street adjacent to the historic Burwell School, the Dozier barn represents perhaps the last appearance of its kind in the town (Figure 6.9). The building is about twenty by twenty-four feet, including the eight-foot-wide shed running the length of the longer north side. Before its interior partitions were removed, the barn had two horse stalls, each with an exterior Dutch door, but the additional space seems not to have been intended for either a wagon or carriage, for the barn lacks a door wide enough for this purpose. The attached shed is unenclosed except at its west end where it becomes a small room. The open section is supported by two posts. The walls are covered with modern vertical metal sheathing except for the exposed wall under the shed, which is unpainted wood. The roof, too, is tin. Nothing about the barn suggests a construction date before the twentieth century.[19]

Since an older house that once stood on the same lot is known to have burned in 1914, it is reasonable to suppose that the barn was built at the same time as the current house, not long after the fire. In 1908 the lot on which the barn stands passed into the possession of T. M. Arrowsmith, who probably built the house that burned and also its replacement. The barn, too, was probably his handiwork.[20]

At one time the barn and a smokehouse close by it were presumed to have been part of the large Hasell-Nash homestead on West Queen Street called Pilgrim's Rest. That assumption was based on the fact that for some seventy years the Nashes owned half a dozen adjoining lots on both West Queen and West Union streets, including the lot the barn stands on

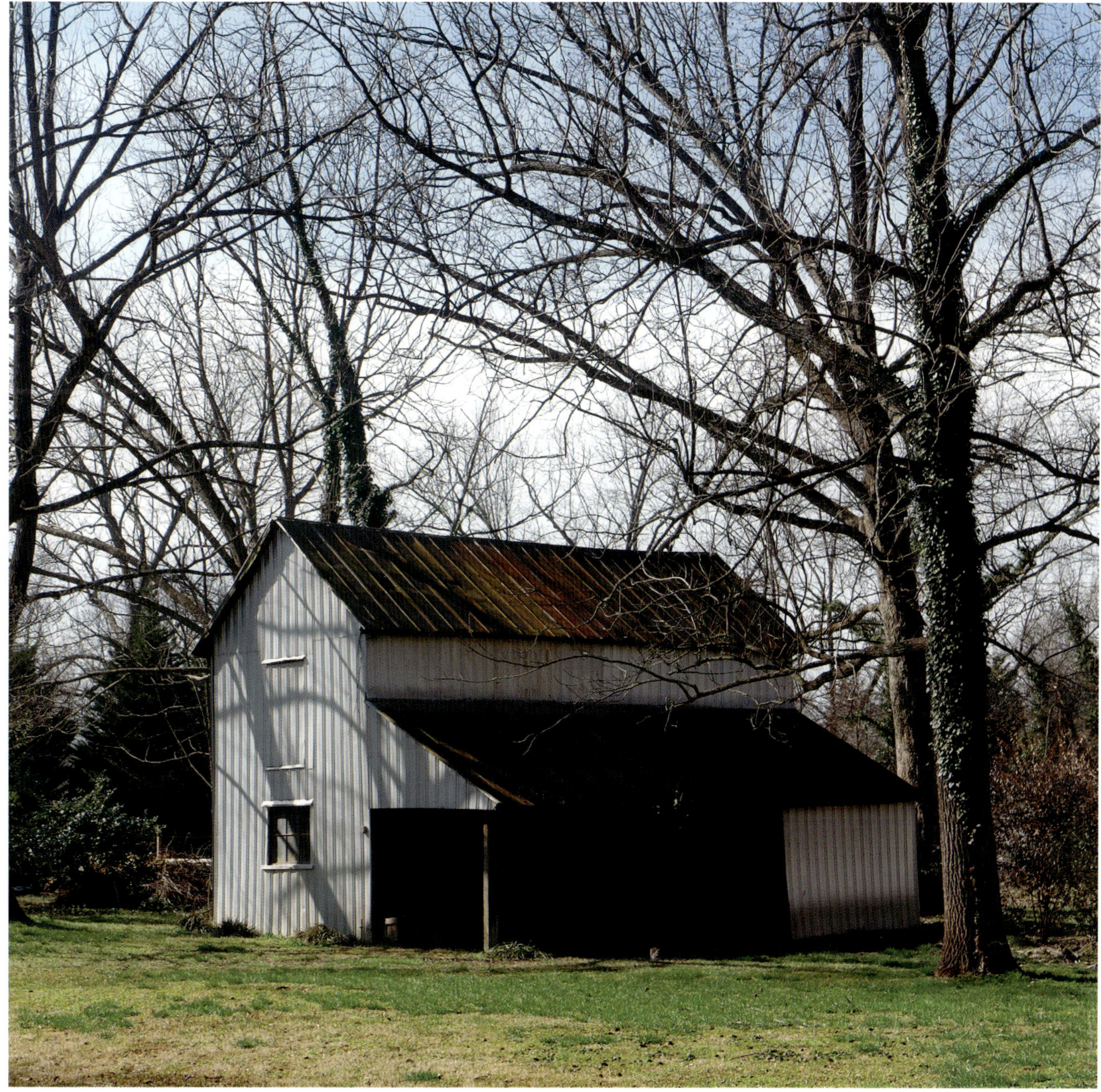

Figure 6.9 / Dozier barn.

and the adjoining lot. However, besides the barn's lack of any structural elements that would support such an early date, it should be noted that the doors to both the barn and the smokehouse face Union Street as does the current house on the lot, not in the opposite direction toward Queen Street where the Nash residence was located.

The Ruffin-Roulhac House now serves as the Hillsborough Town Hall; the property was one of the town's former multi-lot mansion house complexes. The ten-acre tract, which became the Judge Thomas Ruffin homestead after the Civil War, was bounded by East Corbin, Cameron, East Orange, and Churton streets. The main house and outbuildings had been empty for many years and were badly deteriorated when the town purchased the tract in 1972 and undertook a complete restoration and/or reconstruction.[21] The barn and carriage house are two of the reconstructed buildings. While there is nothing original about them, they are built where their counterparts once stood, with their exact dimensions and apertures (Figures 6.10 and 6.11).

The interiors, of course, are changed. Early photographs of the house and outbuildings have aided the town in restoring the entire complex of buildings with great success. (This complex is open to the public.) An early photograph shows that the original dispositions of windows and doors were maintained in the reconstruction.[22]

The barn and carriage house seem now to be part of a single building plan, situated as they are in a row with the office, slave house, and smokehouse, though slightly separated from them to the east. All these dependencies face the rear of the main house. Who the builder of their original counterparts was remains a puzzle. In their present locations they can date only from the Ruffin family's occupation after the Civil War, because the lots they stand on and that of the main house were not owned by the same person until Thomas Ruffin's occupation, when all ten lots in the block came into his possession. Thus it might be fair to conclude that Judge Ruffin built them shortly after 1865. However, from 1830 to 1865 the main house, situated on a lot facing Orange Street, and its adjoining lot were owned by Frances Clark Pollock Connor Blount (later Hill), a member of the Eastern North Carolina establishment. William D. Hill, her second husband, was the North Carolina Secretary of State from 1811 to 1857. Her house would surely have been well supplied with a full complement of dependencies. In fact, an old photograph taken of the front of her house clearly shows a row of outbuildings strung out beside it. Since the office of her house is known to have been moved from its original location near the main house to the row in which it now stands, it

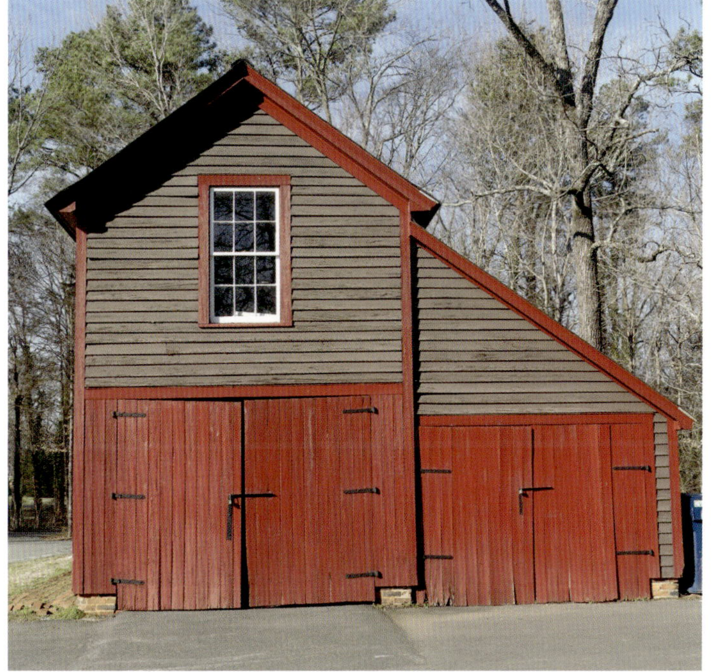

Figure 6.10 / Ruffin-Roulhac carriage house (reconstructed).

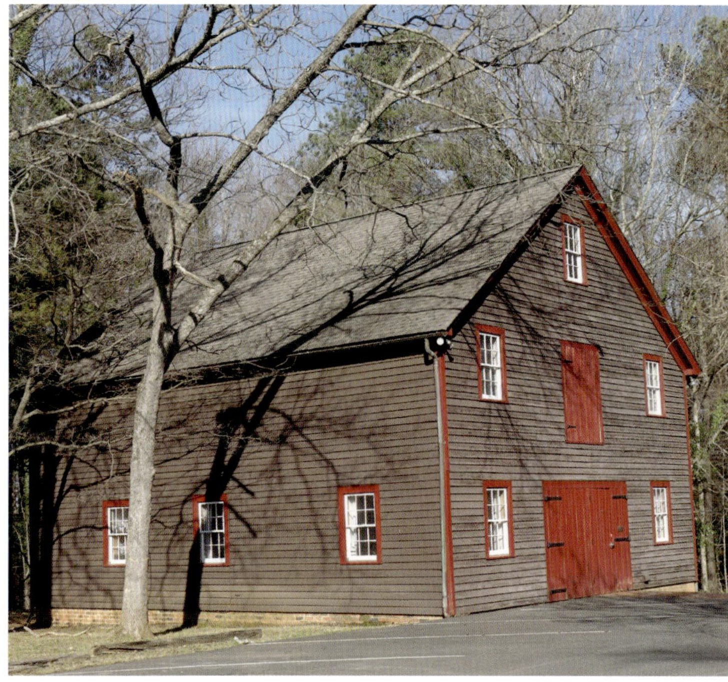

Figure 6.11 / Ruffin-Roulhac barn, now the Town Barn (reconstructed).

is possible to conclude that the other buildings, too, were originally built by her and moved to their current locations either by the Ruffins or their descendants the Roulhacs.[23] Without further evidence it is impossible to know which supposition is correct.

It is not surprising to find so few old barns left in the town. With the rise of taxes and the value of town real estate over the years, maintaining unused and unnecessary structures, particularly if they occupied lots separate from the houses they adjoined, became an unnecessary expense. Over time most of these buildings were torn down or allowed to fall into ruin and be carted away, and the land they stood on sold. By the mid-twentieth century Hillsborough's barns, stables, and carriage houses had become superfluous.

Today, Hillsborough's six barns are found on the following properties: Burnside, Dozier House, Mangum-Ruffin House, Montrose, Robertson-Cheek House, and Sans Souci.

Seven

Other Dependencies

Icehouses

By Stewart E. Dunaway

Icehouses were of two basic types. The first was a structure designed to provide ice storage for personal use on an individual's property; the second was a commercial ice storage building, where people could buy or pay to store ice.

These buildings kept ice frozen by insulating underground chambers with straw or sawdust.[1] The ice was then used as a refrigerant for preserving meats and dairy products within the home.

An icehouse is not an American invention, but existed in antiquity in the Middle East. Icehouses were found in the ancient Mesopotamian town of Terqa, by Zumri-Lim, as early as 1780 BC.[2] They were then introduced to Britain around 1660 AD. Therefore, the design and use had long been known by much of the world.

The most important and largest part of an icehouse was located underground. It consisted of a pit that could be lined with bricks, stones, or squared-off logs. It could be round or square in shape, although the log-lined pits were square. The pit of a small icehouse would usually be more than fifteen feet deep. A log-lined pit would be about twelve feet square on the interior and made of logs about fifteen or more inches thick after being squared off. All icehouses had a ladder inside, leaning up against the wall closest to the door, to access and allow for filling and emptying the pit. The blocks of ice in the pit were packed in sawdust.

The covering over the icehouse was designed to shade the interior and to provide some insulation from the outside temperature. It could be, and frequently was, a simple gabled structure, like a small shed, but with the bottom edges of the gable roof resting near the ground so that it resembled a big pup tent. In a log-lined ice house the gable roof rested on the top log, just a few inches above the surface of the ground. The exterior gable ends were covered with weatherboards, and the door to the interior was located in the front gable end. The Great Burnside Icehouse—a large (twenty-four-feet wide), brick-lined, octagonal ice pit—was state of the art at the time it was built around 1856 (Figure 7.1).[3]

Hillsborough tradition has it that ice was harvested from the Eno River in the winter when it was frozen over. Nearby lakes and ponds were also a source of ice. However, all local ice was dependent on the coldest winter weather to produce ice thick enough to cut and store. *The Hillsborough Recorder,* the local newspaper, documented a number of these cold spells; for example, on 23 December 1882, it reported: "Snow commenced falling last Wednesday afternoon and continued falling until Thursday morning. Messrs. John Laws and Joseph C. Webb filled their icehouses the past week." And on 24 January 1891: "Mr. Isaac R. Strayhorn filled his icehouse two weeks ago with ice one to 2 inches thick. This is the only ice that has been put up in the county, we believe."

The last newspaper article on this subject was dated 4 January 1900:

> We are now having some unusually cold weather. Sunday morning the thermometer registered 3° above zero. Nearly all of the icehouses have been filled with good ice 5 to 6 inches in thickness. Skating on the ponds and River is very fine.[4]

Another source of ice was from points north where colder locales shipped large blocks of ice. When the North Carolina Railroad opened in the middle of the nineteenth century, Hillsborough's depot became a shipping destination for ice from up North.

Icehouses are mentioned in a number of deed records. One icehouse, owned by Paul Cameron, can be seen in the woods behind Cameron Park Elementary School. The Great Burnside Icehouse was restored in 2002 by the Preservation Fund of Hillsborough, and is well documented and photographed.[5] Another, owned by Samuel Strudwick, was mentioned in a number of deed transactions in the 1860s to 1870s as being twenty-four square feet in size, and was situated on part of Lot 77, on the south side of Queen Street. The deed for the Orange Hotel (Lot 15) noted an icehouse in 1849. Also, Lot 9 listed an icehouse beginning in 1849. In subsequent deeds, stipulations were made pertaining to the keeping of the

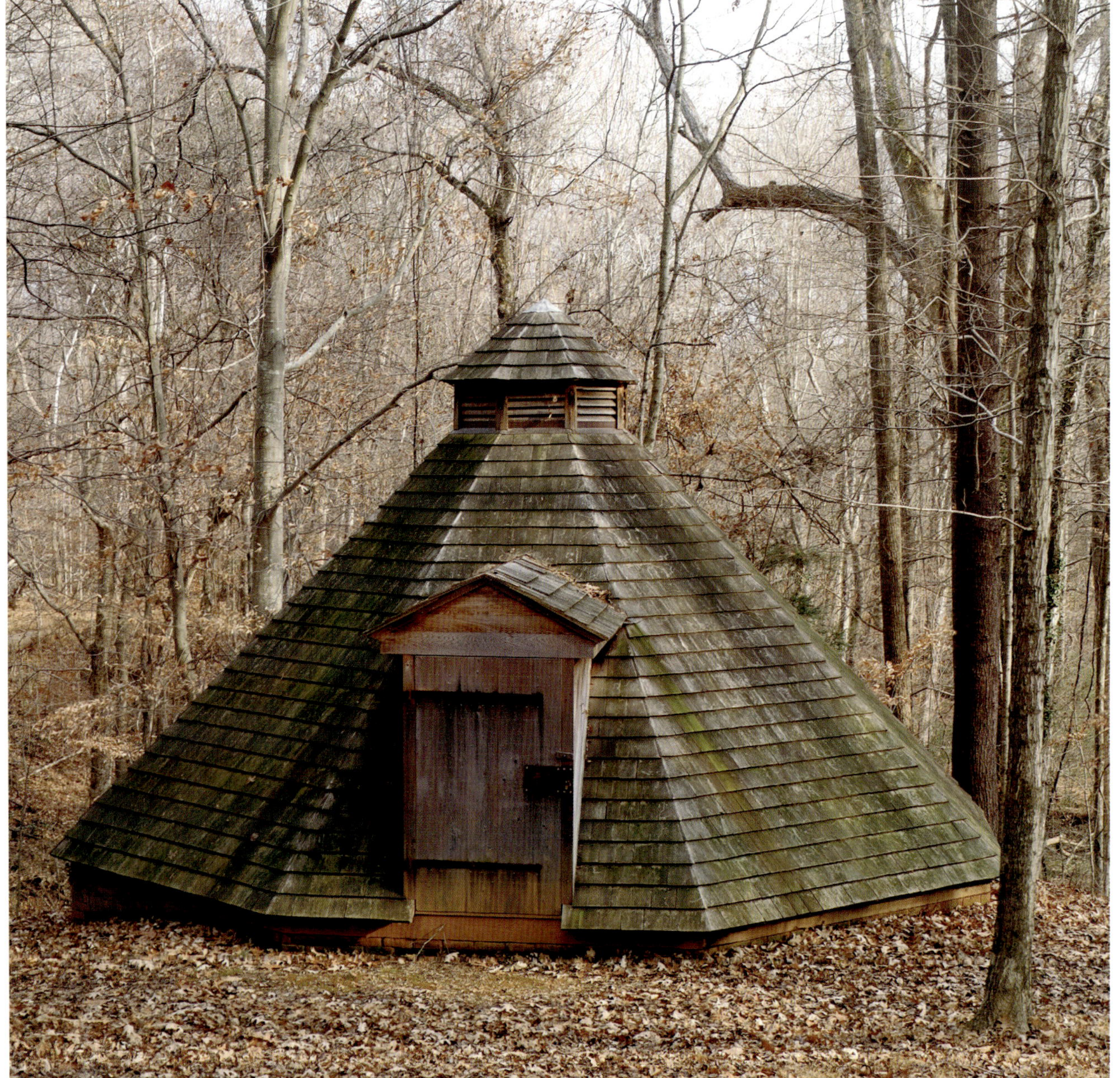

Figure 7.1 / Great Burnside Icehouse, showing octagonal roof and gabled entrance (reconstructed).

icehouse—perhaps inferring a commercial use, for Lot 9 had on it a number of businesses at that time.[6]

In addition to the above references from the *Hillsborough Recorder,* the newspaper often reported on icehouses, both in town and in the county. An article announcing the sale of a fine historic home, Lochiel, included in the inventory of outbuildings an icehouse.[7] According to another article, a local resident lost his icehouse due to a fire:

> An icehouse belonging to Mr. James A. Cheek was burned about 5 o'clock Wednesday morning. . . . Tuesday afternoon about 5 o'clock, it was claimed, was the last time the house was entered. Mr. Cheek's losses amounted to about $300 and a considerable quantity of ice.[8]

Another newspaper article of interest mentions damage to an icehouse:

> Snow commenced falling here last Sunday afternoon at 3 o'clock and continued to fall until the same time Monday. Snow covered the ground to the depth from 12 to 18 inches. Many trees were broken and some buildings were damaged. The rear portion of Mr. Cooley's shop fell in, Mayor Corbin's icehouse gave way, and the shed at Mr. C.W. Brown's Brickyard was wrecked.[9]

Although a number of icehouses are known to have existed in Hillsborough, only one has been preserved and restored, the Great Burnside Icehouse (see Map 7).

Dining Rooms

By Barbara Hume

During the eighteenth and early nineteenth centuries, space used for dining evolved from being combined with other living and eating areas in a dwelling to being important, separate buildings that accommodated larger gatherings or more formal dining at private houses. In the latter part of that period, dining rooms were sometimes located in the basement of a house, as at the Nash House (formerly the Nash-Kollock School located on West Margaret Lane),[10] the Mallett Mill House (Lot 19), and Pilgrim's Rest (the Hasell-Nash House, Lot 58). The Teer House (Lot 29), dated ca. 1870, still continues that practice today.

Freestanding separate kitchens of the eighteenth and nineteenth centuries were busy, crowded, messy places of great activity, focused on food preparation in the era before widespread commercial food processing. The cook was usually assisted by an apprentice cook, frequently a relative, and their children and grandchildren were not far away. For these reasons expensive china and silver cutlery were retained in the dining room and were not brought into the kitchen, although pots, pans, and iron and wooden utensils were used, cleaned, and stored there.

China and silver cutlery, both very valuable at that time, were usually washed and dried in the dining room by the lady of the house or a trusted, experienced servant. She began with the knives whose early steel blades demanded immediate attention to prevent destructive rust.[11] She used two small pans of water for washing and rinsing, and then she carefully dried first the silver cutlery and then the expensive china dishes. These were then stored in cabinets built into the wall of the dining room or in freestanding cupboards also located in the dining room.

Later, when kitchens moved into the house, a butler's pantry, with numerous built-in cabinets, was frequently positioned between the dining room and kitchen to provide for a space—separate and apart from the kitchen—to clean and store the silver cutlery and fine china. After World War I with the expanding middle class and declining use of servants, the butler's pantry evolved into a breakfast room, used by the whole family. Usually, the butler's pantry's many cabinets were retained in the new breakfast room. This preservation of two separate rooms enabled the kitchen to be kept as a space intended primarily for cooking. Following World War II the breakfast room, including its special set of cabinets, was combined with the kitchen, with perhaps a token separation provided by a bar or hanging cabinets. In the last part of the twentieth century, with the declining value of china and silver cutlery (and its replacement by stainless steel utensils), as well as the introduction of dishwashers, washing and storing of dishes moved to the expanded kitchen. Built-in cupboards in the dining room generally disappeared, and separate, formal dining rooms declined in popularity.

Freestanding Dining Rooms in Early Hillsborough

In situations where a number of people dined at the same time, freestanding, exterior dining rooms, separate from the house, were sometimes constructed. An early documented example in Hillsborough of a dining room as a separate dependency was located at John Witherspoon's private boarding school on West King Street, now known as Twin Chimneys

(Lot 21). (In 1818 he enlarged his house in order to use it as a boarding school.) When he offered the home for sale in July 1822, he advertised that "The house contains eight rooms, well finished, with a large garret room; adjoining the house is a dining room 30 by 16 feet, well finished."[12] This exterior room provided dining space for the students, but unfortunately no longer survives.

Another freestanding dining room was constructed across King Street, on Lot 18, behind the building now known as the Inn at Teardrops, a house that was converted into a hotel in the late nineteenth century. The need for additional space for dining was addressed by constructing a separate dependency to be used solely for the purpose of dining. It was located behind and perpendicular to the inn (i.e., perpendicular to King Street and parallel to Wake Street), adjacent to the rear porch of the inn, so that patrons could exit by the back door of the hotel, cross the back porch, and enter the dining room without getting wet when it was raining. About 1937 this dining room was relocated by its new owner, John William (Bill) Richmond, to a position on Wake Street. There, it was converted into a cottage (Figure 7.2).[13] This surviving dining room dependency is now unique in Hillsborough (see Map 7).

Laundries

By Barbara Hume

Laundries were used to clean clothes and linens. They could be located in a freestanding structure or in a separate room inside the house or its basement. In modest households the work would probably have been performed in the kitchen or outdoors. More affluent households had self-contained laundries that were in a separate building detached from the house, which will be discussed here.[14]

Because of their function, laundries were necessarily located near a good water supply and contained a fireplace and a large kettle used to heat the water. They usually adjoined a drying yard. Before the invention of the clothespin, clothes and linens were draped over a line or bush or laid flat to dry on clean green grass.[15]

Laundries were also the place for ironing clothes and linens. The most usual type of iron, the *flat iron,* was heated on the hearth before the fire. Another type of iron, called a *box iron,* was heated by a bar of iron that had been warmed in the fire and then inserted into an

Figure 7.2 / Dining room from the Inn at Teardrops, relocated to its current position on Wake Street.

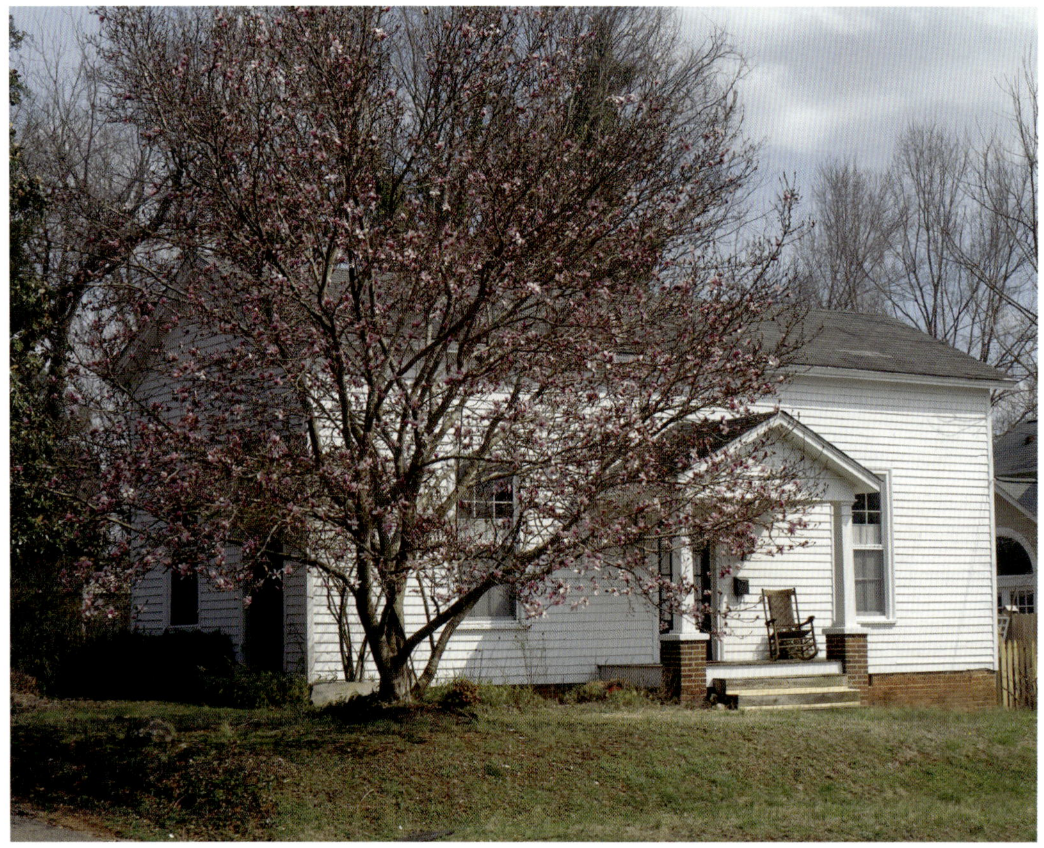

interior cavity, or box, in each iron. A laundry usually contained multiple irons so that as one iron was being used, and was therefore cooling in the process, other irons were being heated in preparation for use. Beginning in the mid-nineteenth century some people acquired cast-iron laundry heaters on which water as well as irons could be heated. Clothes and linens were usually laid flat on a wide board or table to be ironed.

In the eighteenth century, clothes were usually washed with homemade soap. The manufacture of soap by individual households could also have been done in the laundry dependency or in the adjoining yard. The first major advance in reducing the cost and work involved in the production of soap was made by Nicolas Leblanc near the end of the eighteenth century when he discovered a means of producing a cheap alkali, a necessary component of soap-making. Finally, near the end of the nineteenth century, commercially produced soap became generally available for an affordable price, and the process of cleaning clothes and linens required less labor, time, and space.[16] In the first half of the twentieth century, custom-made ironing boards and washing machines (which could easily be accommodated in a modern house) ended the need for a separate dependency for doing the laundry.

Dependencies known as laundries were sometimes combined with kitchens (or spaces for other uses) in the same freestanding building, with two separate entrance doors and a wall dividing the interior into two separate spaces for the two functions.[17] The two surviving dual-purpose buildings in Hillsborough were originally of this type. These buildings, one located at Bellevue and the other at the Mangum-Ruffin House, were both originally four-bay, one-room-deep (called *single-pile*), brick buildings with interior dividers. The Bellevue kitchen building is remembered as being combined with servants' quarters. Originally a story and a half in height with two rooms on each floor, it was covered with a gable roof and had two exterior end chimneys. The finished rooms on the second level were probably used as slave quarters. The Mangum-Ruffin kitchen/laundry is surmounted by a hip roof pierced by one, slightly off-center chimney. Although originally only one room deep, it was enlarged in the later part of the twentieth century with the addition of rooms on the back to convert it into a cottage. For images of these two dual-use buildings, see in Chapter 2, Historic Kitchens, Figures 2.3 and 2.5.

The only surviving frame laundry is located behind the Gattis House on East Tryon Street (Lot 101). It consists of three parts, all under a single gable roof: an open well shelter and two flanking rooms that are both completely enclosed (for Gattis House pump shelter section of laundry, see Figures 5.9 and 7.3). The northern section served as a laundry; the use of the other has not been determined. The laundry section is enhanced by the inclusion of a built-in, full height cupboard with four doors (two over two). It still retains some of its early knob-and-tube electrical wiring. No chimney is currently associated with this building, which has been recently moved about twenty feet to the west of its previous location (Figures 7.3 and 7.4).

Brick or stone laundries were normally plastered and whitewashed inside. Frame laundries were frequently sheathed with flat boards and painted or whitewashed on the interior. Such finishes aided in keeping the clothes and linens clean, and also increased the reflected

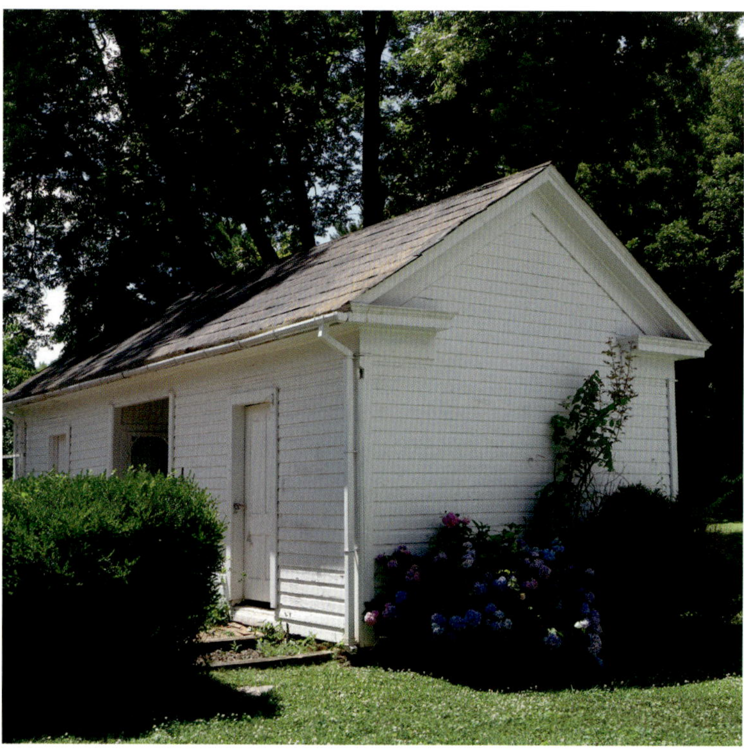

Figure 7.3 / Gattis House, laundry dependency.

light in the buildings. The Bellevue and Mangum-Ruffin dual-purpose buildings were both plastered and whitewashed; the Gattis House laundry was sheathed in horizontal boards and whitewashed. With the improved washing machines and establishment of commercial laundries in the twentieth century, home laundries located in separate dependencies were abandoned and the surviving laundries were converted to other uses.

Necessary Houses

By Jim Parsley

A necessary house was once a *necessity* as one of the least prominent but most important accessory structures on an inhabited property in the eighteenth and nineteenth centuries. After all, bodily wastes had to go somewhere, and the best solution available at that time in a

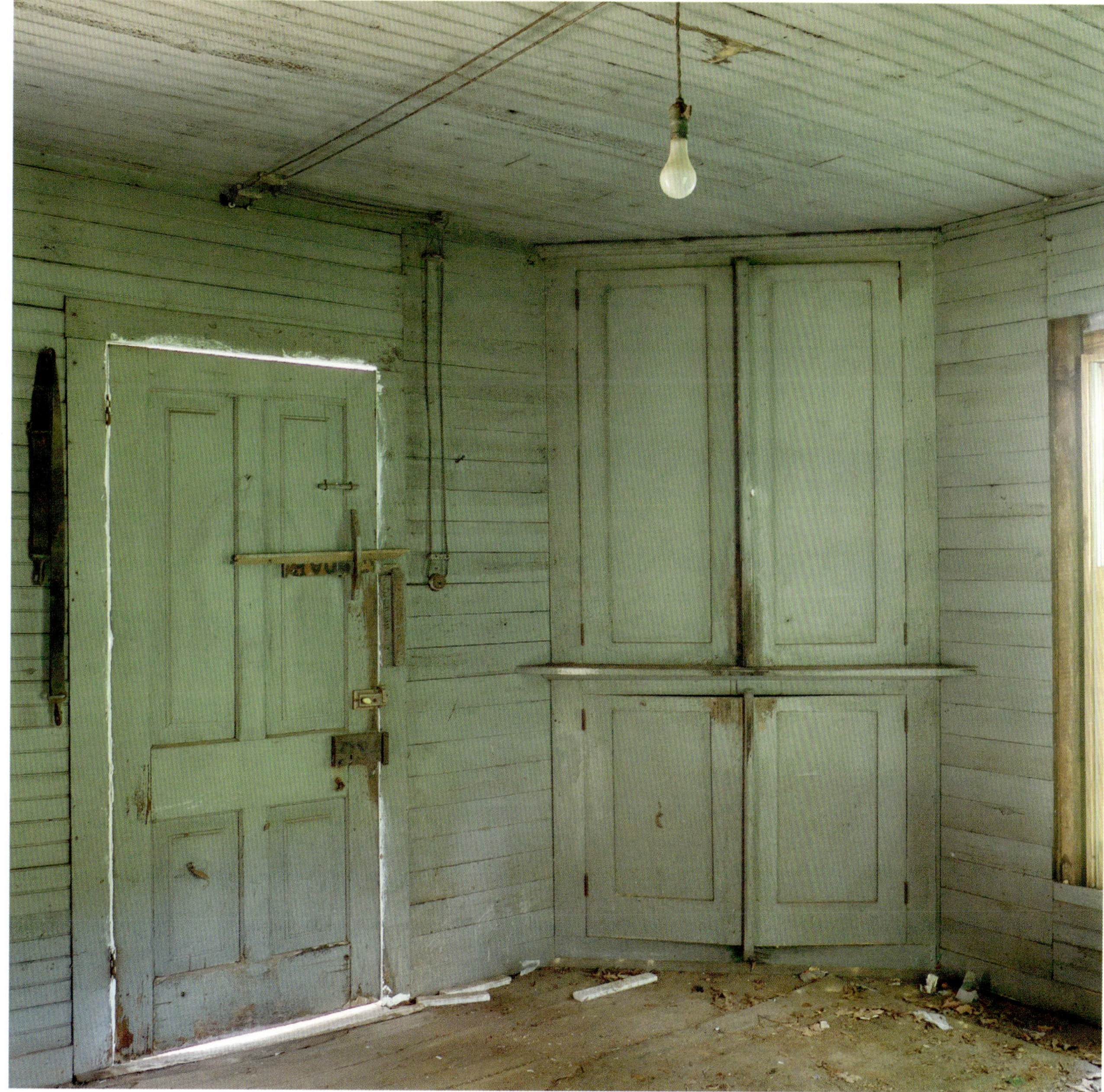

Figure 7.4 / Gattis House, interior of laundry with storage cupboard.

small town like Hillsborough was a system called by various names: the privy, outhouse, necessary house, or simply *the necessary.* Every home and institution had one, and every business at least had access to one nearby. Separate from the main buildings, they were usually inconspicuous but conveniently located, providing privacy and shelter—though often resulting in significant personal discomfort. They served to limit the spread of infectious diseases within the community and were an important public health practice before people fully understood the reasons. They were *necessary,* and every person living in those ages had personal experience using them, although they were seldom mentioned in conversation, records, or literature. They were a classic example of *low technology,* but also *best practice,* for their time. A well-built outhouse could be considered a luxury item, even prestigious.

A detail that people today are often curious about has to do with another aspect of hygiene. Before toilet paper became available, privy users utilized scrap paper (newsprint, catalogs, etc.) or waste vegetation (corncobs, leaves) to satisfy their hygiene needs.

The necessary itself was a simple building dedicated exclusively to its purpose. The structure was usually framed and sided with wood, although sometimes made of masonry, and always roofed for protection from the elements. The footprint was usually square or rectangular, although more elaborate designs were hexagonal or octagonal, and typically measured four to six feet on each side and six to eight feet high. It usually was wood-floored and had an unpainted wood exterior. If the necessary house was a permanent building within a group, its exterior might be trimmed and painted to blend with the others near it.

An open flow of air, via vents or windows, into and through the building was important to minimize unpleasant odors inside. Therefore, the interior temperatures were ambient at best, and uncomfortable in summer and winter. In the daytime, it was dimly lit inside; at night it was very dark, unless the user brought a light. The building featured installed seats with openings of appropriate sizes for adults and children. Most commonly, outhouses were positioned over an open pit in the ground. (The pit also provided a convenient place to dispose of items that one never wanted to be found.) When the pit became full, the lightweight structure could be moved a few feet to access a newly dug pit, while the old pit would be covered with earth. If the outhouse was built to be a permanent building, then its construction had to include some sort of removable container(s) for the accumulated waste.

In Hillsborough, most outhouses were freestanding structures of simple wood frame construction, located at a distance from the house. A few prominent places had outhouses of fine masonry construction, such as the painted brick necessary at the Burwell School (Figure 7.5).

In several cases, the outhouse was integrated with other structures. For example, at Montrose the outhouse was contiguous with and behind the smokehouse (Figure 7.6).

At Tamarind, the outhouse was part of a series of connected outbuildings; it even had an *antechamber* where visitors could await their turns (Figure 7.7). This surviving necessary has been equipped with modern plumbing.

In the late 1800s, the Town of Hillsborough began installing a public water supply system. This enabled homes and businesses to have enough water conveniently available to support flushable indoor toilets. Toilet waste could go into cesspools or septic tanks on the owner's lot. In the 1930s, the town started installing public sewers, a public health improvement that disposed of water and waste directly into the Eno River.[18] The property owners who could afford the expense took advantage of these new conveniences and public utility services, and installed indoor plumbing and toilet facilities. Owners of rental property tended to lag behind that trend, resisting investment in such improvements as long as their renters would accept the old system. Everywhere, enlightened public health concerns led local governments to prohibit or restrict outhouse use, especially in urban areas. Over a period of about fifty years, the necessary house system went from necessity to obsolete and undesirable, from common use to being rare and/or temporary. By the 1970s in Hillsborough, most outhouses had been eliminated through modernization, neighborhood upgrading, and regulation.

As soon as it was no longer a necessity, an outhouse quickly became an undesirable relic, a negative stigma to be removed, or concealed if removal was impractical. For obvious reasons, the privy was one of the few outbuildings on a town lot that did not lend itself to repurposing when it had outlived its original function. As times and needs changed, barns, stables, smokehouses, and woodsheds became garages, storage buildings, workshops, and playhouses. For the outhouse, there was not another job to do. Most were too small, too lightly built, and not well located to adapt to modern living. The outhouse was taken away, leaving behind only a small mound of earth that would eventually settle.

The few examples that remain today are on well-maintained historic properties where the outhouse was a permanent structure in a fixed location, such as the necessary house in the row of outbuildings in back of the brick kitchen at Burnside (Figure 7.8).

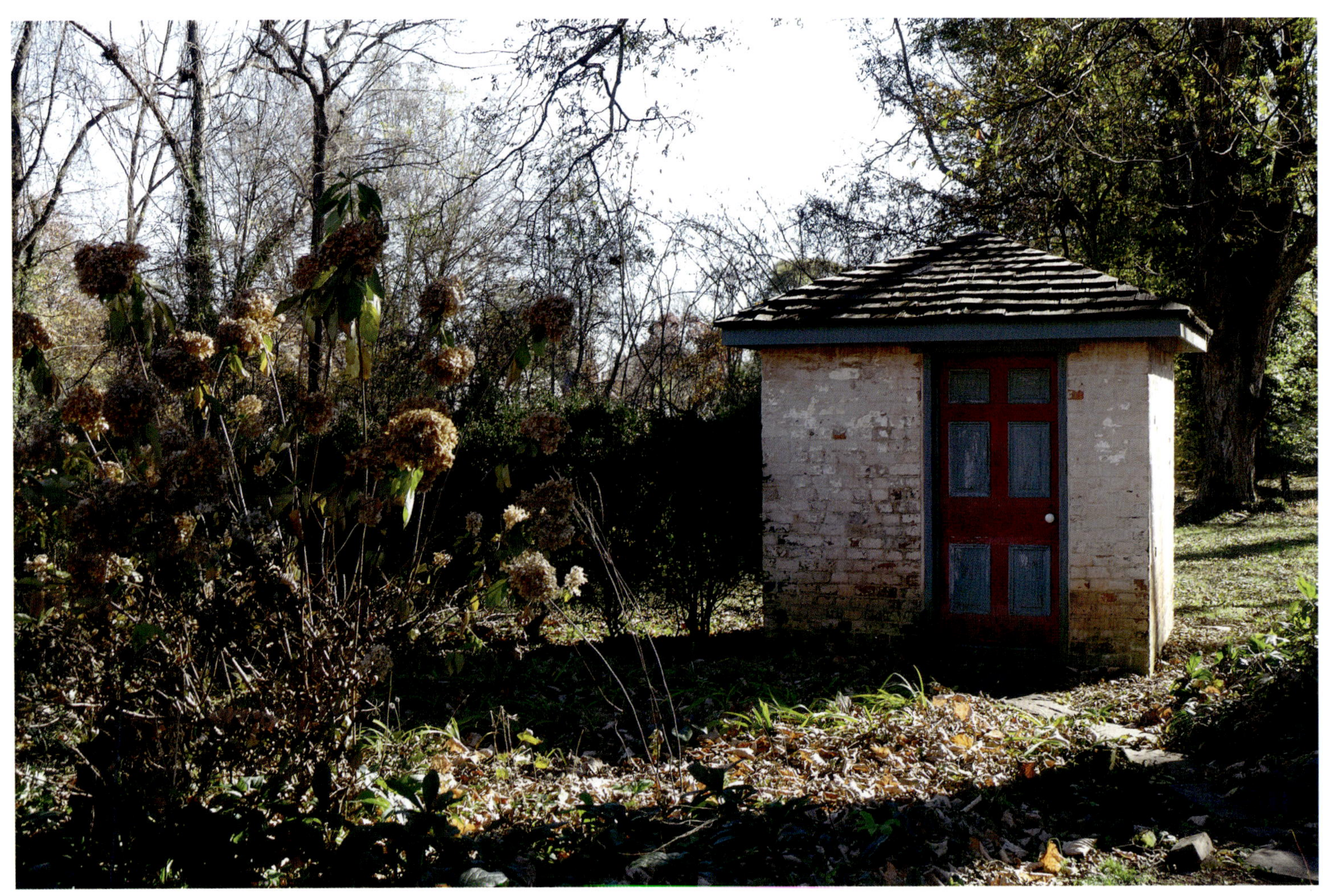

Figure 7.5 / Burwell School necessary house.

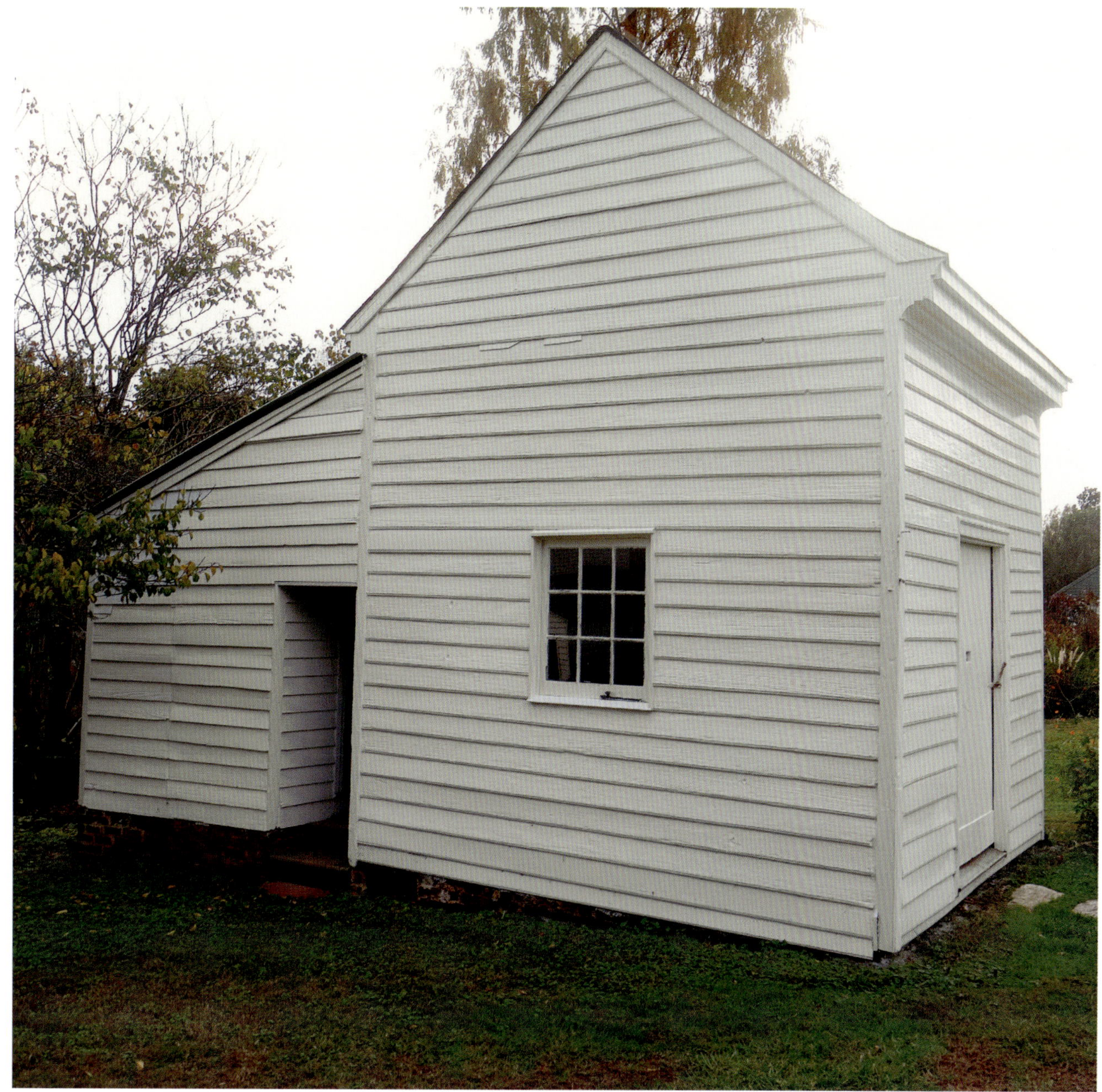

Figure 7.6 / Montrose necessary house (at left), accessed via a covered passage connecting it to the smokehouse.

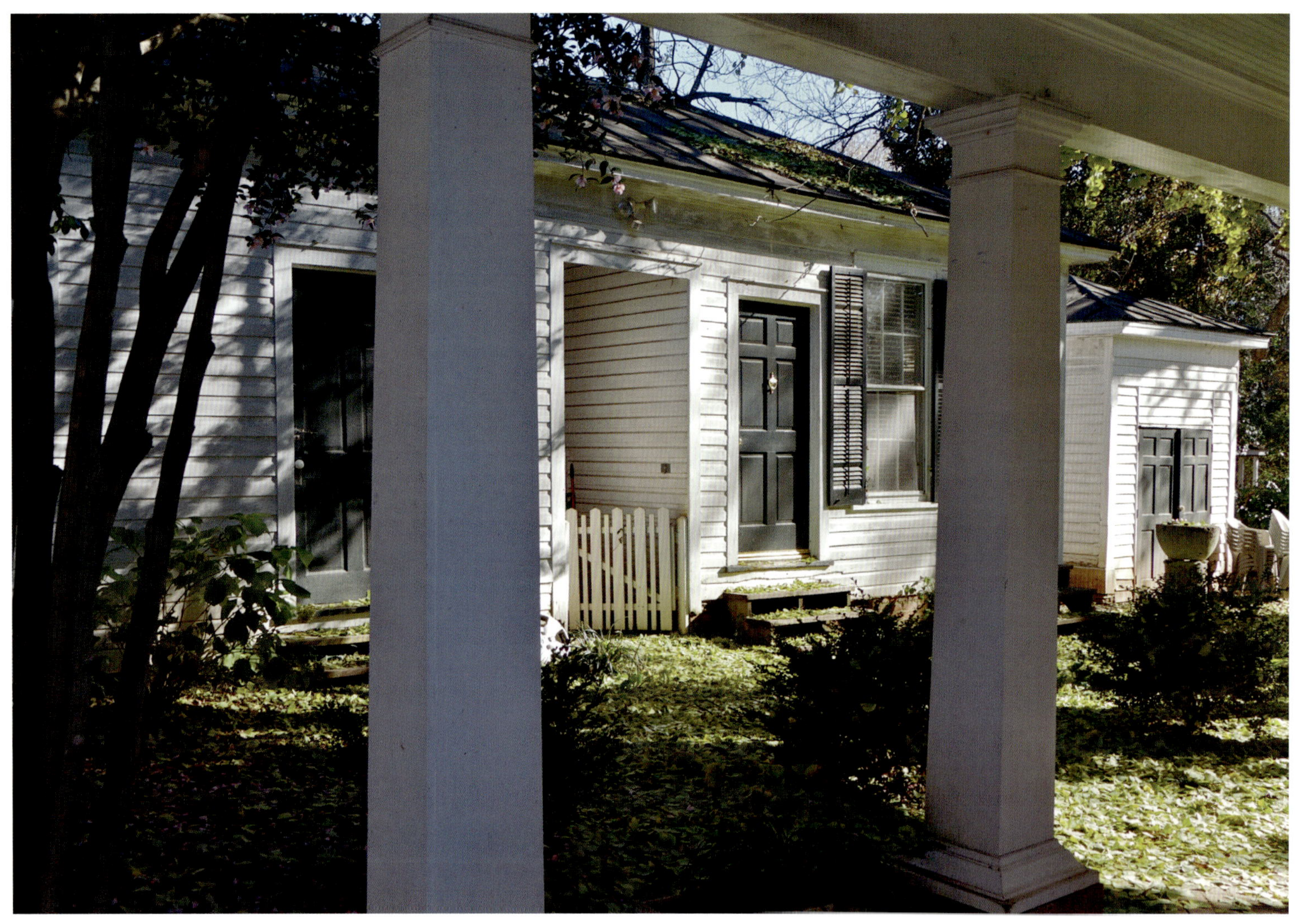

Figure 7.7 / Tamarind necessary house (at center), entered via antechamber.

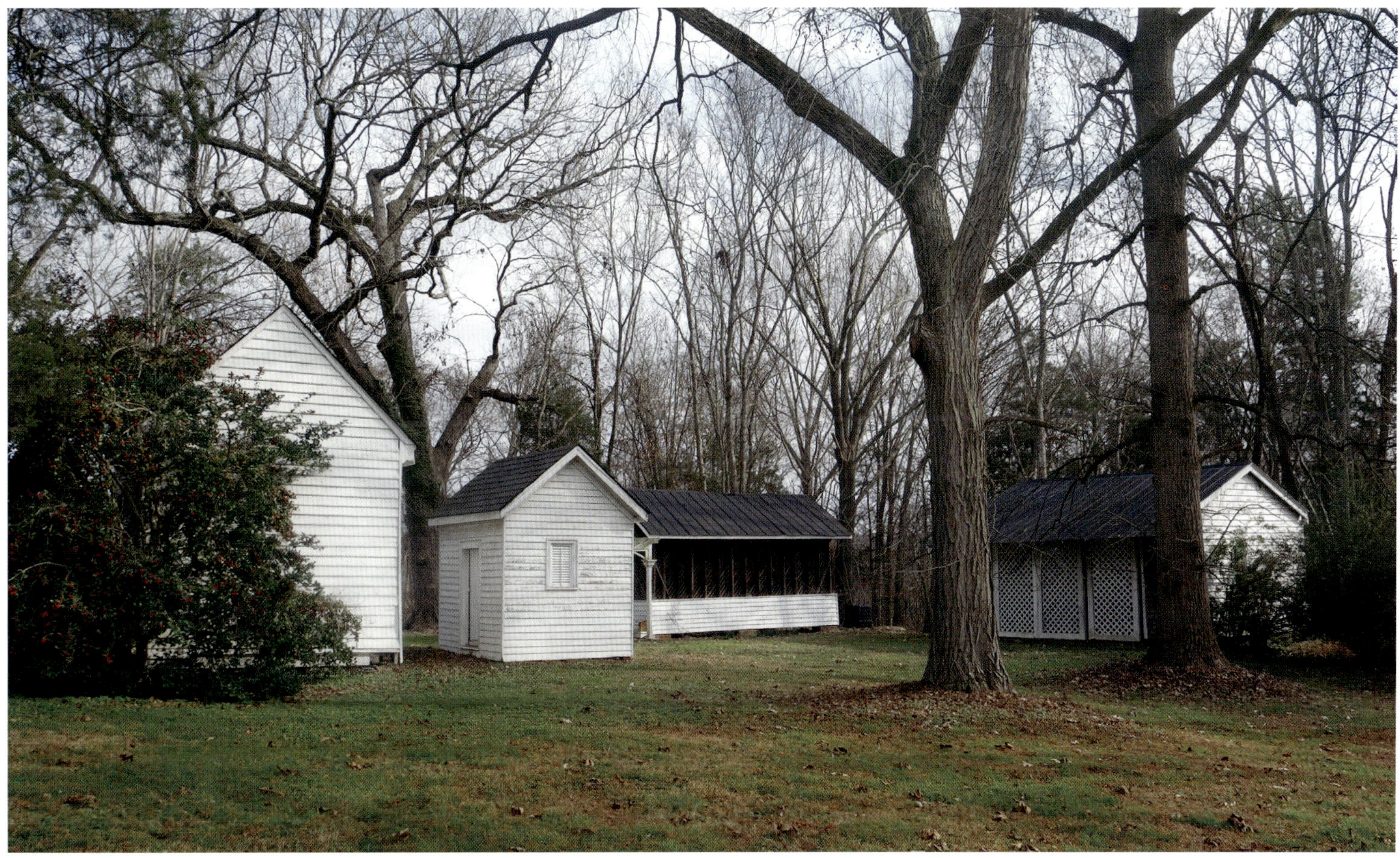

Figure 7.8 / Burnside necessary house (center), in row of outbuildings behind the smokehouse.

The necessary houses discussed here still exist mainly because they have been regarded as historic relics worthy of preservation, as examples of the way life used to be lived. On most town lots, there is no evidence of their once-necessary existence.

There are four surviving necessary houses in Hillsborough today: at Burnside, the Burwell School, Montrose, and Tamarind. (See Map 7.)

Eight

Trees and Gardens

BY CALLIE CONNOR

The trees and gardens, along with other planned landscape features, have long been considered important aspects of Hillsborough's appearance, even from the time of the town's inception. Corbin's carefully laid-out grid plan, recorded in the Sauthier Map of 1768, already provides a rather elegant and orderly concept of the town that includes numerous botanical features: trees, gardens, allées, and hedges, designed around and in relation to the first mansion houses, inns, pubs, and civic buildings (see Map 2). Even though it is unclear whether all of the map's botanical features were in fact implemented by property owners, the overall intent is clear—of evoking a gracious setting for the new town, replete with a number of features stemming from the natural world.[1]

Sixty years after Sauthier's map was drawn, Hillsborough particularly impressed one visitor in 1830 for its well-cultivated and shaded appearance:

> When we drew near Hillsboro, the land became beautifully diversified, with hill and dale fine farms and good land . . . as you approach it from the stream [Eno River], every house is seen at once spread out on this sidelong eminence to a considerable extent. The buildings are neat and many of them display great taste and elegance; these are shaded with handsome trees, to which may be added, beautiful gardens and shrubberies; some of the handsomest county seats in the Union appear in the neighborhood of Hillsboro.[2]

Some of the gardens are shown on the Sauthier map as a checkerboard of square plots, likely referring to vegetable gardens, which were easily accommodated on the large, one-acre lots. Ornamental gardens, or parterres, are also indicated, where geometric designs oriented around circular focal points indicate French formal garden design of the time. A double row of trees, or allée, is shown to the rear of Edmund Fanning's residence on King Street, extending out behind the nucleus of the grand property all the way to Tryon Street. And what appear to be hedges are shown surrounding many properties in lieu of walls or fences.

An interest in mingling the natural world with an orderly townscape apparently continued throughout the nineteenth century. We even have surviving evidence in the form of plantings and designed passages in the Hillsborough of today. According to visitors' impressions and descriptions, or recollections by the residents of their surroundings, the botanical world has played a consistently important role in the townscape.

Perhaps the best-known historic plantings in Hillsborough are the cedars arranged in a double row along Cedar Walk (Lot 12), a path connecting West Margaret Lane with West King Street (see Map 8 and Figure 8.1). Mrs. Frederick Nash, who lived on Margaret Lane, is said to have planted this walk around 1817 in order to facilitate visits with her sister who lived on the next block at Twin Chimneys. The cedars that appear now are likely descendants of the originals, but the concept remains well rooted in contributing to the enjoyable experience of all who care to take Mrs. Nash's shortcut. The lot on which she planted the cedars was known as the "Lucerne Lot" (Lot 12) because it was planted in lucerne, or alfalfa, and is referred to with its associations of relaxation and enjoyment by the girls who attended the Nash-Kollock School fifty years later:

> No matter how great your hurry, you always slackened your pace when you came under its interlocking branches, and felt beneath your feet the resilient carpet spread there, as year after year the cedars shed their spicy tufts in time for spring renewal. You could make up for lost time later, but you could never afford to hurry through the Cedar Walk. . . . On either side was a field of waving green in bright contrast with its dark background of cedars. This luxuriant crop gave the lot its name, provided food for the school cows and beauty for all beholders.[3]

The lot, although located in the center of town, provided pasturage for cows, whose milk was a necessity for any family in which there were children—in this case, for the Nash-Kollock School.

The cultivation of displays of flowers and shrubbery in Hillsborough has been attributed

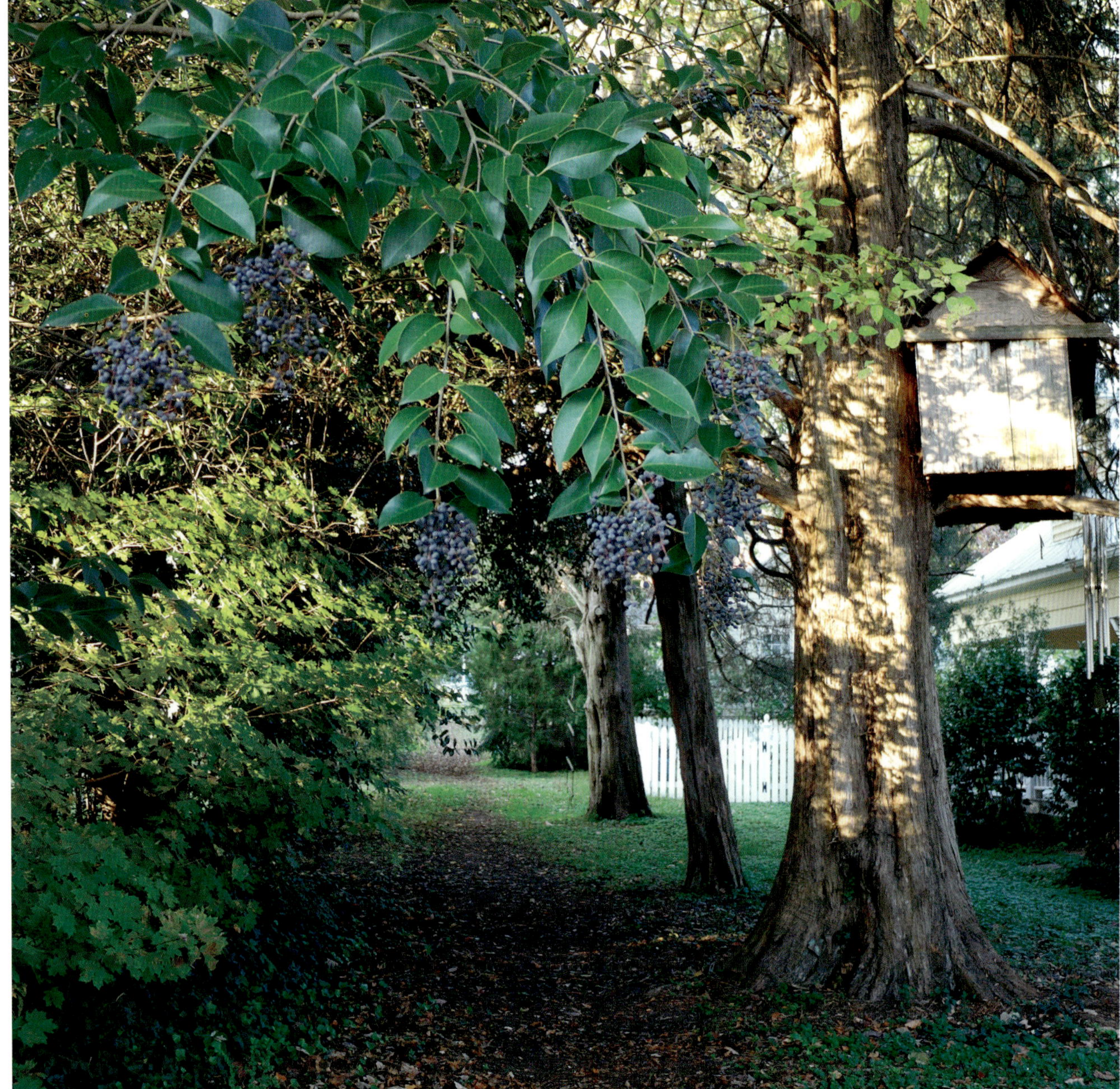

Figure 8.1 / Cedar Walk, showing ancient cedars bordering the path.

to the presence of a renowned botanist and expert in scientific nomenclature, the Rev. Moses Ashley Curtis, rector of St. Matthew's Episcopal Church.[4] A well-documented example of systematic plantings on a large scale can still be detected on the former grounds of Burnside, Paul and Anne Cameron's estate adjoining the town to the east. The Camerons, among the largest plantation owners in the South on the eve of the Civil War, poured their time and resources into the planting of Burnside as an arboretum and specimen gardens in 1858–60; hundreds of varieties of trees, shrubs, and flowers are listed in the invoices from the New York firm that supplied them. The work was implemented by a colorful character, Samuel Parsons, whom the Camerons hired as their gardener. Hand-drawn plans for the planting of the extensive gardens with trees, many imported from abroad, are preserved in the Cameron Family Papers in the Southern Historical Collection at Wilson Library at the University of North Carolina at Chapel Hill. The plans show, in particular, fruit trees and large kitchen gardens; one drawing shows twelve varieties of pear trees on a single section of terraces, and in another field, eleven rows of peaches of various types and thirty Old Apricot slips (Figures 8.2 and 8.3).[5]

Remains of the terracing for the pear orchard scheme can still be seen clearly on the winter landscape of the sloping land behind the main house and outbuildings around the Great Barn and ruins of the Coach House. This terracing may have stemmed from the Mangum Terrace, a system of creating a series of broad hillside ditches running perpendicular to the slope of the land, which served to conserve soil moisture and minimize erosion.[6] The system was named after Priestly Mangum, who resided near Burnside on his farm/estate, the main house of which is known as the Mangum-Ruffin House.

On the north side of the Cameron estate was Cameron Park, an arboretum comprising what are now the grounds of the Cameron Park Elementary School, St. Matthew's Episcopal Church Cemetery, and the Orange County Board of Education property off Cameron Street (Figure 8.4). Access roads to Burnside passed through this large tract planted in numerous species of exotic and collectable trees. At least fifteen individual examples of the very trees listed in the inventory of ca. 1858 can still be seen in the area behind the school, according to a nearby resident; for example, there are a number of stately examples of Chinese fir (*Cunninghamia lanceolata*), and also Japanese fir, linden, Douglas fir, and European fernwood (Figures 8.5 and 8.6).[7]

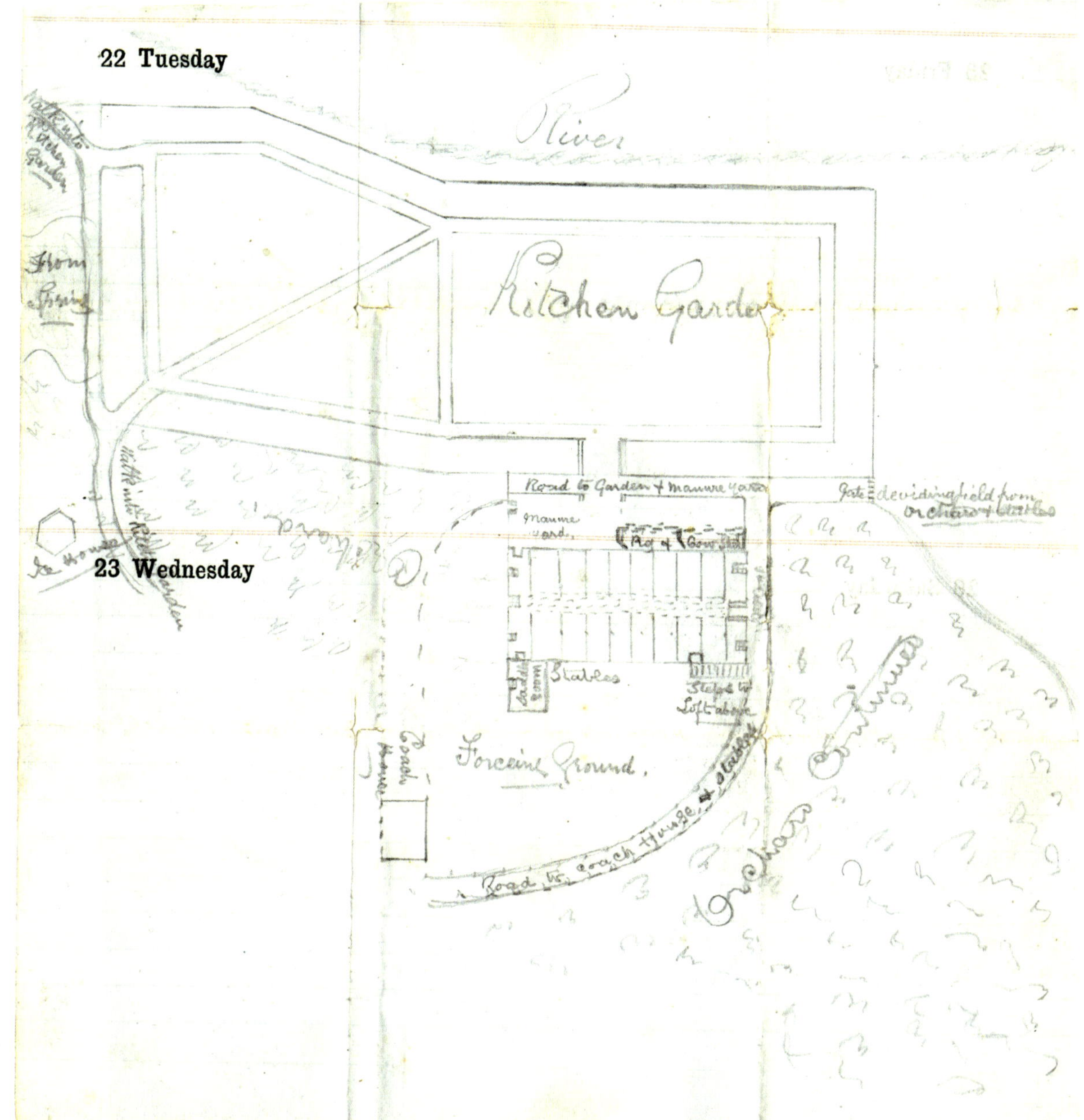

Figure 8.2 / Hand-drawn plan of the grounds of Burnside, ca. 1858–60, showing the area around the Great Barn with its gardens and orchards (courtesy, Southern Historical Collection, Wilson Library, the University of North Carolina at Chapel Hill, Cameron Family Papers, #133).

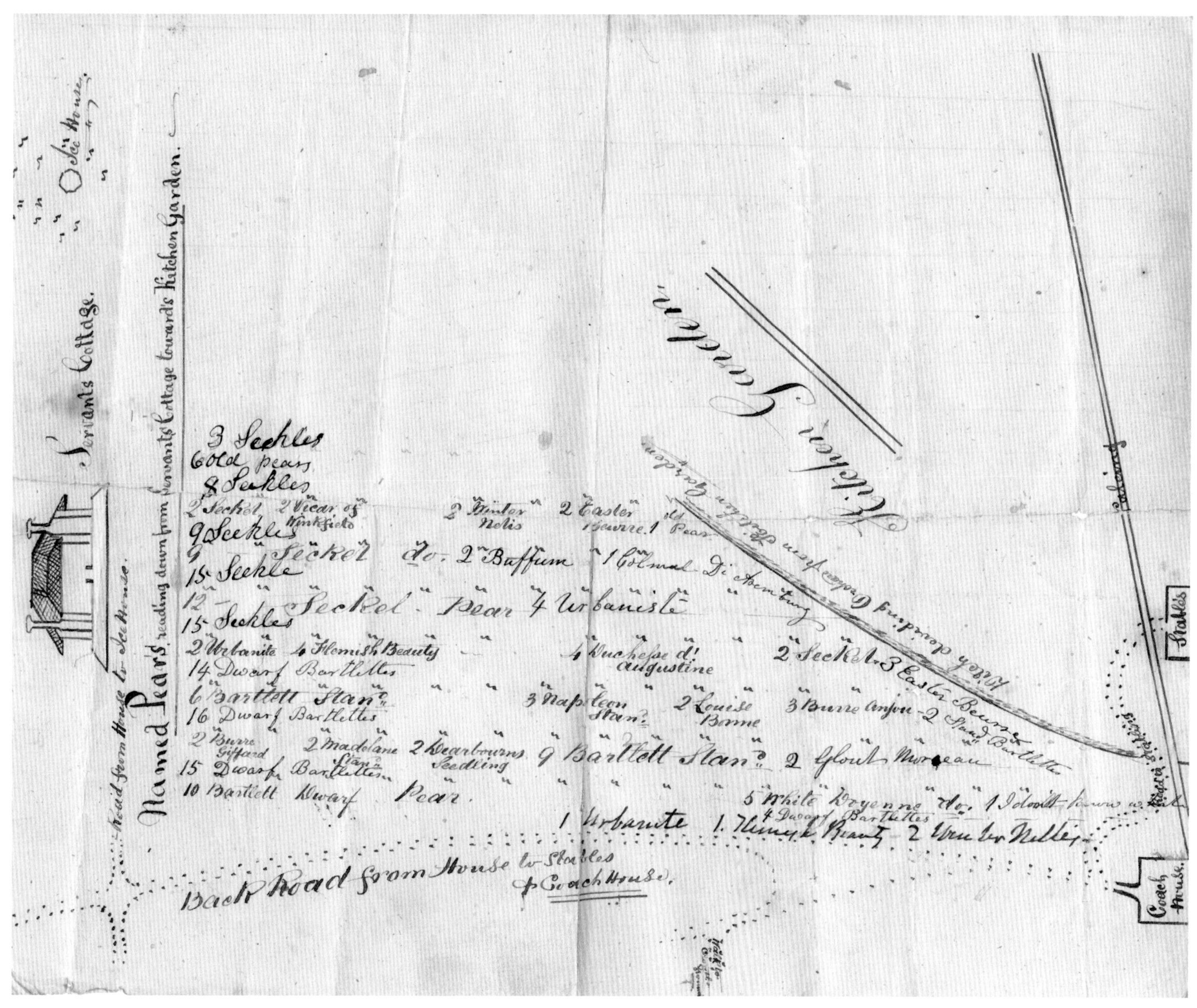

Figure 8.3 / Hand-drawn plan for the planting of a pear orchard at Burnside, ca. 1858–60 (courtesy, Southern Historical Collection, Wilson Library, the University of North Carolina at Chapel Hill, Cameron Family Papers, #133).

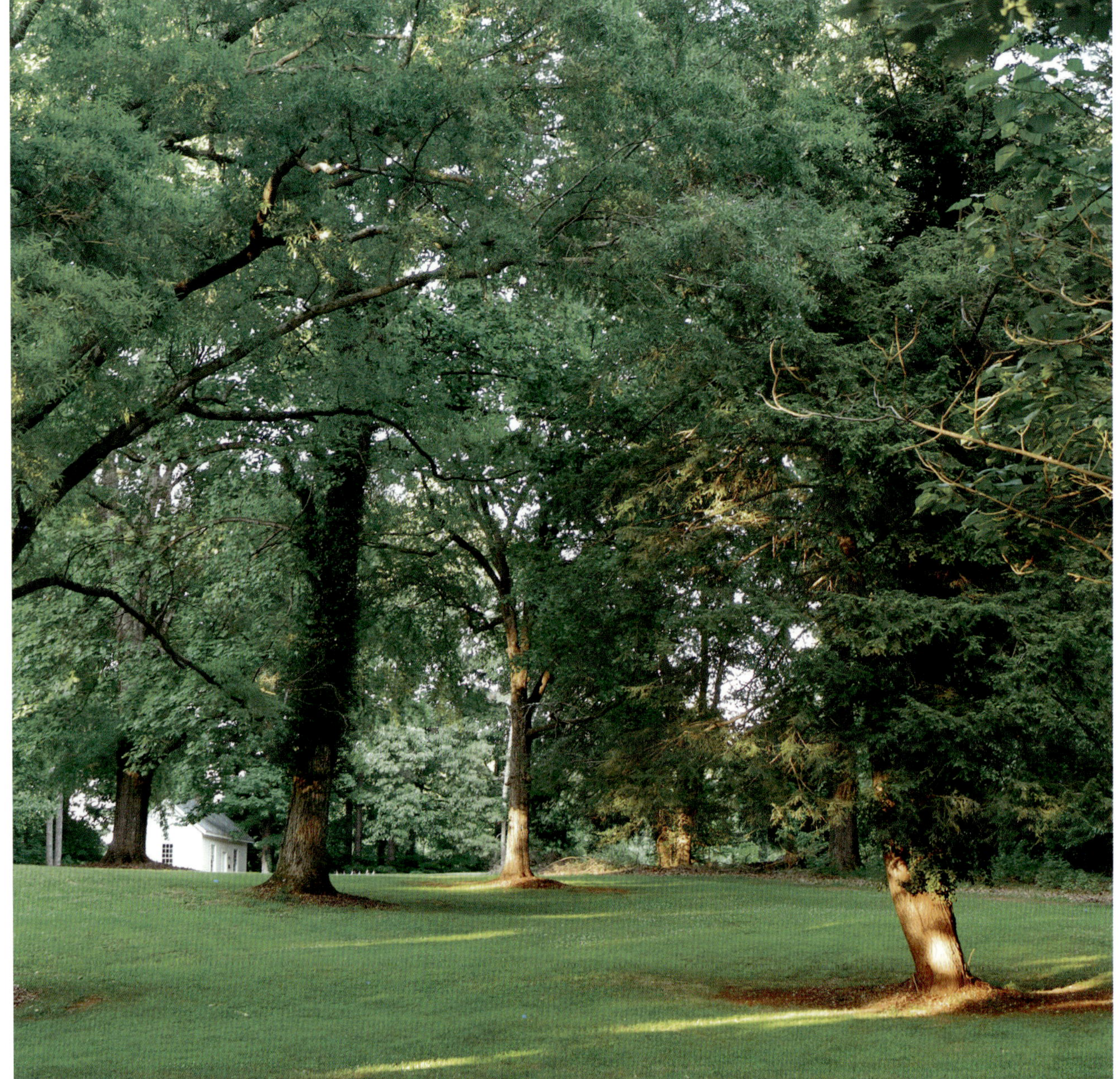

Fig. 8.4 / View of the former Burnside Arboretum with historic trees.

The Chinese firs apparently took firm root in North Carolina soil, for there are other examples of these rare and majestic trees scattered around town.

An earlier, ca. 1818 plat for the extensive property acquired by the Camerons shows it laid out with hedges used to divide areas of the property on the gentle slopes and bottom land along the Eno River; hawthorn and locust hedges are indicated on the plat along the western and northern boundaries, dividing gardens and fields for grazing and cultivation—echoing an old world solution for keeping animals from straying, as well as marking boundaries (Figure 8.7). Remnants of these ancient hedges can still be seen along lower Cameron Street, on the east side of the old road running parallel to the modern paved one.

Boxwood hedges, known for their slow growth and longevity, can be assumed to be survivors in some cases of nineteenth-century plantings in Hillsborough, as for example lining the paths leading to the entrances of a number of the old houses. The Berry Brick House (Lot 54) dating to ca. 1805 is an example in which the boxwood has grown so as to totally block access to the house via the path (see Figure 5.6). At the Mallett Mill House, they have merged into a single, enormous bush. The Old Town Cemetery has numerous old boxwood plantings around the individual family plots and also lining the so-called Students Walk that once served as a footpath between the Burwell School and the Presbyterian church (Figure 8.8).

The huge oak, maple, magnolia, beech, holly, pecan, and poplar trees clearly visible throughout the town are proud remnants of nineteenth-century landscaping; the giant American elms known from descriptions in historical records are gone now, but many oaks in particular survive, immediately bordering the streets today.[8] For example, at the corner of Wake and King streets there is an oak measuring seventeen feet in circumference, having witnessed much of the town's history from this location. In the Old Town Cemetery a handful of towering oaks still survive, and framing a few historic homes are trees that have shaded their dooryards and cooled their rooms for well over a century—some have only recently been lost in storms. One huge tree, known as Old Mahogany, was located on the south side of East Union Street near the intersection with Cameron. Its name, recorded on maps, has now outlived it by at least half a century. Its species has been forgotten, but more likely it was an oak rather than a mahogany tree.

Finally, the flower gardens that once comprised the landscaping around many houses have left little trace, except in literary descriptions. For example, an indelible impression

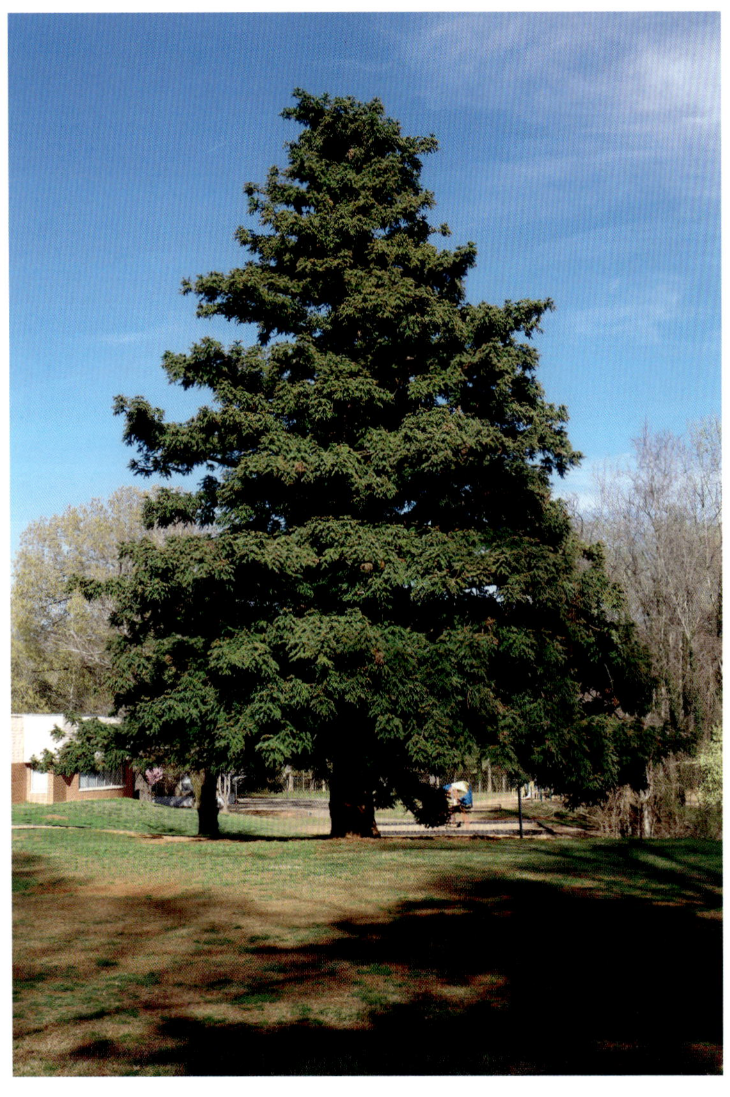

Figure 8.5 / Chinese fir tree near Cameron Park Elementary School, probably one of the original plantings in the Cameron Arboretum.

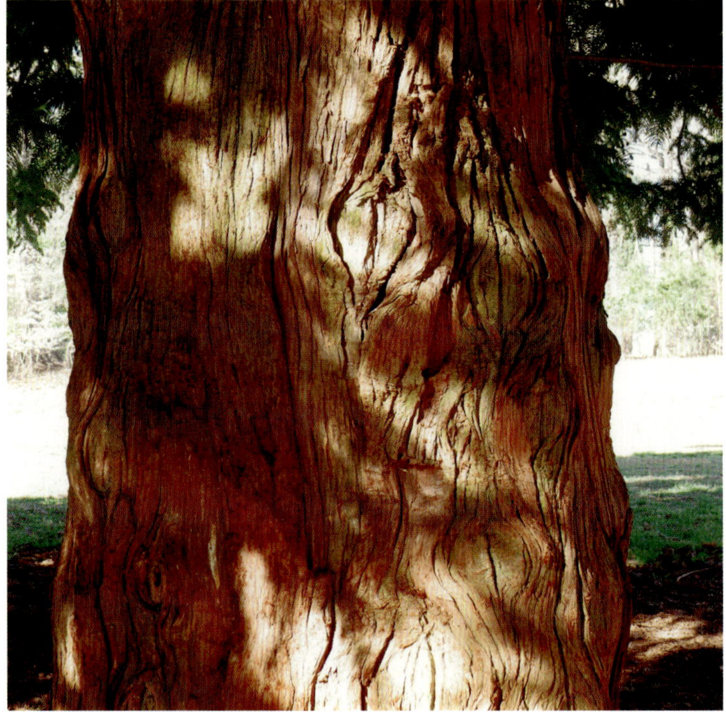

Figure 8.6 / Chinese fir, Cameron Arboretum, detail of trunk.

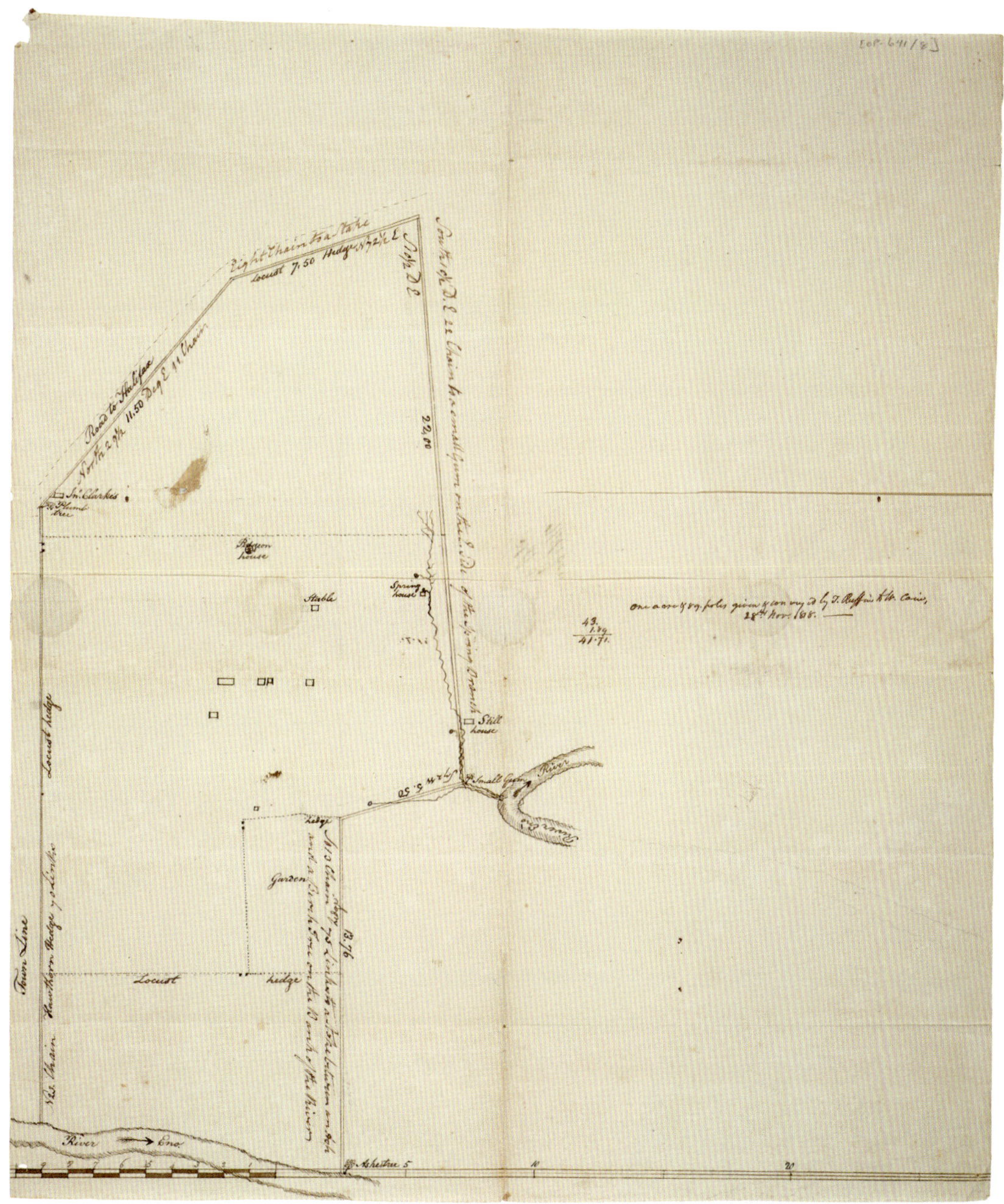

Figure 8.7 / Plat of ca. 1818, showing hedges established along the land boundaries. (Courtesy of Southern Historical Collection, Wilson Library, the University of North Carolina at Chapel Hill, Thomas Ruffin Papers, #641.)

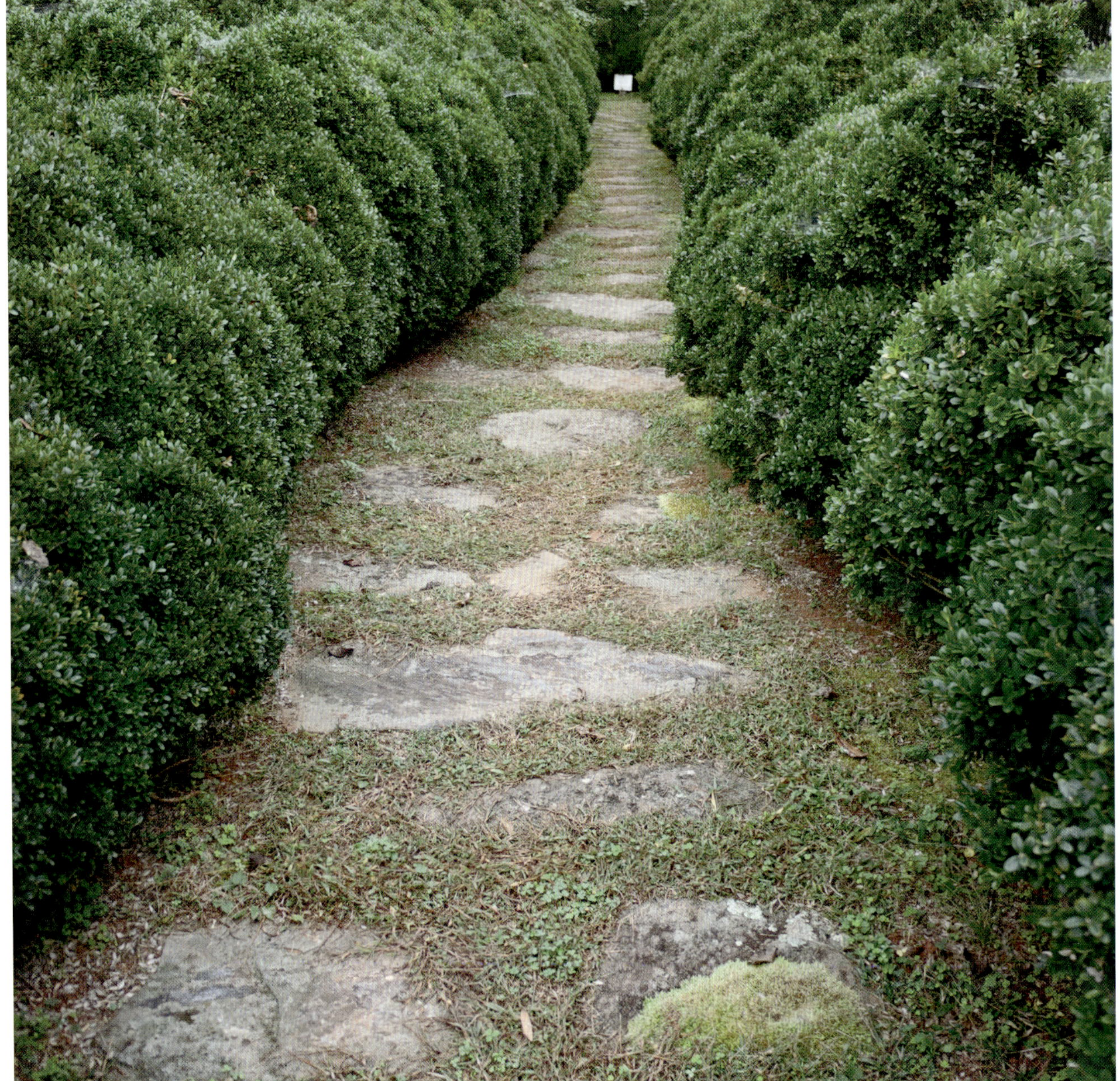

Figure 8.8 / Boxwood plantings along the Students Walk in the Old Town Cemetery.

is created in the descriptions by Ann Strudwick Nash of the plantings surrounding the now-demolished Nash-Kollock School building on West Margaret Lane where she was a student, and of the extensive gardens and crop fields behind it.[9]

> At the right of the front gate, as you entered, grew a tall box bush with a lily-of-the-valley bed near its base. The lilies bloomed in profusion and . . . there were more lilies in shady corners under the parlor windows. . . . The lawn on the east side of the house was a part of the front yard. The round beds in the center were bordered by flint rocks of dazzling whiteness. Old-fashioned roses grew there, our special favorite being the white musk cluster with its tiny crepe blossoms and a fragrance unmatched by that of any other rose I have ever known. *Pyrus japonica*, bridal wreath, wisteria, syringa and other flowering shrubs grew along the fence . . . in springtime, you could make the entire circuit of the yard cutting flowers as you went.[10]

The mention in this passage of the musk rose, *Rosa moschata*, must have been tantalizing to those searching in the 1970s to rediscover this rare, old-fashioned rose, which was also known to have bloomed in the garden of the Burwell School on Churton Street. The story of its rediscovery and propagation by one of the Burwell School's current board members recently brought about its return. Two varieties of this energetic and exceptionally fragrant rose can be seen today climbing its newly re-created arbor on the lawn just south and east of the main building (see Figure 11.1).[11]

Two revivals of historical gardens are nurtured today for the public to enjoy: One is on the grounds of the Burwell School, the Carrie Waitt Spurgeon Garden, dedicated in 1977, complete with its flower pit and ornamental brick walls, based on an account of the garden as it was in the early 1900s; another is Helen's Garden, situated next to the Orange County Visitors Center on East King Street, in a re-creation of a typical, old-fashioned kitchen garden or herb garden, ubiquitously found in close proximity to historic houses, especially their kitchens.[12] The extraordinary Montrose garden developed by Gov. Graham in the 1850s is thriving today under the care of Nancy and Craufurd Goodwin.[13] Gardens are still a major preoccupation of homeowners throughout the Hillsborough Historic District. Many ancient gardens have been revived, others re-envisioned as ongoing works in progress, while others survive only in memories.[14]

Nine

On the Streets

BY STEWART E. DUNAWAY

Streets in downtown Hillsborough today are dotted with traces of a combination of berms, curbs, sidewalks, and walls that date back to the eighteenth and nineteenth centuries. These four elements defined the borders of the town's thoroughfares (see Map 8).

Berms

Carefully engineered earthen mounds alongside and usually above roadways, berms served as the foundations for sidewalks along the street side of a property. Typically they were held in place by gentle grassy slopes or other greenery to prevent erosion of the soil onto the sidewalk; on the street side, they were bordered by stone curbs (see "Stone Curbs" section below).

Well-preserved examples of berms appear along the east side of Wake Street between West Margaret Lane and West King Street (Figure 9.1), as well as along the south side of West Tryon near the intersection with Wake Street and along the south side of West Queen Street for the first five hundred feet. Along the south side of West Union Street near the Churton intersection, another berm serves a double purpose as a raised walkway for a sidewalk and as a retaining wall, with curbstones lining the inside of the berm (Figure 9.2).

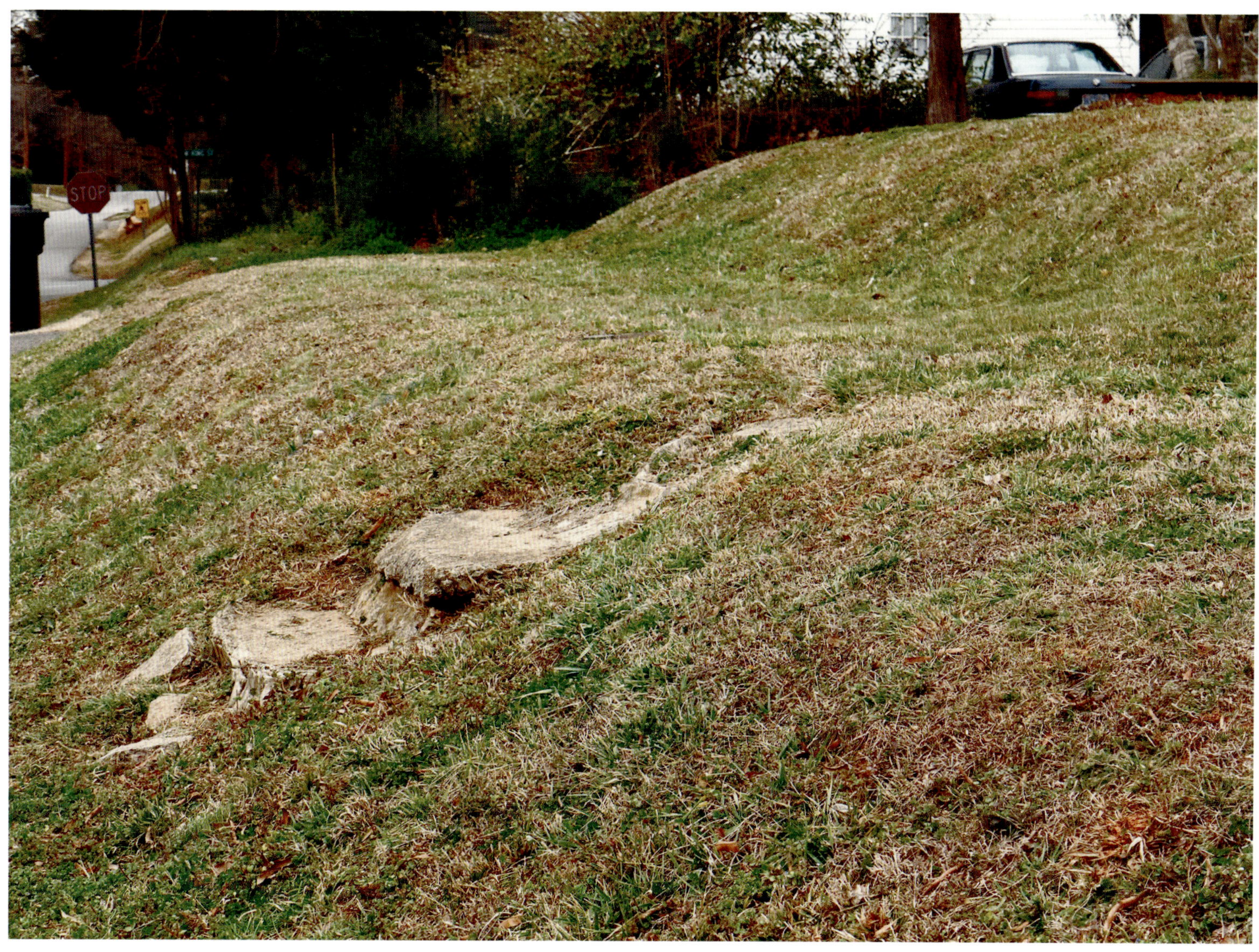

Figure 9.1 / Berm on east side of Wake Street, showing engineered terracing to create setting for former flagstone sidewalk.

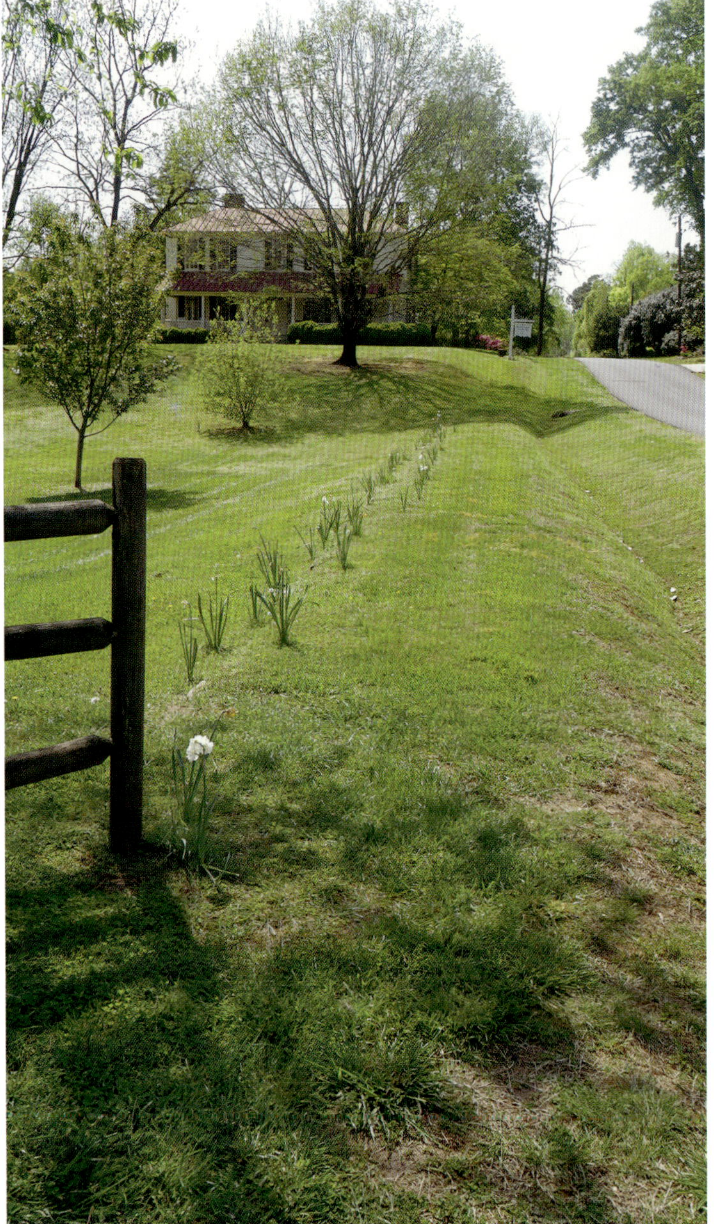

Figure 9.2 / Berm on south side of West Union Street, in front of Burwell School, showing raised path on location of former flagstone sidewalk, with curb stones on the inner side to prevent erosion.

Old Flagstone Sidewalks

Flagstone sidewalks were laid on the horizontal surfaces of the berms, producing a smooth surface for walking; these would have been especially welcome during inclement weather. Large, flat stones appear to have been laid jigsaw fashion on the horizontal surface of the berm at a width of some four to five feet, although it is difficult to say what the exact width or pattern might have been. A flagstone sidewalk is clearly indicated in a sketched site plan of the Nash-Kollock School on West Margaret Lane, suggesting that this was a noteworthy and desirable feature in providing easy and safe access by foot to the rest of the town.[1] A flagstone sidewalk covers the walkways in front of and under the porch colonnade of the Colonial Inn (Figure 9.3). A preserved section of flagstone sidewalk also runs along West King Street in front of the Inn at Teardrops (Figure 9.4). Wide flagstone sidewalks, consisting of flat stones now set in cement, run along the street on the four sides of the Old Orange County Courthouse.

Stone Curbs

Located throughout the town, stone curbs were used to retain the soil along the sidewalks to prevent erosion into the streets where the land sloped away from the sidewalk. Today, these stones appear without any apparent purpose in neat rows along the edges of sidewalks in many sections of town. Sometimes only the tops of the curbstones are seen, still set firmly into the grass; and in other instances they are entangled in tree roots or jutting out of the bank at strange angles, as gravity slowly pulls them out of the embankment and toward the street. The most dramatic example of a dislodged curbstone appears on the south side of West King Street near the intersection with Wake, while its neighboring curbstones still remain aligned (Figures 9.5 and 9.6).

When the sidewalks and curbs were installed some time in the nineteenth century, or earlier, it is unlikely that there was a paved surface on the road itself. So it was worthwhile to construct solid and well-supported sidewalks to protect foot travelers from the mud and other debris in the streets. This was doubtless not only a convenience but a luxury. The most intact section of curbstones appears along the west side of Churton Street running northward from the corner of West Tryon Street for several hundred feet (Figure 9.7).

The old curbstones are easy to miss, especially when they are encased in tree roots

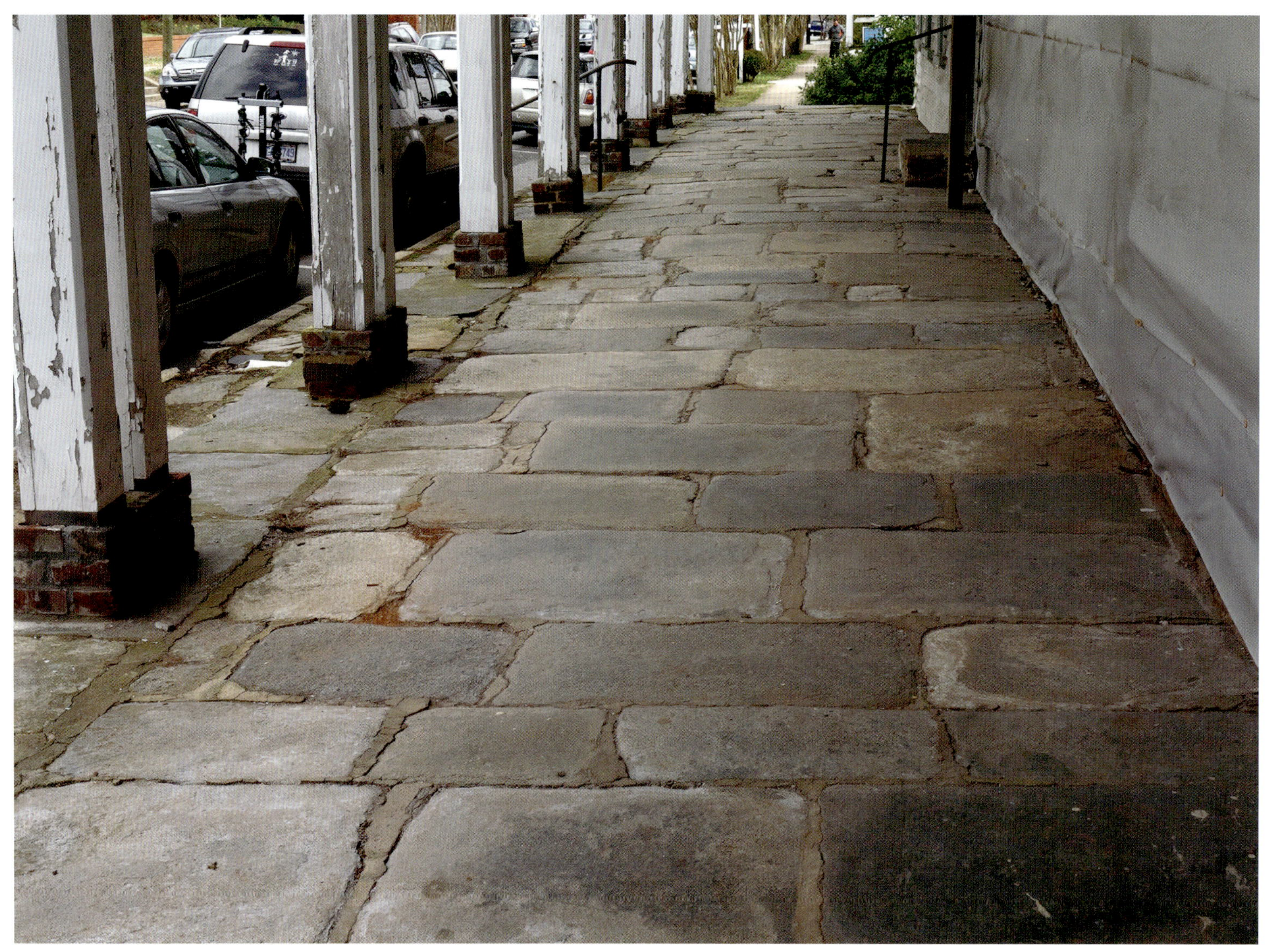

Figure 9.3 / Flagstones on porch walkway and sidewalk in front of the Colonial Inn.

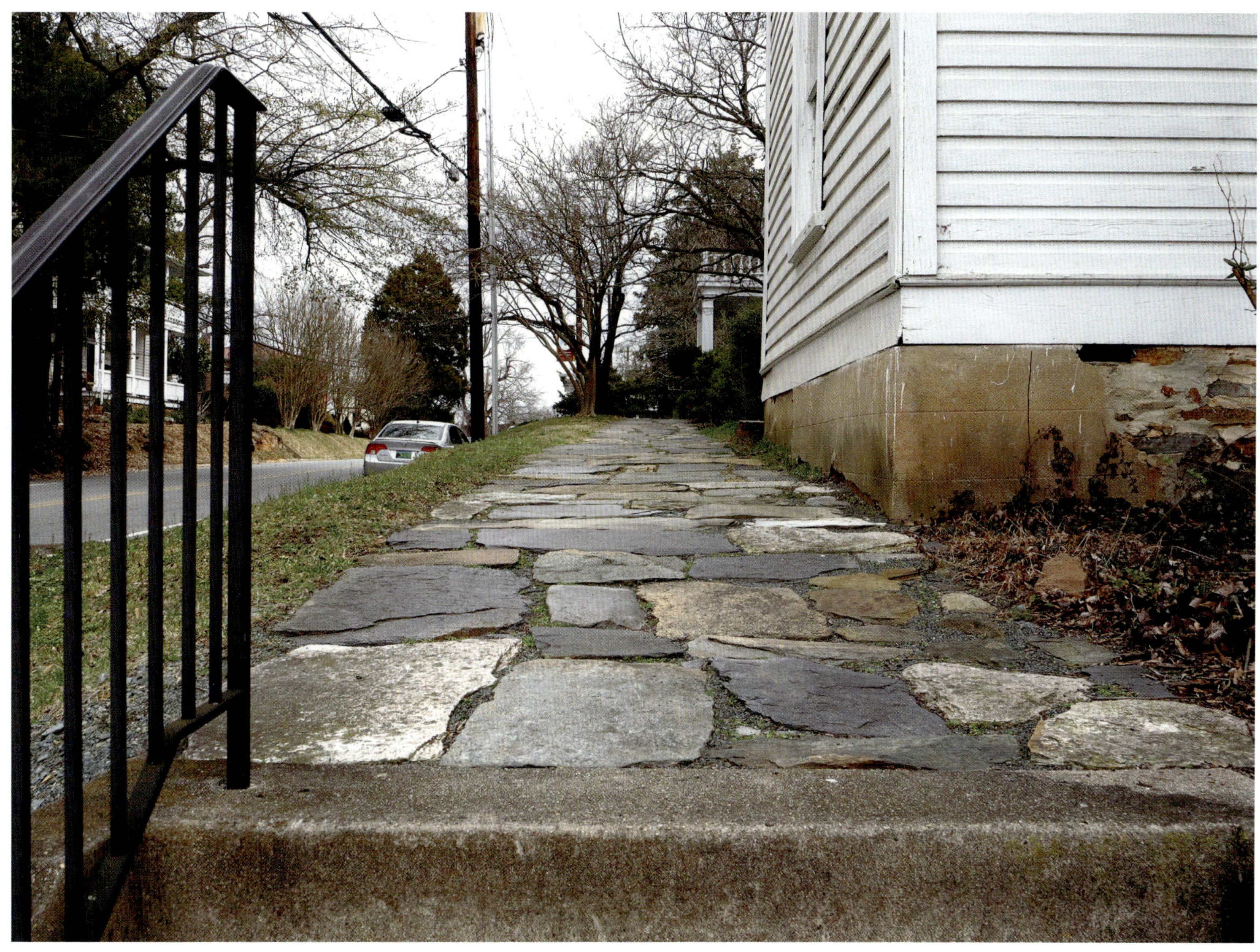

Figure 9.4 / Flagstone sidewalk on West King Street near the intersection of Wake Street.

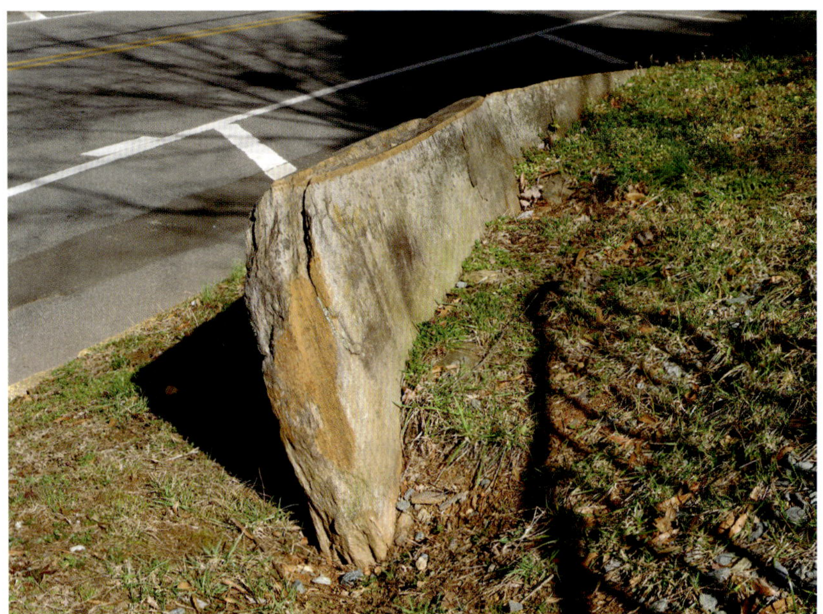

Figure 9.5 / Large curbstone becoming dislodged, at the southeast corner of West King and Wake streets.

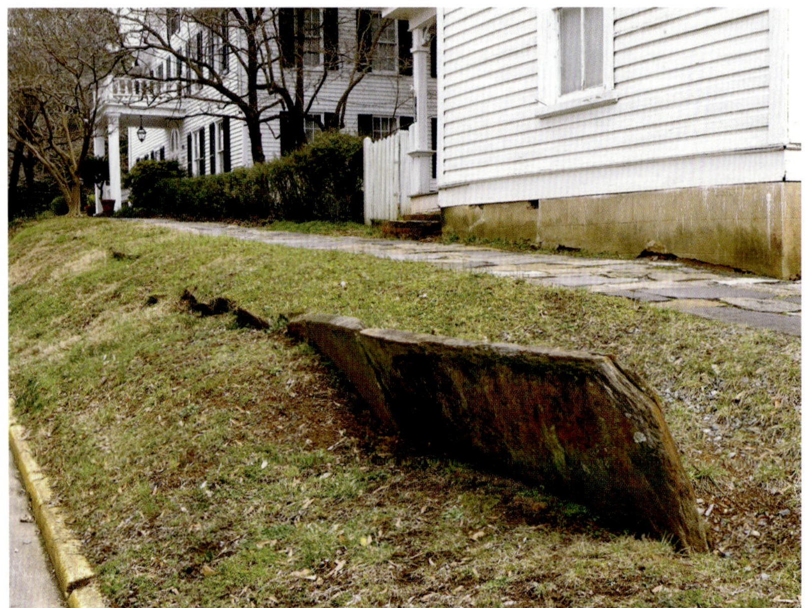

Figure 9.6 / Large curbstone in a line of more secure ones at West King and Wake streets.

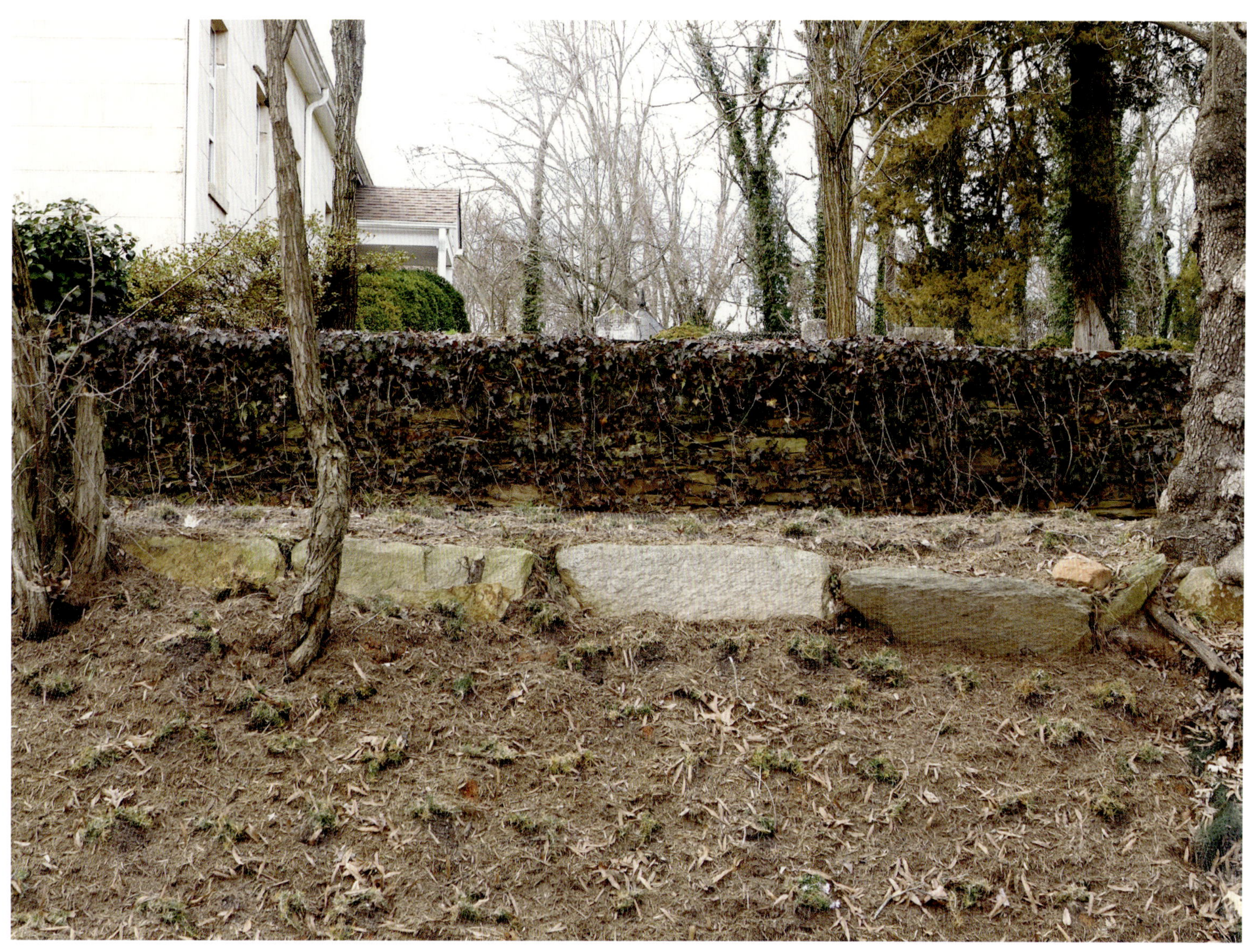

Figure 9.7 / Curbstones along Churton Street.

(Figure 9.8) or, in other cases, when they protrude only slightly and show their regular, flat edges, as they continue to perform their retaining role long after modern cement sidewalks and curbs have been installed around them (Figure 9.9).

Stone and Brick Work in Hillsborough

The source of the plentiful fieldstone slabs around town may be two nearby quarries, although it is difficult to precisely determine this. It is likewise difficult to establish the date of the stonework. Nevertheless, walking around the town, photographing and observing the use of natural stone, one uncovers several common themes or uses, as well as general stone types or coloration.

Stone steps, walls, and sidewalks or paths are easily viewed from the street or from modern sidewalks throughout the town. Natural stone was also used in embankments and the older house foundations. In general, stone was used for foundations earlier than brick. The two local stone quarries mentioned above would have been located to the west of Hillsborough on both sides of the Eno River. Although the quarrying of stone is mentioned in letters from Jesse Benton referencing his quarry in 1786, precise details are lacking. Duke University opened a new quarry west of Hillsborough in the 1920s, but stone outcroppings are also easily found throughout the naturally wooded habitat around the region.[2]

Clay pits near the Eno River also provided the town with a ready source of the material for bricks, which were manufactured at an early brick company near the river on the southeastern section of the old town, near the foot of today's Cameron Street. Bricks were used for chimneys and less frequently to build houses. Occasionally they were used in the building of walls. The wall around the cemetery at St. Matthew's, with its periodic reinforcing buttresses, is the town's best-preserved historic example of a brick wall.

Stone Steps

Steps leading from the street or sidewalk to a house entrance are often made of natural stone. These can be large, hewn stone slabs or a series of stout, flat stones placed one above the other to form the rise. Examples of stone steps are found in many locations, now lacking the former dooryards and house entrances once on their trajectory, and therefore seeming to

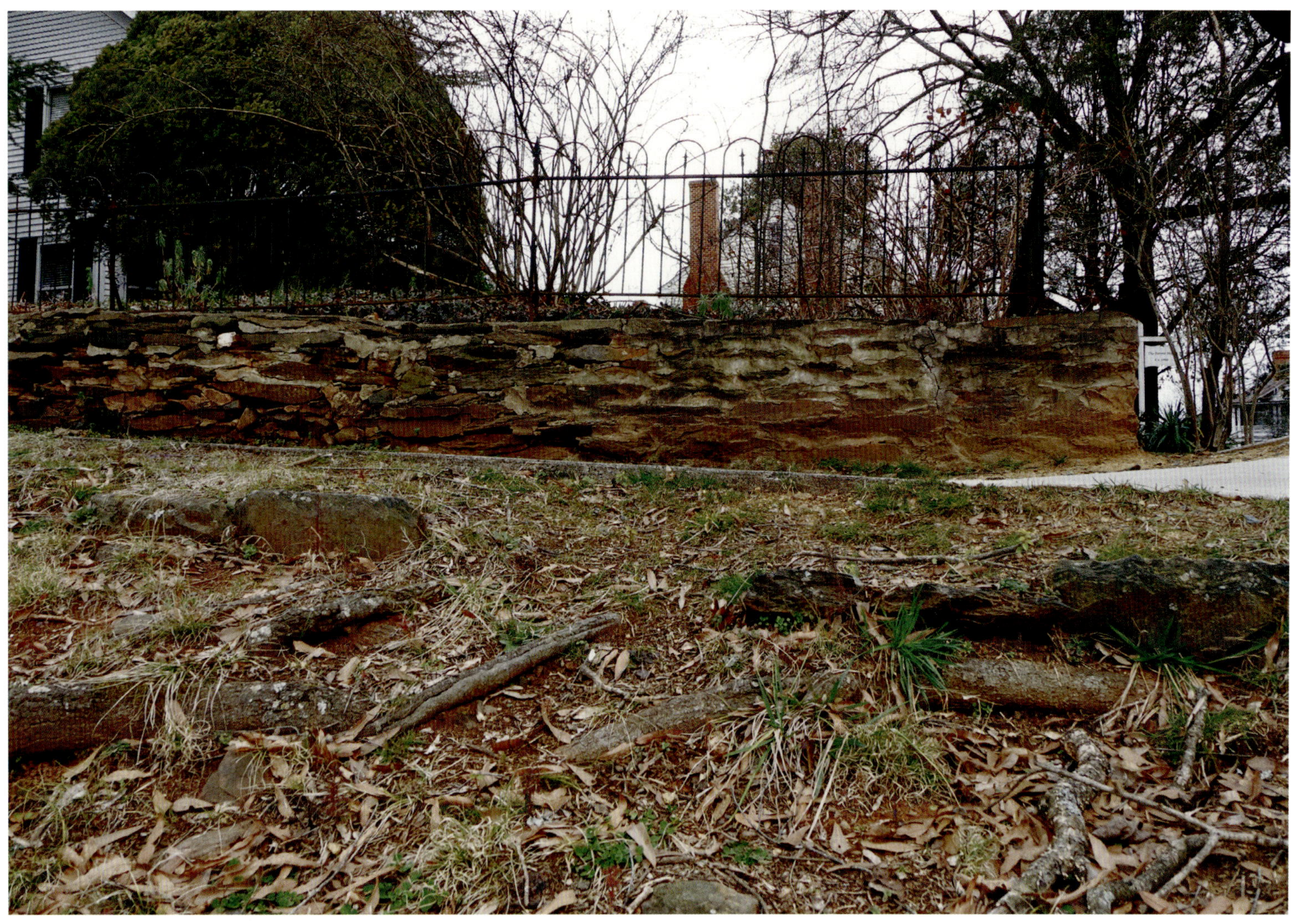

Figure 9.8 / Curbstones encased in tree roots along the east side of Wake Street near the corner of King Street.

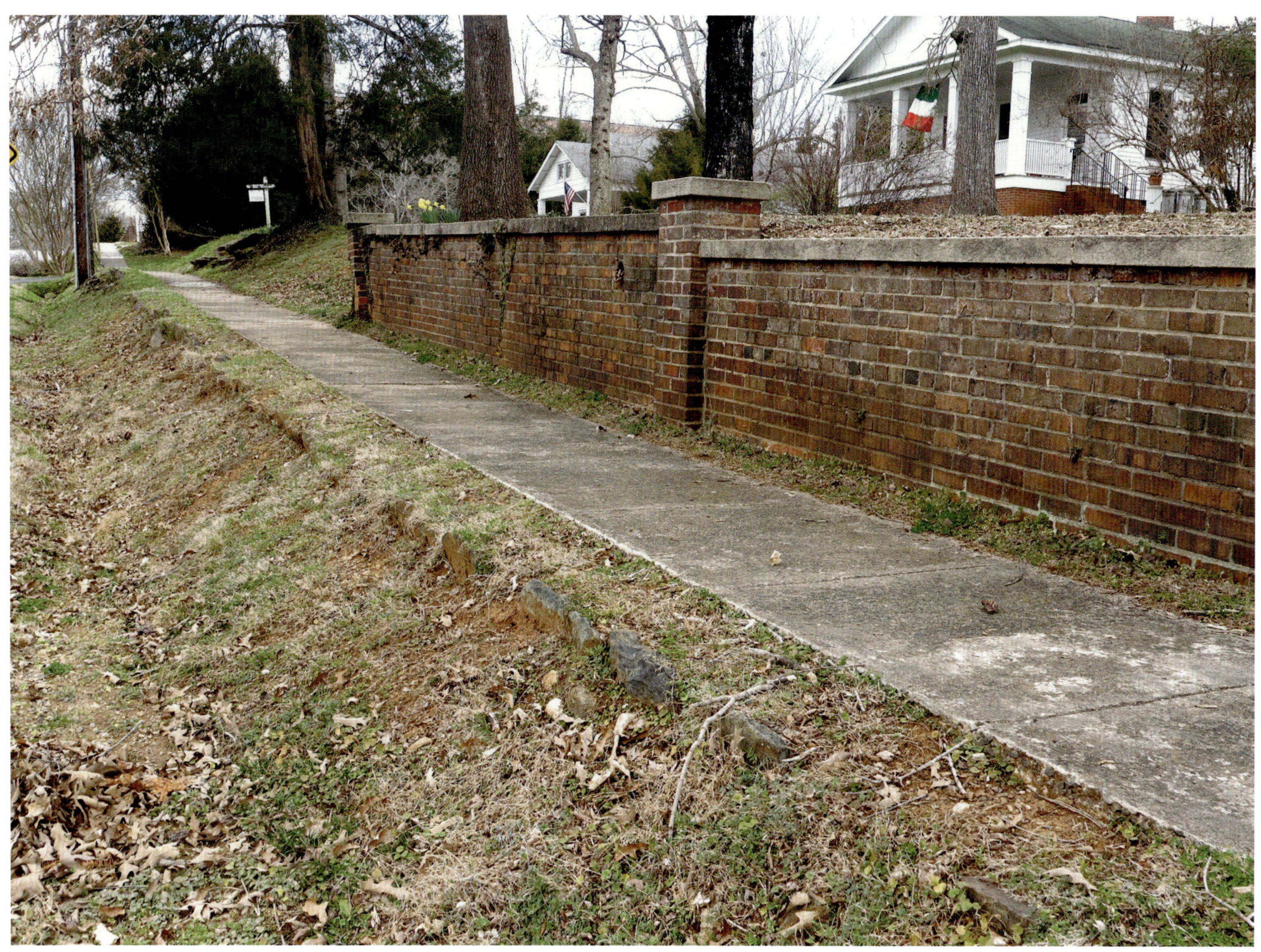

Figure 9.9 / Line of curbstones along north side of West Tryon Street, barely projecting along modern sidewalk.

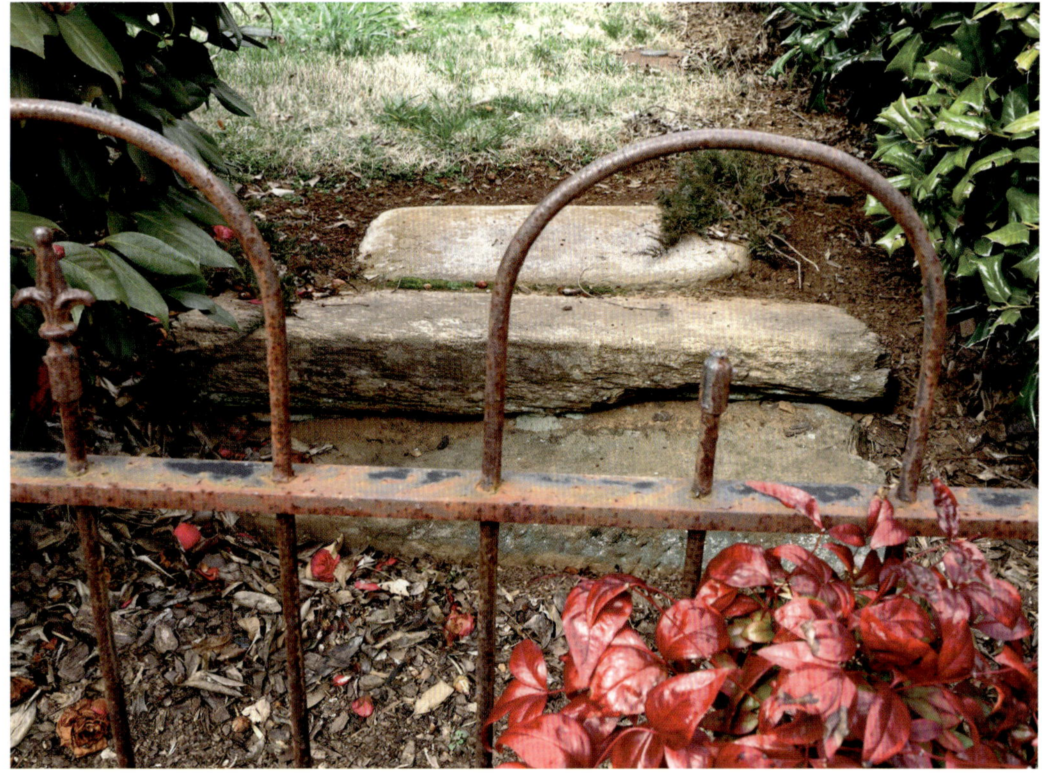

Figure 9.10 / Stone steps ending at a fence on West King Street.

lead nowhere (Figure 9.10). Examples can be found on the first block of West King Street, on Wake Street between King Street and Margaret Lane, on West Tryon in the second block, on West Queen, and in other locations, posing visual riddles for passersby. One series of steps on West Tryon Street has been carefully fashioned with the addition of curb-like stones at the sides, to assist in holding the steps in place (Figure 9.11).

Stone Walls

Natural stone walls of beautiful, carefully selected and placed fieldstone provide contiguous borders around a number of properties and along streets in a number of areas in town. The walls sometimes defined property boundaries in the early town; and their distance of

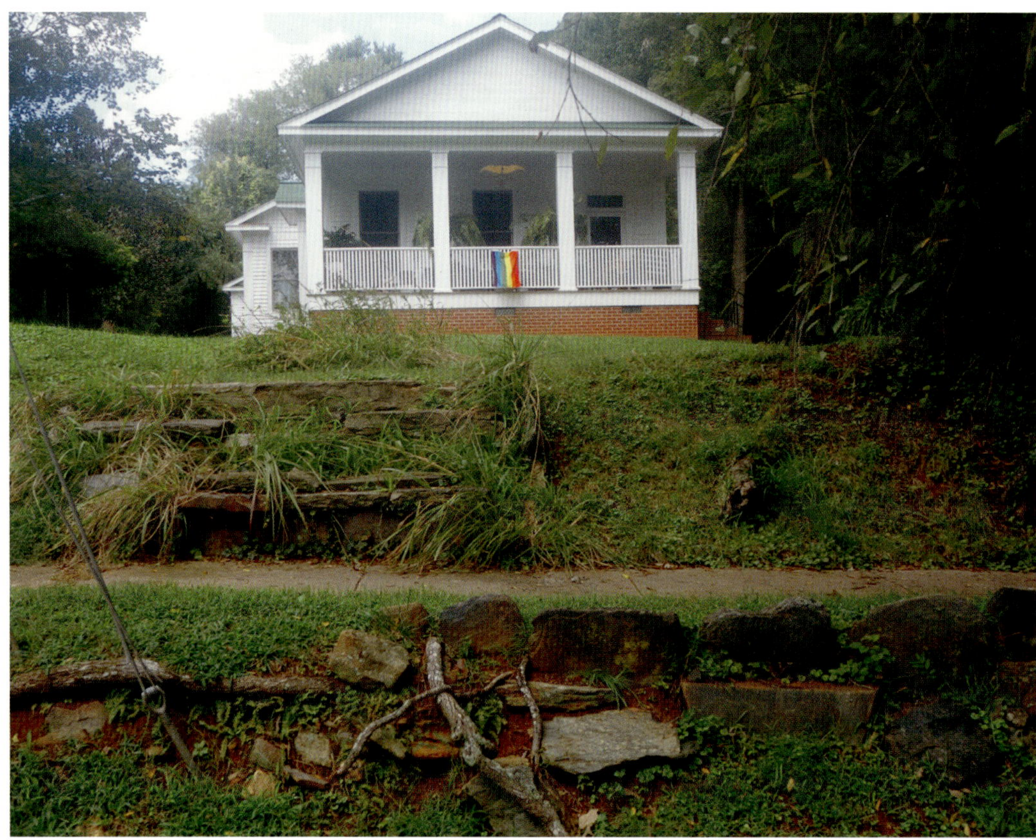

Figure 9.11 / Stone steps with supporting "curb" stones, leading to a house formerly in this location, West Tryon Street.

exactly one chain (or sixty-six feet) apart along the streets still may be seen in a few places, for example at the corner of Queen and Churton streets (Figure 9.12).

In Hillsborough, a tawny or orange color on the fractured sides of many of these stones makes the town walls distinctive, as evident in the walls around the Old Town Cemetery (Figure 9.13).

For the most part, these are dry-stack walls, constructed without mortar; they were laid with such skill that they remain solid centuries later. Many, however, show obvious signs of repair, modern cementing, and substitution of stones. Fieldstone can be found either in flat sheets, like flagstones, or in random-sized boulders that are placed in a way to ensure the

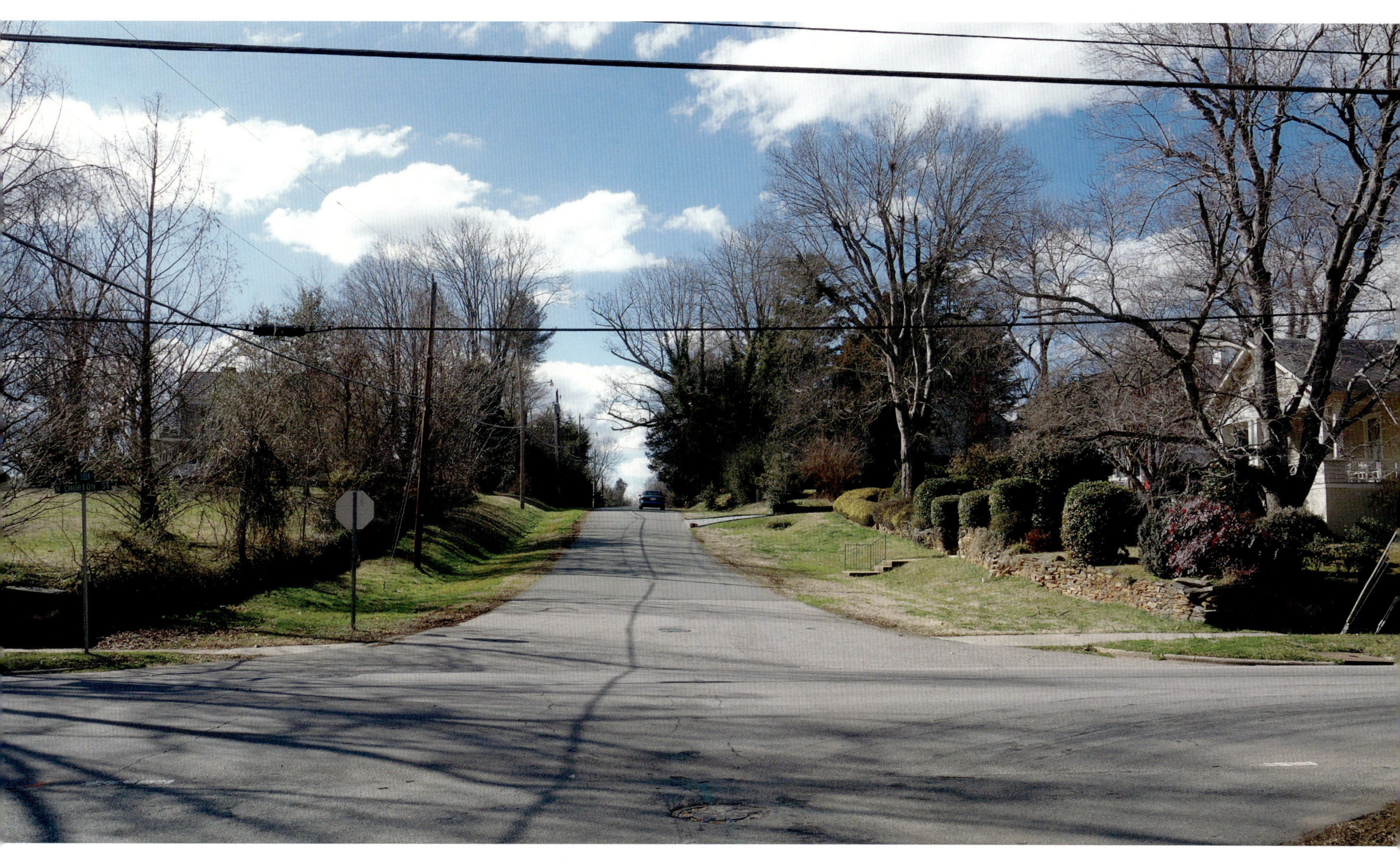

Figure 9.12 / Intersection of Queen and Churton streets, looking west; stone walls border both sides of the street, still defining early property boundaries.

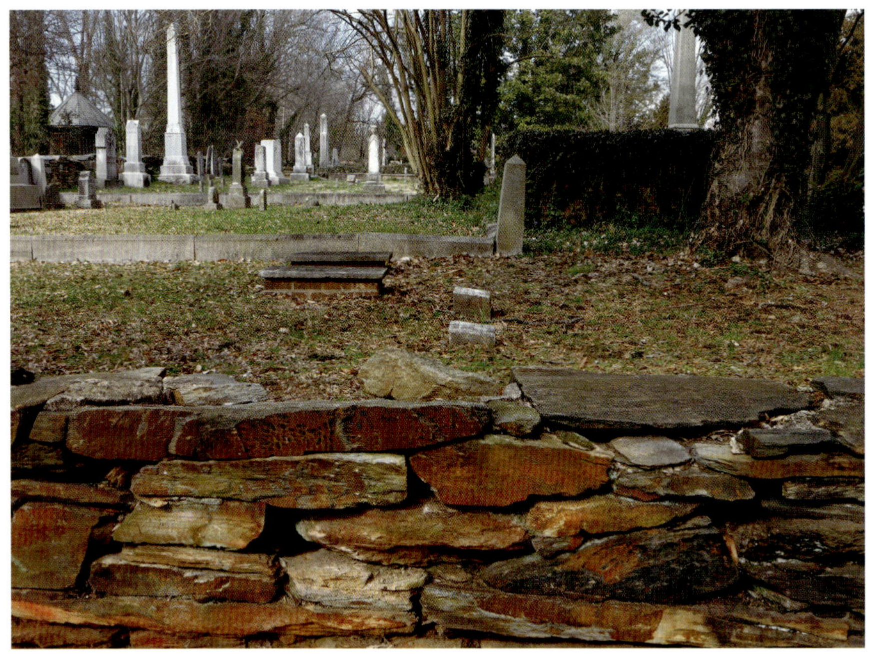

Figure 9.13 / Dry-stack stone wall along south side of Old Town Cemetery, West Tryon Street, showing tawny-orange hue of many Hillsborough stones.

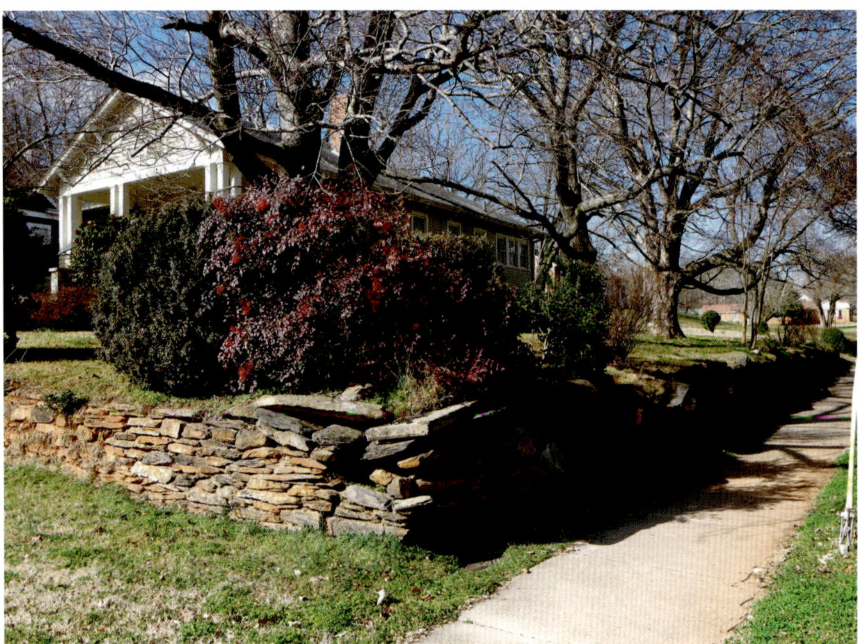

Figure 9.14 / Stone wall near the corner of West Queen and Churton streets showing collapse of some sections.

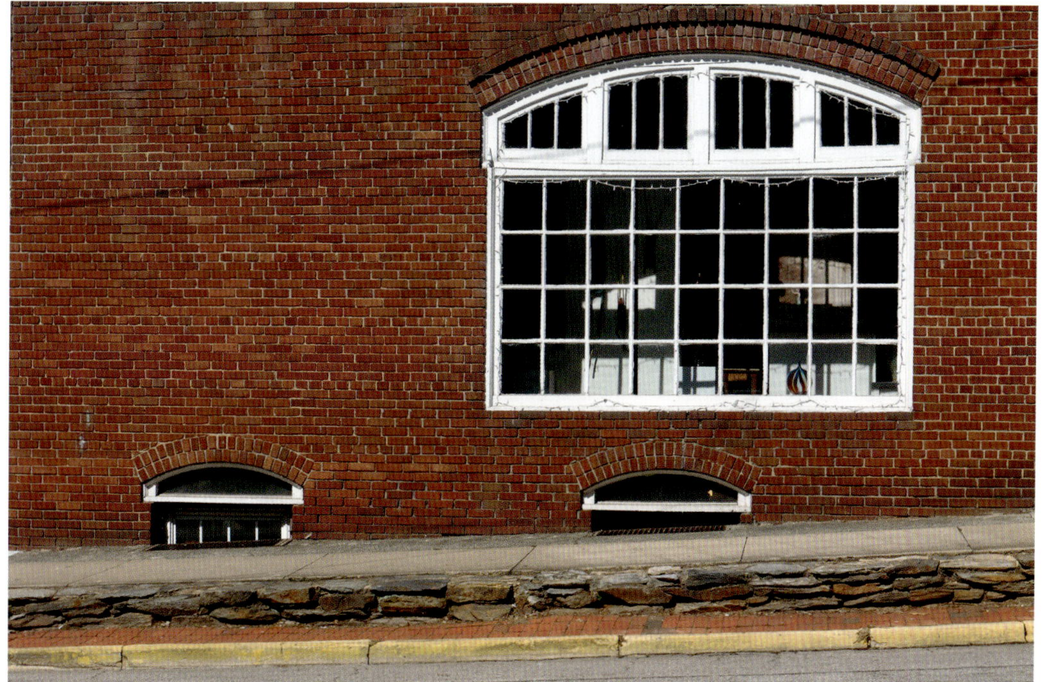

Figure 9.15 / Wall stub encased in modern sidewalk along west side of Churton Street, near King.

wall's stability. The General Assembly of 1784[3] designated that a stone wall be built around the town cemetery. The purpose of the wall was made clear: to keep wandering animals from running loose in the cemetery. Well-shaped, flat fieldstone was utilized in creating the cemetery wall and a number of walls along property boundaries around town, although in some cases the walls are in need of repair (Figure 9.14).

The stub of a stone wall can be seen along the north half of the block of Churton Street between West Margaret Lane and West King (Figure 9.15). Out of place though it appears today, this is a survivor of a wall system of the early town. Modern improvements can clearly be seen in some of the long expanses of walls along North Churton Street, including the addition of white quartz boulders and of small stones that do not conform in color, shape, or size with any of the others, and therefore appear to be out of place (Figure 9.16); many sections of Hillsborough's stone walls now consist only of loosely piled stones arranged in rows.

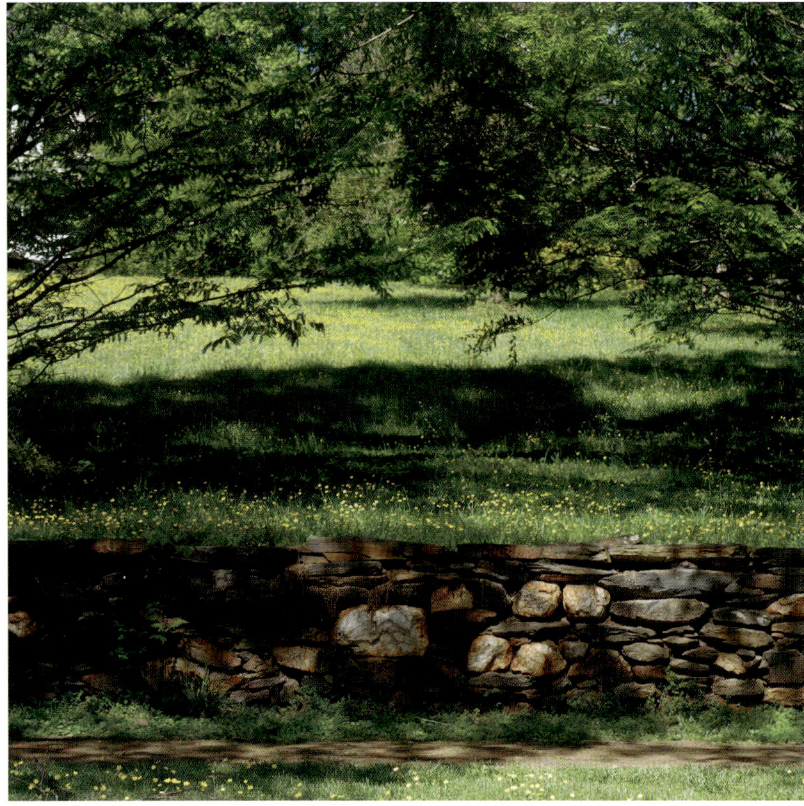

Figure 9.16 / Churton Street stone wall showing inclusions of white quartz boulders.

The Dark Walk

Unique to Hillsborough is the Dark Walk, a well-shaded path or narrow road (or "street") that meanders along the riverbank on the south side of the Eno River. Along the south side of the walk are high bluffs, with the canopy of trees shading the path, thus the term *dark*. A longtime resident of Hillsborough describes the Dark Walk,

> . . . brought us into the Dark Walk. With our eyes accustomed to the stronger light outside, it would take us some minutes to see clearly the beauty of our surroundings. On our right were the slopes of a steep hill. . . . On our left there were more trees to complete the archway, their overhanging branches mirrored in the Eno River. . . .[4]

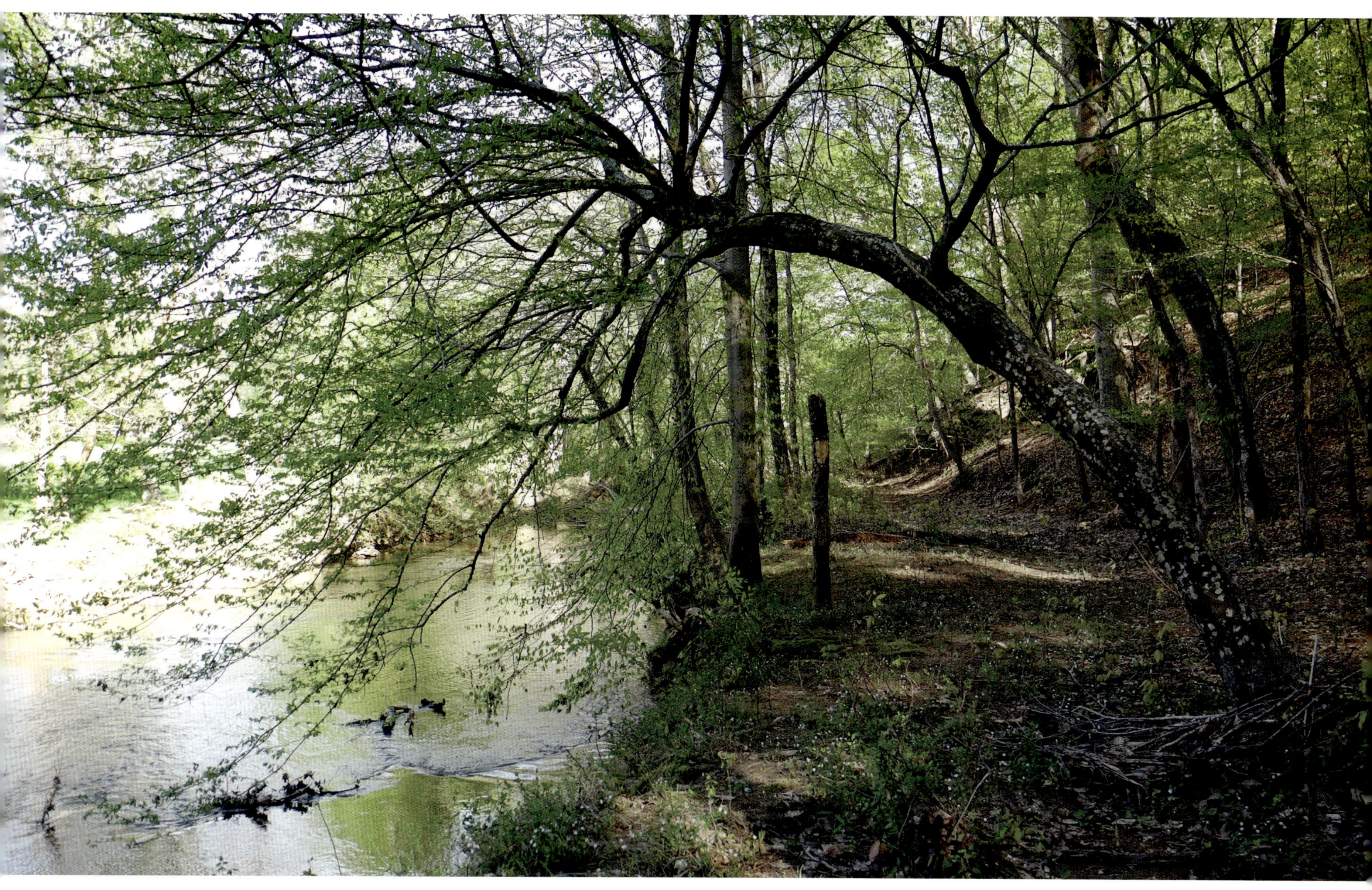

Figure 9.17 / Dark Walk along the south bank of the Eno River in Hillsborough.

Rather than serving as a transportation route, the walk was used by local residents for social visits or lazy strolls along the river (Figure 9.17). Newspaper articles[5] describing visits to Hillsborough in the mid-nineteenth century include the Dark Walk in their description of the town's unique scenes.[6] This well-known site became a favorite subject of local postcards in the twentieth century.[7] Hidden from the hustle and bustle of twenty-first century downtown Hillsborough, the Dark Walk remains a charming and idyllic landscape. One can best view the Dark Walk from across the Eno River on today's Riverwalk.

Ten

Offices and Law Offices

BY CRAUFURD D. GOODWIN

Before the twentieth century there were few structures in downtown Hillsborough that would qualify today as office buildings. Business was conducted elsewhere. The professional persons who flocked to the county seat of this burgeoning part of Piedmont North Carolina as merchants, lawyers, doctors, educators, light manufacturers, and others needed places to meet clients, maintain records, and provide work space for clerical assistants. The solution for some lay in relatively small, compact buildings called *offices,* constructed often, for convenience and security, adjacent to the courthouse or on residential properties. They were located as close as possible to the front or back lawns of homes, depending on the geography of the building lots. These offices were distinctive features of the small commercial and governmental towns of America, not of the larger cities where property values were high.

Because these structures went out of fashion as offices by the twentieth century, without other obvious uses, many were allowed to deteriorate or fall down. Fewer than a dozen of these offices survive in Hillsborough today, saved through adaptation as compact dwellings, storage spaces, or decorative elements in the landscape. Some have been absorbed into larger structures. Most appear to date to the decades before the Civil War when Hillsborough was prosperous as the county seat of Orange County and a commercial center for the agricultural development of the North Carolina Piedmont.

The surviving offices are mainly simple, one-room frame structures, often little more than twenty feet square, with attic space above, sometimes reflecting the architecture of the building to which they were attached or that stood nearby. Most were of white-painted

Figure 10.1 / Cadwallader Jones Law Office on courthouse square.

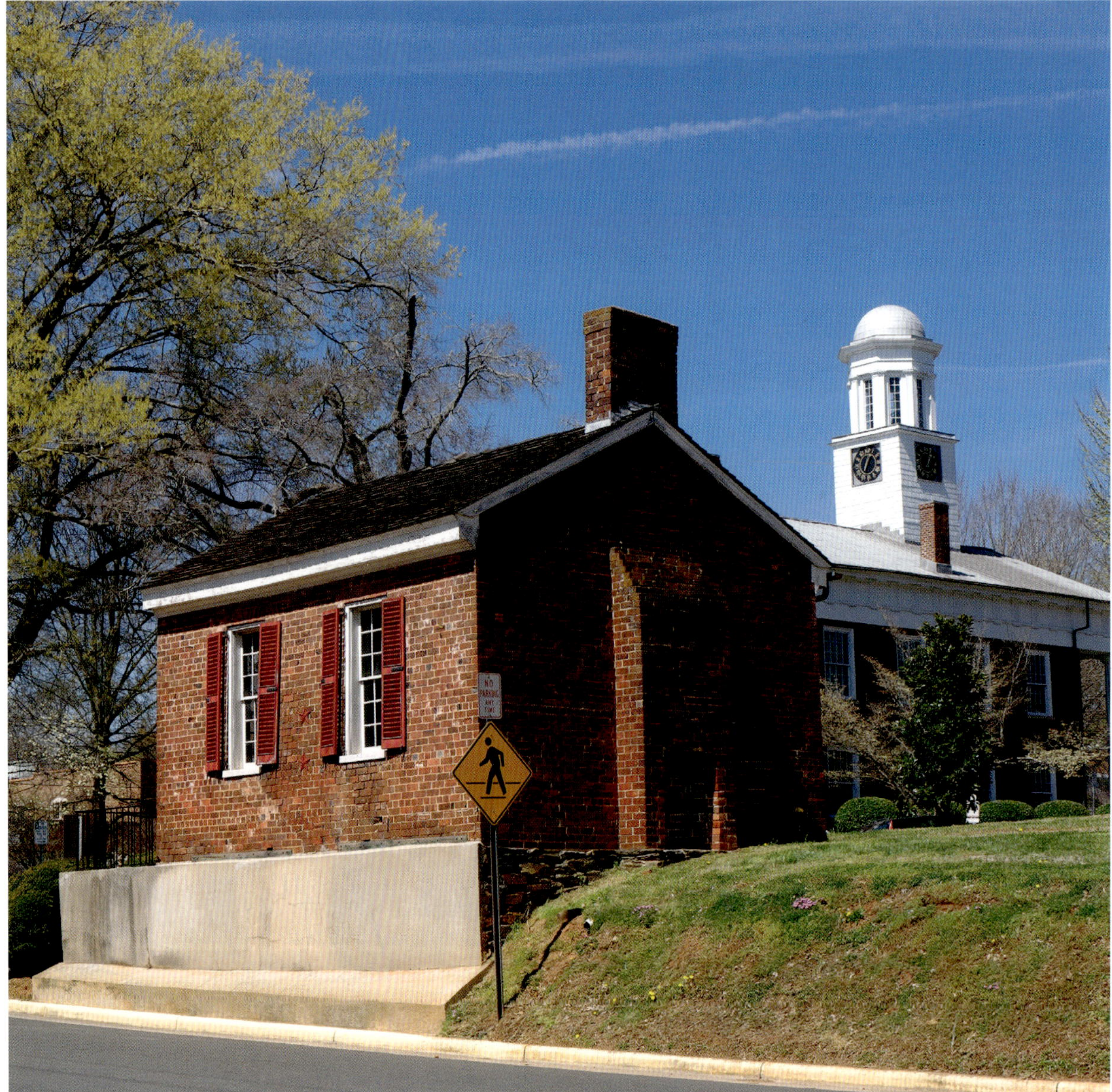

weatherboard but two of those that have survived are of brick. It is hard to be confident of the original appearance of the offices because, like so many other buildings in town, they were frequently modified over the years. Mantels were moved from one building to another, the location of chimneys was changed, doors were replaced, and sometimes whole buildings were moved, presumably on rollers pulled by mules. There was simple woodwork inside that typically included wainscoting, door and window frames, mantels, and, sometimes, bookshelves. Heating came from a fireplace or coal grate. Furniture consisted in most cases of a table, a few chairs, and perhaps a cabinet or desk, as with the Cadwallader Jones Law Office on the courthouse square (Figures 10.1 and 10.2).

The major enemies of these small buildings have been neglect, rising site values, technological change that made the accumulation of paper records less necessary, and shifts in fashion that made it seem odd to have your business in your garden. Termites have always been a problem. It is a surprise and a delight that these few offices have survived in Hillsborough.

Important moments in American history have occurred within Hillsborough offices. We may presume that some of the landmark opinions of Chief Justice Thomas Ruffin on judicial independence, the treatment of chattel slaves, and other matters were prepared in his law office that sits in front of his home, Burnside, on Cameron Street (Figures 10.3 and 10.4).[1]

Toward the end of the Civil War when former Gov. William Alexander Graham worked with his close friend David Swain, president of the University of North Carolina and also a former governor, to arrange for the early surrender of Raleigh to Gen. William T. Sherman, and thereby minimize destruction and loss of life, they met at his home Montrose, very likely in the law office that survives behind the main house (Figure 10.5). [2]

When the remnants of the Confederate cabinet then met to discuss surrender terms to present to Sherman, they gathered at the Alexander Dickson House, Gen. Wade Hampton's headquarters, in the small farm office just behind the main house. Both house and office have now been moved from the edge of town to Lot 46 in the center of town where they serve as the Orange County Visitors Center (Figure 10.6). Like many other offices, this one has opposite doors on two sides. It was reported that one of the Confederate conferees joked that this was an ideal setup, for if the Yankees came in one of the doors they could go out the other.

The offices also harbor mysteries. Gov. Graham's law office at Montrose is a combination of two similar but not identical one-room offices, bolted together and with a door

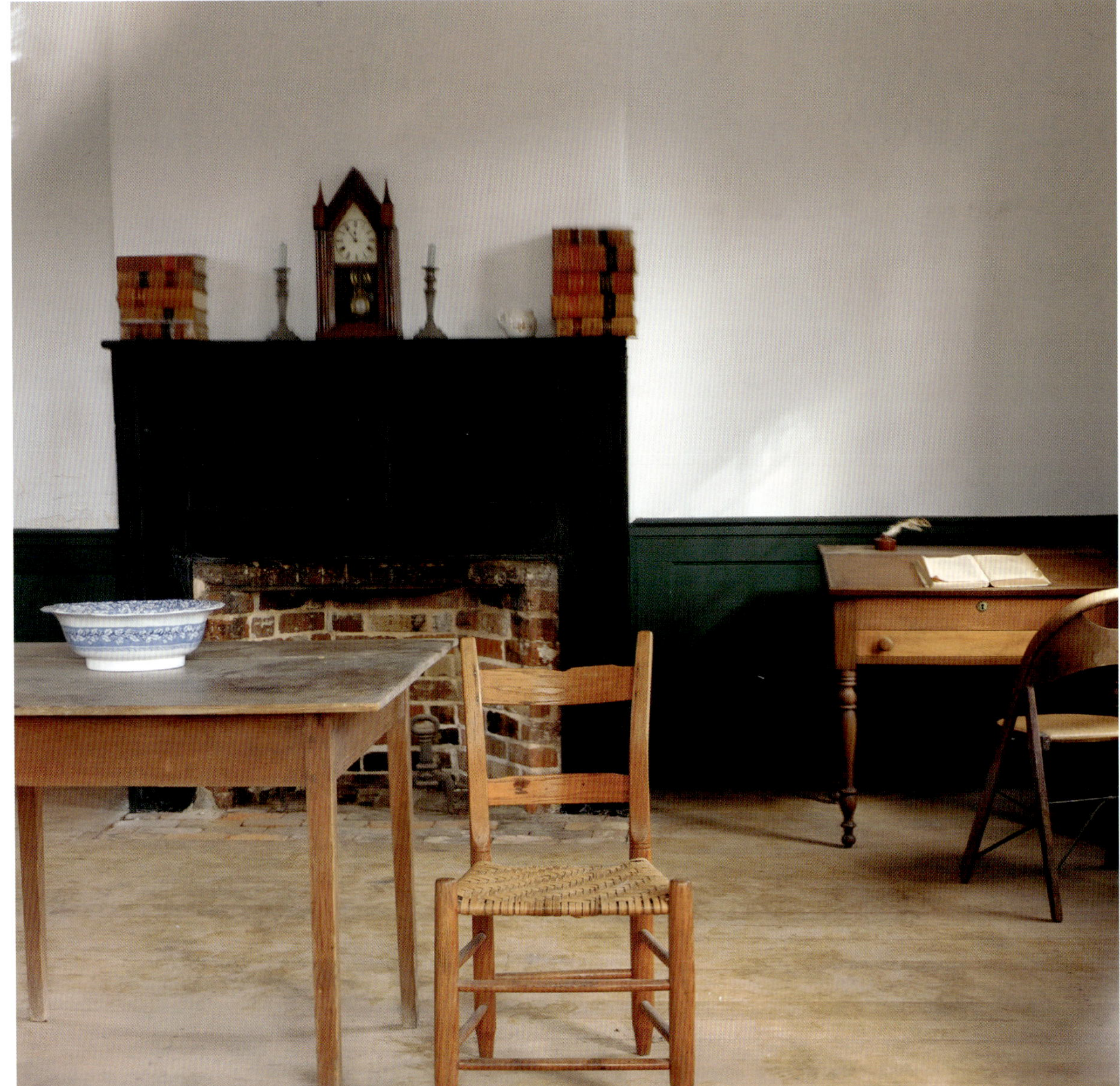

Figure 10.2 / Interior, Cadwallader Jones Law Office.

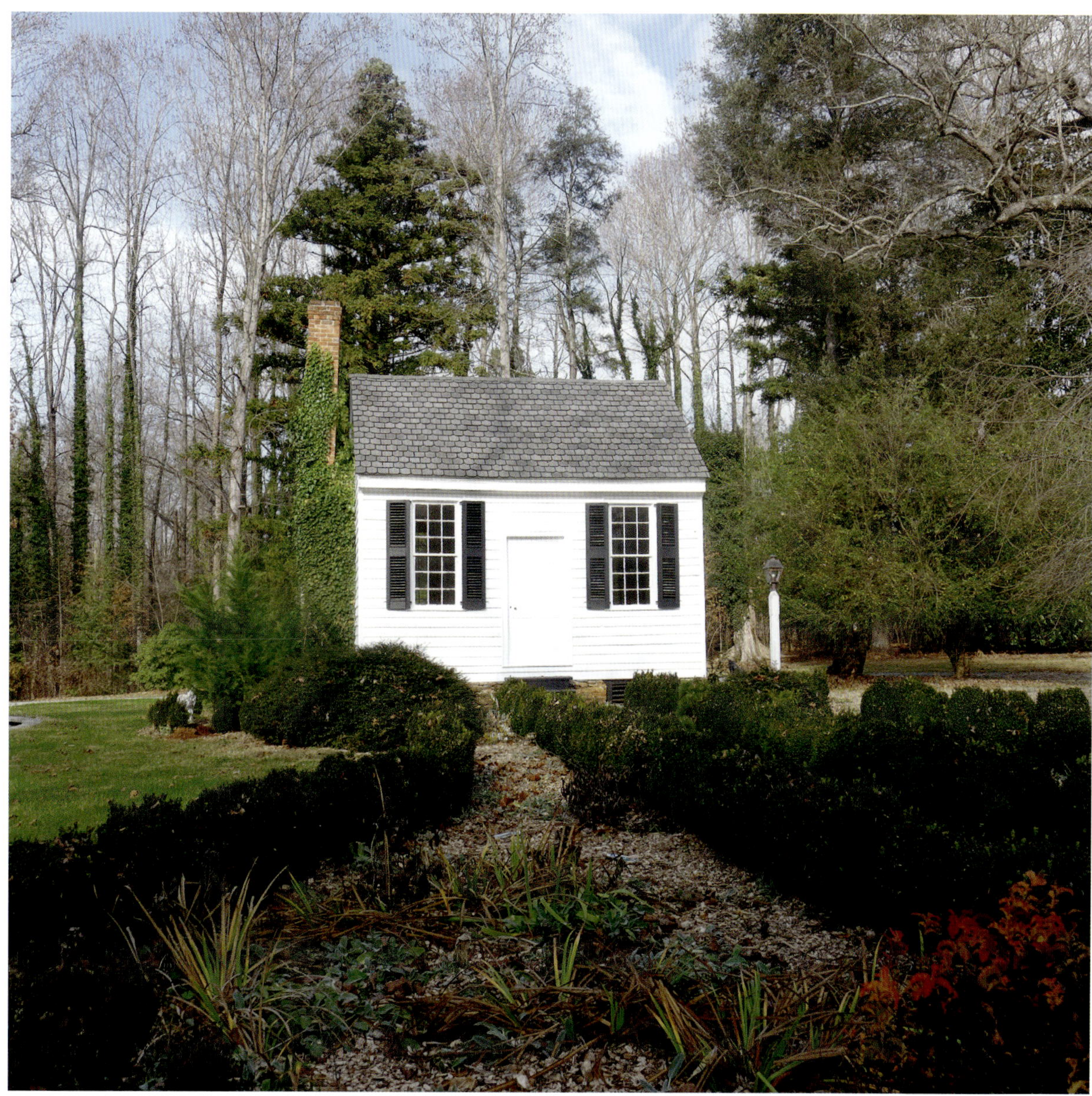

Figure 10.3 / Ruffin Law Office, Burnside, ca. 1818.

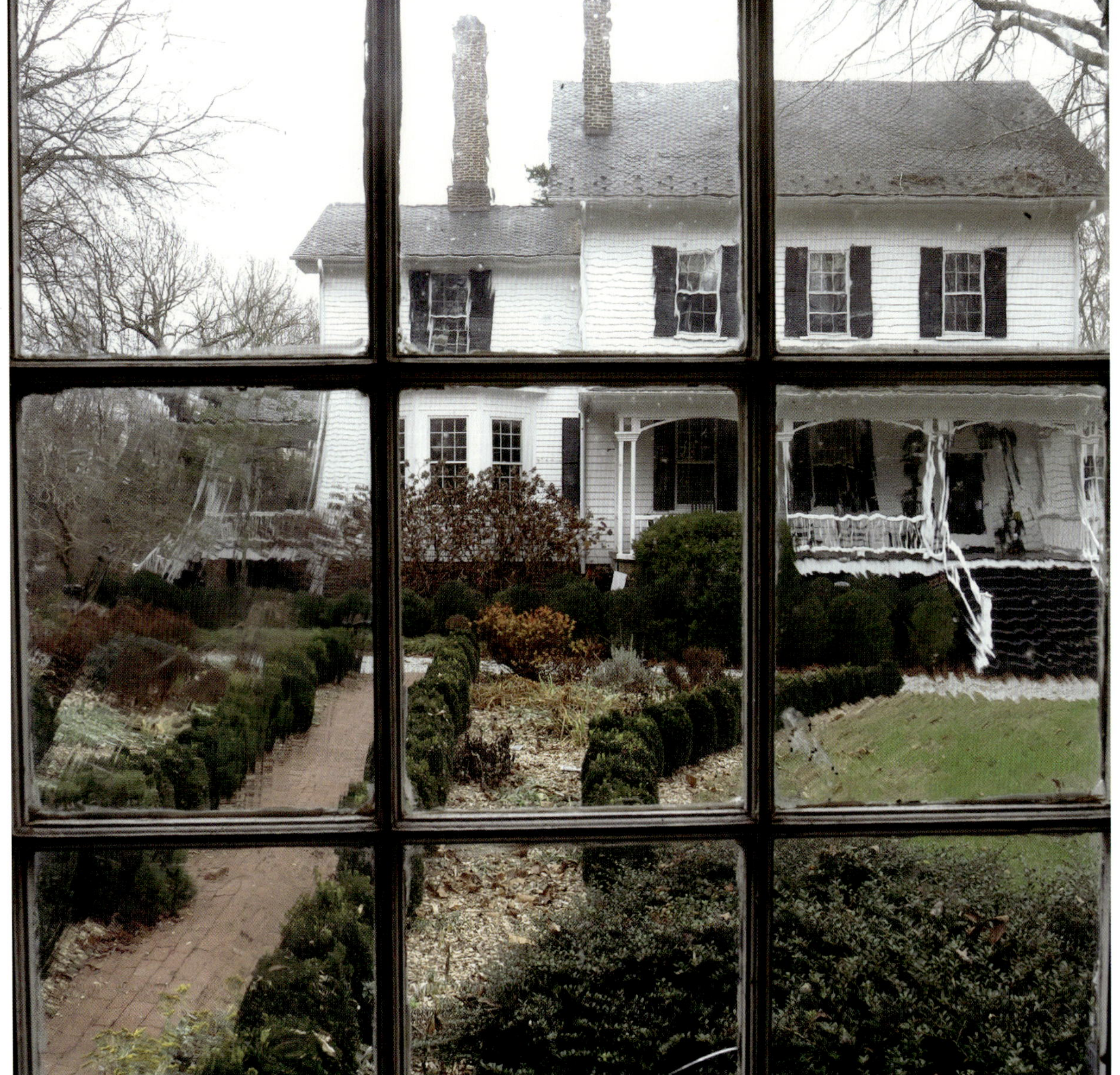

Figure 10.4 / View from Ruffin Law Office toward main house, Burnside.

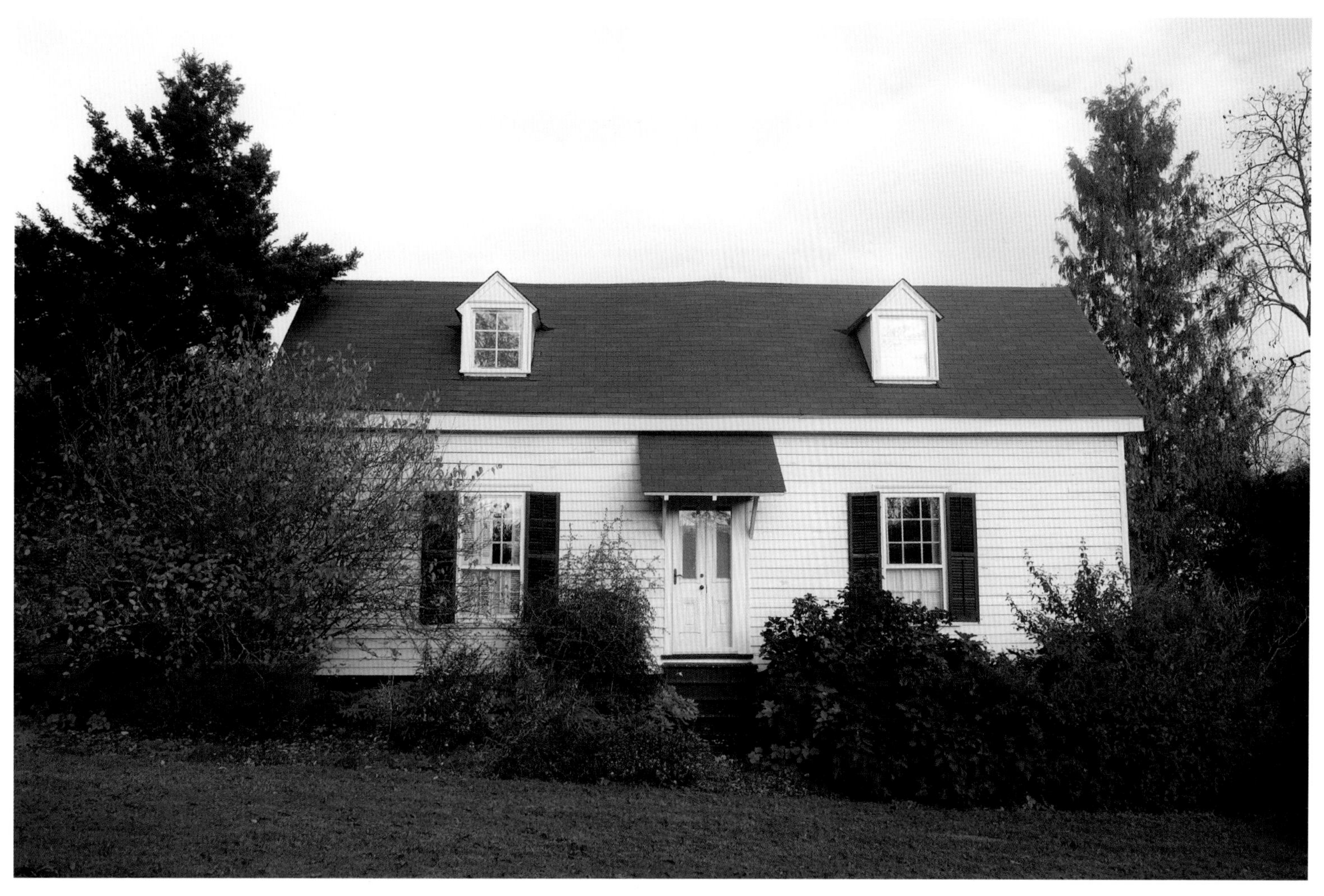

Figure 10.5 / Graham Law Office, Montrose.

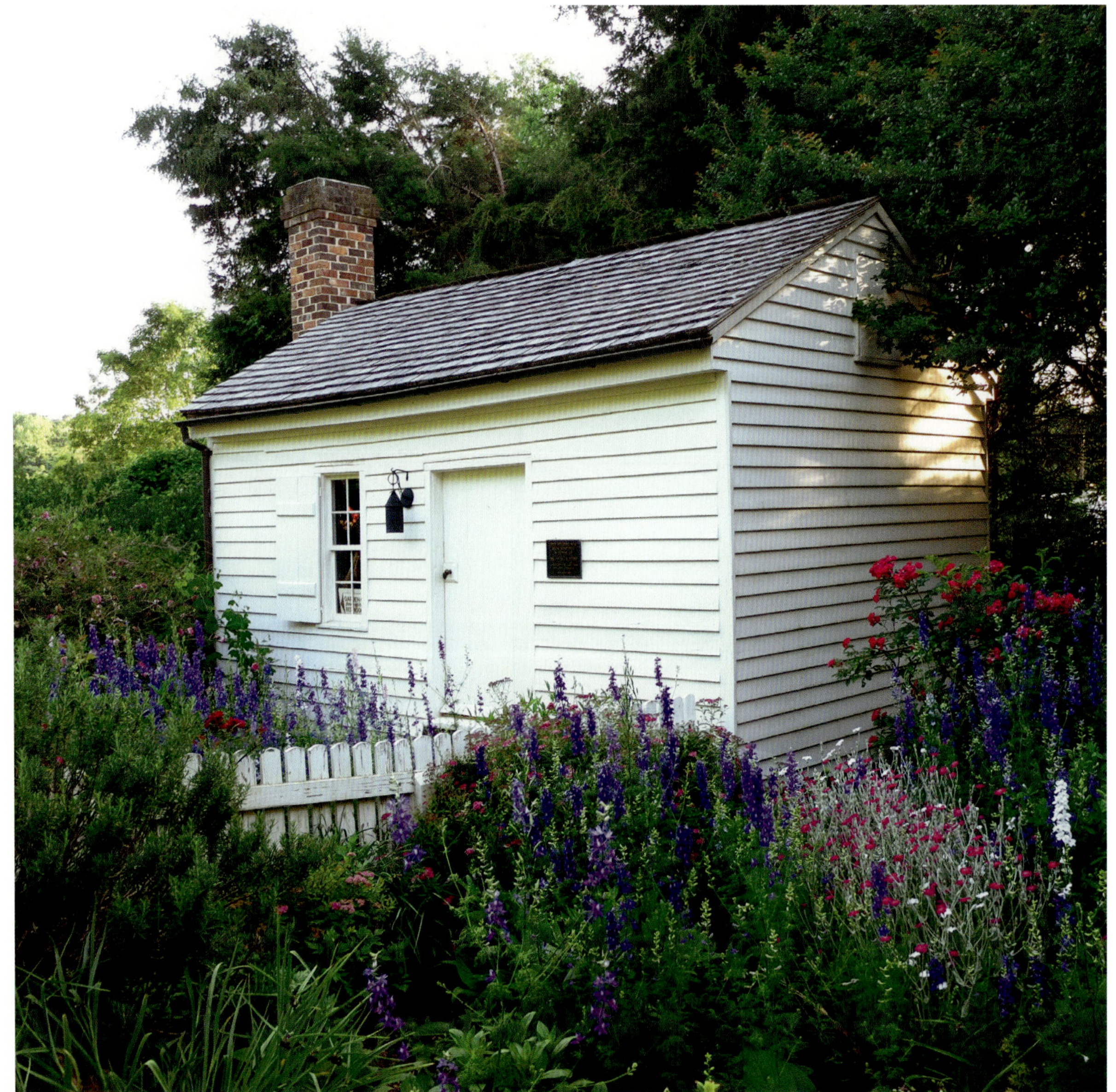

Figure 10.6 / Alexander Dickson Office, ca. 1780, Orange County Visitors Center.

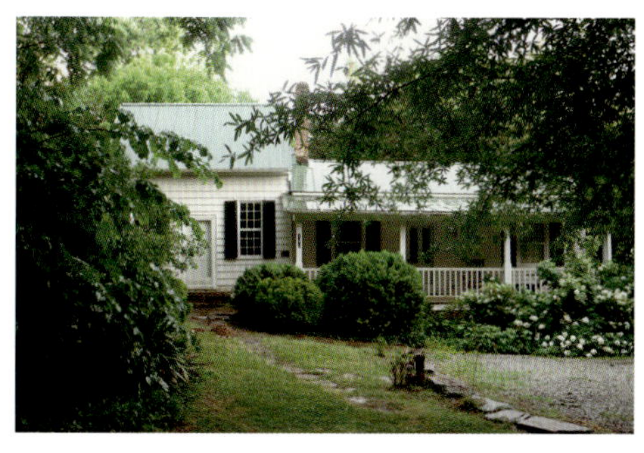

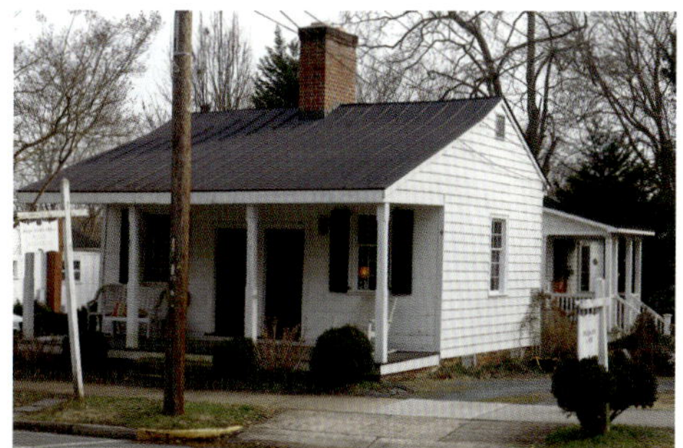

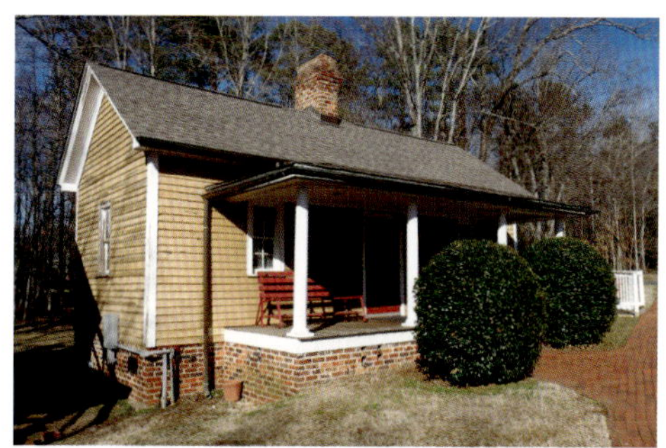

(left to right)
Top row:
Figure 10.7 / Cameron-Nash Law Office, Margaret Lane.
Figure 10.8 / Frederick Nash Law Office, West King Street.
Figure 10.9 / Ruffin-Roulhac Law Office, Town Hall Campus, East Corbin Street.

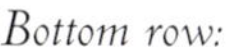

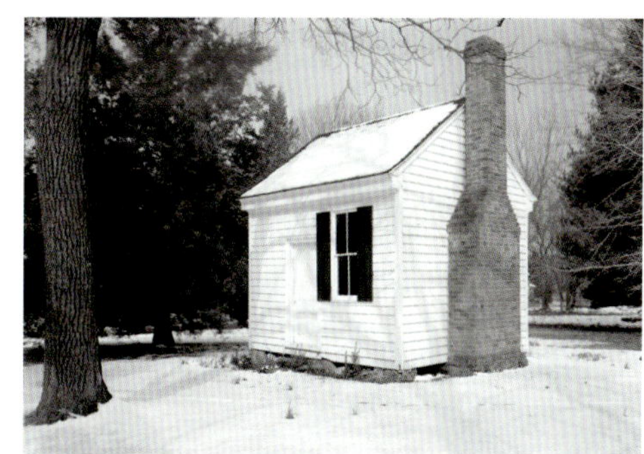

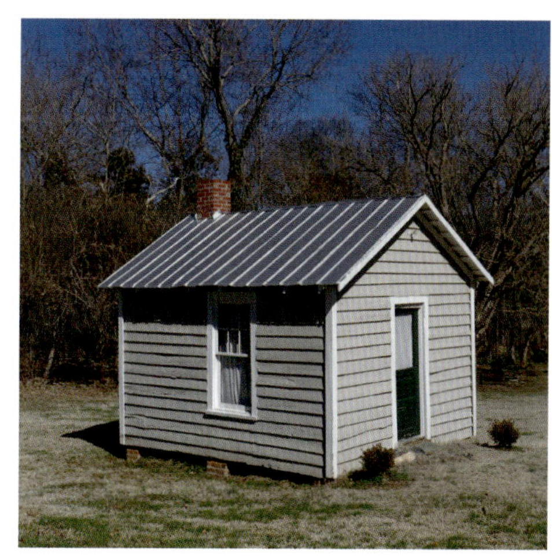

Bottom row:
Figure 10.10 / Sans Souci Office, Cain Street. (Photograph from the 1930s, Historic American Buildings Survey. Courtesy, Library of Congress, No. NC-221-B-1.*)*
Figure 10.11 / Basket Factory office, South Occoneechee Street.

between. Where did these two offices come from and how did they get there? Up the hill from downtown, pulled by mules? Another mystery can be observed at the Cadwallader Jones Law Office. On the back of this brick structure is a chimney with an open fireplace that now seems intended only to increase global warming (see Figure 10.1). But does this fireplace facing outward suggest that another structure once was attached to the back of the office and the fireplace warmed an interior room? Or might this fireplace have warmed the hands and hearts of coachmen and clients who had come to see the lawyer and were waiting their turn under a primitive carport?

We do not know with certainty how many offices remain in Hillsborough because some may be tucked away out of sight and others enveloped by larger buildings. But we are confident of at least nine: Cadwallader Jones Law Office on the courthouse square; Cameron-Nash Law Office, Margaret Lane (Figures 10.7); Alexander Dickson House Office, now on East King Street; Frederick Nash Law Office, West King Street (Figure 10.8); Ruffin-Roulhac Law Office, Town Hall Campus, East Corbin Street (Figure 10.9); Ruffin Law Office, Burnside; Sans Souci Office, Cain Street (Figure 10.10); Graham Law Office, Montrose; Factory office, South Occoneechee Street (Figure 10.11). (See Map 7.)

Happily the first five offices listed above, some of which are on private property, are easily visible from public walkways. The aforementioned Dickson House Office at the visitors' center is open to the public.

Eleven

Schools and School-Related Buildings

BY CALLIE CONNOR

The exceptional number of schools founded in Hillsborough in the nineteenth century sets the town apart from most places in the South. The town was a center of state politics as well as the county seat for Orange County, and therefore attracted many well-educated and distinguished lawyers, doctors, state officials, and educators, along with ordinary citizens and merchants who chose to live and raise their families here. Young boys and girls were sent from around the state—and the country—to attend Hillsborough's many secondary educational institutions. Schools quickly gained reputations for excellence, and some served as preparatory schools for the University of North Carolina at Chapel Hill, founded in 1789 and located only twelve miles away.[1] The sizes and types of school buildings were as diverse as their founders.

Surviving today in and around Hillsborough are a half dozen buildings that served as schools or as annexes to schools during the nineteenth century. Many more appear in records, but have disappeared without a trace. The best-known surviving school is the Burwell Academy for Young Ladies, or the Burwell School (Lots 152–53 and 170–71), at the corner of Churton and Union streets, a school for girls that operated from 1837 to 1857. It enrolled around two hundred students over this period, at the beginning of the institutionalization of women's education in North Carolina.[2] The Rev. Robert Burwell moved to Hillsborough with his family in 1835 to serve as minister of the Presbyterian Church. In 1837, the church's parsonage, a two-story, hip-roofed, frame house built in 1821, became home not only to the family but also to the school the Burwells founded (Figure 11.1).

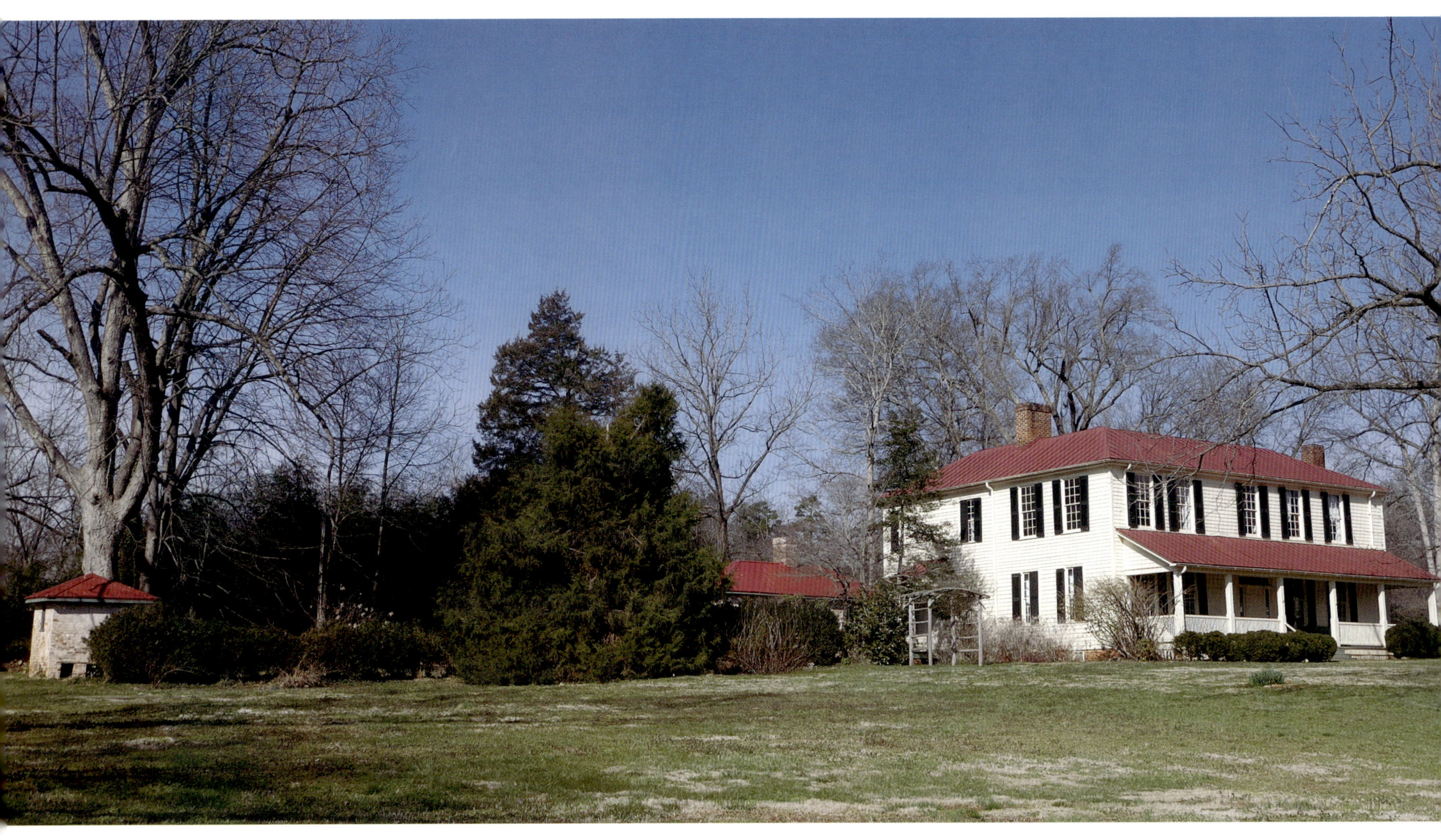

Figure 11.1 / Burwell School from the southeast, showing (from the left) necessary house, classroom building, and main house. (The arbor built for the musk rose on near side of main building.)

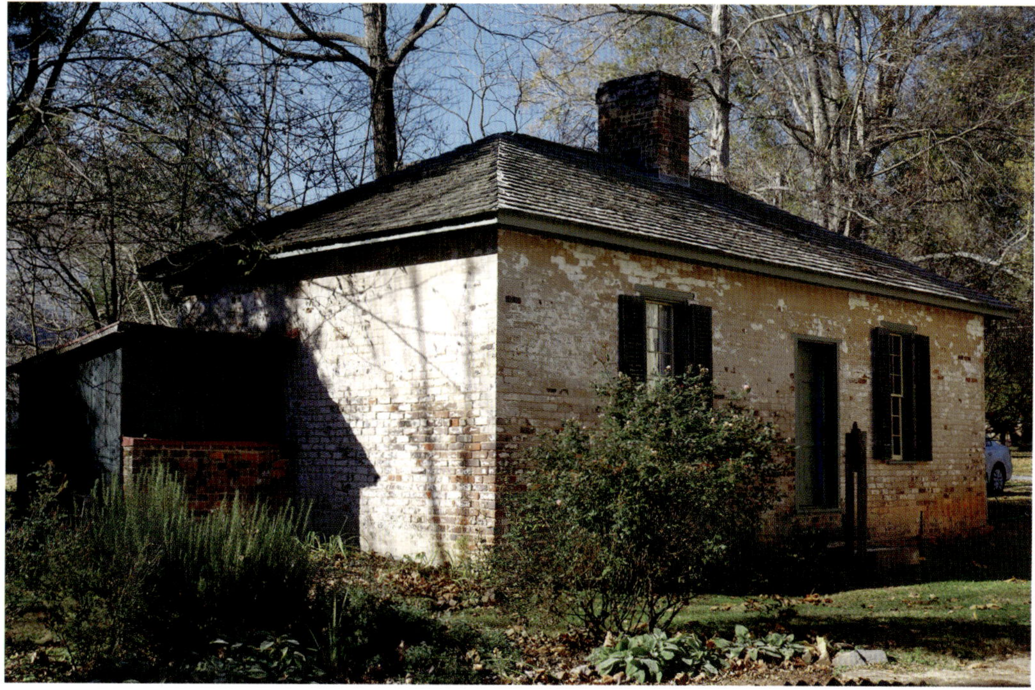

Figure 11.2 / Burwell School, brick classroom building.

Margaret Anna Burwell directed its daily operation for both boarding and day students. In addition to overseeing teachers and instruction, Mrs. Burwell also supervised the family's slaves and cared for her own family of twelve children. Some students were given accommodations in the main house, while the downstairs rooms served as refectory (dining room) and schoolrooms or parlors. Behind the main building is the Brick House, or Brick Room, a one-story, hip-roofed, brick structure with an off-center chimney, built in 1837 as a two-room classroom building. Its rooms measure approximately twenty by twenty feet, and eleven by twenty feet, with nine-foot ceilings; each is lit by large, east- and west-facing windows (Figures 11.2 and 11.3).

This was later referred to as the Music Building, for piano lessons were an important part of the curriculum in female education.[3] Academic subjects taught at the school included Latin, philosophy, literature, astronomy, history, and algebra; music, drawing, and French lessons were offered for an additional charge.[4] A kitchen south of the house, an office for

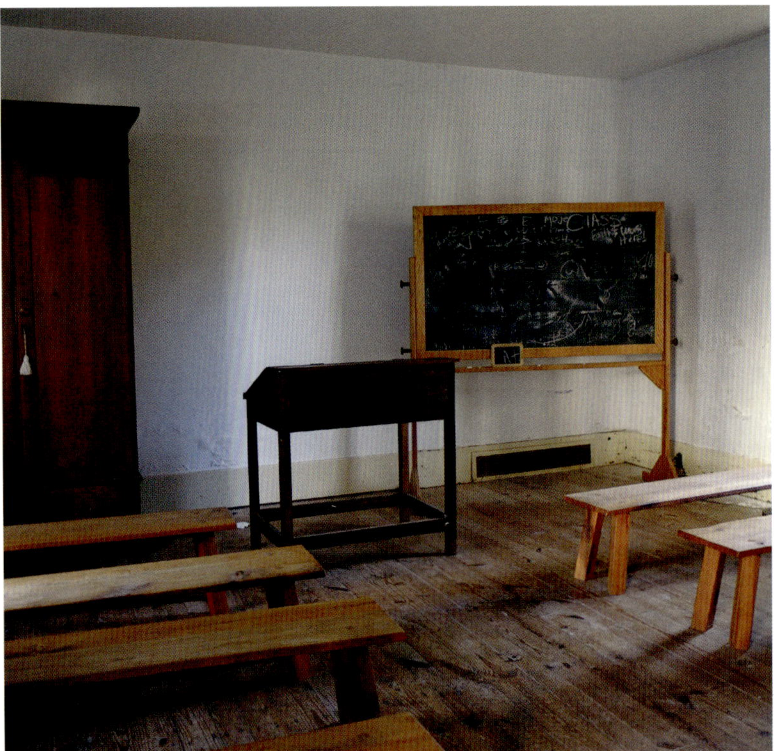

Figure 11.3 / Burwell School, classroom building interior.

the Rev. Burwell on the north, and a slave house and dormitory for students, located across Union Street, have all disappeared, although a brick necessary house does survive on the property (see Figure 11.4 for a sketch of the school as it appeared in the mid-nineteenth century).

In 1965 the school was acquired by the Historic Hillsborough Commission (HHC), restored, and put on the National Register of Historic Places. It is currently owned and run by the HHC as a house museum and educational center for schoolchildren.[5]

The Nash-Kollock School (Lots 10, 11, 13, 14, and 16) on West Margaret Lane occupied the former residence of Frederick Nash, chief justice of the North Carolina Supreme Court; a law office adjacent to this residence served as an annex to the school. Today, while the house and its numerous outbuildings have completely disappeared, the law office, known as

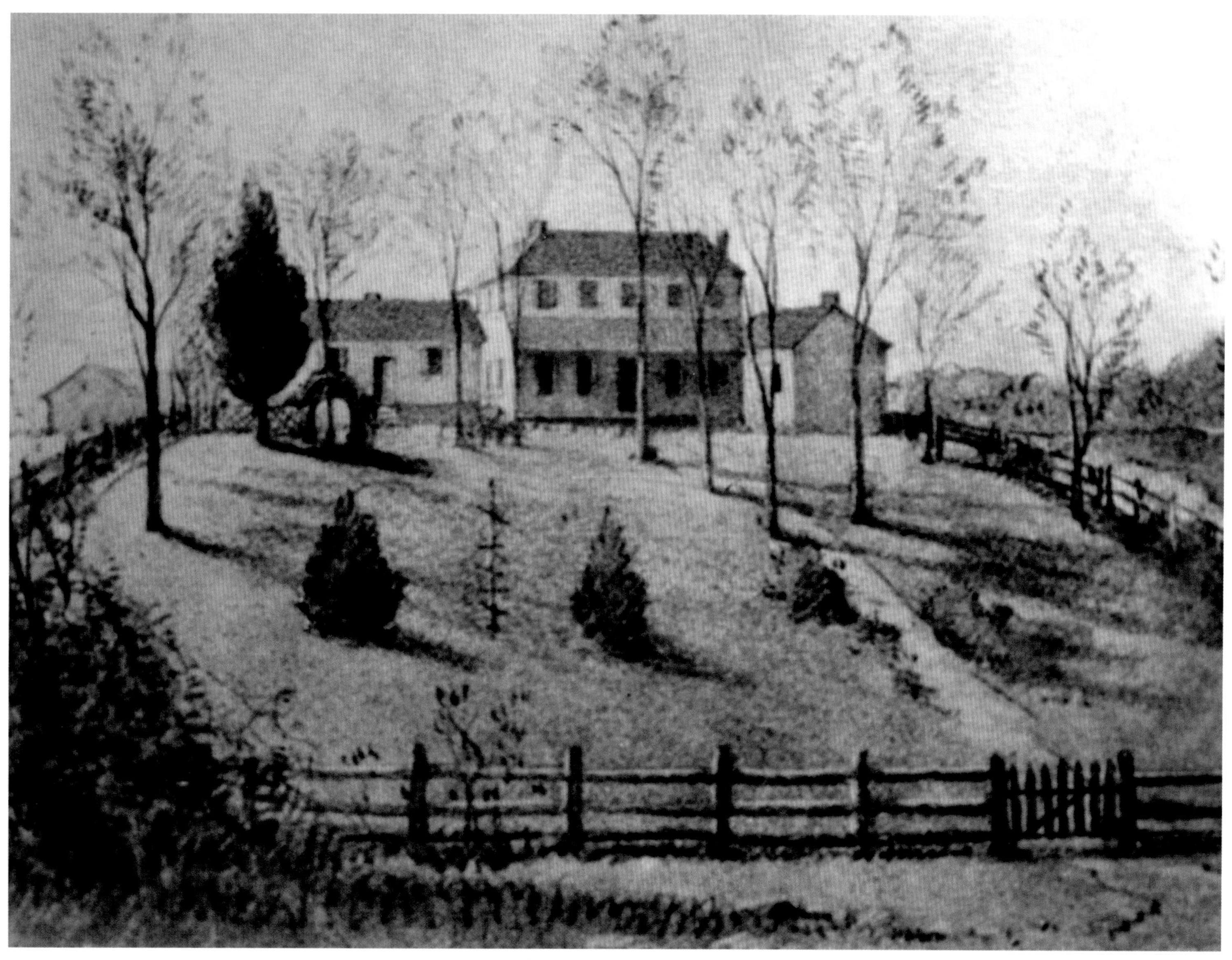

Figure 11.4 / Burwell School, pencil sketch, mid-nineteenth century, showing main house with two flanking buildings that no longer survive: a kitchen on the left and office on the right (courtesy, Historic Hillsborough Commission).

the Cameron-Nash Law Office, is still in use as a private residence (see Figure 10.7).[6] In order to make ends meet after Nash's death in 1858, his two daughters, Misses Maria Jane Nash and Sally Kollock Nash, along with their cousin, Sarah Kollock, founded and operated the school from 1858 to 1892. Sara(h) Kollock had been a student and later a teacher at the Burwell School, four blocks to the north, which likely served as the model for the Nash-Kollock School; it too was a boarding and day school for girls (or "young ladies" as they were styled), with a strong religious element.[7]

The Cameron-Nash Law Office, measuring sixteen by eighteen feet, plus a two-room addition (ca. 1839) to the west, served as an annex to the school (see Figure 10.7). It was also the residence of one of the principals, Sarah Kollock, with the two-room addition doubling as music room and classrooms, with their separate entrances.[8] Daily life at the school is recorded in lively and informative detail in *Ladies in the Making*, a book by a former student, Ann Strudwick Nash. On the book's endpapers are plans of the house and the site, indicating the layout not only of the ground-floor rooms, but also locations of the annexes and outbuildings, and other features; included are a detached kitchen, slave house, well house, cowshed, cow pasture, flagstone walks, and fields and gardens. It is worth noting here that the little one-story, frame law office itself had had an even earlier role, when it was built as a law office by Duncan Cameron, ca. 1801. It later served as a law office for Francis Nash, and the two western rooms were added in 1839 as a dormitory for the boys attending the law school he operated for "a few students."[9]

Miss Polly Burke's School (Lot 63) consisted of a one-room log schoolhouse. One of Hillsborough's earliest private schools, it was built by Dr. James Webb on East Queen Street around 1812 to provide a place for his children's elementary education.[10] Mary W. (Polly) Burke, the well-educated daughter of Gov. Thomas Burke, lived in the house next door, named Heartsease, when Dr. Webb engaged her as the teacher for his and other children in the neighborhood. She operated the school until around 1837 when she sold Heartsease and moved to Alabama. The log building is now incorporated into what is known as the Webb House, for it was a Webb residence for many years after it ceased to function as a school. Its numerous accretions added on all sides and on different levels, with varying sizes of windows and dormers added over the years, give it its present picturesque appearance. A section of the original log wall can be revealed in the present owner's living room (Figure 11.5).

The Hughes Academy, a country schoolhouse, survives in its original form, if not its original location, just to the east of the town center behind the present Orange County Board of Education building on Cameron Street (Figure 11.6).

The Hughes Academy, built in around 1862, was named for Northern Orange County educator Samuel Wellwood Hughes; it was moved to Cameron Park from its original location near Cedar Grove, about five miles north of town on the west side of N.C. State Road 86, when it was threatened with demolition in 1997. The Preservation Fund of Hillsborough sponsored its moving and restoration. A frame building about thirty feet long by sixteen feet wide, with twelve-foot ceilings, it has a massive stone center chimney that divides the interior into two rooms; three large windows provide natural lighting to each of the rooms (Figure 11.7).

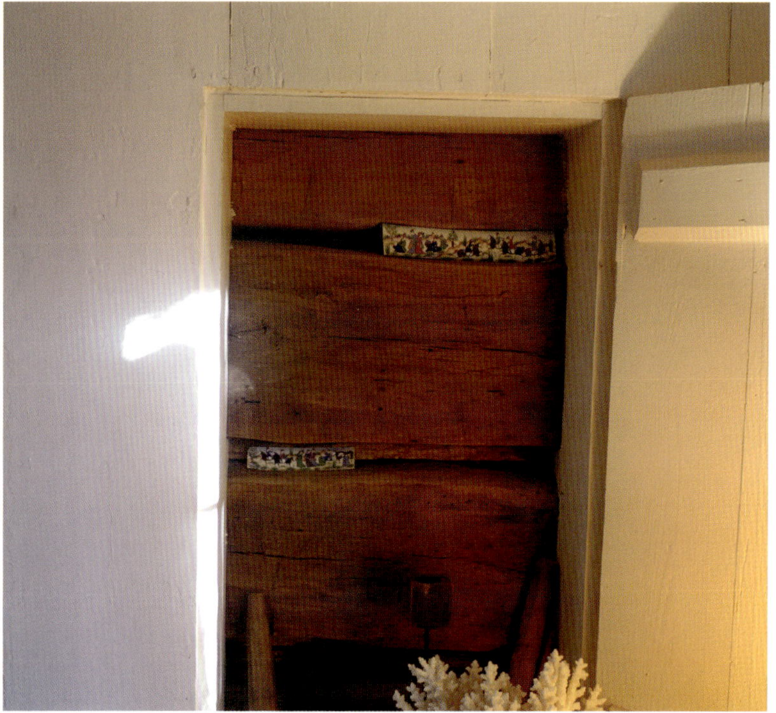

Figure 11.5 / Webb House, log wall of Miss Polly Burke's School, revealed behind paneling.

The Hughes Academy resembles countless rural one- or two-room schoolhouses that dotted the American landscape in the nineteenth and early twentieth centuries; in fact, many of them operated well into the twentieth. Some have been repurposed, but most have disappeared.[11]

The custom of operating schools in individual residences in Hillsborough is also well attested.[12] John Witherspoon's Private Boarding School (1825–39, or later) was located in Twin Chimneys, a downtown residence on King Street; it received up to twenty-two pupils.[13] The boarding school at Lochiel, an estate to the west of town, was called Anderson's Female Boarding School, and operated from 1830 to 1836.[14] Boys and girls also attended the school of Miss Alice Heartt and Mrs. Mary Bragg around the turn of the twentieth century in Heartsease on East Queen Street (1899).[15] The cottage at Midlawn, at the intersection of Queen and Cameron streets, was used as a schoolhouse where kindergarten was taught by Mrs. David Patterson for fifteen years starting in 1919 (Figure 11.8).[16]

The majority of Hillsborough's schools only survive in historical records: Lot 43 had a long and interesting history as the Brick Schoolhouse Lot, as revealed in county court

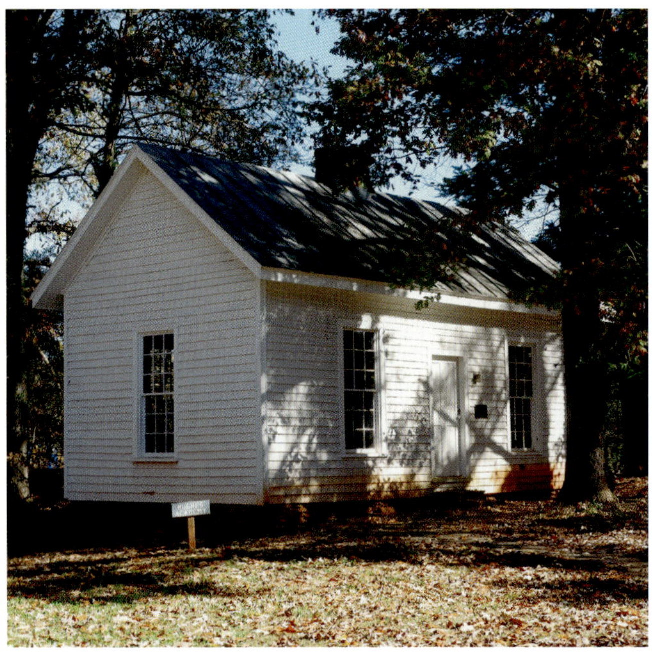

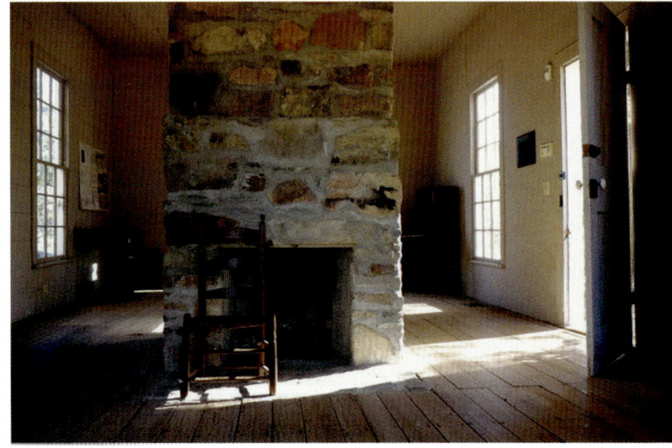

(above, top) *Figure 11.6 / Hughes Academy.*
(above, bottom) *Figure 11.7 / Hughes Academy, interior view.*

records of 1834; the building was only demolished in the 1960s.[17] The Hillsborough Female Seminary, also known as the Episcopal Seminary, was located on East Tryon Street (1825–38). It distinguished between *Ordinary* tuition classes, and tuition for the *Ornamental Branches* (music, drawing and painting, and needlework).[18] The Hillsborough Academy operated from 1801 to 1844; in 1821 a substantial two-story, four-room brick building was constructed on the hill known as Academy Hill in the northwest sector of town, near where the water tower is today. It was built to accommodate up to one hundred and fifty students. Although it initially accepted both girls and boys, it was later re-chartered as a *Classical School* or *Classical Academy,* and accepted only boys, either preparing them for the university in Chapel Hill or providing a general education in an *English Department.*

Distinguished educators were among the principals at the Hillsborough Academy, including the Rev. William Bingham and his son, William J. Bingham, who, along with his brother and sons, were highly influential in North Carolina education, starting in 1812.[19] Courses were in Latin, Greek, English, geography, mathematics, reading, writing, and bookkeeping, and later, French and moral philosophy.[20] The family members directed Bingham Schools at a number of locations in and around Hillsborough in the second quarter of the nineteenth century.

For a time (1845–59) the Caldwell Academy, an elite academy for boys, had occupied the old Hillsborough Academy building; it enrolled one hundred students in 1848.[21] From 1852 to 1890 it occupied Lots 147–51 as the Caldwell Academy, or Caldwell Institute. Another elite school, the Hillsborough Military Academy, chose as its location a site on the North Carolina Railroad west of town, at a spot known for its healthful climate. It operated between 1859 and 1868, and drew its cadets from most of the Southern states. Although the huge castle-like school building was demolished, the Commandant's House, built in the same neo-Gothic style, still survives on Barracks Road in West Hillsborough.[22]

Public education was established in North Carolina in 1839 and

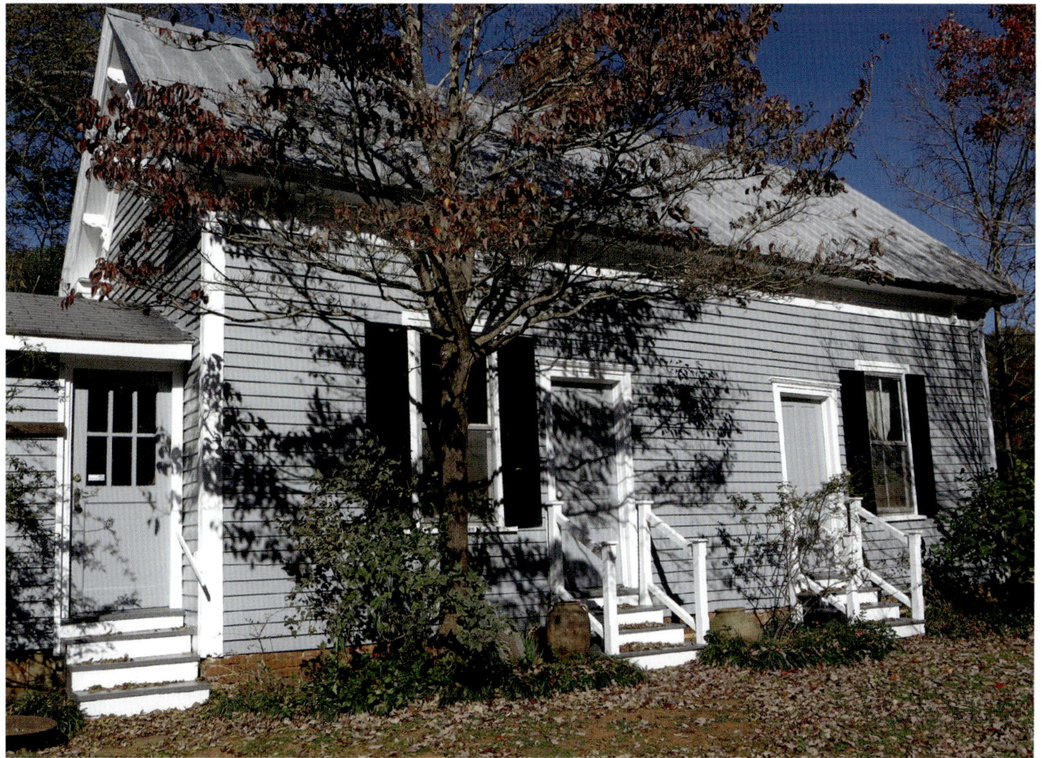

Figure 11.8 / Midlawn Cottage, once used as a schoolhouse.

overlapped with the operation of some of the schools mentioned above. An important forerunner of Hillsborough public schools was the Sunday School, later referred to as the Session House, on the corner of Churton and Tryon streets, built in 1836. This was a free school for poor children whose work on the surrounding farms left them only with Sundays to attend school. Dr. James Webb was behind the building of this one-room Sunday School building, which measured twenty by thirty feet, and had a bell tower; the bell was rung to signal the beginning of each Sunday's school day. Dr. Webb enlisted the subscriptions of nine townspeople to join with his own to finance its construction.[23] The building was later used as the town library. The movement to organize Sunday Schools started in North Carolina around 1820. Slaves were not among the students at the Sunday Schools, but were educated at the discretion of their owners until the end of the Civil War.[24]

One of the great forces behind public education in North Carolina was the educator, lawyer, and statesman, Archibald DeBow Murphey (1777–1832). This influential man left a brief and modest record of his later life in Hillsborough in a notice in the local newspaper, *The Star*:

> Study of the Law, In Hillsborough. A.D. Murph[e]y having settled himself in Hillsborough, will receive a few Law Students. Dec. 10, 1831.[25]

He died a few months later.

The surviving schools and school-related buildings in Hillsborough are the following: the Burwell School and Classroom Building; Hillsborough Military Academy (Commandant's House); Hughes Academy moved from Cedar Grove; Midlawn Cottage; Miss Polly Burke's School, now incorporated into the Webb House; Nash-Kollock School site and its annex known as the Cameron-Nash Law Office.

Twelve

Cemeteries

BY ELLEN C. WEIG AND PIP MERRICK

The town of Hillsborough has five prominent cemeteries: two that exemplify the qualities of plantation or family cemeteries (the Lockhart-Phillips Cemetery and the Kirkland Family Cemetery), two that are historic churchyard cemeteries (the Old Town Cemetery and the St. Matthew's Episcopal Church Cemetery), and the Margaret Lane Cemetery (see Maps 4 and 7). In each case, they are referred to as *cemeteries,* although it will be clear that some of them began as simple burial grounds or family graveyards.[1] All five cemeteries are registered as part of the Hillsborough Historic District Additional Documentation for the National Register of Historic Places.[2] However, our knowledge and understanding of them are incomplete because of the scarcity and loss of colonial and post-colonial records, and the weathering, absence, and removal of old gravestones.

An Act of the North Carolina General Assembly (1715) ensured:

> That every Planter, Owner, Attorney or Overseer of every settled plantation . . . shall be set apart a Burial Place & fence the same for the Interring of all such Christian Persons whether Bond or Free that shall die on their Plantation.[3]

Public records in North Carolina were sketchy, at best, due to inconsistent record-keeping and the fact that people were dispersed around the countryside.[4] In fact, colonial Gov. William Tryon had documented that there was "no regular register of . . . burials . . . kept in any county in the province" in 1767.[5] There are no extant colonial burial records in Hillsborough.

Early-eighteenth-century family burials were commonly at home in enclosed graveyards. As missionaries of various denominations began establishing meetinghouses and churches throughout Orange County, rural churchyards and more organized burial grounds developed with loosely organized rows of graves rather than family clusters.[6] In contrast, Hillsborough presented a landscape of family homes and a town-centered society of educated and culturally minded merchants, physicians, lawyers, and statesmen, and therefore invited a more sophisticated approach to creating cemeteries. The town's cemeteries developed accordingly and were organized in family clusters.

Cemeteries were generally located on higher ground than the surrounding land and were enclosed either by stone or handmade brick walls, or wood and later gated-iron fencing. Both the location and the enclosure addressed health concerns. Colonial laws underscored the necessity of securing cemeteries from pigs and wandering animals. Siting cemeteries on high ground reduced the risk of flooding, which could raise buried bodies to the surface.

Fencing later served as a way to establish family clusters and create places where family members could visit the dead and embellish gravesites with plantings. In 1855, Mrs. Margaret Anna Burwell, head of the Burwell Academy for Young Ladies and wife of the Presbyterian pastor, walked from her home at Union and Churton streets to visit several graves at the Old Town Cemetery. She wrote in her diary, "went to the graveyard & planted some violets on Lizzie Coit's grave, on Mr. Heartt's, on our own dear little baby's & Dr. Witherspoon's—planted a willow in the corner near Mary's baby's grave."[7]

Another significant consideration was the pattern of burial alignment in cemeteries. Customarily, Christian burials face west to east, with the head lying to the west and the feet to the east; similarly, it was a convention in church architecture to align the portal at the west end of the building and the altar and sanctuary to the east. Traditional Christian explanations for this vary, but usually suggest that if the dead face east, they will witness the Second Coming of Christ. Hillsborough cemeteries generally reflect this burial pattern with headstones at the west end of gravesites. Some graves have small footstones that help to configure the grave and give it the appearance of a bed from which to rise.

Changing headstone and monument styles were reflected by the use of fieldstone, slate, sandstone, marble, or granite for grave markers. This variety can be seen in the Old Town Cemetery and St. Matthew's Churchyard. As cemetery landscapes moved more toward park-like settings during the mid-nineteenth-century rural garden cemetery movement, marble and granite stones with ornate or decorative elements and extensive engravings became the choice for memorializing loved ones. Graves of soldiers were often memorialized; this was particularly true of Confederate soldiers' graves, which are identified with *CSA* (Confederate States of America) engraved on small, square footstones. There are also unmarked graves in all the cemeteries.

Visitors may notice uneven terrain in cemeteries. Commonly, old graves have a sunken appearance as wooden coffins deteriorate and the ground subsides accordingly.

Individual sketches of each cemetery offer a sense of their unique and personal character and an understanding of the strength of family ties in Hillsborough. Many families today have a spiritual investment in Hillsborough's historic cemeteries and know that they invite us to carry on traditions, invoke memories, and create the bridge between past and present.

The Lockhart-Phillips Cemetery (ca. 1792) on East Tryon Street

By Ellen C. Weig

The casual passerby might easily miss the simple family cemetery on a rise on the north side of East Tryon Street, midway between Churton and Cameron streets. While unassuming, this cemetery offers visitors a look back to the early days of Hillsborough and two families who were significant in the early history of a Piedmont town in central North Carolina. Nineteen members and descendants of the Lockhart and Phillips families were laid to rest here. The name plaque, nestled behind red-berried nandina bushes, identifies the cemetery and dates it to 1792. The cemetery measures forty-two feet square, and five stone steps lead up to a narrow entrance (Figure 12.1).

The wall was originally constructed as a *dressed-dry* wall of roughly stacked fieldstone.[8] Only a few remaining ledgers (low, horizontal, rectangular slabs) and upright stones mark the gravesites, while other markers simply lean against the stone wall (Figure 12.2).[9]

In the 1960s, the cemetery was significantly restored and extensively researched. Hugh Conway Browning, a Lockhart descendant and local Orange County historian, identified family members buried there and wrote a beautiful history of the cemetery for the *Hillsborough Historical Society Newsletter.*[10]

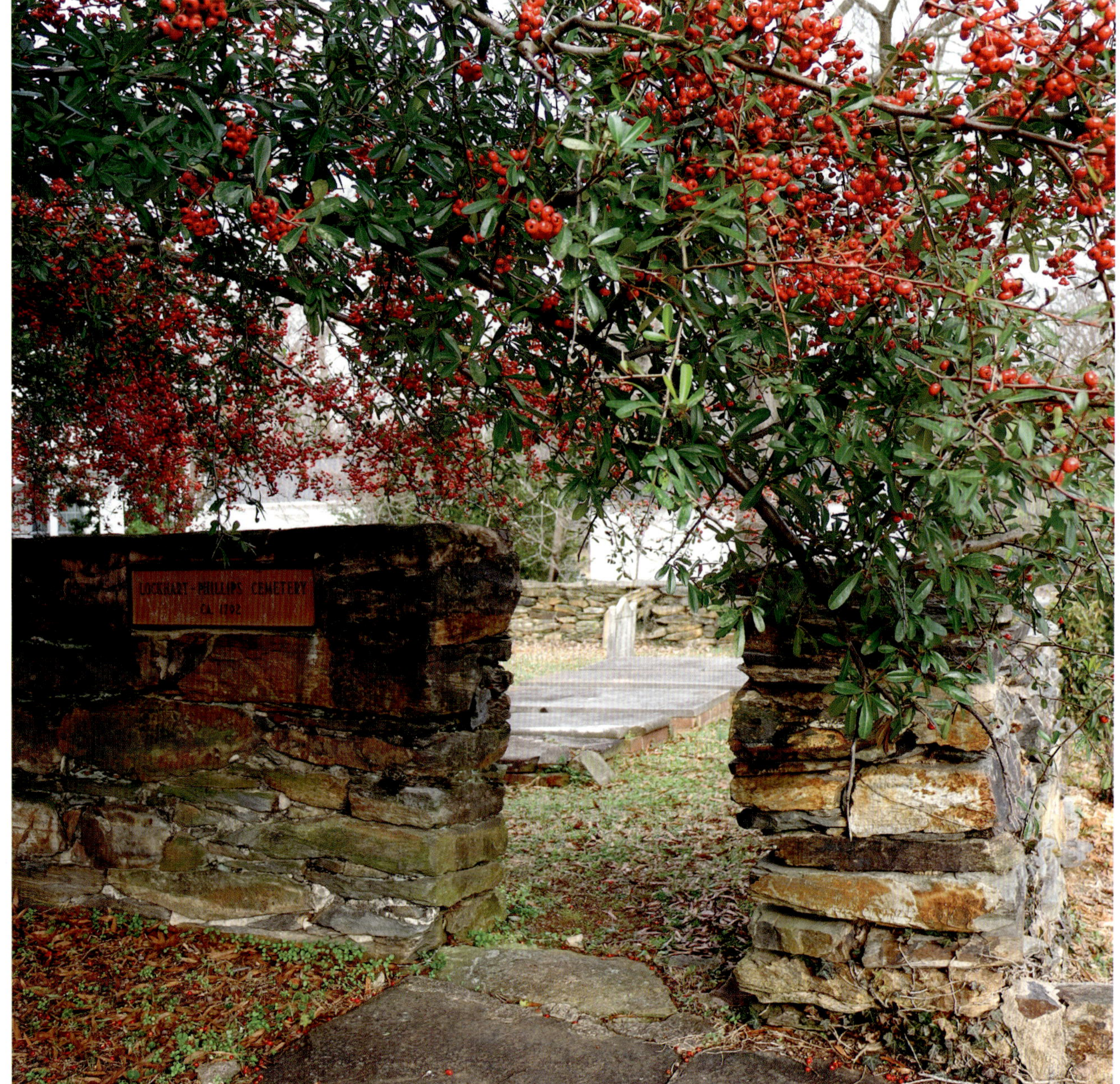

Figure 12.1 / Entrance to Lockhart-Phillips Cemetery.

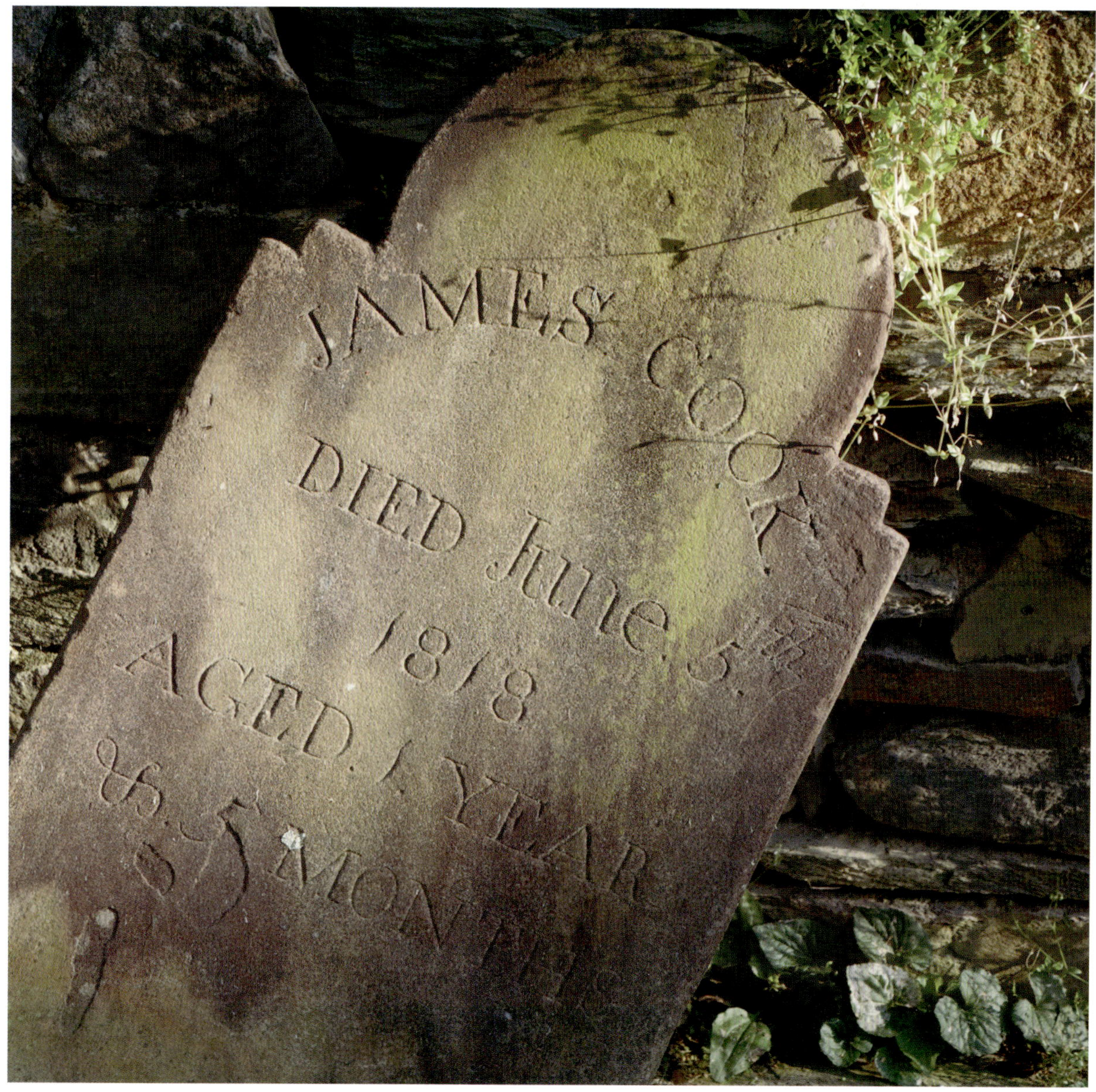

Figure 12.2 / Lockhart-Phillips Cemetery headstone.

As the colonial era faded and Hillsborough began to emerge as a center of politics, commerce, law, and literacy, Samuel Lockhart's widow, Catherine Lockhart, and her children, and James Phillips, who married one of Catherine's granddaughters, were part of town society and two new churches. Between the location of the colonial St. Matthew's Parish church (ca. 1768–69) and the present 1825 site of St. Matthew's Episcopal Church, there were several old eighteenth-century roads. The Sauthier Map of Hillsborough (1768) shows a view of this portion of town (see Map 2). Roads from the north and east merged on the way into town, heading west toward the lot designated for the church. Dowell's Ordinary, a place for lodgers and travelers, and a barn stood where some of the roads merged, near a high point midway down East Tryon Street.[11] By the end of the 1700s the ordinary no longer existed and the land belonged to the Lockhart family. As the high spot on the property, it naturally became a place for family burials.

Across from the area marked *A* (the location of the town's church and churchyard), the Sauthier map indicates several buildings—a house and barn with extensive gardens (Lot 99). Catherine Barrett Bennett Lockhart (1727–92), originally from Virginia, had purchased this lot in 1766, the same year that an Act of the North Carolina Assembly designated the land for the church. Catherine lived on this property with her son, William, and five daughters until her death. When she died, she left to "my dearly beloved son William Lockhart the dwelling House square and Lot whereon I now Live in possession of with every other part and partanent [permanent] there unto belongings."[12] Catherine was buried on the rise behind her home, thus initiating the use of the land as a family cemetery. Browning wrote in his history of the cemetery that Catherine's son, William, purchased the two lots (Lots 100 and 101) east of the Lockhart property in 1798 but also commented that the two lots were acquired earlier. It would be logical to assume that because Catherine was buried there in 1792, the graveyard location (the southeast corner of Lot 101) was part of that earlier acquisition.

Marriage united the Lockharts with another old Hillsborough family. James Phillips was a prosperous saddler in Hillsborough in the late 1700s. As an elder, he helped to organize the Presbyterian church on the site of the old Anglican church in 1815 and, later, left the church to sponsor a small O'Kelly's Chapel.[13] That chapel, which has not survived, was built on Lot 103 on East Tryon Street, east of the location of the Lockhart family graveyard on Lot 101. When Phillips courted and married Catherine's granddaughter, Nancy, in February 1797,[14] he purchased the two eastern Hillsborough lots adjoining the Lockhart land (Lots 102 and 103) as a home for his bride.[15] The Lockharts' cemetery bordered the Phillips property. In 1885 it is referred to as the "grave yard lot" and as the "Phillips Grave yard" in the sale of Lot 101,[16] probably because of its proximity to their home.

Hugh Conway Browning put the date of Catherine Lockhart's death as 1792, and identified the cemetery accordingly. He also recorded that James Phillips built the stone wall, somewhat higher than it is now, to surround a square graveyard about 1820. There are seventeen visible graves—nine of them are marked, including five with sandstone slabs. Browning tentatively identified an additional five unmarked graves along the west wall of the cemetery as belonging to Lockhart family members, and wrote that the center area contains the graves of children. As younger Lockhart and Phillips generations married into other families—Lewellings, Fullers, and Adams—they were returned to the family graveyard for burial.

In 1966, the cemetery wall was lovingly restored by Browning; the weedy turf was replaced with grass, and the bronze plaque was put into place. Today the cemetery remains under the watch of family descendants and bears a new memorial, placed in 2014 as a family Christmas present: *Lockhart/Dedicated by the family of Clara Frances Lockhart*.[17]

The Kirkland Family Cemetery at Ayr Mount (ca. 1815)

By Ellen C. Weig

On the grounds of Ayr Mount, less than a mile east of the Hillsborough town line, on St. Mary's Road is a family plantation cemetery. William Kirkland (1768–1836), a Scotland-born merchant, and his wife, Margaret Blair Scott (1773–1839), established their homestead in the early 1800s along the Old Indian Trading Path, then a colonial road from Petersburg, Virginia, to the Georgia border. Generations of the Kirkland family lived there until the last direct Kirkland descendant sold the property in 1985. Approaching the house, the cemetery is to the right, on the west side of the stately brick plantation house. Family members could look out the window and see the graves from the house (Figure 12.3).

The cemetery, measuring fifty by eighty feet, is enclosed now by a low, cemented stone wall with iron fencing and a gate with the Kirkland name; there are both marked graves and unmarked graves. Large, table-top ledgers mark four graves, including those of William and Margaret. William's is known to have been installed by Samuel Hancock, "the brickmason in Hillsborough, [who] walled the grave and laid the tombstone, a marble slab, ordered from

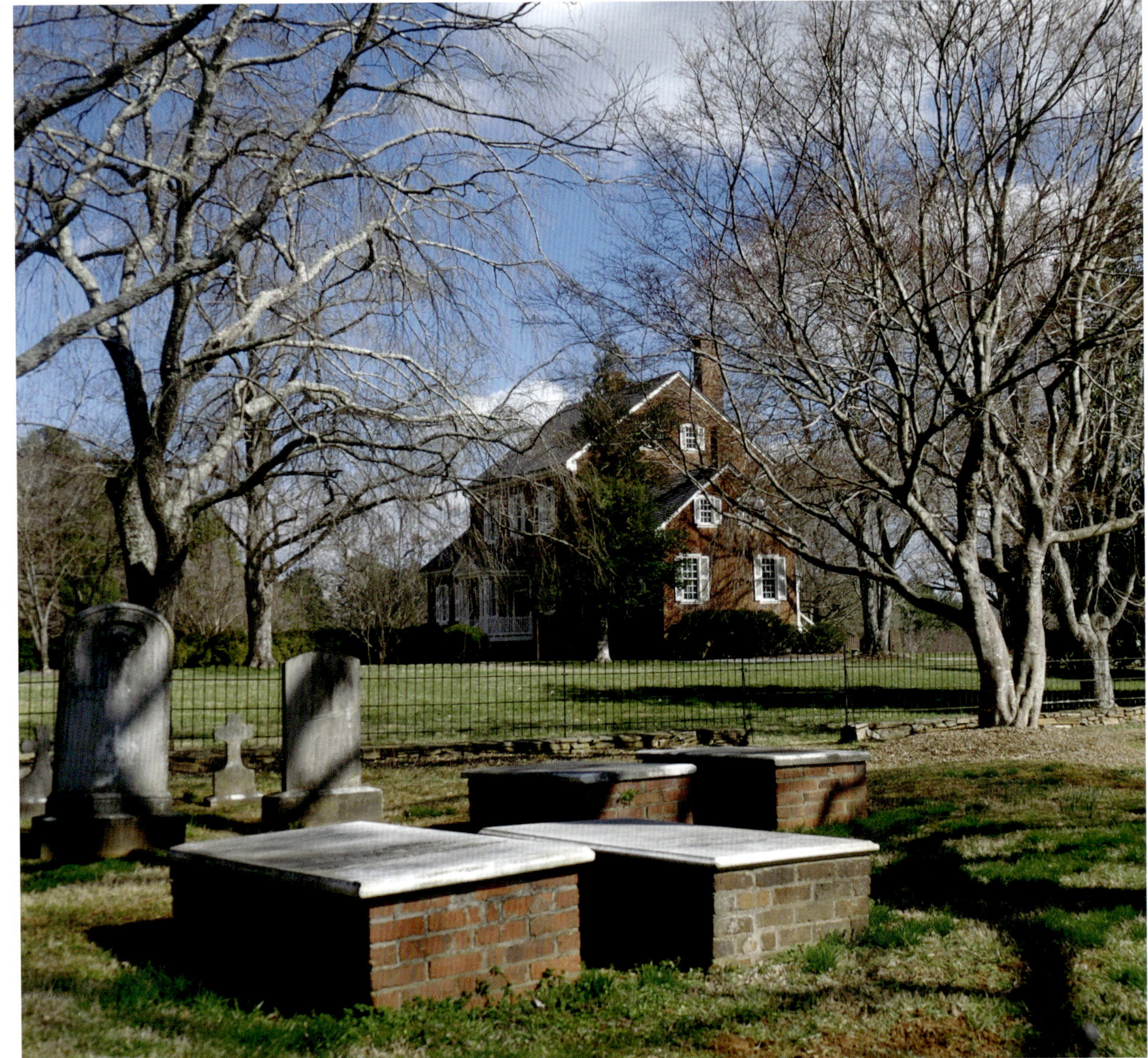

Figure 12.3 / Kirkland Family Cemetery at Ayr Mount, with ledgers marking Kirkland graves.

Petersburg."[18] Four of the Kirklands' sons are buried in unmarked graves in the cemetery. A daughter, Elizabeth M. McNeill (1796–1822), has one of the most elaborate stones, described as an "elaborate Baroque headstone,"[19] while the gravesite of their granddaughter Margaret "Maggie" McLester (1842–1921) is marked only by a rough fieldstone.

Jean Anderson, in *The Kirklands of Ayr Mount,* explains the reasons for Maggie's poverty over the course of her life. Maggie was only two when her mother Phoebe Bingham Kirkland McLester (1811–44) died; Phoebe's sister, Mary, raised Maggie. When Nelson McLester, Maggie's father, died not long afterwards in 1850, his inheritance was left to Maggie with a request that she remain under the care of the Kirkland family. Maggie's finances were strictly managed by neighbor and state Supreme Court Chief Justice Thomas Ruffin. Her board and living expenses, education at Burwell School, and spending money all came out of her inheritance.[20] By the end of the Civil War, Maggie was left in poverty.[21] She never married, but spent her life caring for younger members of the Kirkland family and, in her later life, working as a housekeeper at the Nash-Kollock School.[22] When she died, there was no money for an elaborate stone to mark her grave.

Throughout the rest of the cemetery, other graves are marked by upright markers. Most are illegible and worn by time. Nature has changed the trees shading the gravesites, and although the house's historic magnolias, hollies, oaks, and a craggy old hackberry tree stand nearby, some landscape features have been lost. The Kirkland Family Cemetery Census online describes two deodar cedars, a flower-bordered path that led to the entrance gate, and a four-foot-wide walk. Additionally forsythia and rose bushes once grew inside the cemetery fence.[23] Mary Claire Engstrom's photographic collections include a series of twenty-six images of the cemetery taken in 1974 that provide a nostalgic perspective of the cemetery.[24]

St. Matthew's Episcopal Church Cemetery

By Ellen C. Weig

By 1826 families from Hillsborough's colonial Anglican church had re-organized as an Episcopal church and established a new church building at the end of East Tryon Street, on St. Mary's Road, and with it, a cemetery. The earliest known burial there is that of Maria Octavia Jones in 1834. Her grave is marked with a ledger and engraving that has been worn away by time and weather. Shortly after that, in 1838, the Rev. William Mercer Green was granted permission by the church vestry to relocate the body of his infant son to the churchyard, thus helping to establish the area to the east of the church as a burial ground.[25] Marble plaques in the east wall of the church memorialize Sarah Green, the Rev. Green's first wife, and three of their children who were also buried in the early churchyard (Figure 12.4).

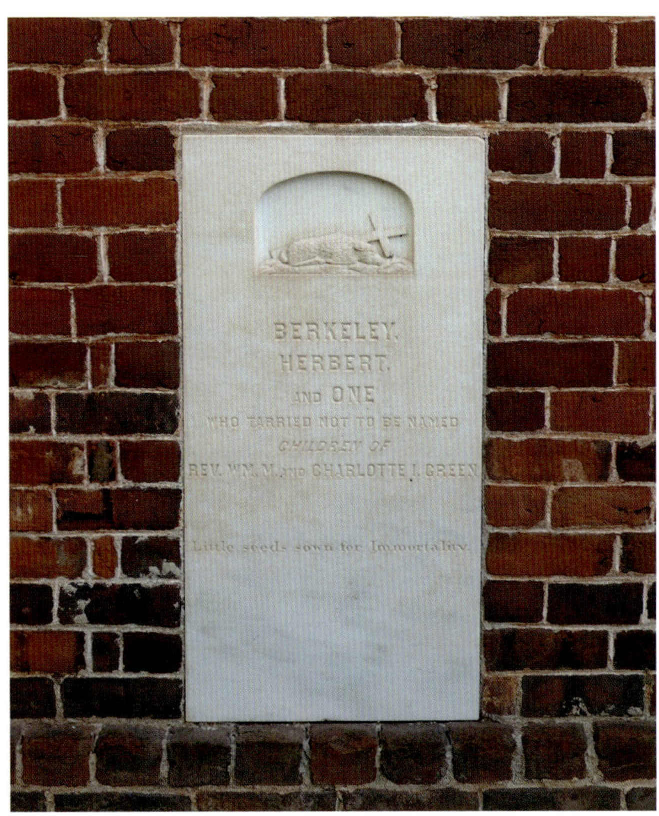

Figure 12.4 / Marble plaque, St. Matthew's Episcopal Church Cemetery, memorializing children of the Rev. William Mercer Green.

Years later, in 1854, North Carolina Chief Justice Thomas Ruffin deeded to St. Matthew's the one and a third acres that included the parcel of land on which the church building had been located, as well as the space for a cemetery (Figure 12.5).[26] The church agreed to his request that its cemetery be enclosed with a stone wall along the road, with wooden fencing to the side and rear.[27] The remains of this stone wall can barely be seen on the bank covered with vegetation along St. Mary's Road. In the cemetery, visitors can find a sundial that marks the northeast corner of this first cemetery tract. Ruffin's gift meant there was properly designated space in the churchyard for parish family burials, beginning with his own. The churchyard continued to develop as other families established their own burial lots. Cameron, Cain, Webb, Kirkland, Graham, Hill, and Roulhac are names seen in family clusters and throughout the cemetery as families grew and married. Paul Carrington Cameron, Ruffin's son-in-law, and family descendants became instrumental in the growth of the churchyard. When Cameron died in 1891, an additional half acre was added to the east of the cemetery. More land was added in the first half of the twentieth century with gifts from the Cameron family in 1909, 1934, 1950, and finally, in 1951, by Rebecca B. Wall.[28]

A significant feature of the cemetery is the landscaping (Figures 12.6 and 12.7). Phyllis Roberson Hoots wrote, "A cemetery itself is a symbol of the civilization which created it." In her article "Cemeteries as Outdoor Museums," she added, "Every aspect of . . . cemetery reflects the culture that created it: its vegetation, grave markers, ornamentation, and boundaries (fences, walls, trees), even its orientation."[29] The significance of the changes in the cultural understanding of nineteenth-century cemeteries, from colonial family graveyards to simple rural burial grounds, to the more

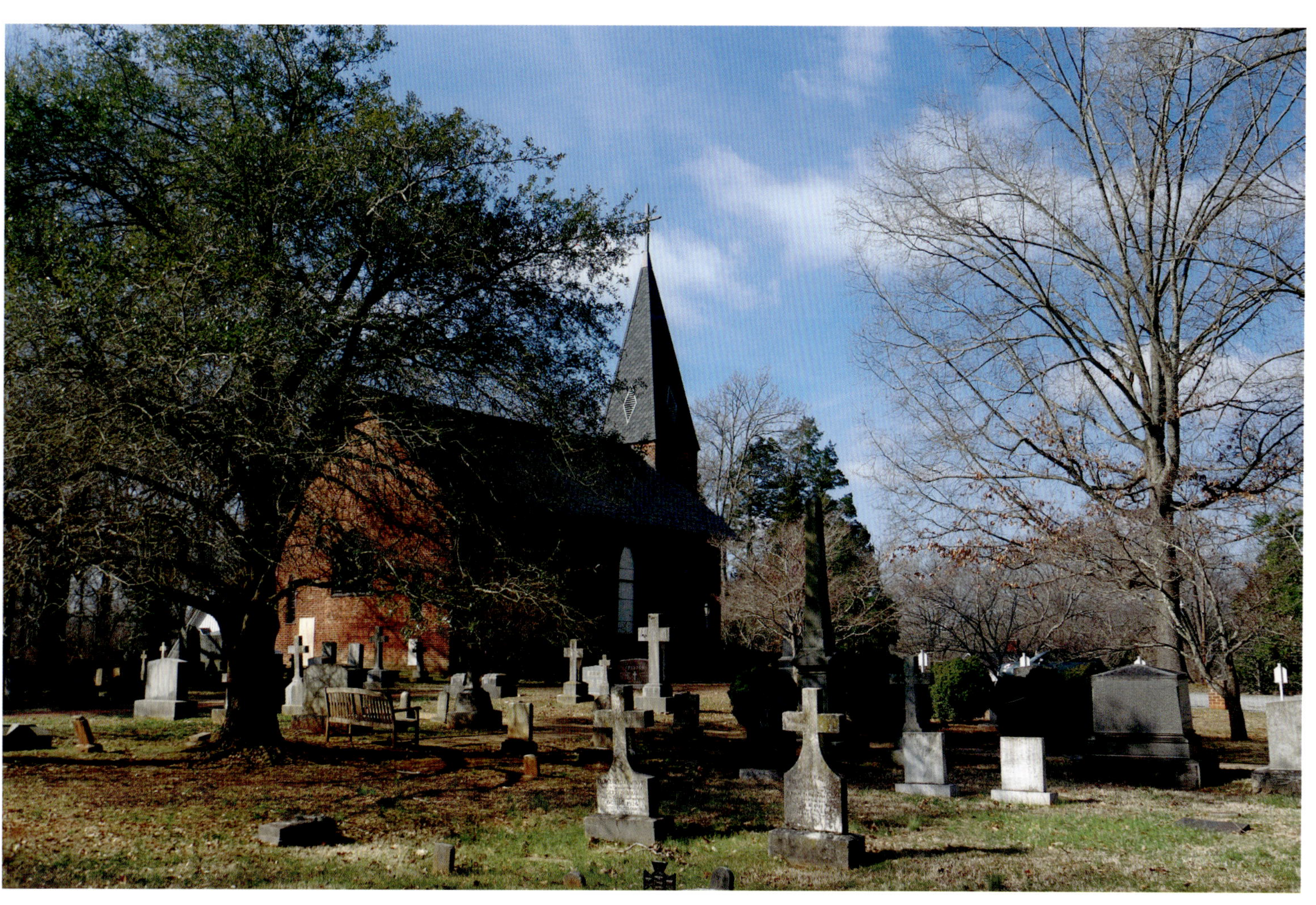

Figure 12.5 / View of St. Matthew's cemetery from the northeast.

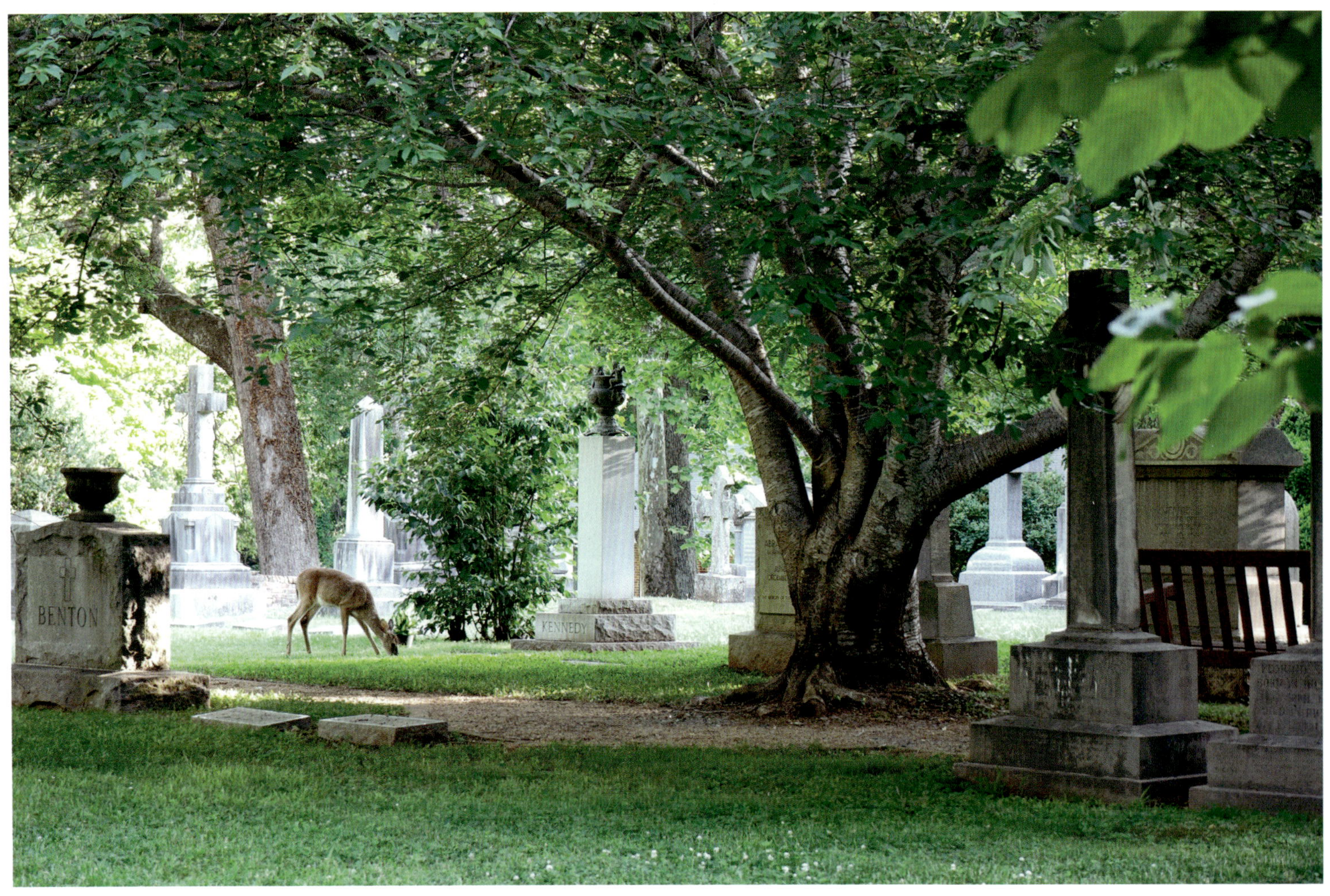

Figure 12.6 / St. Matthew's cemetery.

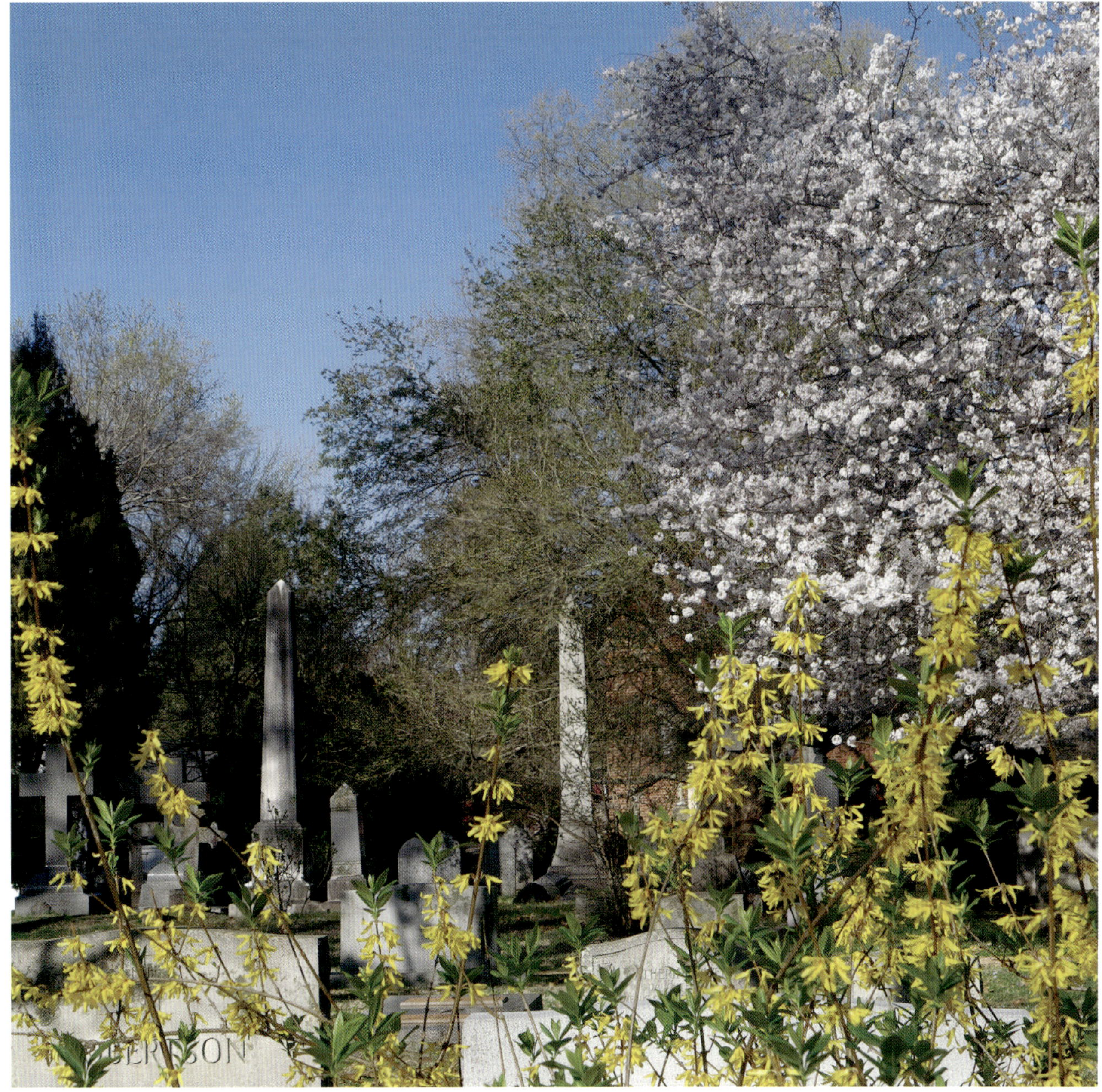

Figure 12.7 / St. Matthew's cemetery, showing garden-like setting.

garden-like cemeteries, is evident in the work of four St. Matthew's families and neighbors of the church: the Ruffins, Camerons, Grahams, and Webbs. Four men in particular shared a friendship and common passion for landscaping and the culture of plantation gardening.[30] Paul Carrington Cameron (1808–91) and his wife, Anne Ruffin (1814–97), daughter of Chief Justice Thomas and Anne Ruffin, lived at Burnside, next door to the church. The Camerons' gardens were filled with plants, trees, and shrub specimens, tended by the English gardener, Thomas Adams.[31] The Camerons' grand arboretum, Cameron Park, once extended into what is now part of the cemetery and church grounds. Their close neighbor to the east at Montrose, William A. Graham (1804–75) was the second of the four men. In *Gardens of Old Hillsborough,* by Mrs. Charles (Helen) Blake, it is noted that the Grahams developed the gardens at Montrose in 1852 with the aid of the University of North Carolina's gardener, Thomas Paxton, who reportedly was related to the famous English gardener and designer of the Crystal Palace in London.[32] The Graham family is prominent in St. Matthew's cemetery. One portion of the cemetery in the southwest corner, known as the Cameron Exception, is the resting place of members of the Cameron and Graham families.[33] An iron fence once enclosed a fifty by fifty foot area known as Cameron Square.[34] The square is also noted on the cemetery survey based on the survey work of J. Watts Copley.[35]

The return of the Rev. Moses Ashley Curtis (1808–72), church rector and an internationally known botanist, to St. Matthew's in 1857 after a ten-year absence, completed a setting in which the transition from a simple country churchyard set aside for family burials to the establishment of a garden cemetery could occur.[36] Curtis's expeditions into the western North Carolina mountains provided him with the opportunity to collect native specimens. Additionally, the Rev. Joseph Blount Cheshire (1814–99), the rector of Calvary Church in Tarboro, North Carolina, and himself a botanist, was a close friend of Curtis. He had two sisters married and living in Hillsborough: Sarah Frances Cheshire, wife of James Webb, who lived at Over the River, and Elizabeth, wife of Duncan McNair who lived at Highlands, across the road from Sarah. Cheshire often visited them in Hillsborough and brought plants, trees, and shrubs for Curtis. In *Gardens of Old Hillsborough,* Mrs. Blake writes:

> Dr. Cheshire . . . procured plants from all over North Carolina, and requested missionaries in many foreign parts to send him plants. . . . Some he planted . . . in the yard of St. Matthew's church, notably the Western Arborvitaes, and weeping cedars, which he grafted on native cedar stumps.[37]

(Curtis must have shared them with Cameron for his arboretum since several of the Chinese firs [*Cunninghamia*] are still seen on church grounds near the cemetery.) It is generally acknowledged that Cheshire was instrumental in the design of St. Matthew's cemetery. Many of the old trees are gone, as is fencing around family lots. Scattered through the cemetery one can find some of the old cedars and English boxwood, as well as some American varieties of boxwood planted in the 1960s to designate the corners of a family cluster.[38] Some of the oldest trees are the red oaks, tulip poplars, and black walnuts, which are the most valuable.[39]

Throughout the family clusters in the cemetery, the graves are marked with headstones that exemplify the stylistic development and classic ornamentation of memorial stones that reflect generations of family burials. There are graves marked by the flat ledger stones over simple stone or brick foundations. Strikingly beautiful are the family crests for the Mayo and Cameron families engraved into two later Cameron ledgers.[40] Many graves have more elaborate upright and obelisk designs, integrating enlarged crosses, urns, scrolls, floral and ivy embellishments, elaborate memorial writings, or tender memorabilia for children. At least one grave has a stone by Thomas and Miller, prominent Massachusetts manufacturers and designers of monuments made of Quincy granite.[41] For the casual observer, however, family clusters may be difficult to distinguish since families honored each other by naming children after parents and past generations, and because they married into other local families. As important as the graves of clergy, statesmen, and Hillsborough's prominent businessmen are the graves of the women, many of whom worked diligently for their husbands, their church, and their country.[42] Anne Ruffin Cameron served as the president of the Churchyard Society in the late nineteenth century. A number of the well-educated daughters of St. Matthew's families attended Hillsborough's schools, including the Hillsborough Female Academy, the Burwell School, and the Nash-Kollock School, and eventually were buried at St. Matthew's.[43]

Near the eastern edge of the cemetery is an open area. Three Confederate soldiers who died far from home are buried there and recorded in the St. Matthew's Parish register.[44] No other graves appear in this section of the cemetery along the eastern wall, although no formal written record offers an explanation. The burial sites of local Confederate soldiers, with additional small footstones marked *CSA,* are scattered among the family lots. One of the cemetery's most beautiful trees[45] spreads long branches over the grave of Willie Hardee, the sixteen-year-old son of Col. William and Elizabeth Hardee, who was mortally wounded in March 1865 at the Battle of Bentonville, the last full-scale battle of the Civil War in the South.[46]

The brick walls that encompass the cemetery were constructed at different times following the donations of land. They have been repaired numerous times, and sections have been rebuilt. While there were once interior brick- and stone-walled plots with iron railings, they are gone now and the cemetery is an open space. There are some brick paths, but the Rev. Brooks Graebner relates that the paths are "the product of our work in the early 2000s" and that they "[mostly] follow the lines of previously demarcated paths."[47]

Old Town Cemetery

By Pip Merrick

Since colonial times, the Old Town Cemetery at the corner of Churton and West Tryon streets (Lot 98) has held an important place in Hillsborough history. The church site and original public graveyard (which predates the building of the Anglican church) were set aside by an Act of the North Carolina General Assembly in 1758. The Sauthier Map of Hillsborough 1768 delineates the graveyard and possibly indicates the potential church site with a large *A*.[48] Sometime after that, the Anglican church was built; it was the meeting place of the North Carolina Constitutional Convention of 1788.[49] The original Anglican church deteriorated over time, and in 1816 the current Presbyterian church was built on this site.

The oldest part of the graveyard is on the north and west sides of Strudwick Hall, a northern extension of the Hillsborough Presbyterian Church. The graveyard was public, and although the original records are missing, by 1758 it was considered the burial place for the townspeople. Currently, this area contains only a few of the original markers, but was once filled with graves, some on top of one another. This was discovered during the building of Strudwick Hall, adjacent to the church, in 1948. Other early graves are tucked between the church and the Orange County Historical Museum. Many graves in this area date from the period of the Civil War. Missing from this colonial graveyard is a flagstone walk, uncovered in 1962 by the Hillsborough Historical Society. It bisected the lot leading from the iron gate on Churton Street to the row of large boxwood.[50]

Standing on West Tryon Street, one immediately notices among the cemetery's monuments the high granite obelisks, ledgers, and a vault facing the entrance of the Hillsborough Presbyterian Church (Figure 12.8).

The land for this part of the cemetery (Lot 97) on the west side of the boxwood path originally belonged to the Hooper family. Initially, William Hooper, a signer of the Declaration of Independence, was buried (1790) in his cultivated garden, part of an open field, known at that time as Rye Patch, a short distance east of his house on West Tryon Street and adjacent to the public cemetery. Years after he died, his gravesite was enclosed by a high brick wall, which encircled the Hooper-Norwood plot.[51] In 1846, his grandson William Hooper enlarged the cemetery. Most of the parcels of Rye Patch were sold separately over a twelve-year period for private family plots. The sale to the Richards family in 1858, extended the cemetery to its current boundary on West Tryon Street.[52] The final plot from Hooper's original garden, just outside the west wall, was purchased in the 1860s by the Turrentine family who lived on King Street.[53] Perhaps the plot was needed for the burial of three-year-old Eugene Turrentine, who died in 1866.

The variety of styles of gravestones in this cemetery shows changes in economic means, technology, and transportation, along with a shift in the perception of death. Types of grave markers evolved from the very plain slab, with inscribed name and date (e.g., *James Hogg, died 1805*) (Figure 12.9), to more elaborate marble and granite carvings. Some of the stones in this private section reflect contemporary wealth and fashion.

A focus on the brevity of life, inevitability of death, and the Resurrection evolved to include a variety of depictions taken from nature showing a sentimentality concerning death. In fact the term *graveyard* was replaced with *cemetery,* a Latin word meaning sleeping chamber.[54] Although simplicity remained the norm in the Old Town Cemetery, the new European movements in decoration influenced the choices of motifs and are also exemplified here.

The Neoclassic revival style, beginning in the late eighteenth and early nineteenth centuries, brought a new sentiment called *mourning art,* as seen in this stone marker exemplified by lilies of the valley (Figure 12.10).

In the 1820s, Neoclassical depictions of the urn (Edwin Heartt, died 1855) and the weeping willow (Elizabeth Coit, died 1852) became popular.[55] In the mid-nineteenth century the Greek Revival movement introduced the rose (Nancy C. Watson, died 1852), and the crown and wreath (Dr. Edmund Strudwick , died 1879). The Renaissance revival brought about the motif of acorns and oak leaves (Rosanna Berry, died 1860).

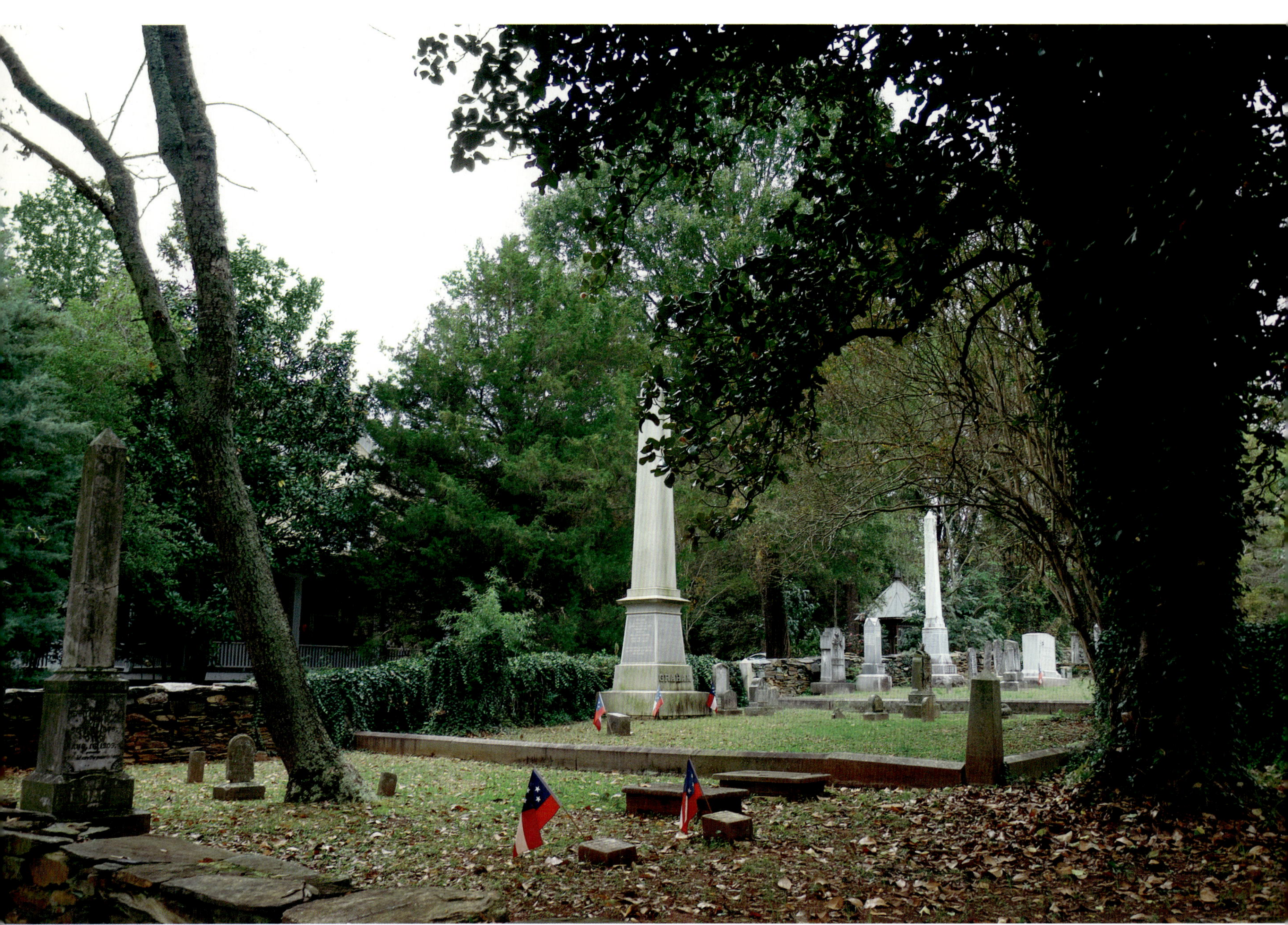

Figure 12.8 / Old Town Cemetery, showing a section of the cemetery near the west wall, which was originally on William Hooper's land.

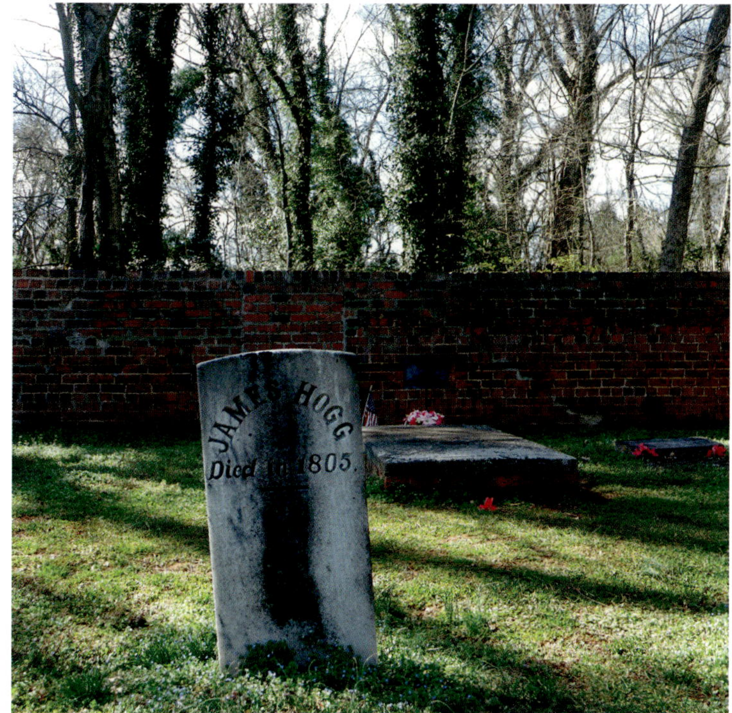

Figure 12.9 / Old Town Cemetery, grave marker of James Hogg.

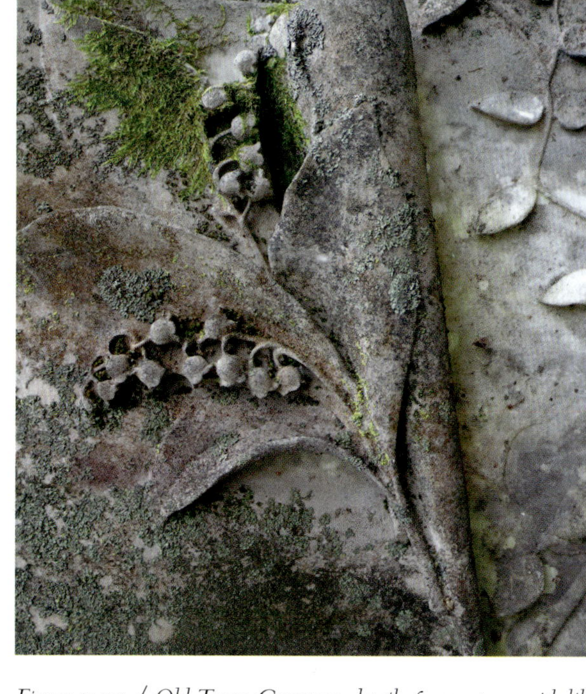

Figure 12.10 / Old Town Cemetery, detail of gravestone with lilies of the valley.

A Romantic rendition appears on the carved marble gravestone of eight-year-old Sophronia Graham, who died in 1855. A dove appears to have just landed on the stone with its wings still open; lilies of the valley, signifying humility and sweetness, are under the dove's feet and tucked into the marble scroll. A lamb rests on the footstone, carved and signed by Van Gunden and Young (Figure 12.11). Another example of Victorian Romanticism is found in the carving for the grave of Lily and Rosaline (both girls are presumed to be Strudwicks). A nosegay, with ribbon carved in high relief, appears as though purposely left by a mourner on top of the gravestone.

Perhaps the most famous gravestone is also among the oldest.[56] It belongs to William Hooper, whose grave was temporarily moved to Greensboro to commemorate North

Carolina's Signers of the Declaration of Independence. Hooper's ledger was moved at dawn on 24 April 1894 to the Guilford Courthouse National Military Park, along with an envelope of relics removed from his Hillsborough grave. This slab of William Hooper served as a temporary marker there until the funds for a permanent statue for the Signers could be raised. Shortly thereafter the ledger of William Hooper was returned to Hillsborough with the addition of six words carved in a large font: "Signer of the Declaration of Independence."[57]

The ledger gravestone was favored by wealthy and prominent citizens. Although the dimensions of the ledger allow for an extended epitaph, it is revealing that Hooper's revolutionary activities were not deemed important at the time of his death. It was later generations who attached importance to a Signer of the Declaration of Independence (Figure 12.12).[58]

A particularly iconic gravestone shows incised carving on the stone of Dr. Michael W. Holt (died 1858) which depicts a well and rope, classical building, and broken urn. It is signed by Maunder. The Raleigh stonemason firm of Maunder and Campbell was active in the early nineteenth century. Other examples of their stones can be found in the Old Chapel Hill Cemetery in Chapel Hill and in the Stoner's Church Cemetery in Alamance County, N.C.

Other signed stones came from the firms W.E. Wilson from Durham and H.J. Hege from Lexington, N.C. Stones made outside the state, and therefore more expensive, were produced in Baltimore (A. Gaddess), Philadelphia (Van Gunden and Young), and Richmond (D.C. Duncomb); stones are usually signed in the lower-right corner.

In addition to tablet-shaped stones, more expensive granite obelisks and ledgers (Jahaziel Richards, died 1851), and vaults could be purchased as grave markers. Some gravestones in the town cemetery were replaced at a later date with granite obelisks, such as that of Archibald DeBow Murphey who died in 1832. The use of Elbertine granite and ready-made monuments appeared in the 1920s in N.C.[59] Granite could be polished to a high finish that provided enough contrast to read the chiseled names and dates easily. After the advent of mechanized precision tools, the craft and individual artistry of the older marble and sandstone work were replaced with reproducible designs from pattern books. These designs have not evolved significantly from the 1930s.

The wall around the cemetery and those walls within are testimony of the ever-changing life of the graveyard from its conception to the present day. The north side of the cemetery was always enclosed by hedgerows, whereas the west side was enclosed by stone and brick walls. A dry-stack stone wall was built on the east and south sides of the cemetery, as authorized by the N.C. General Assembly in 1804.[60] The most recent addition, built around 1858, was the stone wall on West Tryon Street along the Richards' plot. These walls have been restored periodically. Much of the long dry-stone wall to the west and the nine private cemetery walls were leveled and re-laid in 1964 by the Hillsborough Historical Society.[61] It is probable that the tops of the stone walls that now contain remnants of cement were capped with top slates which was customary in England. Some of the high brick walls still retain their finishing top bricks to keep out the water and ice. Fingerprints can be found in a few of the handmade bricks that were probably made at a local brickyard.

Two openings in the west wall are of interest. Access from the Hooper garden to Hooper's grave is quite apparent having been filled in with newer brick. Another possible old opening in this wall that is now filled in with stone can be seen from inside the Berry family plot. Artifacts from an iron gate or fence—including post holes, a large glob of cement, and an old iron gate- or fence-post holder embedded in the dirt—can be seen just in front of the west wall. Looking carefully one can discern a finished slate slab at the bottom of the stone wall. The straight vertical edge of the wall stones above the slate slab may be all that marks the original opening of this gate into the cemetery.[62] A similar iron artifact is sticking out of the ground in front of Annie Brown's grave which could be the base of a former fence. John Roberts, a life-long Hillsborough resident, remembers the cemetery filled with fences and gates when he was young.

An outstanding sight in this graveyard is the double straight line of ancient looking English boxwood which separates the public cemetery from the private plots. Boxwood line the flagstone path generally known as the Students Walk,[63] which was uncovered in 1963 by members of the Hillsborough Historical Society. Students from the nearby Burwell School may have used this as the most direct walkway to the Presbyterian church. The Burwell students never saw these particular boxwoods as they were only planted in 1964 (see Figure 12.13). The Hillsborough Historical

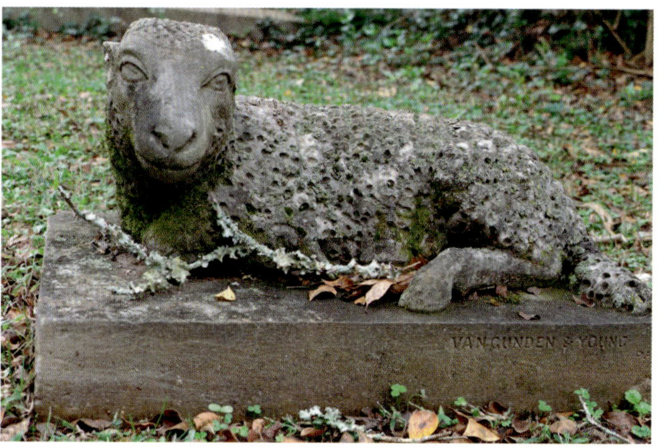

Figure 12.11 / Old Town Cemetery, carved lamb on a footstone made by Van Gunden and Young.

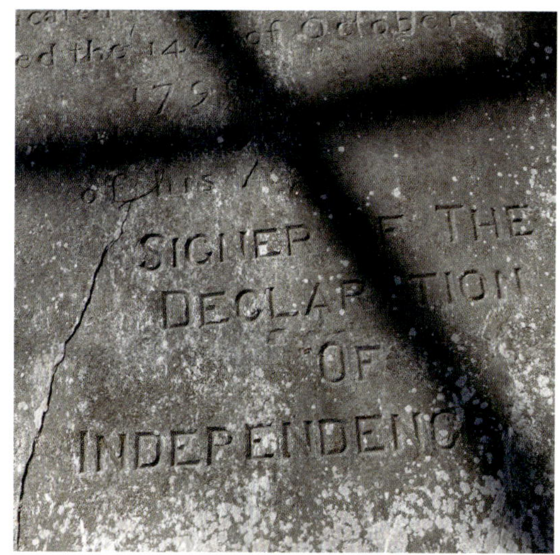

Figure 12.12 / Old Town Cemetery, gravestone of William Hooper, clearly labeled "Signer of the Declaration of Independence."

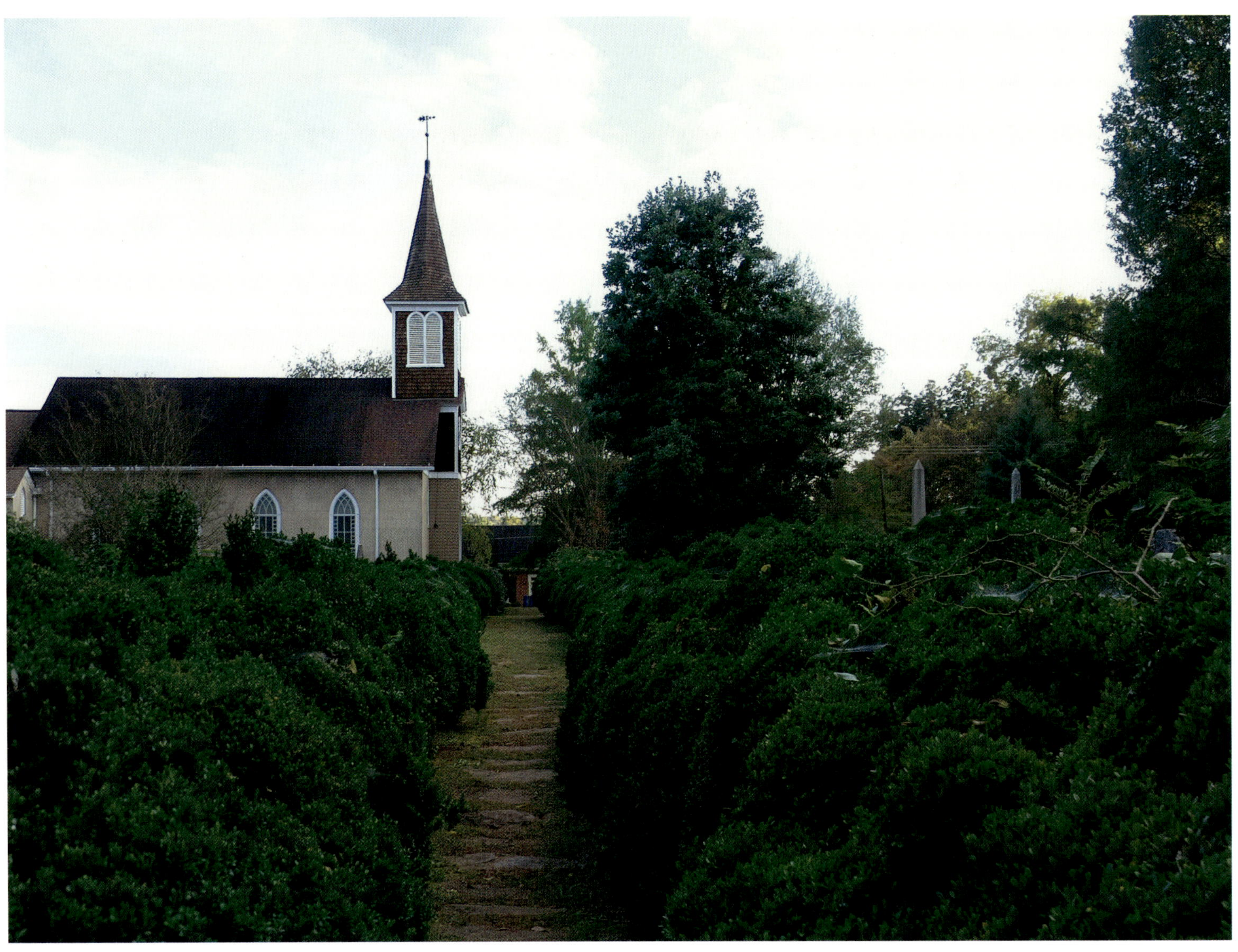

Figure 12.13 / Old Town Cemetery, Students Walk lined with old boxwood plantings.

Society was intent on encouraging the conservation of boxwood[64] and planted eighty-seven small ones in the cemetery along with four sizable ones.[65] They are reminiscent of the old colonial boxwood abundant in Hillsborough in former times. In 1964, the *Hillsborough Historical Society Journal* reported:

> In the earlier day, we have been told, people could smell the clean, spicy, pungent odor of Hillsborough boxwood some miles away when they were driving their buggies and wagons into town.[66]

Until Hurricane Fran in 1996 this graveyard was shaded by oaks and hardwoods, giving a feeling of perpetuity. Today only a few stumps remain of the trees.

Margaret Lane Cemetery

By Pip Merrick

At the top of the hill on West Margaret Lane, old oak trees shelter a peaceful park, edged by crepe myrtles. This is Margaret Lane Cemetery, bordered by Occoneechee Street, Margaret Lane, and Hillsborough Avenue South, and it comprises Town Lots 233 and 234 (Figure 12.14).

Margaret Lane Cemetery is thought to have originally been a burial ground for the slaves of neighboring landowners, as well as employees of the Ruffin tannery and members of the Faucette family. Peter B. Ruffin owned land to the north, and Cadwallader Jones the land to the west. Trustees for the cemetery were appointed in 1854 but the cemetery may have existed earlier. After the Civil War, the cemetery continued as a burial ground for blacks until it was filled to capacity by 1931.[67]

The local historian Mary Claire Engstrom wrote in 1973 that at one time the cemetery was enclosed by a traditional low stone wall on the west and north sides.[68] In later years the cemetery fell into disrepair and the surrounding stone walls were dismantled, grave markers disappeared, and weeds took over. Neighbors who lived on Hillsborough Avenue during 1950s recall piles of stones in the west and north corners of the cemetery. Currently all that remains of original enclosures is a single small wrought-iron fence and gate in the southwest corner.

After an ownership dispute was settled in 1987, a rededication of the cemetery took place under the Rev. William P. Price, former rector of St. Matthew's Episcopal Church, and a

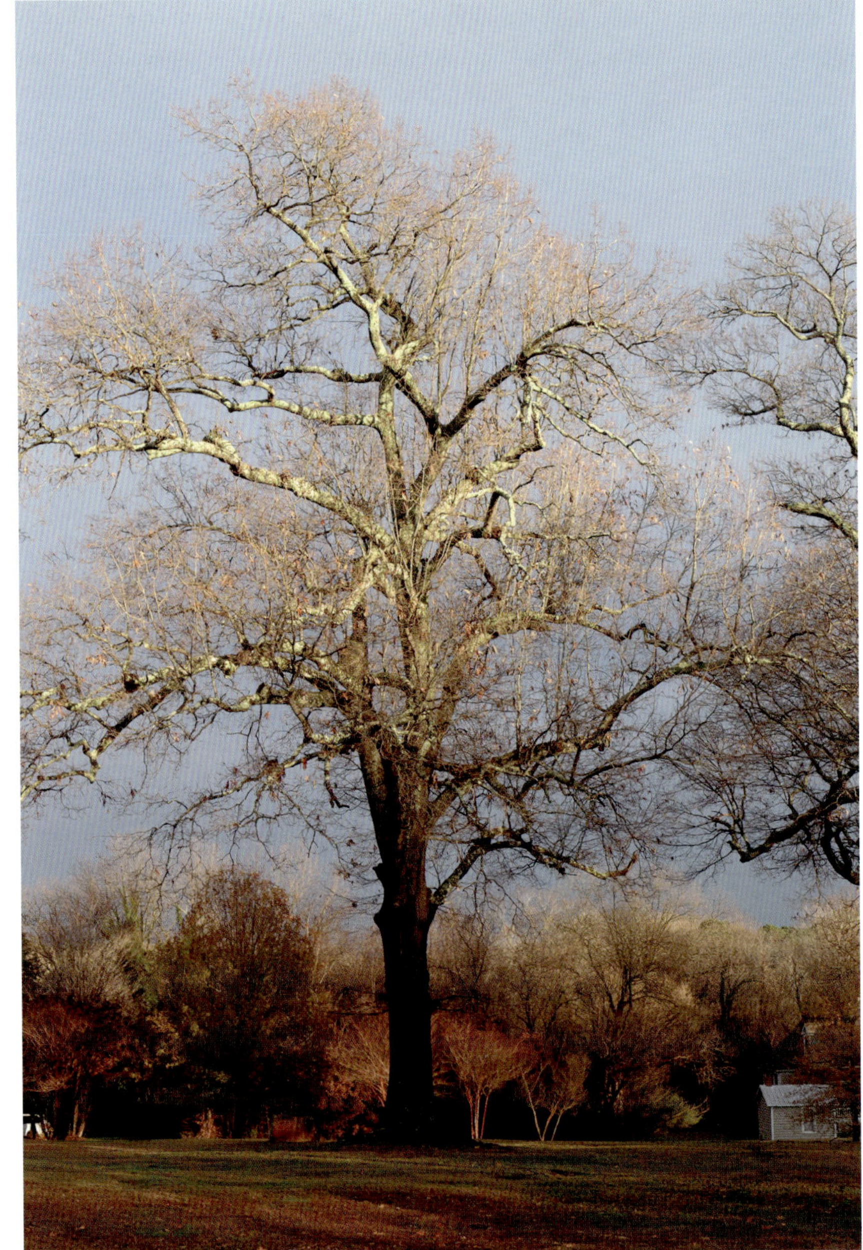

Figure 12.14 / Margaret Lane Cemetery, monumental oak trees shelter the few headstones that remain.

citizen's committee was formed to care for the grounds.[69] The contemporary brick entrance posts facing Occoneechee Street mark vestiges of an old road into the cemetery that leads toward its center (Figure 12.15).

The following excerpt is the remembrance of the wife of a Confederate officer who attended a slave funeral in Charlotte County, Virginia, in 1861. A similar procession may have taken place along this road leading into this cemetery.

> We had a long warm walk behind hundreds of Negroes, following the rude coffin in slave procession through the woods, singing antiphonally as they went, one of those strange, weird hymns not to be caught by any Anglo-Saxon voice. . . . Words of immortal comfort to the great throng of Negro mourners who caught it up, line after line, on an air of their own, full of tears and tenderness, a strange weird tune no white person's voice could ever follow.[70]

Only six identifiable gravestones remain in the cemetery today. One can see three of them preserved in a brick memorial on the site. Two graves remain in the small wrought-iron enclosure: husband, Willy Johnson, died in 1898, and his wife, Mary Collins, died in 1899. The Neoclassical obelisk, the most elite type of monument, marks the grave of George Hill, who died in 1900. Mary Claire Engstrom noted, "Various brick tombs above ground, obelisks and handsome gravestones are remembered as having stood in the cemetery around 1918." She added that "the bases of other stones are hidden in the grass."[71] It is thought by local citizens that some of the gravestones were reused for walkways and as foundations in nearby houses.

Based on other North Carolina slave cemeteries, one would have expected to see a variety of grave markers. Masters sometimes erected markers giving the name and dates of favored slaves. Many graves may have been decorated with objects, such as lamps, bowls, and vases, used by the deceased and designated by wooden markers or fieldstones made of local schist stone, neither dated nor inscribed.[72] A few such stones survive here, without inscriptions, so it is impossible to authenticate them. However, those people who attended the rededication ceremony in 1987 would have seen a sixth inscribed stone leaning against the dedication stone with the name of the slave, Dinah Thompson (died 1859). Dinah's name was roughly chiseled into this slate slab. The gravestone was returned to the cemetery for the dedication, but only survived a few days before it was destroyed by vandals. Members of the Faucette,

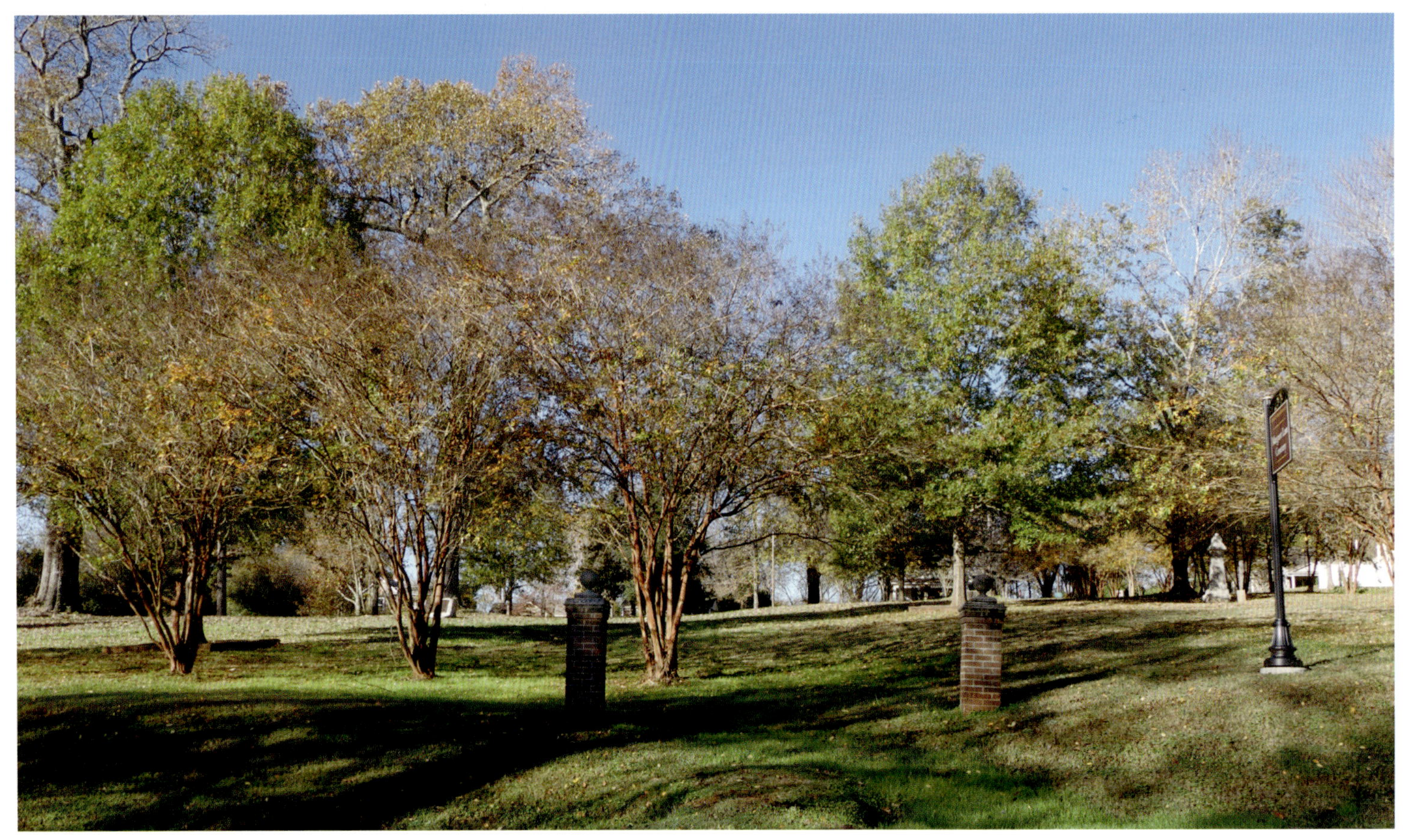

Figure 12.15 / Margaret Lane Cemetery, brick posts marking former road into the cemetery.

Brower, Payne, Whitted, Ellison, and Jones families, to name just a few, were also buried here.[73] Some must have been freedmen and -women, because people of color could not be buried elsewhere in Hillsborough. It is generally believed that Native Americans were also included in this graveyard, although that has not been verified.[74]

In 2006, personnel from the firm Of Grave Concerns, under the principle investigator John Clauser, positively identified 142 graves through a combination of surface inspections of depressions or mounds and through controlled probing. Although this type of field method is only 80 percent accurate, their report estimates that as many as thirty more graves could exist in the cemetery.[75] Presently, each authenticated grave is distinguished by two small marble markers at ground level, square at the head and round at the foot. With a light snowfall many other unmarked six-foot-long depressions are visible, a possible indication of additional gravesites.

Margaret Lane Cemetery was probably landscaped in the nineteenth century, and at one time a grove of large oak trees shaded the graves. Because of storm damage and age, only a few of the old oaks remain. The Margaret Lane Cemetery Committee and Hillsborough Tree Board recently planted ornamental trees and oak trees. Periwinkle and lilies grew in the small wrought-iron family enclosure until weed-whacking in the 1990s eliminated them. Old-fashioned early daffodils planted around the gravesites are now the only reminders of beloved family members.

Conclusion

BY CALLIE CONNOR

If Hillsborough now looks a little different from the way you found it, it must be . . . your imagination, for an informed eye is a trusty helpmate.

The Hidden Hillsborough Committee has tried to bring into focus a past reality that colored a way of life, making up for those many pieces of our historic built and engineered environment that are forever missing. As the committee pursued its project of assembling this picture, members were constantly hearing from property owners about buildings that had been lost only recently; they had either collapsed, burned, or been demolished. A memory, or rather, a visual image of what was now only a memory, sometimes accompanied by stories recollecting people and their ways, was still vivid in some cases. The absence of these buildings was still felt (call it nostalgia if you like), although it was difficult to say why. In other cases, the memory was accompanied by a sense of relief from what can be substantial maintenance costs of old buildings. We hope *Hidden Hillsborough* has kindled an interest in those who are uncertain about how one might approach these anachronistic structures or puzzling features of our town. For their historic value as artifacts is incalculable, and their power to evoke the silent past begs for their preservation.

Historic dependencies and barely discernable landscape features contribute a tangible and authentic form of history, as they serve as witnesses to the life that once depended on them in the course of its routines. They performed a definable, albeit ordinary, role as they functioned in relation to a round of daily activities, pursuits, and chores, ones that involved many long-departed people over many more years. The dependencies with which we are concerned did not lose their utility or associations all at once, for some residents remember seeing summer kitchens still in use before WWII. At that time cooking was not over an open fire but rather in a woodstove vented out through a stovepipe and up the chimney, as at the Robertson-Cheek kitchen or Dr. Edmund Strudwick's kitchen. Somewhere in Orange County there *is* doubtless an old-timer who prefers to cook certain dishes in a woodstove or even over an open fire. This reminds us, too, that there is a perceptible rural character in our Southern towns that affirms their connection to the farm and plantation life of the South in past centuries. It appears in subtle ways, even in the outlying lots of the historic district in Hillsborough—a goat pen here, or at least a clearly audible bleat, a horse's name still legible on the split door of her stall: *Maude.* Take a drive and see for yourself the open character of some of the lots to the north and west of the town center. Or alternatively, take a look at the Orange County Soil and Water Conservation Aerial Maps for a glimpse of the tracts that were still productive farmland in, say, 1955 but are now scrubby forest, housing developments, or shopping centers.

The life of the self-sufficient family farms that lived off the soil during the Great Depression is never far from today's high-tech organic farms with their solar-powered pumps and efficient, grid-enhancing, compact wind turbines. One might take pride and enjoyment in this persistent rural character, for it is an historical reality to be cherished. The old wooden water tower at the Ruffin-Roulhac House, remembered by many, was perhaps the last of these old-style practical necessities to disappear, replaced by the town water tower on West Union Street. With the diverse features and buildings surviving around Hillsborough, rural aspects of the Old South live on in every encounter with our town environment.

The 1839 flagstone walks with their berms still buttressed by enduring curbstones, preserved only on a few stretches around town, keep reminding us of the daily scenarios they witnessed, with horse-drawn vehicles clopping by on the unpaved streets. Until well into the twentieth century, many families had a horse, or a mule, as well as a cow, chickens, and a goat, sheep, or pigs in the yard behind the house; vegetable gardens were ubiquitous in backyards—and still are in many. Close by were the kitchen and herb gardens, the milk house, henhouse, woodshed, and barn. Many in-town families had a wagon or a carriage for transport of animals and foodstuffs, as well as themselves. Until the mid-nineteenth century there was the old market house where vendors could sell their foodstuffs at the intersection of King and Churton streets, while now we have the new market shelter to the east of the new courthouse, where the farmers still come to town to sell produce—in trucks. Waved greetings and conversations in passing were surely issued from horseback or between passing open carriages or travelers on foot; both horses and vehicles were housed near the residences, in carriage houses, stables, and barns tucked into the backs of lots, some of which still serve as a reminder of their associations.

The original one-acre lots of the old town are still present in the boundaries and measurements of residential lots today, having been determined in the mid-eighteenth century when the town was first surveyed and laid out in lots. The carving-up or reshaping of present property boundaries often retains an echo of the dimensions of all or part of the original one-acre Town Lot. We hope that references to the numbers of lots have proved enriching as a form of orientation to the maps of the early town in relation to surviving structures. With the help of Stewart Dunaway's maps, it is not difficult to see the relationship of the old divisions to the new shapes and dimensions of house lots after only a minute of study. Most of all, these lots serve to explain the very essence of Hillsborough's character—as a town of constant variation and alternating architectural types. After realizing that the colonial *mansion house* requirements dictated the dimensions and material durability of the first dwellings, we now understand the reason behind the alternation of historic houses with more recent bungalows, colonials, brick ranches, mill houses—a whole range of architectural types. Many of the owners of mansion houses accumulated additional lots, as we have seen, to accommodate the needs of their in-town *farmettes.* They sold off these adjoining lots as the need for a feedlot, a horse lot, a lot for the cow (or her alfalfa), or field crops or gardens became dispensable. These lots were often subdivided as they were sold, and so the quarter-acre lot became part of the mix. In fact the only property in town that retains anything like it's former dimensions is the Ruffin-Roulhac House (Town Hall), which preserves four of its original ten one-acre town lots—one of Hillsborough's fortunate legacies in historic preservation and repurposing for public use.

The committee does not claim completeness in publishing this record, although the enchanting photographs of Elizabeth Matheson help provide documentation of these treasured traces of the past. For *Hidden Hillsborough* is in effect a seed planted to help raise consciousness about certain features of the town that are easy to overlook. There are surely examples that have not been noted or photographed, and there may even be new categories—does anyone have an historic dovecote? For this reason, we urge you, readers, to contact members of the committee with information you would like to see added to the project. Email addresses change, but with a little inquiry, for example at the local bookstore, the Purple Crow, the Alliance for Historic Hillsborough, or the Orange County Visitors Center, we encourage you to contact a committee member and have your information included in updated versions, either in a new edition or an online addendum. We urge you to savor the uniqueness of our small town, or of your town, wherever that may be, not least for its preservation of features and small buildings that tell an ordinary story of life in the past, but because these aspects of the town become extraordinary when they are considered for their evocative qualities when combined with a visual imagination.

One of the property owners has, tucked into a corner of her property, an historic barn, a handsome structure with board and batten siding, hand-hewn timbers, and well-preserved traces of stalls and carriage parlor, and therefore, technically, a carriage house. One can read it like a book. The owner remarked when we returned to observe and photograph details of the building that she thought we'd be able to see more now than on our first visit, because she had had the barn repaired by a historically knowledgeable carpenter the preceding summer—roof patched, siding replaced in places—and had cleaned out the stuff that was stored there so that the bugs and critters could be dealt with more effectively. Music to our ears, for this kind of stewardship of historic features of a property enhances not only its appearance but also its market value. Historic preservation is in the end a service to us all.

A change in one's experience through a visual imagination can be demonstrated in the case of one of our most famous local landmarks, Historic Ayr Mount, dating to the early nineteenth century, and now owned by the Classical American Homes Preservation Trust. The harmonious proportions and regal silhouette of the house set in its carefully landscaped grounds are a memorable sight, indeed. But this house was never intended to be seen as pristine and isolated on the land, as noted in the account of the Kirkland family by Jean Anderson, a beloved local author:

> Although some of the outbuildings originally at Ayr Mount were standing well into the present century, all are now gone. Those that are remembered include a two-room kitchen, icehouse, well, another outbuilding (possibly a slave house), and a massive stone barn, which was demolished in this century and the stone sold. A stable and

> carriage house were located to the east at the end of the carriage drive. . . . Patterns of depression in the ground and rudimentary remains of stone foundations here and there in the yard suggest the original disposition of the outbuildings at Ayr Mount. Clustered behind the main house at the east end and running south in a line and then west, creating in the backyard a work area surrounded by buildings on three sides, would have stood the kitchen, dairy, smokehouse, corncrib, a slave house or two for house servants, and small barns for poultry and milch cows. The daily work conducted in these buildings and the yard and the continual passage of servants to and from the big house would have made the backyard the busiest place at Ayr Mount.[1]

She then goes on to describe what is known of the fenced fields, hedges, pastures, and terraced gardens. Taking in the house's appearance today, we might find it in one sense sadly lacking without its dependencies, but then with a secret smile, we can use our imagination to fill in what we know was once part of the picture, enriching it immeasurably.

Notes

INTRODUCTION

1 Don Higginbotham, ed., *The Papers of James Iredell*, 2 vols. Raleigh: N.C. Department of Cultural Resources (1976), 2:8.

2 Elkanah Watson, *Men and Times of the Revolution*. New York: Dana (1856), 290.

CHAPTER ONE

1 Stewart E. Dunaway, *Road, Bridge, Mill, and Ferry History of N.C.* This book details the state laws as they were changed, defining bridge and road design and dimensions, etc., from early British era into American law.

2 Stewart E. Dunaway, *Orange Co., N.C.–Bridge Records (1787–1865)*, 12–14.

3 William P. Cumming, *The Southeast in Early Maps*, Chapel Hill: University of North Carolina Press, 3rd ed., rev. (1998): 28.

4 Stewart E. Dunaway, *Henry McCulloh & Son, Henry Eustace McCulloh* (2011), 212–19. This survey map allocated twelve 100,000–acre tracts, of which Tract 11 was on the west side of Hillsborough and Tract 12 on the east. Rowan's survey shows the trading path extending all the way to near Mecklenburg County.

5 Cumming, *The Southeast in Early Maps*. Many of these maps are online at UNC Digital Map collection: http://www2.lib.unc.edu/dc/ncmaps/.

6 See Stewart E. Dunaway, *Claude J. Sauthier and His Map of North Carolina*, 13. Claude Sauthier (1736–1802), cartographer, was a native of Strasbourg, France. He drew maps of ten North Carolina towns between 1768 and 1770. He departed from North Carolina with Governor William Tryon in 1771. For prior grants, ownership, and names of the town (Corbinton [1754–59] and Childsburg [1759–66]—after Lord Granville's land agents Francis Corbin and Francis Child), see Dunaway, *History of Town Lots* (2012), 17–22.

7 Claude J. Sauthier drew maps of Edenton, Newbern, Cross Creek, Bath, Brunswick, Salisbury, Hillsborough, Wilmington, Beaufort, and Halifax.

8 The roads within a town were regulated by the same state laws as those governing all other roadways.

9 Petersburg is located on the fall line of the Appomattox River, which was navigable below that line by large ships in the eighteenth century. The Appomattox River flows into the James River, which provided ready access to the Chesapeake Bay and the Atlantic Ocean.

10 When six judicial districts were created in North Carolina in 1777, the courthouse in Hillsborough was selected as the location where its District Superior Court would meet.

11 Both of these one-and-one-half story houses, which date from the very earliest years of the town, survive today, although now enlarged.

12 Duncan Cameron (1777–1853) was the son of the Rev. John Cameron, who emigrated

from Scotland in 1770, and his wife, Ann Owen Nash. He studied law, was admitted to the N.C. bar in 1798, and settled in Hillsborough about 1800. His office in Hillsborough was constructed in 1801. He owned a five-acre estate on the south side of Margaret Lane (Lots 10, 11, 13, 14, and 16), which he sold in 1807 when he moved to the country and became a planter. He owned a large and successful plantation with a country house, Fairntosh, in northern Durham County and a town house in Raleigh.

13 Dr. James Webb (1774–1855) was born in Granville County, N.C., into a family that had been long established in Essex County, Va. He studied medicine under Benjamin Rush at the University of Pennsylvania about 1798 and established his medical practice in Hillsborough about 1799. In addition to his practice, he invested in several mercantile businesses and also in a brick-making company. Throughout his life in Hillsborough, he supported the construction of local churches, schools, and academies. He constructed a log schoolhouse in 1817. He owned a five-acre estate situated on both sides of East Queen Street (Lots 63, 64, 65, 83, and 102) and is buried in the Old Town Cemetery.

14 Sauthier's map of Hillsborough, drawn in 1768, seems to show a stone wall around the perimeter of the church lot (Lot 98). A portion of this wall was incorporated into the foundation of the Sunday School building constructed in 1836 to be a schoolhouse. Later, after it was no longer needed for a schoolhouse, the building became known as the Session House. A portion of the original enclosing wall was completely removed when the present stone museum building was constructed in the 1930s on the site of the old Sunday School/Session House.

15 The David Anderson House was constructed on Lot 229 about the 1840s by David Anderson, a professional carpenter, for his family.

16 Edmund Fanning was born in New York about 1737–39 (his memorial stone in St. Mary Abbotts near Kensington indicated he was born in 1739; see *Life & Times of Edmund Fanning* [2016], Dunaway, pp. 17–23, 76, 77), graduated from Yale College, and moved to Hillsborough where he became a colonial official. His house in Hillsborough was destroyed by Regulators in 1770, and he followed Gov. William Tryon to New York in 1771. As a loyalist, he fought on the side of the king during the Revolutionary War. He served as lieutenant governor of Prince Edward Island, Canada, from 1786 to 1805. He retired to England and died there in 1818.

17 Ann Strudwick Nash, *Ladies in the Making*, 71.

18 Carl R. Lounsbury, ed. *An Illustrated Glossary of Early Southern Architecture & Landscape*, 222. See also Dunaway, *History of Town Lots*, App. A, 494–98, for Acts of the North Carolina General Assembly of 1760; and Chapter VII (1766–67) at the incorporation of the town. Chapter XVI further specifies that mortar, clay, or wooden chimneys could not be built, for the safety of the town.

19 The term *lot*, when used in the eighteenth and nineteenth centuries and in the context of property usage, also referred to a small pasture, not far from the house, for the horses used by the family who owned and lived on the property.

20 Francis Lister Hawks (1798–1866) was a grandson of John Hawks, architect of Gov. Tryon's palace. He studied law and was admitted to the bar. In 1826 he abandoned the practice of law and prepared for the ministry while living in Hillsborough. He was ordained a priest and quickly rose to prominence in the Episcopal church.

21 Throughout most of the nineteenth and twentieth centuries, Montrose was owned by members of the Graham family, beginning with Gov. William A. Graham and descending through his son and grandson until 1977.

22 John Hawks was an English architect brought to North Carolina by Gov. William Tryon to design government buildings, including Tryon's Palace in New Bern. Although neither the plan nor the elevation is signed or dated, the handwriting on it appears to match that of Hawks.

23 William Kirkland was one of the young Scottish merchants sent out in the eighteenth century to staff one of the branch stores in the backcountry. By 1793 he was an independent merchant in Hillsborough where in the early nineteenth century his success in commerce coincided with, and perhaps benefited from, his Scottish family's rise in prominence and wealth. He became a planter and established himself at Ayr Mount, his new house. For a comprehensive study of William Kirkland and Ayr Mount,

see Jean Bradley Anderson, *The Kirklands of Ayr Mount* (Chapel Hill: University of North Carolina Press, 1991). He is buried in the Kirkland family cemetery.

24 The design of the Hillsborough clock is typical of English tower clocks of the mid- to late eighteenth century.

25 Adelaide L. Fries, ed. *Records of the Moravians in North Carolina,* 10 vols. Raleigh: N.C. Historical Commission (1941), 5:2188. The clockmaker in Guilford County "who knows his trade well" reported "the Hillsborough clock is good and will last a long time." See also, Frank P. Albright, *Johann Ludwig Eberhardt and His Salem Clocks* (Chapel Hill: University of North Carolina Press, 1978), 133–35.

26 George W. Bruce, "Benton & Hogan's Fight," *Hillsborough Recorder,* 30 June 1875. The market house, which predated St. Matthew's, clearly did not have a cupola originally or the clock would have been installed in it; there would have been no need to design a special holding place for it in the church. But Bruce reported that in the early 1800s, the clock was in the cupola of the market house, which was surmounted by a rooster weathervane, a design normally found on churches. This sequence and combination strongly suggest that when the cupola was removed from St. Matthew's, it was immediately installed on top of the market house, with the clock, weathervane, and all. (I am indebted to Jean B. Anderson for bringing to my attention Bruce's article.)

27 Dunaway, *History of Town Lots, Addendum* (2015), 313.

28 Because Hillsborough had a sawmill on the Eno River before the Revolution, many of the early houses in town were constructed of wood framing; a few, such as the house of John (Jack) Wilson (the Carpenter's House, Lot 135), were constructed of logs.

29 Dunaway, *History of Town Lots,* 353. Nathaniel Rochester was born in 1752 in Westmoreland County, Va. Following the early death of his father and the remarriage of his mother, the family moved to Granville County, N.C., about 1760. Orange County court records place him in Hillsborough in the 1770s, where he bought and sold property. Later he moved to Maryland and then to New York where the city of Rochester bears his name.

30 Frederick Nash (1781–1858), lawyer, chief justice of the N.C. Supreme Court, and son of Gov. Abner Nash, was born in New Bern in the colonial Tryon Palace. In 1807 he moved to Hillsborough where he spent the remainder of his life. He owned Town Lots 10, 11, 12, 13, 14, and 16. He is buried in his family plot that adjoins the Old Town Cemetery.

31 Dr. Edmund Strudwick (1802–79) was born near Hillsborough. He studied medicine at the University of Pennsylvania and received his degree in 1824. Following a two-year internship, he returned to Hillsborough and established his medical practice in 1826. He was involved in re-establishing the North Carolina Medical Society. In 1837 he acquired the house on Town Lot 59. The brick kitchen behind that house survives today; his house was razed in the twentieth century. Financial reversals after the Civil War forced him and his wife to sell their house and to live in a two-room office owned by their nieces. He is buried in a plot that adjoins the Old Town Cemetery.

32 William Alexander Graham (1804–75) was born in Lincoln County, N.C., attended the Hillsborough Academy, and graduated from the University of North Carolina. He studied law under Thomas Ruffin and opened his own law office in Hillsborough in 1828. His political career included his election to the State House, the U.S. Senate, the Governorship of N.C. He also was the Vice Presidential candidate of the Whig Party in 1852. He supported education and internal improvements, and he opposed secession. He lived at and named Montrose. He is buried in his family plot that adjoins the Old Town Cemetery.

33 The five antebellum churches in Hillsborough are Dickerson Chapel (1790), constructed to be a courthouse; Presbyterian church (1815); St. Matthew's Episcopal Church (1824–26); Hillsborough United Methodist Church (1861); Hillsborough Baptist Church (1861). For a discussion of the history of these churches, see Brooks Graebner, "Antebellum Church Buildings of Hillsborough," *Hillsborough Historical Society Journal* 7, no. 1 (2004), 35–48.

34 The three surviving courthouses from south to north are the 1954 courthouse, the 1845 courthouse, and the 1790 courthouse, now a church.

35 William Nichols was a native of Bath, England, and had come to North Carolina

before 1800. For a summary of his extensive work in the antebellum South, see C. Ford Peatross, *William Nichols, Architect* (University of Alabama Art Gallery, 1979).

36 These two builders combined their expertise and built the Person County Courthouse.

37 *Hasell* was the name of a prominent family in Charleston, S.C., and also in Wilmington, N.C. It is pronounced like the woman's name *Hazel,* and sometimes even spelled that way on early maps and deeds. *Hasell* is the correct spelling and *Hazel* the correct pronunciation of a street in Hillsborough named for that family. Eliza Hasell was originally from Charleston, but had lived for about a decade in Wilmington, before moving to Hillsborough.

38 The existing Courtney's Yellow House was extended to the east in order to create alcoves. Arched alcoves were part of the original design of Lochiel, constructed shortly after Pilgrim's Rest.

39 Dunaway, *History of Town Lots,* 137.

40 Ibid., 137.

CHAPTER TWO

1 See Allen, *Uncommon Vernacular,* 122–25, and Vlach, *Back of the Big House,* 43–62.

2 This information comes from the current owners, Virginia Smith and Mark Bell, who uncovered traces of the rotation and moving of the kitchen, as well as later rebuilding of the chimney with a smaller firebox.

3 Nash, *Ladies in the Making,* 75.

4 Nash, *Ladies in the Making,* 76–77.

5 Virginia Smith in a quotation from Mrs. Berry's journal.

CHAPTER THREE

1 Gwenyth and William Reid, the current owners of the Coachman's House, had the building restored. The author is grateful to them for allowing her to see it and for information about its restoration.

2 Peter Wood and Holly Reid, "The Coachman's House." Unpublished essay.

3 Mangum Papers, I:97, V:200; Dunaway, *History of Town Lots,* 605–6. The author wishes to thank Mary Ann Plambeck for permission to see her property.

4 Anderson, "A Rationale for Sans Souci"; *Town of Hillsborough,* 203–7.

5 Ryan, *Orange County Trio,* 86.

6 The author is indebted to Jeanne Frederick, Amy Roach, and Betty Eidenier for information about Price Boyd.

7 Dunaway, *History of Town Lots,* 431–2; 446–9. The author wishes to thank Peter Sandbeck for information about these town lots and the slave house.

8 Margaret Schucker, *The Ruffin-Roulhac House* (Hillsborough, N.C.: HPT); Lloyd and Lloyd, *Town of Hillsborough,* 192.

CHAPTER FOUR

1 See Wikipedia (en.wikipedia.org/wiki/Smokehouse); How to Build a Smokehouse www.goodshomedesign.com/how-to-build-a-smokehouse/Meathouse definition. http://en.wiktionary.org/wiki/meat_house. Lounsbury, *Illustrated Glossary,* s.v. smokehouse.

CHAPTER FIVE

1 Poplar Hill was moved to the north side of the river in the latter part of the twentieth century.

2 Nash, *Ladies in the Making,* 122–23.

3 Dunaway, *History of Town Lots,* 18.

4 Ibid., 219–20.

5 Allen, *Uncommon Vernacular,* 140–43.

6 Vlach, *Back of the Big House,* 79–80.

7 Thanks are extended here to Ashley DeSena, who contributed the initial research on wells and well houses.

8 Lloyd and Lloyd, *Town of Hillsborough,* 21; for the pump, see Dunaway, *History of Town Lots,* 69, and *Addendum,* 289.

9 Dunaway, *History of Town Lots,* 68.

10 Dunaway, *History of Town Lots, Addendum,* 290.

11 Ibid., 131.

12 Nash, *Ladies in the Making,* 66.

CHAPTER SIX

1 See Dunaway, *History of Town Lots* (2012), 498–9, for Acts of Assembly, 1757 and 1766, that legalized the laying out and establishment of the town and common.

2 Anderson, *Piedmont Plantation,* 19–20.

3 Ibid., 128.

4 *Hillsborough Historical Society Journal* 5, no. 1 (Fall 2002), 15.

5 The author is grateful to the current owners of the stable/house, Gwenyth and William Reid, for permission to examine their house, and also to Jeanne Frederick and

Amy Frederick Roach for photographs of the stable before its reconstruction.

6 *Hillsborough Historical Society Journal* 5, no. 1.

7 The author is indebted to Holly Reid for relaying a photograph taken in 1938 showing the stable when it was still in use. The photograph is courtesy of the Research Laboratories of Archaeology, University of North Carolina at Chapel Hill.

8 Details of the reconstruction are found in Gwenyth Reid's unpublished account, "The History of the Horse Barn," based on an interview with Jeanne and Frank Frederick, who did the reconstruction; the author also thanks Amy Frederick Roach for her memories of the reconstruction in which she participated.

9 The author is indebted to Craufurd Goodwin for details of the barn's construction.

10 Anderson, *The Kirklands of Ayr Mount*, 144.

11 Cameron Family Papers, letter of Paul C. Cameron, 16 Nov. 1869.

12 Anderson, *Piedmont Plantation*, 122.

13 The author wishes to thank Mary Ann Plambeck for permission to see her barn and for providing information about it and the slave house also on her property. She also wishes to thank Peter Sandbeck and Dean Ruedrich, restoration specialists, who were vital in analyzing the barn's structure.

14 The author is indebted to Stewart Dunaway for deeds information concerning the Mitchell ownership of the land: Orange County Deed Book 94:108, Deed Book 108:144.

15 Anderson, "A Rationale for Sans Souci;" Lloyd and Lloyd, *Town of Hillsborough*, 203–7.

16 Samuel Tillinghast Papers, letter from J.C. Norwood, 15 Nov. 1830.

17 Lloyd and Lloyd, *Town of Hillsborough*, 206. The author is grateful to Dean Ruedrich and Peter Sandbeck for their information about the building.

18 The author is grateful to Lee Smith for permission to see the Robertson-Cheek barn. The author also wishes to thank Dean Ruedrich for his inspection and analysis of the barn's construction.

19 Thanks again to Dean Ruedrich for an expert analysis of the barn.

20 Dunaway, *History of Town Lots*, 413. The author wishes to thank Larry and Dinah Dozier for permission to examine their barn.

21 Ryan, *Orange County Trio*, 86.

22 Lloyd and Lloyd, *Town of Hillsborough*, 299.

23 Dunaway, *History of Town Lots*, 431–32, 446–49; Margaret Schucker, *The Ruffin-Roulhac House.* The author wishes to thank Peter Sandbeck for information about these buildings. The old photograph is in Lloyd and Lloyd, 192.

CHAPTER SEVEN

1 Vlach, *Back of the Big House*, 80–81.

2 Wikipedia: Icehouses; also note references to Ice Wagons and Ice Cutting as related topics.

3 Holly Reid, "The Paul and Ann (Ruffin) Cameron Icehouse," in *Hillsborough Historical Society Journal* 5, no. 1 (Fall 2002), 13–25.

4 *Hillsborough Recorder*—Newspaper.com or Orange County Public Library, N.C. Room microfilm collection of early newspapers for Hillsborough and Orange County.

5 Reid, "Cameron Icehouse," 13–25.

6 Dunaway, *History of Town Lots.*

7 *Hillsborough Recorder*, 30 October 1849.

8 Ibid., 26 August 1893.

9 Ibid., 31 March 1883.

10 Nash, *Ladies in the Making*, 73.

11 Stainless steel knife blades did not become available until about the time of World War I.

12 Dunaway, *History of Town Lots*, 137.

13 Telephone interview on 19 November 2015 with James Richmond, son of John William (Bill) Richmond, who remembered the relocation of the dining room dependency.

14 The terms *laundry* and *washhouse* were synonymous. Because of the rarity of surviving examples, we do not know which term was favored by the majority of Hillsborough's inhabitants.

15 The first clothespin, a one-piece wooden design still in production today, appeared in the early nineteenth century. The modern design, two pieces connected by a wire spring, was patented in 1853.

16 Jane Ashelford, *Care of Clothes* (London: National Trust, 1997), 8.

17 For a combined-use building, as both a kitchen and a laundry, see Vlach, *Back of the Big House*, 57.

18 "Building an Outhouse," www.MotherEarthNews.com.

CHAPTER EIGHT

1 Dunaway, *Sauthier and His Maps* (2016).

2 Ann Royall, *Mrs. Royall's Southern Tour, or Second Series of the Black Book* 1 (1830), 13, cited in R. Ireland, "Hillsborough's Natural History: An Introduction," *Hillsborough Historical Society Journal* V, no. 1 (Fall 2002), viii–ix.

3 Nash, *Ladies in the Making*, 61.

4 Ibid., ix–x.

5 Kenneth McFarland, "Landscape Gardening in Antebellum Hillsborough, North Carolina: The Camerons at Burnside," *Magnolia, Bulletin of the Southern Garden History Society* XI, no. 3 (Spring 1995), 1–11; invoices for the hundreds of specimens that were planted give us a precise idea of the Camerons' ambitious undertaking. An unpublished paper by Mary Claire Engstrom, "The Planting of Cameron Park, 1858–59," was also consulted. See also Leah Burt, "The Beginnings of Cameron Park in Hillsborough, North Carolina," *Hillsborough Historical Society Journal* 5, no. 1 (Fall 2002), 1–11, including bibliography; see esp. drawing on p. 8.

6 See "Priestly H. Mangum Jr.," by H. Thomas Kearney Jr., 1991, in *NCpedia* in *Dictionary of N.C. Biography*, ed. William S. Powell; "Mangum Terrace," by Douglas Helms, in Powell, *Encyclopedia of North Carolina*, online (consulted April 2016). Mangum, a Wake County farmer, had lived in Hillsborough and built a substantial house (on the site of today's Mangum-Ruffin House) on St. Mary's Road, opposite Montrose. His invention greatly affected the cotton-growing South, and was an ideal solution for farmers trying to make the most of their land on the slopes leading to the Eno River.

7 Holly Reid graciously supplied me with this information.

8 An informative and evocative letter of a visitor walking around Hillsborough in October 1855 appeared in the *Hillsborough Recorder* of 14 November 1855; in it he describes the "stately mansions embosomed in gigantic oak groves," and in particular the view of the Burwell School from Churton Street, "adorned by a shady, roomy and beautiful front yard."

9 The gardens and other landscape features that surrounded the Nash-Kollock House on West Margaret Lane were captured by Ann Strudwick Nash in her book, *Ladies in the Making*; see p. 71 for a plan of the flower and vegetable garden in the back of the property. See Robert Ireland, "Gardens in the Making: A Sketch of the Gardens Captured in Ann Strudwick Nash's *Ladies in the Making*," *Hillsborough Historical Society Journal* 5, no. 1 (Fall 2002), 27–36.

10 Nash, *Ladies in the Making*, 62–63; for a description and plan of the Rear Garden, see 70–73.

11 See Liz Druitt, "Cherchez le 'Musk,'" *Magnolia* X, no. 3 (Spring 1994), 1–4. See also Marie Butler, "Discovering the Musk Rose in America," and Helen Watkins, "The Early Garden at Chatwood," *Hillsborough Historical Society Journal* 5, no. 1 (Fall 2002), 41–55 and 37–40, respectively.

12 The garden at the Alexander Dickson House was dedicated to Mrs. Helen Blake Watkins and her first husband, Dr. Charles Blake, in October 1990. Mrs. Watkins and her husband donated the land where the Dickson House and Office were to be relocated; they were moved and restored by the Preservation Fund of Hillsborough in 1982.

13 Nancy Goodwin and Ippy Patterson, *Montrose: Life in a Garden* (Duke University Press, 2005); see also *Gardens of Old Hillsborough: A Project of the Horticulture Committee of the Hillsborough Historical Society* (Hillsborough Historical Society, 1971), 4–5. This garden can be seen by special arrangement.

14 *Gardens of Old Hillsborough*. Another sure sign of a former garden can be seen on spring walks in the woods. Often clumps of flowers will appear blooming along old roads or paths, indicating the location of the dooryard of a long-vanished house. One instance of this in Hillsborough is at the foot of Cameron Street, on the right, a few dozen feet from Riverwalk. Half a dozen thick clumps of daffodils stand in a row in the woods.

CHAPTER NINE

1 See Nash, *Ladies in the Making*, 67.

2 Dunaway, *History of Town Lots, Addendum*, Appendix D (Rock Quarries and Brickyards).

3 Act of the North Carolina General Assembly in 1784 mandated that a stone wall be constructed to enclose the churchyard and burial ground. Another act in 1804 requested the church and burial ground have

a stone wall erected. Was the 1804 act due to disrepair or due to the wall not having been built in accordance to the 1784 act? It is plausible that the wall was in disrepair and the 1804 act was in response to that—although not worded as such (i.e., repair).

4 Nash, *Ladies in the Making*, 122–23. Note: book provides detailed insight to Hillsborough from 1859 to 1890, when perhaps the trees were much larger. Today the trees along the trail appear to be less than fifty to seventy-five years old. Yet, mountainous vegetation—such as rhododendron, or laurel, also mentioned in this book (p. 122)—still remains.

5 *Fayetteville Semi-Weekly Observer*, 8 Nov. 1844; *The Weekly Standard* (Raleigh, N.C.), 27 March 1857; *Orange Co. Observer*, 4 June 1881 and 20 May 1893; *The Alamance Gleaner* (Graham, N.C.), 11 June 1895.

6 Ibid., newspaper account lists all three well-known outdoor sites of interest along the Eno River: Lovers Leap, Dark Walk, and Panther's Den.

7 Dunaway, *History of Town Lots, Addendum*. See Appendix J (Dark Walk), for more details, GPS references, and images of these postcards. See UNC Digital website for its collection of N.C. Postcards, dc.lib.unc.edu—North Carolina Postcards.

CHAPTER TEN

1 See *Dictionary of North Carolina Biography* (Chapel Hill: University of North Carolina Press), biography of Thomas Ruffin. Also available on ncpedia.org.

2 Ibid., see biography of Gov. William Alexander Graham.

CHAPTER ELEVEN

1 Coon, *Schools and Academies, 1790–1840*, and Blackwelder, *Age of Orange*.

2 Powell, *Encyclopedia of North Carolina*, 159.

3 A letter of 15 March 1856 written by Mrs. Burwell to her daughter Fanny mentions a new piano being acquired, making it the fourth or possibly the fifth at the school; see the unpublished 1855–56 Letters of Mrs. Burwell, Burwell School Archives.

4 Engstrom, *Book of Burwell Students*, 11.

5 See Engstrom, *Book of Burwell Students*, for records pertaining to the girls who attended the school. For a glimpse of the Burwell School from the perspective of Elizabeth Keckley, one of the Burwells' slaves, see Keckley, *Behind the Scenes*.

6 The residence was first built by Duncan Cameron, a wealthy lawyer and entrepreneur, in 1802, and he located his law office a short distance to the west of his house. Other buildings added to what eventually became a five-acre property in the years that followed were a kitchen, corn crib, well house, wagon shed, barn, dairy, smokehouse, carriage house, and stables. Frederick Nash purchased the entire property in 1807; see Anderson, *Piedmont Plantation*, 18–20 and n.s. 24–30.

7 See Lloyd and Lloyd, *Town of Hillsborough*, 145–49, for a sketch and photographs of the school and its annex. See Chamberlain, *This Was Home*, 221–30, for a first-hand description of her life at the school in the 1880s.

8 For an archival photograph of the building with its annex showing the original two-door arrangement, see Lloyd and Lloyd, *Town of Hillsborough*, 149.

9 Coon, *Schools and Academies*, 314; Blackwelder, *Age of Orange*, 135; Bellinger, *Photocensus*, 70.

10 Lloyd and Lloyd, *Town of Hillsborough*, 198–99.

11 *Country School Association of America: countryschoolassociation.org*.

12 See Coon, *Schools and Academies* in his list and descriptions of Orange County Schools (280–324), most of which are in Hillsborough.

13 Coon, *Schools and Academies*, 310–12; Blackwelder, *Age of Orange*, 126.

14 Coon, *Schools and Academies*, 312–14.

15 For an 1899 photograph of the teachers and students at this school, see Lloyd and Lloyd, *Town of Hillsborough*, 139; see also 141–43 for more about the school.

16 Dula, *The Pelican Guide to Hillsborough*, 69.

17 Anderson, "Town Lot 43." Unpublished paper.

18 Coon, *Schools and Academies*, 300–10.

19 Ibid., 286–95; 310–12; see esp. 292–94. For Bingham Schools around North Carolina, see Robert I. Curtis, "The Bingham School and Classical Education in North Carolina, 1793–1873," *North Carolina Historical Review* (July 1996), 328–77.

20 See Blackwelder, *Age of Orange*, 126–29; Coon, *Schools and Academies*, 280–95.

21 See Blackwelder, *Age of Orange*, 122–26.

22 Blackwelder, *Age of Orange*, 129–31; Lloyd and Lloyd, *Town of Hillsborough*, 149–54.

23 James Webb Papers, 3760, Southern Historical Collection, University of North Carolina Library at Chapel Hill.

24 Blackwelder, *Age of Orange*, 118. For the education of blacks after the end of slavery, see Rosetta Austin Moore, *The Impact of Slavery on the Education of Blacks in Orange County, North Carolina, 1619–1970*, Lulu, 2015.

25 Coon, *Schools and Academies*, 314. For a recent account of the impact of A.D. Murphey and a bibliography, see Houston, George, *National American Biography*, s.v. "Archibald DeBow Murphey." http://www.anb.org.libproxy.lib.unc.edu/articles/asearch.html?which_index=both&meta-dc=10&func=simple_search&field-Name=archibald+murphey&search_text=&Login=Quick+Search.

CHAPTER TWELVE

1 U.S. Department of the Interior, National Park Service. "Types of Burial Places and Associated Features" in *Guidelines of Evaluating and Registering Cemeteries and Burial Places.* Accessed online November 2015. http://www.nps.gov/nr/publications/bulletins/nrb41/nrb41_6.htm. (*Note:* Terminology used in the sketches of these five historical cemeteries follows the descriptions. Cemeteries considered "elements of historic districts" and "in association with churches" can be included in the Historic Register if they contribute to the historical nature of a town, date from a historical period, or are historical in their own right.)

2 National Register of Historic Places Registration, "'Hillsborough Historic District Additional Documentation.' Hillsborough, Orange County OR0077ad." Listed 1/24/14. Accessed online June 2015. http://www.hpo.ncdcr.gov/nr/OR0077ad.pdf.

3 "Colonial and State Records of North Carolina (CSR) 1715–1716," Vol. 23, Chap. XLVII, 66. *Documenting the American South* website. Accessed online 2015. http://docsouth.unc.edu/csr/index.html/volumes.

4 CSR, 29 June 1767, Vol. 7, 488.

5 Ibid.

6 Orange County Cemetery Census website: http://cemeterycensus.com/nc/orng/cem155.htm.

7 Margaret Anna Burwell's diary entry, 26 November 1855. Courtesy of the Burwell School Archives, Hillsborough, N.C. Accessed August 2009. *Note:* Elizabeth Coit (1837–52) of Cheraw was a student at Burwell when she died and was buried in the Old Town Cemetery. Mary's baby was Mrs. Burwell's first grandchild, Mary Strudwick (1853–55). Mr. Heartt was Edwin A. Heartt (1819–55), the superintendent of the Presbyterian Sabbath School. The Rev. John Witherspoon (1791–1853) was the organizer and pastor of Hillsborough's Presbyterian church who preceded the Rev. Robert Burwell.

8 Hugh Conway Browning, "The Lockhart-Phillips Cemetery," *Hillsborough Historical Society Newsletter* V, no. 30 (1967).

9 "Lockhart-Phillips Cemetery Census." Orange County Cemetery Census website: http://cemeterycensus.com/nc/orng/cem155.htm.

10 Browning, "The Lockhart-Phillips Cemetery."

11 Dunaway, *History of Town Lots*, 329.

12 Browning, "The Lockhart-Phillips Cemetery."

13 The Rev. James O'Kelly, a Methodist missionary in North Carolina in the 1780s, broke away from the Methodist church and established a number of small congregations of followers. This movement eventually became the foundation of the Christian church in Virginia and the upper Piedmont of North Carolina.

14 Browning, "The Lockhart-Phillips Cemetery."

15 Dunaway, *History of Town Lots*, 332–33.

16 Ibid., 333.

17 Christina Oakes (Lockhart-Philips family descendent and great-great-great-great-granddaughter of Clara Frances Lockhart) to Ellen C. Weig. 30 January 2014.

18 Anderson, *The Kirklands of Ayr Mount*, 129.

19 Ayr Mount (NR1971), National Register of Historic Places Registration, "'Hillsborough Historic District Additional Documentation.' Hillsborough, Orange County OR0077ad." Listed 1/24/14. Accessed online June 2015. http://www.hpo.ncdcr.gov/nr/OR0077ad.pdf.

20 Anderson, *The Kirklands of Ayr Mount*, 88.

21 Ibid., 166–7.

22 Nash, *Ladies in the Making*, 130.

23 Kirkland Family Cemetery at Ayr Mount (ca. 1817). Orange County, North Carolina Cemeteries website: http://cemeterycensus.com/nc/orng/cem150.htm.

24 Mary Claire Engstrom, "Kirkland Family Cemetery Circa May 1974." Color Film Box 03, Mary Claire Engstrom Photographic Collection (P0050), North Carolina Collection Photographic Archives, Wilson Library, University of North Carolina at Chapel Hill. Accessed online July 2015. http://www2.lib.unc.edu/ncc/pcoll/inv/P0050/P0050.html.

25 "The Minutes of St. Matthew's Hillsborough, 1838–1939." St. Matthew's Episcopal Church Archives, Hillsborough, N.C. 23 April 1838.

26 Thomas Ruffin to St. Matthew's Church. Orange County Deed Book 34/404. 7 July 1854.

27 J.B. Donnelly to Thomas Ruffin, letter of 23 September 1853. J.G. deRoulhac Hamilton, ed. *The Papers of Thomas Ruffin*, II, 405.

28 St. Matthew's Archives.

29 Phyllis Roberson Hoots, "Cemeteries as Outdoor Museums." Forsyth County Historical Association, http://www.forsythnchistory.com/files/cemeteries.pdf. Accessed online August 2012.

30 Miranda Seymour, "This Blessed Plot," *Sunday Book Review, New York Times*, 10 April 2009: 8. See also Andrea Wulf, *The Brother Gardeners: Botany, Empire and the Birth of an Obsession* (2008).

31 Kenneth McFarland, "Landscape Gardening in Antebellum Hillsborough, North Carolina: The Camerons at Burnside," *Magnolia, Bulletin of the Southern Garden History Society* XI, no. 3 (Spring 1995): 1–11.

32 Mrs. Charles (Helen) Blake, *Gardens of Old Hillsborough*, Hillsborough Historical Society, 1971.

33 The Rev. N. Brooks Graebner, "Expansions and Evolution of the Churchyard of St. Matthew's, Hillsborough 1824–2003." Adult Forum Presentation. St. Matthew's Episcopal Church, 2 September 2012.

34 Elizabeth Matheson to Ellen Weig. 2015.

35 St. Matthew's Church Cemetery Plat. St. Matthew's Church Archives. (*Note:* This is a copy of an original survey by Copley, probably resketched by Mary Claire Engstrom.) Other surveys showing locations of family lots and a census of names are in the St. Matthew's archives.

36 Moses Ashley Curtis was the author of several books on plants, including catalogs of North Carolina woody plants, *The Woody Plants of the State with the Descriptions of Trees, Shrubs, and Woody Vines* (1860).

37 Blake, *Gardens of Old Hillsborough.*

38 Graebner, "Expansions and Evolution of the Churchyard of St. Matthew's" (2012).

39 Fred White, St. Matthew's parishioner and retired director of Duke Forest and Assistant State Forester, from St. Matthew's Churchyard Spring History Day presentation, 2011.

40 Bennehan Cameron (9 September 1854–1 June 1925), the son of Paul Carrington Cameron, and his wife, Sallie Taliaferro Mayo (9 November 1865–11 April 1932).

41 See *The Churchman* LXXXI, no. 3 (1900), for advertisements. Accessed online March 2016: https://books.google.com/books?id=IQIQAAAAYAAJ&vq=thomas+and+miller&dq=carolina+churchman+1900&source=gbs_navlinks_s.

42 Weig, "The Churchyard at St. Matthew's: A Spiritual Investment." Adult Forum Presentation, St. Matthew's Episcopal Church. 9 April 2010.

43 Burwell School Historic Site website, "Burwell School Students": http://www.burwellschool.org/research/.

44 St. Matthew's Episcopal Church Vestry Minutes, 1824–81. The deaths of two soldiers from South Carolina and one from Missouri are recorded in the Spring of 1865.

45 White, Spring History Day presentation, 2011.

46 He was brought to Hillsborough to the home of his cousin, Susannah Hardee Kirkland at Ayr Mount, where he died and was buried at St. Matthew's.

47 The Rev. N. Brooks Graebner to Ellen C. Weig, 22 January 2016.

48 Dunaway, *History of Town Lots* (2012), 560–65.

49 "The Old Town Cemetery," pamphlet published by Historic Hillsborough Commission, 1966.

50 *Hillsborough Historical Society Newsletter* II, no. 8 (1963), 4.

51 *Hillsborough Historical Society Newsletter* II, no. 9 (1963), 5.

52 "The Old Town Cemetery," pamphlet.

53 Dunaway, *History of Town Lots* (2012), 359.

54 S.H. McGahee, *South Carolina's Historic*

Cemeteries: A Preservation Handbook. Columbia: South Carolina Department of Archives and History (2007), 5.

55 Ruth Little, *Sticks and Stones*. Chapel Hill: University of North Carolina Press (1998), 179.

56 Mary Claire Engstrom was responsible for the cemetery census found in the pamphlet, "Old Town Cemetery," by the Historic Hillsborough Commission (1966). Among the prominent citizens buried in the Old Town Cemetery are the following: the Hon. William Hooper, Esq., who died in 1790, was a signer of the Declaration of Independence, a lawyer, and an orator; Capt. John Berry, who died in 1870, was a bricklayer and architect and built the Berry Brick House on West Queen Street and the Old Orange County Courthouse; Dr. James Webb, who died in 1855, was a physician and founder of the State Medical Society and Miss Polly Burke's School, now the Webb House, as well as helped found the Burwell School; Archibald Murphey died in 1832 and was an N.C. historian, judge, UNC professor, and trustee (Murphey Hall is named for him); Frederick Nash, born in Tryon Palace, died in 1858, and was chief justice of N.C. Supreme Court; Sally and Maria Nash died in 1893 and 1907, respectively, and taught at the Nash-Kollock School; William Graham, who died in 1875, was governor of N.C. and lived at Montrose. In the last years of his life (1869–75), he lived at the Nash-Hooper House.

57 This story, found in Engstrom's *The Book of Burwell Students* (2007), was told to the author by historian Steve Peck who gives walking tours around this cemetery in conjunction with the Burwell School and the Alliance for Historic Hillsborough.

58 Steve Peck's observation.

59 Little, *Sticks and Stones,* 231.

60 "The Old Town Cemetery" pamphlet.

61 *Hillsborough Historical Society Newsletter* III, no. 16 (1964), 2.

62 Normally a gatepost is located in the middle of the wall so that the gate is within the wall, not on the other side of it. This iron artifact is on the near side and not in the middle. However, it is possible that when the wall was rebuilt by the Hillsborough Historical Society in the 1960s, the wall was straightened and moved to the other side of this iron post, and the opening was closed up.

63 Engstrom, *Book of Burwell Students,* 69.

64 *Hillsborough Historical Society Newsletter* III, no. 15 (1964), 3.

65 *Hillsborough Historical Society Newsletter* III, no. 13 (1964), 5.

66 Ibid.

67 Mary Claire Engstrom, *Old Margaret Lane Cemetery Survey*. Hillsborough, NC; published by author (1973).

68 Ibid.

69 For a discussion of additional gravesites, see Dunaway, *History of Town Lots: Addendum* (2015), 209–17.

70 Little, *Sticks and Stones,* 38.

71 Engstrom, *Old Margaret Lane Cemetery Survey.*

72 Little, *Sticks and Stones,* 248.

73 Engstrom, *Old Margaret Lane Cemetery Survey.*

74 Personal communication with Beverly Payne and John Jefferies, 2013.

75 Of Grave Concerns, 2006.

CONCLUSION

1 Anderson, *Kirklands of Ayr Mount,* 34–35.

Selected Bibliography

Allen, John. *Uncommon Vernacular: The Early Houses of Jefferson County, West Virginia*. Morgantown, WV: West Virginia University Press, 2011.

Anderson, Jean Bradley. *The Kirklands of Ayr Mount*. Chapel Hill: University of North Carolina Press, 1991.

———. *Piedmont Plantation: The Bennehan-Cameron Family and Lands in North Carolina*. Durham: University Press of America, 1985.

———. "A Rationale for Sans Souci." *Hillsborough Historical Society Journal* 7:1 (Winter 2001), 73–78.

———. "Hillsborough Town Lot 43 and the Brooks Family" (unpublished paper, n.d.), Anderson Archives, Durham Public Library.

Ashelford, Jane. *Care of Clothes*. London: Trafalgar Square Publishing, 1997.

Bailey, William Henry, "A Visit to the Athens of North Carolina," manuscript map, ca. 1870s, John Lancaster Bailey Papers, Southern Historical Collection, University of North Carolina at Chapel Hill.

Bellinger, Susan McArtor. *Photocensus: A Photographic Survey of Buildings in the Hillsborough, NC Historic District Built Prior to 1950*. Hillsborough, NC: printed by author, 1992.

Betts, E. *Thomas Jefferson's Garden Book, 1766–1824*. Philadelphia: American Philosophical Society, 1947.

Blackwelder, Ruth. *The Age of Orange: Political and Intellectual Leadership in North Carolina, 1752–1861*. Charlotte: William Loftin, 1961.

Blake, Mrs. Charles (Helen), and the Horticulture Committee of the Hillsborough Historical Society. *Gardens of Old Hillsborough: A Project of the Horticulture Committee of the Hillsborough Historical Society*. Hillsborough, NC: privately printed, 1971.

Burt, Leah. "The Beginnings of Cameron Park in Hillsborough, North Carolina." *Hillsborough Historical Society Journal* 5, no. 1 (Fall 2002): 1–11.

Burwell, Margaret Anna. "Anna Burwell's Diary" (unpublished document), Burwell School Archives, Hillsborough, NC.

Carr, John W. "Secondary Hillsborough Houses," *Durham Morning Herald*, 17 Feb. 1963.

Chamberlain, Hope Summerell. *This Was Home*. Chapel Hill: University of North Carolina Press, 1938.

Coon, Charles L. *North Carolina Schools and Academies, 1790–1840: A Documentary History*. Raleigh: Edwards & Broughton, 1915.

Dula, Lucile Noell. *The Pelican Guide to Hillsborough, Historic Orange County, North Carolina*. Gretna, LA: Pelican Publishing, 1989.

Dunaway, Stewart E. *Hillsborough, N.C.: History of Town Lots: The Complete Reference Guide*. Hillsborough, NC: printed by author, 2012.

———. *Hillsborough, N.C.: History of Town Lots: The Complete Reference Guide, An Addendum (2015)*. Hillsborough, NC: printed by author, 2015.

———. *Claude J. Sauthier and His Maps of North Carolina*. Hillsborough, NC: printed by author, 2016.

Engstrom, Mary Claire. *The Book of Burwell Students: Lives of Educated Women in the Antebellum South*. Hillsborough, NC: published by Historic Hillsborough Commission, 2007.

———. *Old Margaret Lane Cemetery Survey*. Hillsborough, NC: self-published, 1973.

Fries, Adelaide L., ed. *Records of the Moravians in North Carolina*, 10 vols. Raleigh: North Carolina Historical Commission, 1941.

Goodwin, Nancy, and Ippy Patterson. *Montrose: Life in a Garden.* Durham: Duke University Press, 2005.

Graebner, Brooks. "Antebellum Church Buildings of Hillsborough." *Hillsborough Historical Society Journal* 7, no. 1 (2004): 35–48.

Higginbotham, Don, ed. *The Papers of James Iredell,* 2 vols. Raleigh: N.C. Department of Cultural Resources, 1976.

Historic American Building Survey (HABS), National Park Service. 1965. https://www.nps.gov/hdp/habs/.

Historic Hillsborough Commission. *The Old Town Cemetery.* Hillsborough, NC: published by the organization, 1966.

Holaday, Chris. *Images of America: Hillsborough.* Charleston: Arcadia Publishing, 2002.

Ireland, Robert. "'Gardens in the Making': A Sketch of the Gardens Captured in Ann Strudwick Nash's *Ladies in the Making.*" *Hillsborough Historical Society Journal* 5, no. 1 (Fall 2002): 27–36.

______. "Hillsborough's Natural History: An Introduction." *Hillsborough Historical Society Journal* 5, no. 1 (Fall 2002): viii–ix.

Keckley, Elizabeth. *Behind the Scenes: Thirty Years a Slave and Four Years in the White House.* 1868; 2016 edition, with Introduction by Dolen Perkins-Valdez. Hillsborough, NC: Eno Publishers.

Kennedy, John P., Jr. "Tamarind: The History of a Hillsborough House." Briefing paper prepared as background information for Hillsborough House Tour, April 1977.

Little, Ruth. *Sticks and Stones.* Chapel Hill: University of North Carolina Press, 1998.

Lloyd, Allen Alexander, and Pauline O. Lloyd. *History of the Town of Hillsborough, 1754–1991.* Published by authors, n.d.

Long, Mary Alves. *High Time to Tell It.* Durham: Literary Licensing, 1950.

Lounsbury, Carl R. *An Illustrated Glossary of Early Southern Architecture and Landscape.* Charlottesville and London: University of Virginia Press, 1994.

Magnuson, Tom. "The Roads Made the Town: The Approaches to Hillsborough in Pre-modern Times." *Hillsborough Historical Society Journal* 2, no. 1 (July 1999): 1–12.

Matheson, Elizabeth, and Elon G. Eidenier. *Sense of Place: A Hillsborough Memoir.* Hillsborough, NC: Hillsborough Historical Society, 1991.

McFarland, Kenneth. "Landscape Gardening in Antebellum Hillsborough, North Carolina: The Camerons at Burnside." *Magnolia, Bulletin of the Southern Garden History Society* XI, no. 3 (Spring 1995): 1–11.

McGahee, S. H. *South Carolina's Historic Cemeteries A Preservation Handbook.* Columbia: South Carolina Department of Archives and History, 2007.

McMurry, Sally, and Nancy Van Dosen, eds. *Architecture and Landscape of the Pennsylvania Germans, 1720–1920.* Philadelphia: University of Pennsylvania Press, 2011.

Moore, Rosetta Austin. *The Impact of Slavery on the Education of Blacks in Orange County, North Carolina, 1619–1970.* Hillsborough, NC: published by author, 2015.

Nash, Ann Strudwick. *Ladies in the Making (also a few gentlemen) at the Select Boarding and Day School of the Misses Nash and Kollock, 1859–1890, Hillsborough, North Carolina.* Hillsborough, NC: privately printed, 1964.

Nash, Francis. *Hillsboro, Colonial and Revolutionary.* Chapel Hill: Orange Printshop, 1953.

Powell, William S., ed. *Encyclopedia of North Carolina.* Chapel Hill: University of North Carolina Press, 2006.

Reid, Gwenyth T. "The History of the Horse Barn." Unpublished paper, 2004.

Reid, Holly. "The Paul and Ann (Ruffin) Cameron Icehouse." *Hillsborough Historical Society Journal* 5, no. 1 (Fall 2002): 13–16.

Ryan, Elizabeth S. *Orange County Trio: Hillsborough, Chapel Hill and the University of North Carolina, and Carrboro.* Chapel Hill: The Chapel Hill Press, 2004.

Schucker, Margaret. *The Ruffin-Roulhac House Then and Now: A Historic Structure Report.* HPT (May 5, 2003), 233.

Shanks, Henry T., ed. *The Papers of Willie P. Mangum,* 5 vols. Raleigh: N.C. Department of Archives and History, 1952–56.

Vlach, John Michael. *Back of the Big House: The Architecture of Plantation Slavery.* Chapel Hill: University of North Carolina Press, 1993.

Waddell, Alfred Moore. *Some Memories of My Life.* Raleigh: Broughton & Edwards, 1908.

Watson, Elkanah. *Men and Times of the Revolution.* New York: Dana, 1856.

Wood, Peter H., and Holly Reid. "The Coachman's Bricks: Celebrating Passage of the Thirteenth Amendment in Hillsborough, North Carolina." Unpublished paper, 2012.

Wulf, Andrea. *The Brother Gardeners: Botany, Empire and the Birth of an Obsession.* London: Alfred A. Knopf, 2008.

List of Contributors

JEAN B. ANDERSON received her MA in English at the University of Pennsylvania, where she worked as an instructor. She also taught at Duke University and Duke Divinity School; she later worked as a genealogist and then as a contract researcher in the Historic Sites section of the North Carolina Division of Archives and History. She has published over a dozen articles on topics in North Carolina history, industry, and genealogy. Her books include *Piedmont Plantation: The Bennehan-Cameron Family and Lands in North Carolina* (1985; repr. 2002); *Durham County: The History of Durham County, North Carolina* (1990); *The Kirklands of Ayr Mount* (1991), among others. She received the 1986 Mary Claire Engstrom Award for Distinguished Service, and has served on numerous boards and foundations in Orange and Durham counties, including the Historic Hillsborough Commission, Historic Preservation Commission, and Preservation Fund of Hillsborough.

CALLIE CONNOR has lived in Hillsborough for twenty-two years, and is Professor Emerita of Classics at the University of North Carolina at Chapel Hill. She has published extensively in her field of Byzantine Studies, her most recent book being *Saints and Spectacle: Byzantine Mosaics in Their Cultural Setting* (2016). Locally, she has served on the Historic District Commission (Chapel Hill), Historic Preservation Commission (Orange County), Historic Hillsborough Commission, Orange County Cultural Center, and Preservation Fund of Hillsborough (secretary).

STEWART E. DUNAWAY, a fifth generation Floridian and retired vice president of Siemens Telecom, has resided in Orange County for the past fifteen years. He is a researcher in North Carolina colonial and Revolutionary War history; he photographs and transcribes original records from the State Archives (Raleigh), then publishes these records in book form. Among his 203 titles are *Hillsborough, N.C.: History of Town Lots* (2012); *Chapel Hill, N.C.: History of Town Lots (1790–1930's)* (2014); *Hillsborough, N.C.: History of Town Lots, An Addendum* (2015); *Claude J. Sauthier and His Maps of North Carolina* (2016). He is a board member of the Friends of the State Archives.

CRAUFURD D. GOODWIN is James B. Duke Professor of Economics Emeritus at Duke University, where he has served as department chair, vice provost, and dean of the graduate school. He was director of the European and International Affairs Program at the Ford Foundation (1971–77) and received a Guggenheim Fellowship and a Smuts Fellowship at Cambridge University. The author of over eighty articles and book chapters, he is author of eleven books and editor of nine more. His most recent book is *Walter Lippmann: Public Economist* (2014). He is co-president of the Preservation Fund of Hillsborough.

BARBARA HUME, a resident of Hillsborough for the last twenty-six years, earned her MAH from the University of Virginia School of Architecture, Charlottesville. She worked in historic architecture preservation for twenty-six years, during which she first directed the State Historic Preservation Office's National Register program and later was in charge of the Historic Architecture Section of the North Carolina Department of Transportation. That section produced parts of environmental impact statements and ensured compliance with relevant laws and regulations. She has published a number of articles on historic architecture. She has served on the Hillsborough Historic District Commission and currently is on the board of directors of the Hillsborough Preservation Fund.

ELIZABETH MATHESON, a native of Hillsborough, earned her BA at Sweet Briar College, and later studied photography at the Penland School of Crafts. Her photographs have been exhibited in numerous museums and galleries around the Southeast. She has published portraits of two old North Carolina towns, Edenton and Hillsborough. Other books include *To See* (1991), *Blithe Air: Photographs of England, Wales and Ireland* (1995), and *Shell Castle: Portrait of a North Carolina House* (2008). In 2004 she was awarded the North Carolina Award for Excellence in the Arts, the state's highest civilian honor. She is on the board of directors of the Preservation Fund of Hillsborough.

PIP MERRICK, a thirty-year resident of Hillsborough, earned her BM in music theory from Manhattan School of Music and her MS and PhD in cell biology from New York University. She came to UNC Medical School for a post-graduate fellowship in burn surgery, then served as an instructor of physiology and comparative anatomy in the UNC Biology Department. She has served on the Hillsborough Planning Board, Arts Council, Tree Board, and the Alliance for Historic Hillsborough.

JIM PARSLEY is a Hillsborough native who moved away to pursue an engineering education at Duke University, followed by a thirty-seven-year career with Procter & Gamble, where he held five jobs in four different states. He and his wife moved back to Hillsborough in 2003 and contribute in many ways to the community. He participates in activities and groups at St. Matthew's Episcopal Church, and maintains a keen interest in local history and historic preservation.

MARY ANN PETER earned a PhD in education from the University of North Carolina at Chapel Hill and BS and MS degrees in nursing from Duke University. She was on the faculty at UNC-Chapel Hill School of Nursing for ten years and held a variety of positions in nursing at Duke University Hospital for twenty-five years, including that of director of nursing. She received numerous awards and honors during her nursing career, wrote a number of articles in professional journals, and holds a patent for a medical device. She was chair of the board of trustees of Durham Technical Community College for eight years. Among her local community service activities are Alliance for Historic Hillsborough Board of Directors (chair), Historical Foundation of Hillsborough and Orange County (chair); Preservation Fund of Hillsborough. She received the 2013 Mary Claire Engstrom Award.

ELLEN C. WEIG has lived in Hillsborough for the past twelve years and has been a parish historian for St. Matthew's Episcopal Church. Her research focuses on the stained glass windows and churchyard, and women of the church. She recently moved to Wilmington, North Carolina, where she is the archivist and historian for St. Paul's Episcopal Church. She is a retired child life specialist, with a master's degree in early childhood education, specializing in the hospitalized child, from Worcester State College. She has worked in child life and early childhood education programs in Massachusetts, Pennsylvania, New York, and North Carolina. In the 1990s she worked at the University of Massachusetts Medical Center with their Child Life Program, Child Abuse Team, Pediatric Oncology Team, ID/HIV/AIDS Team, and Pulmonary/Cystic Fibrosis Team. She has made numerous local presentations on historical topics over the past ten years and continues to do so.

Index

All numbers refer to page numbers; italicized numbers indicate images.

academy, 14, 15
Academy Hill, 140
Act of the North Carolina General Assembly of 1715, 143
Act of the North Carolina General Assembly of 1758, 158
African American community, 15
Alexander Dickson House, 125
Alexander Dickson Office, 125, *130*, 132
allée, as feature of garden design, 10, 93
Anderson, Jean B., 173
Anderson's Female Boarding School, 139
animals
  accommodation of on town lots, 60
arboretum, at Burnside (Cameron Park), 95
architecture
  of Hillsborough, 9, 15
Ayr Mount, 5, 6, 12, 16, 173
  cemetery at, 14, 15, *150*
  Few Farm and, 6
barns, 59–75
basement dining rooms, 79
Basket Factory Office, *131*, 132
Belleview, *21*, 31
  kitchen, *21*, *24*, *25*, *26*, *27*, 30
  dual-purpose building at, 83
berms, 9, 104
Berry Brick House, *54*
  boxwood plantings at, 99
  well house at, 52, *54*
Berry, John, brickmason, 16, 17
Berry, Mary Elizabeth Strayhorn, 31
Bingham schools in North Carolina, 140
Bingham, William, 140
Bingham, William J. (son), 140
botanical world, importance of, 93
boxwood plantings, 99
Boyd, Price, coachman and freed slave, 38
brick manufacturing, 112
Brick Schoolhouse Lot, 139–40
brick work, 112
bridges, 6
Browning, Hugh Conway, historian, 145
Burke, Mary W. (Polly), 138
Burke, Thomas, 138
Burnside, 12, 25, 33, 36
  arboretum at, 95
  barn at (also called, Great Barn), 60, *61*, 62, 63, *64*
  Coachman's House at 33, *34*
  dependencies of, 14
  development of by Paul Cameron, 60
  gardens at, 95
  hedges at, 99
  icehouse at, 76, 77, *78*
  kitchen, *20*, *29*
  law office at, *127*, *128*
  necessary house at, 87, *91*
  plantings at, 95
  Samuel Parsons, gardener at, 95
  smokehouse at, *46*
  terracing for gardens at, 95
Burwell, Margaret Anna, 135, 144
Burwell, Robert, 133
Burwell School, 99, 103, 133, *134*, 144, 151
  academic subjects at, 135
  classroom building at, 135, *135* 136
  dormitory at, 136

Burwell School *(continued)*
historic sketch of, *137*
kitchen at, 135
as model for Nash-Kollock School, 138
Music Building at, 135
music lessons at, 135
necessary house at, 87, *88*
office at, 135–6
butler's pantry, 89

Cadwallader Jones Law Office, *124*, 125, *126*
Caldwell Academy (*also called* Caldwell Institute), 140
Cain, Thomas R., 36
Cain, William, Jr., 36, 67
and Hardscrabble Plantation, 67
Cameron, Duncan, 9, 59
Cameron Family Papers, 63, 95
Cameron-Nash Law Office, *131*, 132, 138
as built by Duncan Cameron, 138
Cameron Park, plantings in, 95
Cameron, Paul Carrington, 33, 35, 36, 60
Carrie Waitt Spurgeon Garden, 103
Cedar Lane, 93, *94*
cellar kitchens, 25
cemeteries, 14, 15, 143–69. *See also* St. Matthew's Episcopal Church Cemetery, Kirkland Family Cemetery at Ayr Mount, Lockhart-Phillips Cemetery, Margaret Lane Cemetery.
burial conventions in, 144
Confederate graves in, 145
headstone styles in, 144
landscaping styles of, 145
laws regarding, 144
locations of, 144
unmarked graves in, 145

Chapel Hill
and population expansion of Orange County, 1
Church of England, 14
church lot, 14
churches, 14. *See also* St. Matthew's Church.
Churton, William, surveyor, 9, 59, 93
Civil War, 19, 33, 74, 95, 123, 125, 141, 151, 158, 165
clay pits, 112
Coachman's House, *34*, 35
Colonial Inn
flagstone sidewalks and, 107
commons, 9, 59
courthouse, 8, 9, 14, 15, 16
courthouse square, 14, 16, 125
Courtney's Yellow House, 16
well house at, *57*
curbs and curbstones, 10, 107–12
curing meat, smokehouses and, 43
Curtis, Moses Ashley, botanical interests of, 94

Dark Walk, 120–22, *121*
David Anderson House, 10
dependencies, 17
at Burnside, 47
dual-purpose, 83
loss of, 14
original contexts of, 2, 3
at Ruffin-Roulhac House, 11
types of, 2
Dickerson Chapel, 16
dining rooms, 25, 79–81
freestanding, 80, 81
as location for washing and storage of china and silver, 80
as refectory, 135
dogtrot, 21, 28

Dozier House
barn at, 72, *73*
smokehouse at, *45*, 47

Edmund Strudwick's kitchen, 25, 28, *29*
Edmund Fanning's house, site of, 10, 93
educational institutions, 8. *See also* 133–42.
ell, 21
Engstrom, Mary Claire, xxvi, 151, 165, 167
Eno River, 6, 7, 60, 99
harvesting ice from, 77
Exchange Street Bridge, 6

Fanning, Edmund, 10
Faucett, John, carpenter, 17
Faucette Mill
ford at, 6
fire, loss of houses to, 13
danger of, 19
Fish Dam Road, 7
flagstone sidewalks, 107, *108*, *109*
flower gardens, 99, 103
fords, 6, 7
and bridges, 6
Frederick Nash Law Office, *131*, 132
Fry-Jefferson map, 6
furniture industry, 1

gardens, 93–102
at Burnside, drawings for, 95
historic, 99, 103
Gattis House
laundry at, 83, *84*, *85*
well shelter, 57
Graham, Rebecca Cameron, 66
Graham, William A., 16, 66, 125
law office of, 125, *129*, 132

Graham Law Office, 125, *129*, 132
graveyards
in the 18th century, 144
Great Barn at Burnside, 35, 60–64
Green, William Mercer, 66
grid system
for streets, 7, 93
Gunter's chain, 9

Halifax Road, 5, 7
Hampton, Wade, 125
Hancock, Samuel, mason/bricklayer, 8
Hasell, Eliza, 17
Hasell-Nash House (*see also* Pilgrim's Rest), 16, 17, 25, 72, 79
well house at, 57, *57*
Haw River, 6
Hawks, Francis Lister, 11, 38
Hawks, John, architect, 14
hedges, 93, 99
Heartsease, 138
school of Miss Alice Heartt and Mrs. Alice Bragg at, 139
well house at, *57*
Helen's Garden, 103
Henderson Jones House, *32*
Hill, Frances Clark Pollock Connor Blount, 38, 74
Hillsborough (*for sites and properties, see by name*)
architectural development of, 9
climate of, 8
colonial settlement of, 7
commercial factor in colonial settlement of, 8
as county seat, 8, 9, 123, 133
division into lots, 9
early appearance of, 1, 93
evolution of townscape, 2
factors in early settlement of, 7, 8
garden design in, 10
and landscape design, 93
maps of, 6, 7
mercantile companies and, 8
Occoneechee as early name for, 6
public buildings, 14
Pump and Spring Committee, 52
townscape of, 93
Hillsborough Academy, 140
Hillsborough Female Seminary, 140
Hillsborough Military Academy, 140
Commandant's House at, 140
historic gardens, 99, 103
historic plantings, 93
historic preservation, 170–74
Hogg, James, 60
grave of, 159
Hooper, William, signer of Declaration of Independence, 159
grave of, 161–2
Hughes Academy, 138–9, *140*
Hughes, Samuel Wellwood, 139

ice, shipping of, 77
icehouses, 76–79
history and design of, 76
published references to, 77, 79
types of, 76
Inn at Teardrops
freestanding dining room of, 81, *82*
Iredell, James, 1, 14
ironing, of clothing, 81–83

jail, 9, 14, 16
John Witherspoon's Private Boarding School, 139

Jones, Pride, 69
Judge Gattis House
well house at, 52, *55*

Kirkland Family Cemetery at Ayr Mount, 143, 149–51
Kirkland, William, 15, 66, 149
entrepreneurial interests in Hillsborough, 8
kitchens, 19–32
designs of, 21
moving of, 21
social implications of, 19
Kollock, Sarah, 138

Ladies in the Making, on Nash-Kollock School, 138. *See also* Nash, Ann Strudwick.
landscape design, 93
landscape features, 17, 18, 93–102
types of, 2, 9, 10
laundries, 81–84
location of, 81
law offices, 123–32
woodwork in, 125
Locheil, 17
Anderson's Female Boarding School at, 139
Lockhart, Catherine Barrett Bennett, 148
Lockhart-Phillips Cemetery, 15, 143, 145–9, *146*, *147*
development of, 148–9
Sauthier Map and, 148
lots, 9, 92–3. *See also* town lots.
"Lucerne Lot," 93
Lyman, Theodore B., 69

Mallett Mill House, 16, 25, 79
boxwood plantings at, 99
Mangum, Priestly, 36, 95

Mangum Terrace, 95
Mangum-Ruffin House, 12, 13, 21, 23, 35, 95
barn at, 67, *68*
dual-purpose building at, 83
kitchen at, 21
slave house at, *37*
smokehouse at, *44*
mansion house, definition of, 10, 11
mansion house complex, 2, 10
definition of, 11
compared with plantation, 11
Margaret Lane Cemetery, 14, 143, 165–9, *166*, *168*
burial of Native Americans in, 169
burial of slaves at, 165
grave markers in, 167
rededication of, 165
technical analysis of, 169
market house, 8, 14, 15
Masonic Lodge, 17
Mason's Ordinary, 8
McLester, Maggie, 151
meat house, as synonym for smokehouse, 43
meat, preservation of, 46, 47
Midlawn, *32*
cottage at, as Mrs. David Patterson's kindergarten, 139, *141*
kitchen at, *32*
Miss Polly Burke's School, 138
log wall of, *139*
Montrose, 12, 13, *32*
barn at, 64, *65*, 66, *66*
kitchen at, 27–28
law office at, 125, *129*
necessary house, 87, *89*
smokehouse at, *42*, *89*
Montrose Garden, 103
Moseley, Edward, maps of, 6, 7
mounting blocks, 10
Murphey, Archibald DeBow, 142
musk rose (*Rosa moschata*), 103

Nash, Ann Strudwick, author, 48, 52, 103
Ladies in the Making, written by, 138
Nash, Frederick, 16
Nash, Mrs. Frederick Nash, 93
Nash, Mariah Jane, 138
Nash, Sally Kollock, 138
Nash-Hooper House, 66
Nash-Kollock School, 10, 25, 28, 31, 52, 57, 103, 136, 138, 151
basement dining room at, 79
as former residence of Chief Justice Frederick Nash, 136
gardens at, 103
Ladies in the Making, as source on, 138
law office at, 136, 138
National Register of Historic Places, 2
necessary houses, 84–91
hygiene in, 86
location and construction of, 86
location at Montrose, 43
public health concerns and, 87
public water system and, 87
requirement of, 86
Nichols, William, 16
North Carolina Constitutional Convention of 1788, 14
North Carolina Railroad
used for shipping of ice, 77
Norwood, Joseph, 67

Occoneechee, Native American Village, 6, 60
Occoneechee Mountains, 8
offices and law offices, 123–32
Old Indian Trading Path, *4*, 5, 6, 8, 14, 149
Old King Street Tavern, 9
Old Mahogany (a tree), 99
Old Town Cemetery, 14, 99, 143–4, *160*, *161*
boxwood plantings at, 99, 163, *165*
grave art in, 159, 161
grave markers in, 159, 162
Hooper-Norwood plot in, 159
Sauthier Map and, 158
stone walls at, 116, 118–19, 162–3
Students Walk in, 163, *164*
Old Town Clock, 15
moving of, 15
one-room schoolhouses, 139
Orange County
population changes of, 1

Palmer, Martin, carpenter/joiner, 8, 14
pantry, 27
Parsons, Samuel, gardener at Burnside, 95
parterres, as feature of garden design, 10, 93
Petersburg, Virginia, 8
Phillips, James, saddler, 148
Phillips, William H., 38
Piedmont of North Carolina
furniture and textile industries in, 2
as having safe and healthful climate, 8
Pilgrim's Rest. *See* Hasell-Nash House.
plantations, 2, 59
as distinguished from mansion house complexes, 12
plantation cemeteries, 143
Poet's Walk at Ayr Mount, 5
Pollock, Thomas, 60
poor children
free schools for, 141

Poplar Hill, 48
  spring at, 48
population, makeup in eighteenth century, 8
Presbyterian church, 14, 16, 99, 133, 158–9
Price, William P., 165
privies. *See* necessary houses.
public education in North Carolina, 140

race track, 60
rain barrels, 52
Revolution, American, 14, 15
roads, roadways and roadbeds, 7
  early establishment of, 6
  traffic patterns across state and, 7
Robertson-Cheek House, 25, 29
  barn at, 69, *71*, 72
  dependencies at, 69
  kitchen at, 25, *29*
Rochester, Nathaniel, 15
Rowan, Matthew, early surveyor, 6
Ruffin, Chief Justice Thomas, 11, 14, 41, 60, 151
Ruffin Law Office, 125, *127*, *128*
Ruffin, Thomas, Jr., 67
Ruffin-Roulhac House, 11, *32*, 36
  barns at, 75
  dependencies, 41, 74
  law office at, *131*
  restoration of, 74
  slave house, *40*
  smokehouse, *46*, 47
  well and well house, 52, *53*
Ruffin-Roulhac Law Office, *131*, 132

St. Matthew's Church, 14–17, 95
St. Matthew's Episcopal Church Cemetery, 143, 151–8

Sans Souci, 12, 27–28, *30*, 36
  barn at, 67
  carriage house at, 69
  contemporary description of, 69
  dependencies of, 13, 67, 69
  kitchen, 28, *30*
  office at, *131*, 132
  slave house, *39*
Sauthier, Claude J., cartographer, 7
Sauthier Map, 9
  and garden design, 10
  grid plan of, 93
  mansion house complexes and, 10
  Spring Lot on, 48
  springhouses on, 49
  streams, stillhouses on, 48
  vegetable gardens on, 92
school of Miss Alice Heartt and Mrs. Mary Bragg, 139
schools and school-related buildings, 8, 133–42
Sherman, William T., 125
Session House, 141. *See also* Sunday Schools.
sidewalks, 9–10
slave funeral procession, 167
slave houses, 21, 33–41, 38
slave quarters, 41
slavery, 19
slaves, 135
  burial of, 165
  education and, 141
  roles of, 25, 31
smokehouses, 42–47
Spring Lot, 48
  Act of Assembly of 1766 and, 48
spring, public, 48
springhouses, colonial style, 49
  uses of, 49
  remains of, 49, *50*
  springbox of, 49, *50*, 51
springs and spring houses, 48–58
stable, *as subcategory of* barns
  Burnside barn as example of, 62
Stagville, plantation, 35, 41, 60, 63
stillhouse lot, 48
  Josiah Lyons', 48
  William Courtney's, 48
stone curbs, 107
stone steps, 112
stone walls, 115–20
  dry stack, 10
  Sauthier Map and, 48
streets, historic features of, 104–22
Strudwick, Edmund, 16
Students Walk, 99, *102*
summer kitchens. *See* kitchens.
Sunday School
  as forerunner of public school, 141
  as free schools for black children, 141

Tamarind
  necessary house at, 87, *90*
  well house at, *57*
Teer House, basement dining room at, 79
terracing, for gardens at Burnside, 95
textile industry, 1
Thirteenth Amendment to the U.S. Constitution, 35
Town Hall, 38
  as former Ruffin-Roulhac House, 11
Town of Hillsborough, public water system, 87
town lots, 7, 9, 59
  allocation of, 60
Town Pump, 52
  abuse of, 52

town well, 51
townscape
early appearance of, 93
Trading Path. *See* Old Indian Trading Path.
transportation
as factor in colonial settlement, 7, 8
trees and gardens, 92–103
trees, historic, 99
Tryon, William, 7
Tryon Palace, New Bern, 38
Turner-Strudwick House
well house at, 52, 56
Twin Chimneys, 16, 21, 22, 31
freestanding dining room at, 80–81
as John Witherspoon's Private Boarding School, 139
kitchen at, 21, 31

University of North Carolina at Chapel Hill, 1
Hillsborough schools as preparatory for, 133, 140

vegetable gardens, 92

washing of clothes, 82
soap used in, 82–83
Webb House, 138
as Miss Polly Burke's School, 138
well house at, 58
Webb, James, 9, 16, 138
as builder of Sunday School, 141
wells
digging of, 51
monitoring of, 52
on private property, 52
public and private, 51
wells and well houses, 48–58
displacement of springs by, 51
Whitted House, 21
well house at, 57
kitchen of, 21
Whitted-Johnson House, 16, 21, 32
Witherspoon, John Knox, 16, 17
women's education in North Carolina, 133

Yarborough, David, 36, 67